REAGAN AND THE STATES

Reagan
and the
States

RICHARD P. NATHAN,
FRED C. DOOLITTLE,
AND ASSOCIATES

Princeton University Press

PRINCETON, NEW JERSEY

Contents

Conclusions

Contributors

ARIZONA

John Stuart Hall
School of Public Affairs
Arizona State University

Richard A. Eribes
West Campus
Arizona State University

CALIFORNIA

Cristy Jensen
Center for California Studies
California State University at Sacramento

Ruth Ross
Graduate Center for Public Policy and
    Administration
California State University at Long Beach

FLORIDA

Lance deHaven-Smith
Department of Political Science
Florida-Atlantic University

Allen W. Imershein
Center for Human Services Policy and
    Administration
Florida State University

ILLINOIS

Charles J. Orlebeke
School of Urban Planning and Policy
University of Illinois at Chicago

MASSACHUSETTS

Arnold M. Howitt
John F. Kennedy School of Government
Harvard University

R. Clifford Leftwich
Crownpoint Institute of Technology

MISSISSIPPI

Lewis H. Smith
Department of Economics
University of Mississippi

Robert S. Herren
Department of Business Administration
    and Economics
North Dakota State University

NEW YORK

Sarah F. Liebschutz
Rockefeller College of Public Affairs and
    Policy
State University of New York at Brockport

Irene Lurie
Graduate School of Public Affairs
State University of New York at Albany

OHIO

Charles F. Adams, Jr.
School of Public Administration
Ohio State University

Joseph M. Davis
The Peabody Group

Marilyn T. Davis
Blue Cross and Blue Shield of Ohio

WASHINGTON STATE

V. Lane Rawlins
University of Alabama System

Betty Jane Narver
Institute for Public Policy and
    Management
University of Washington

Advisory Committee

Preface

This is the final summary volume on a study begun shortly after Ronald Reagan was elected president of the United States and it became clear that he would seek to make substantial changes in domestic policies and programs of the national government. The study focuses on the effects of Reagan policies for federal grant-in-aid to state and local governments. This is an area in which the president made many of his deepest cuts and most basic changes in national policy.

The study is a collaborative effort, using a field network evaluation methodology involving an interdisciplinary group of academic social scientists (political scientists and economists). Field researchers in fourteen states studied the effects of Reagan's changes in grants on these state governments, plus forty local governments within the sample states. Two previous volumes and a number of shorter reports and articles have been issued on findings of this research. This volume focuses on the states, and particularly on the effects of Reagan's policies on state governments and on American federalism. A major effort has been made to place Reagan's actions in historical perspective.

The previous publications on this study combined the field data across the sample sites. By contrast, this volume presents individual case studies, along with overview chapters analyzing the observations made in the fourteen states.

The book consists of six overview chapters—five introductory and one concluding chapter—which we have written. In addition, there are nine case-study chapters, which have been selected, as explained in chapter 1, because they represent a cross section of responses to the Reagan changes. Four of the five case studies belonging to the complete research study have been published in other places.[1] The field research for the case studies was begun in the spring of 1981. The case studies were first submitted in June 1984; revisions of the nine case-study chapters included in this volume were completed as of January 1986.

The overall project is a team effort, and there are many people who deserve credit and thanks for their participation. First and foremost, we extend thanks to the field researchers who authored the fourteen case studies on which the volume is based. Our own staff at the Woodrow Wilson School of Public and International Affairs at Princeton University did yeoman service in checking, conforming, and managing the editorial process of this volume. We especially pay tribute to John Lago at the Princeton Urban and Regional Research Center of the Woodrow Wilson School. Others at the Center who aided in this work are Nan Nash, Loretta Haggard ('86), Andrea Nervi ('85), and Alison Tracy ('84). Anne Marie DeMeo provided word processing assistance. David L. Aiken provided editorial assistance on the introductory overview chapters. Mary Capouya provided editorial assistance on the case-study chapters; Catherine Claxton proofread the manuscript.

We would also like to thank Dean Donald E. Stokes, Ingrid W. Reed, Agnes M. Pearson, and Audrey J. Pitman for making Princeton's Woodrow Wilson School a happy home for our research.

Funding for this research was provided by the Ford Foundation and the Commonwealth Fund. Appreciation should be expressed to Susan V. Berresford, vice president, and David Arnold and Shepard Forman, program officers, at the Ford Foundation. At the Commonwealth Fund, we would like to thank Margaret E. Mahoney, president, Thomas W. Moloney, senior vice president, and Susan Aldridge, senior program officer.

Sanford G. Thatcher, Elizabeth Gretz, and Ann Hirst at the Princeton Uni-

---

[1] Lynn Rittenoure, Larkin Warner, and Steve B. Steib, "Oklahoma's Legislative Process in a Period of Fiscal Change," *Public Budgeting and Finance* 4, no. 2 (Summer 1984):42–57; William O. Farber, *The Impact of Reagan Federalism on South Dakota and South Dakota State Government* (Vermillion, S.D.: Governmental Research Bureau, University of South Dakota, December 1984); Richard W. Roper, John R. Lago, Nancy G. Beer, and Martin A. Bierbaum, *Federal Aid in New Jersey, 1981–84*, Council on New Jersey Affairs working paper no. 9 (Princeton, N.J.: Princeton Urban and Regional Research Center, March 1986); Susan A. MacManus, Robert M. Stein, and V. Howard Savage, "The Texas Response to Reagan's New Federalism," in Lewis Bender and James Stever, eds., *Managing the New Federalism* (Boulder, Colo.: Westview Press, 1986).

The case study on Missouri was written by George Dorian Wendel and Mary Collins Wendel. This case study focuses on health policy issues and has been used as a major component of this overall research on the effects of the changes made under the Reagan administration in the Medicaid program. This research is directed by Dr. Gilbert S. Omenn, Dean of the School of Public Health and Community Medicine, University of Washington at Seattle. See *Restructuring of Medicaid* (Baltimore, Md.: Johns Hopkins University Press, forthcoming).

versity Press were wonderfully supportive and helpful throughout the process of assembling and reviewing the material for this volume. Among our professional colleagues, a number of people deserve special thanks: Thomas J. Anton at Brown University and the anonymous readers who reviewed this manuscript. We also were aided by an advisory committee, whose members are listed on pages xi-xii.

Finally, this research could not have gone forward without the help of the literally thousands of people who provided assistance and information to us and to the field researchers on the character and effects of Reagan's policy shifts. We thank them all.

Richard P. Nathan
Fred C. Doolittle
Princeton, New Jersey
January 1987

Overview Chapters

RICHARD P. NATHAN AND FRED C. DOOLITTLE

Introduction

✳

Woodrow Wilson said in 1908 that "the question of the relation of the states to the federal government is the cardinal question of our constitutional system." It cannot be settled, said Wilson, "by one generation, because it is a question of growth, and every new successive stage of our political and economic development, gives it a new aspect, makes it a new question."[1] The focus of this book is on the way in which this central debate in federalism was reopened during the first term of the Reagan administration, a period in which basic changes were occurring in the mood of the country and the attitude of the public on the role of the government in domestic affairs.

The analysis presented in this volume is based on research begun in 1981 when it became evident that Ronald Reagan's new administration was likely to achieve significant cuts and changes in federal grants-in-aid. A network of field researchers was established to study a sample of state and local governments in order to assess the resulting changes in their policies, operations, and roles as the effects of the Reagan changes were felt. Two books and several other publications have been produced based on this research.[2] This book, which pre-

---

[1] Woodrow Wilson, *Constitutional Government in the United States* (New York: Columbia University Press, 1908; reprinted 1961), p. 173.

[2] The books are John W. Ellwood, ed., *Reductions in U.S. Domestic Spending: How They Affect State and Local Governments* (New Brunswick, N.J.: Transaction Books, 1982), and Richard P. Nathan, Fred C. Doolittle, and Associates, *The Consequences of Cuts: The Effects of the Reagan Domestic Program on State and Local Governments* (Princeton, N.J.: Princeton Urban and Regional Research Center, 1983). Articles include Richard P. Nathan, "State and Local Governments Under Federal Grants: Toward a Predictive Theory," *Political Science Quarterly* 98, no. 1 (Spring 1983):47–57; Richard P. Nathan and Fred C. Doolittle, "The Untold Story of Reagan's 'New Federalism,' " *The Public Interest*, no. 77 (Fall 1984):96–105; and Richard P. Nathan and Fred C. Doolittle, "Federal Grants: Giving and Taking Away," *Political Science Quarterly* 100, no. 1 (Spring 1985):53–74.

sents the main findings of this research, is based on these earlier publications plus fourteen state-focused case studies summarizing the effects of cuts and changes made in federal grant-in-aid programs during the first term of the Reagan administration. The fourteen states in the sample are listed below:

Arizona	New Jersey
California	New York
Florida	Ohio
Illinois	Oklahoma
Massachusetts	South Dakota
Mississippi	Texas
Missouri	Washington

The sample was chosen to be representative in terms of size, location, and economic and social characteristics. This volume includes nine individual case-study chapters written by the researchers who conducted the field research and six chapters of general analysis drawing on the findings of the case studies.

In both the study and in this book, we have tried to do two things. First, we have looked at budget cuts and other changes in federal grant-in-aid programs and how state and local governments responded to them. Much of the business of the federal government in domestic affairs is transacted in the form of grants-in-aid. Reagan's policies in this area, in effect, have two aspects. His efforts to cut spending under federal grants-in-aid (an area in which budget cuts have been concentrated under Reagan) reflect the administration's *retrenchment* objective. Also under grants-in-aid, Reagan has proposed changes reflecting his federalism reform objective of *devolving* power and responsibility from the federal government to state governments.

Reagan's biggest successes in pursuing both types of changes under federal grant-in-aid programs—retrenchment and devolution—came in 1981. The cuts made in grants-in-aid in Reagan's first year in office were historic. This was the first time in over thirty years that there had been an actual-dollar decline in federal aid to state and local governments. The cuts produced a 7 percent reduction for fiscal year 1982 in overall federal grants-in-aid to state and local governments as shown in table 1.1. This amounted to a 12 percent decline in real terms. The same legislation which contained these cuts, the Omnibus Budget Reconciliation Act of 1981, also included major changes in the structure of federal aid programs to create block grants that assigned a greater role to state governments.

In addition to describing and analyzing the effects of Reagan's cuts and changes in federal grants, our second objective in this book is to assess how changes in the domestic policies of the national government made during Pres-

Table 1.1. *Federal Grants as a Percentage of Total Federal Outlays*

Federal fiscal year	Federal grants in millions of dollars	Federal grants as a percentage of total outlays
1981	94,762	14.0
1982	88,195	11.8

SOURCE: Table 12.1, "Summary Comparisons of Total Federal Grants-in-Aid (Including Shared Revenue) to State and Local Governments, 1940–1990," Executive Office of the President, U.S. Office of Management and Budget, *Historical Tables, Budget of the United States Government, Fiscal Year 1986* (Washington, D.C.: Government Printing Office, 1985), p. 12.1(2).

ident Reagan's first term have affected the roles and relationships of the three levels of government in our federal system: national, state, and local. Although this subject was largely neglected in 1981 in the debate about the merits of eliminating or trimming particular programs and cutting taxes, we believe the policies of the Reagan administration in the domestic public sector have contributed to a fundamental shift in the balance of power and responsibility in American federalism. This shift involves the enhancement of the role of state governments vis-à-vis both the national government and local governments.

The purposes of the overview chapters in this volume are to describe the Reagan program, its roots and significance; to summarize the responses made by the sample state governments to the Reagan changes; and to analyze the reasons for the differences in these responses both on a program-by-program and a state-by-state basis. We begin by examining the theory of federalism advanced by the Reagan administration and its relationship to other objectives which the administration has pursued in the field of domestic policy.

Reagan's Theory of Federalism

President Reagan's domestic policy initiatives during his first term reflect a theory of federalism grounded in the Tenth Amendment to the Constitution which reserves to the states or to the people all powers not delegated to the national government. One of Reagan's major goals throughout his public career has been devolution to the states, that is to curtail the role of the federal government in domestic affairs and enlarge the role and responsibilities of state governments.[3] As governor of California he argued strongly for such a shift. When he

[3] The term "decentralization" is often used interchangeably with "devolution." We prefer the former term because its meaning, to transfer authority, is broader, although both terms are used in this volume. The term "federal government" is used in a number of places in this volume in

was running for the Republican presidential nomination in 1976, he delivered a speech calling for a "systematic transfer of authority and resources to the states." This set of proposals, affecting $90 billion in federal programs, evoked widespread criticism because of the inability of Reagan and his advisers to spell out the details and explain its consequences. But the proposals did accurately reflect the candidate's basic position.

These views had not changed by 1980 when Reagan was elected president. In his inaugural address in 1981, he promised to curb federal powers and to "demand recognition of the distinction" between federal powers and "those reserved to the states." News accounts at the time said that Reagan's comments on federalism brought a cheer from the section where the governors were seated at the inaugural.[4]

Thirty days after his inauguration as president, Ronald Reagan told a group of governors at the White House that it "is a long-time dream of mine, this thing of balancing up the divisions of government."[5] A few months later, he told state legislators that the federal system is like a masonry wall, and that what is needed is "a proper mix" of the bricks (i.e., the states) and the mortar (i.e., the federal government). "Unfortunately," according to the president, "over the years, many people have come to believe that Washington is the whole wall— a wall that, incidentally, leans, sags, and bulges under its own weight."[6]

Reagan's "dream" (a term he has used often in this context) of bringing about a "proper mix" between federal and state roles needs to be viewed in relation to what we consider to be the preeminent goal of the Reagan administration in the domestic public sector—social program retrenchment. Not only did Reagan wish to increase the authority of the states, but he also had strong opinions about how they should exercise that authority: they should join the federal government in its effort to reduce the size of the public sector. Since his conversion to conservatism and Republicanism in the early 1960s, Reagan has strongly opposed the values or at least the methods associated with many domestic social and urban programs at every level of government. He has consistently criticized welfare and redistributive social service programs, which conservatives believe undermine the work ethic and encourage dependency. In addition, Reagan has

---

the conventional way it is used in the United States to refer to the national government. We have sought to make clear where we use the terms "federal system" or "federalism" that we are referring to the larger political system including the national, state, and local governments.

[4] *Congressional Quarterly*, January 24, 1981, p. 164.

[5] "National Governors' Association" (Remarks at a White House meeting, February 23, 1981), *Weekly Compilation of Presidential Documents* 17, no. 9 (March 2, 1981):177.

[6] "National Conference of State Legislatures" (Remarks at the annual convention in Atlanta, Georgia, July 30, 1981), *Weekly Compilation of Presidential Documents* 17, no. 31 (August 3, 1981):834.

viewed subsidy programs to distressed areas as distorting markets and market relationships. His speeches and policies reflect steady opposition to "social engineering" and generally to the values which conservatives identify with the domestic programs that grew rapidly both in size and number at every level of government in the United States in the 1960s and 1970s.

Many conservatives and liberals alike have assumed that devolution and retrenchment would go hand in hand. As program responsibility was devolved to the states, less would be done by the states because of competition among states to attract business and higher income residents with low taxes and the generally more conservative orientation of state governments. The assumption was that if social program retrenchment occurred at the federal level in combination with devolution, the states, too, would pull back on social programs. The service reductions implied by the federal aid cuts would stick, and perhaps even be compounded by parallel state and local action.

It is our contention based on the field research we have conducted that this assumption has not proven true in many cases in the first term of the Reagan administration. It is true that public service levels in some program areas are lower than they were in 1981 because of cuts at the federal level. But it is also true that the state and local government responses to the 1981 federal aid cuts— through replacement funding, through a wide variety of financial coping and delaying measures, and through administrative reforms—has produced higher service levels than otherwise would have been the case due to the Reagan cuts. We also believe that the developments at the state level outlined in the case studies suggest that the states are poised to do even more in the future to protect and even extend service levels.

In sum, during this period in U.S. history, liberals seeking support for social programs have fared better in many states than they have in the nation's capital. Social programs have had a larger constituency in many states than expected. This is not the first time that liberals have found the states more receptive than the federal government. During the 1920s, Washington kept cool with Coolidge, while some states were passing child labor laws, experimenting with unemployment insurance plans, and expanding social services and benefits to mothers and children, the aged, the disabled, and other groups.

The lesson here is an important one for American federalism. A general pattern in the United States in the period since World War II has been for liberals on social issues to favor central government action, while conservatives tend to favor devolutionary strategies from the national government to states and localities. What we have now added is the observation that these positions may not be that astute, at least not as a general rule for political behavior.

In liberal periods (here, we refer to periods in which there is widespread support for social spending), it is true that it is likely to be easier and more efficient for the supporters of social programs to seek resources from one central source. But the flip side of this proposition is often ignored. In conservative periods, the supporters of social programs are likely to find that in many instances their best strategy is a devolutionary one. They may well find in particular areas of domestic policy that the best approach is to seek support from those states and major local governments which for various reasons are sympathetic to proposals for increased social spending.

These observations have important implications for the Reagan administration. Our initial assumption, and we believe the same assumption was made by officials of the Reagan administration, was that devolutionary measures would aid and abet the administration's overarching domestic commitment to retrenchment in the sphere of social policy. But this was not always the way it worked out. There is evidence from this study and from other sources that Reagan's federalism reforms have stimulated and are continuing to stimulate state governments to increase their efforts to meet domestic needs in the functional areas in which the national government either was cutting grants-in-aid or threatening to do so.[7]

Like most generalizations, there are caveats to be entered. We found that even the most active and responsive state governments did not step into the breach in all of the federal aid areas in which the Reagan administration was pursuing its retrenchment and devolutionary policies. On the whole, the more highly targeted a program was on the poor, the more likely it was to be cut by the national government and the less likely it was that these cuts would be replaced by state and local governments.

In addition, the American federal system, as the case-study chapters in this volume amply demonstrate, is a many splendored and varied political system; the roles of different political institutions are influenced by many forces. In the case of state governments, federal aid policy is but one of the forces that affects the relative standing and influence of these middlemen of our political system.

Economic conditions also have a major effect. The steep 1981–82 recession hit some states much harder than others and caused changes in the relative re-

---

[7] George E. Peterson, "Federalism and the States: An Experiment in Decentralization," in John L. Palmer and Isabel V. Sawhill, eds., *The Reagan Record* (Cambridge, Mass.: Ballinger, 1984). See also reports published by the U.S. General Accounting Office in Washington, D.C.: *Maternal and Child Health Block Grant: Program Changes Emerging Under State Administration*, May 7, 1984; *States Used Added Flexibility Offered by the Preventive Health and Health Services Block Grant*, May 8, 1984; *States Fund an Expanded Range of Activities Under Low-Income Energy Assistance Block Grant*, June 27, 1984; *Public Involvement in Block Grant Decisions: Multiple Opportunities Provided but Interest Groups Have Mixed Reactions to States' Efforts*, December 28, 1984; *Block Grants Brought Funding Changes and Adjustments to Program Priorities*, February 11, 1985.

sponsibilities of states and localities. Moreover, in a number of states, important causes of changes in the state role predated the Reagan presidency. In several of the study states, for example, a major factor in bringing about changes was the passage in the 1970s of referenda that limited state and local taxes and spending. Nevertheless, in the pluralistic environment of the American political system, we believe that the behavior of state governments in response to the Reagan brand of federalism reform is notable and surprising.

The authors of the case-study chapters in this volume have in our view made a good effort to put Reagan's program in perspective. They repeatedly call attention to other forces at work affecting the role of state governments in the period of this study. At the same time, there is a strong and consistent theme across the sample states to the effect that the policy-making, administrative, and often the financial role of state governments is becoming more important, both relative to the central government and relative to local governments as a result of the way in which the Reagan system of ideas in domestic affairs has shined a spotlight on the state level. In many of the case studies, state efforts have focused on ways to continue services cut by Congress at President Reagan's urging.

One additional point needs to be made here before we take a closer look at the Reagan program; it concerns timing. Although there is no definitive barometer or scale of the health and vitality of state governments, the consensus among the experts who work in this field is that over the past two decades there have been a series of changes in the structure and procedures of state governments that have improved both their standing and capability. In January 1985, the U.S. Advisory Commission on Intergovernmental Relations published a summary report on the capability of state governments. Drawing on a wide range of studies on the finances, management, and institutional behavior of states, the report reached a very upbeat conclusion: "This study concludes that state governments have been transformed in almost every facet of their structure and operations."[8] The situation, says the report, is vastly different from that of the 1930s when one expert quoted in the report said, "The American state is finished."[9]

The point here is that the timing of Reagan's federalism-reform program was propitious from the point of view of supporters of social programs. The states were ready; and the strong signal and action of Reagan's program for federalism reform appears to have had a deep effect on the policy agenda in many states.

[8] U.S. Advisory Commission on Intergovernmental Relations, *The Question of State Government Capability* (Washington, D.C.: Government Printing Office, January 1985).
[9] Ibid., p. 1. The quote is from an article by political scientist Luther A. Gulick. The article was published in 1933.

The American political system is intrinsically change-resistant. This is why we so often understand and interpret policy change as incremental rather than fundamental. And it is also for this reason that strong and highly visible policy shifts are required to bring about basic institutional changes in American government. We believe the Reagan program, and the way in which it has been discussed and understood in the field of domestic affairs and the media, is an event of sufficient importance that it appears to have permeated the political system and is likely as a result to have a lasting effect on American federalism.

Cuts and Changes in Federal Grants-in-Aid under Reagan

In Reagan's initial set of budget recommendations put forward in the spring of 1981, both of the objectives discussed above—social program retrenchment and devolving national government responsibilities to the states—were prominent. Despite the hope of David Stockman that "weak claims rather than weak clients" would be the target of federal spending reductions, the Reagan cuts were concentrated primarily on lower income groups—and especially the working poor, which had benefited most heavily from the spurt in social spending that had occurred since the inception of Lyndon Johnson's Great Society programs.[10]

Reagan explicitly linked many of his proposed cuts to the objective of the devolution of federal responsibilities. This linkage was most clearly reflected in Reagan's advocacy of block grants, i.e., merging groups of so-called "categorical" grant programs into broader and more flexible grants. In the address before a joint session of Congress announcing his economic recovery program in February 1981, the president said:

> . . . while we will reduce some subsidies to regional and local governments, we will at the same time convert a number of categorical grant programs into block grants to reduce wasteful administrative overhead and to give local governments and States more flexibility and control. . . .
>
> Now, we know of course the categorical grant programs burden local and State governments with a mass of Federal regulations and Federal paperwork. Ineffective targeting, wasteful administrative overhead—all can be eliminated by shifting the resources and decisionmaking authority to local and State government. This will also consolidate programs which

[10] William Greider, *The Education of David Stockman and Other Americans* (New York: E. P. Dutton, 1982) and Jack A. Meyer, "Budget Cuts in the Reagan Administration: A Question of Fairness," in D. Lee Bawden, ed., *The Social Contract Revisited: Aims and Outcomes of President Reagan's Social Welfare Policy* (Washington, D.C.: The Urban Institute, 1984).

are scattered throughout the Federal bureaucracy, bringing government closer to the people and saving over $23.0 billion over the next 5 years.[11]

Our initial analysis of the cuts and changes in grants made in Reagan's first year as president showed five things:

1. The cuts in 1981 were appreciable.
2. These cuts fell more heavily on actual or potential welfare beneficiaries (notably the so-called "working poor" group) than on state or local governments.
3. Several changes, especially the creation of new block grants and the passage of provisions giving states new authority to reshape the Medicaid program, shifted responsibilities from the national government to the states.
4. State and local governments responded initially to federal aid reductions in many programs with coping strategies using carryover funds, shifting funds among accounts, and in other ways putting off the day of reckoning for the cuts enacted in 1981.
5. These kinds of coping actions generally did not occur for welfare programs (such as AFDC and food stamps) and the public service employment program, where the 1981 cuts tended to be passed on directly to recipients.

After 1981, the momentum of Reagan's retrenchment policies in domestic affairs was dissipated as Congress rejected most of the administration's proposals for further cuts and approved some new domestic spending to stimulate the economy and reduce unemployment during the steep 1981–82 recession.

Two major pieces of legislation enacted at the initiative of the Congress in 1982 and 1983 provided large new infusions of federal aid funds. The Surface Transportation Assistance Act of 1982 raised the federal excise tax on gasoline from 5 cents to 9 cents per gallon, producing an increase of nearly 50 percent in the amount of federal aid available for highway and mass transit programs from the highway trust fund. In March 1983, the Congress followed suit with the emergency jobs act, which added $2.8 billion for a wide range of existing grant programs, including some which had been cut in 1981. The overall result was a jump in federal aid spending in nominal terms, as shown in table 1.2. Nevertheless, even in fiscal year 1985, federal aid was 5 percent below fiscal 1981 levels in real terms. In many functional areas, these antirecession increases in federal aid, plus state-local coping actions, the unwillingness of the

[11] "Program for Economic Recovery" (Address before a joint session of Congress, February 17, 1981), *Weekly Compilation of Presidential Documents* 17, no. 8 (February 23, 1981):131–33.

Table 1.2.   *Historical Trend of Federal Grants-in-Aid Outlays, Federal Fiscal Years 1976–85 (dollars in millions)*

Federal fiscal year	Total grants-in-aid[a]	Federal Grant as a Percentage of	
		Total budget outlays	Domestic outlays[b]
1976	$59,094	15.9	21.4
1977	68,415	16.7	22.4
1978	77,889	17.0	22.5
1979	82,858	16.5	21.8
1980	91,451	15.5	20.6
1981	94,762	14.0	18.7
1982	88,195	11.8	16.1
1983	92,496	11.4	15.8
1984	97,577	11.5	16.0
1985 est.	107,016	11.2	15.6

SOURCE: Executive Office of the President, U.S. Office of Management and Budget, *Special Analyses, Budget of the United States Government,* 1986 (Washington, D.C.: Government Printing Office, 1985), p. H-19.

NOTES: [a] Includes outlays that are off budget under current law; legislation is proposed to include them on budget. Such outlays began in 1973.

[b] Excludes outlays for national defense and international functions.

Congress to accede to Reagan's later requests for federal aid cuts, and actions by state and local governments to replace federal aid cuts out of own-source funds, meant that the service impact envisioned for the 1981 cuts simply never occurred. Some federal policy shifts that enhanced the role of states did take place even after 1981, however. The most notable was the 1982 passage of the Job Training Partnership Act, which gave state governments the lead role in setting policy for job training programs.

Even though Reagan's early cuts were large, we observed a tendency by both politicians and scholars to exaggerate their size and scope and to downplay the political effects (namely, the devolutionary effects) of Reagan's policies. The view commonly expressed in the media was that the president failed to follow through on his "new federalism" proposals. This label was used in the press (although not by the administration) to refer to the proposals Reagan made in 1982 to "swap and turn back" a wide array of domestic programs on a basis that would shift authority from the federal government to the states. Though less radical than Reagan's 1976 campaign proposal, the 1982 plan resembled it in its scope and basic character.

Reagan devoted the bulk of his January 1982 State of the Union message to his "swap and turnback" initiatives. Programs with total 1982 appropriations of

$46.6 billion were to be realigned between 1984 and 1991. The federal government was to assume responsibility for Medicaid, which is administered by state and local governments. In exchange, the states were to assume responsibility for the aid to families with dependent children (AFDC) program and food stamps. The plan also called for establishing a trust fund to finance "turnbacks," i.e., programs that would be devolved to the states. Certain federal taxes were to be relinquished to the states to help finance the programs to be turned back to them. Despite the fact that these "swap and turnback" proposals were never even introduced in Congress, our interpretation, as stressed in this volume, is that Reagan in his first term significantly advanced his federalism reform ideas, reflecting his state-centered theory of American federalism.

The Impact of Economic and Fiscal Conditions

We need at this junction to look more closely at the economic and fiscal setting of the Reagan changes in federal aid. In 1981, when Congress accepted many of President Reagan's proposals to cut federal aid, it took even stronger action in following up on the administration's proposals for large "supply-side" federal tax reductions. Later, when congressional enthusiasm for further budget cuts waned and tax revenues leveled off because of the income tax cuts of 1981, the national government as a result faced large and growing deficits. In this situation, Reagan's advocacy of federal spending restraint gained credibility. Even in the depths of the 1981–82 recession, new federal spending initiatives were modest in comparison with countercyclical programs in previous recessions.

Politicians and program advocates will debate for a long time whether the Reagan administration deliberately created the federal deficit to force Congress to cut further spending.[12] But what is not debatable is the inhibiting effect of the deficit on proposals for new federal programs. The signal from Washington was clear; new social program initiatives would have to occur elsewhere.

In an important way, the business cycle also influenced the responses of state governments to the changes in federal policy. By far the biggest federal aid cuts were made in 1981. Shortly after the 1981 budget act was adopted, the nation entered a sharp recession. Typically in a recession period, state and local governments overreact. Fearing the worst, and forced by state constitutional mandates to balance their budgets, they cut spending, increased taxes, and, generally speaking, "battened down the hatches." This behavior was clearly manifest in the 1981–82 period, since the recession came on so suddenly and hit so hard.

[12] Daniel Patrick Moynihan, "Reagan's Inflate-the-Deficit Game," *New York Times*, July 21, 1985, p. E-21.

Thirty-eight states raised taxes in 1983. According to the U.S. Bureau of the Census, the tax revenues of state governments in 1984 showed a dramatic 14.8 percent increase in 1984. State fiscal analyst, Steven D. Gold, notes that "Real state general fund spending rose at a significant rate in 1984, 1985, and 1986."[13] Focusing on the condition of state finances in 1984, Steven D. Gold and Corina L. Eckl note a marked improvement: "State finances are in much better shape today than they have been in the past several years. . . . The up-turn is the result of the unexpectedly vigorous economic recovery, large tax in-creases in 1983, and restraint in spending."[14]

As a result of these actions and the sharp economic upturn, many state gov-ernments were relatively flush near the end of 1983.[15] Moreover, since it always takes time for policy changes made in Washington to percolate through the sys-tem, it was not until the economic recovery was under way that many of the cuts in federal grants made in 1981 were felt with full force.

This volatile pattern of state finances and the delayed effects of federal policy changes meant that many states were in a position to consider claims from groups that either experienced federal aid cuts or feared them.

Long-Term Changes in Domestic Politics and Intergovernmental Relations

At this point in the analysis, a basic political observation needs to be added. Re-trenchment involves more than money: *It sends a signal*. Reagan sent a signal to the domestic public sector—and it was strong and explicit—that the federal government should and would do less, and that states and localities, especially nonprofit institutions that provide social services and the private sector, should do more. Not surprisingly, the politics of social programs changed in ways that reflect the seriousness which service providers attributed to Reagan's policies. Increasingly, the proponents of federal domestic programs turned to others for succor. In particular, claims were made at the state level at just the time, as it turns out, that many states could respond to them.

It will take a while before we can analyze census and other data on govern-ment finances to assess the magnitude of state responses to these new and

[13] Steven D. Gold, "Developments in State Finances, 1983 to 1986," *Public Budgeting and Finance*, forthcoming.

[14] Steven D. Gold and Corina L. Eckl, "State Budget Actions in 1984," Fiscal Affairs Pro-gram, National Conference of State Legislatures, Legislative Paper no. 45 (September 1984):1.

[15] David Levin, "Receipts and Expenditures of State Governments and Local Governments, 1980–83," *Survey of Current Business*, September 1984, pp. 19–23 and John Herbers, "States Discover Large Surplus in Their Income," *New York Times*, December 4, 1983, p. 1.

stronger claims. Moreover, such analysis is never easy due to the large number of factors that influence governmental finances. The evidence from our research, however, suggests that state governments have been—and still are being—activated by the Reagan program, and as a result are playing a larger role in domestic affairs. In these terms, political dynamics can be seen to be changing.

These shifts have been commented on by other observers. A 1985 article in the *National Journal* reported that organizations which support social programs have produced a level of liberal and minority-group political activism heretofore unknown in state capitals.[16] Similarly, a lead survey article in the *New York Times* in May 1985 noted an increase in the activities at the state level on the part of the leaders of civil rights groups and lobbyists for the poor. "On a wide range of social issues, including education, civil rights, and health care for poor people, they [the leaders of these organizations] said the states had been quicker to respond to their appeals than the federal government in the last few years."[17]

These developments can be expected to disappoint conservatives to the extent that they hoped that shifting responsibilities from the national government to the state level would bring about a general decline in governmental activity. According to the article in the *National Journal* quoted above, "[C]onservatives who gleefully assumed that shifting the responsibility for social programs to the states would mean the end of the programs have discovered that state governments were not as conservative as they thought."[18]

Past research suggests that "innovative" policies tend to be adopted by the larger, generally more liberal or progressive state governments.[19] Our research provides support for these findings in that the most pronounced response to the Reagan changes usually—but not always—came in states that fit this definition. This is particularly true for the states that were from the outset most willing to commit new or additional revenues from their own sources to replace actual or anticipated federal aid cuts. But there is also evidence of the beginning of a broader response, in some cases involving traditionally less progressive states, where the political ideology was seen to be shifting during the period of our study.

We can only speculate about the future: We see a likelihood that as state gov-

[16] Jerry Hagstrom, "Liberal and Minority Coalitions Pleading Their Cases in State Capitals," *National Journal* 17, no. 8 (February 23, 1985), p. 426.

[17] Robert Pear, "States are Found More Responsive on Social Issues," *New York Times*, May 19, 1985, p. 1.

[18] Hagstrom, "Liberal and Minority Coalitions," p. 426.

[19] Jack L. Walker, "The Diffusion of Innovations Among the American States," *The American Political Science Review* 63 (September 1969):880–99 and Virginia Gray, "Innovations in the States: A Diffusion Study," *The American Political Science Review* 67 (December 1973):1174–85.

ernments take on a larger role—initially perhaps concentrating on increased policy and administrative responsibilities for devolved federal programs—they will eventually commit additional resources to these functions, and that, over time, though it is very hard to measure in a close way, this will be reflected in higher levels of state spending than would otherwise have occurred. As the program advocates in the areas in which the federal government is pulling back turn increasingly to the state level as a new arena of action, the link between devolution and retrenchment, in our view, is likely to be even weaker.

Up to now, we have dealt with Woodrow Wilson's cardinal question about the relationship between the federal government and the states in the customary way—*involving money*. It is true, as many experts in the field have stressed, that money has increasingly become the glue of American federalism.[20] Grants-in-aid and their attendant regulatory requirements have influenced the character of state and local governmental activities and the levels of funding devoted to different public purposes. This is the area of our expertise and it is the focus of this study. We have tried to deal not just with grants and their requirements in a mechanical way, but also with the signals transmitted by Reagan's changes and proposed changes in the grant system.

There are, however, other federalism policy issues that are outside the scope of this study or only tangentially fall within the purview of the federal aid system. Some involve admonitory ("bully pulpit") tactics presidents can use to influence the behavior of state and local governments that do not involve the federal aid system. Although Reagan's changes in federal aid policy in the field of education, for example, would have to be described as modest, his actions in other ways have had a decided effect on educational policies and practices and on American federalism that this study does not capture. Reagan's position on school prayer, for example, as well as the dramatic national report issued by a commission, which was appointed by his secretary of education in August 1981, have influenced state governments and local school districts in important ways. In some cases, they have increased the influence of the national government, as in the case of school prayer, although this is not an area in which concrete policy change was accomplished in Reagan's first term. In other cases, these actions, as was true in the case of the 1983 report, A *Nation at Risk*, have catalyzed state action and appear in this case to have increased the relative position of the states in the field of elementary and secondary education.[21] These

[20] Michael D. Reagan, *The New Federalism* (New York: Oxford University Press, 1972), chapter 3, argues grants-in-aid make cooperative federalism "a functioning reality instead of a constitutional lawyer's phrase."

[21] In the introduction of the 1983 report, the commission stated: "If an unfriendly foreign power had attempted to impose on America the mediocre educational performance that exists today, we might well have viewed it as an act of war. As it stands, we have allowed this to happen to

issues and others like them—for example, involving the way in which federal power in the Reagan period was used to enforce the twenty-one-year-old drinking-age requirement—are not covered in this study, which focuses on grants-in-aid.

We point this out to remind readers that one needs to consider this broader landscape in assessing our thesis that Reagan's actions on grant-in-aid policy issues are stimulating states to play a larger and more important leadership role in American federalism. Although we see the need to put our findings in this broader context, the consideration of other developments in the Reagan period that have influenced federal-state relations and American federalism does not in our view diminish the strength of importance of the findings of this research.

Research Methodology

Our research approach in this study and in previous field evaluation studies we have conducted emphasizes the need to go beyond centrally available statistical data in studying both the effects and implementation of major changes in the intergovernmental policies of the U.S. national government.[22] In field evaluation studies of the effects of changes in federal grant-in-aid policies we have conducted, beginning with the general revenue sharing program enacted in 1972, we have based our analysis on observations about political processes and relationships as well as financial and program data. This research has been conducted on an interdisciplinary basis; economists and political scientists have participated both in the field and in the conduct of the central analysis to combine the field data. Frequently in these studies, we have focused on questions of economic analysis; we have been interested in the *impacts* of new federal aid policies. Our previous research projects, for example, have asked whether a particular new grant-in-aid program expanded the public or the private sector (in the case of revenue sharing); aided the poor or other groups (in the case of

---

ourselves. . . . We have, in effect, been committing an act of unthinking, unilateral educational disarmament." National Commission on Excellence in Education, A *Nation at Risk: The Imperative for Educational Reform* (Washington, D.C.: U.S. Department of Education, April 1983), p. 5.

[22] See, for example, Richard P. Nathan, Allen D. Manvel, Susannah E. Calkins, and Associates, *Monitoring Revenue Sharing* (Washington, D.C.: The Brookings Institution, 1975); Richard P. Nathan, Charles F. Adams, Jr., and Associates, *Revenue Sharing: The Second Round* (Washington, D.C.: The Brookings Institution, 1977); Paul R. Dommel and Associates, *Decentralizing Urban Policy: Case Studies in Community Development* (Washington, D.C.: The Brookings Institution, 1982); Richard P. Nathan, Robert F. Cook, V. Lane Rawlins, and Associates, *Public Service Employment: A Field Evaluation* (Washington, D.C.: The Brookings Institution, 1981); and James W. Fossett, *Federal Aid to Big Cities: The Politics of Dependence* (Washington, D.C.: The Brookings Institution, 1983).

the community development block grant); or caused more employment as opposed to displacing jobs that would have been filled anyway (in the case of the CETA public service jobs program under the Comprehensive Employment and Training Act, CETA).

In studying the Reagan domestic program, we are again interested in impact issues: Were the services affected by Reagan's cuts in grants-in-aid replaced or in other ways protected by state and local governments, or did these governments ratify the cuts by passing them on to the programs and people who otherwise would have been served?

It is our experience that the answers to questions such as these cannot be provided on the basis of the analysis of centrally available data from the U.S. Bureau of the Census, the Office of Management and Budget, and the Treasury Department. The data from these sources are aggregated at too high a level; they often do not provide the needed information or sufficient detail to analyze the effects of changes in federal grant-in-aid and policies on the finances and services of state and local governments.

Our conclusions are based on research in the sample of fourteen states shown earlier. In each of the case-study states for this research on the effects of Reagan's cuts and changes in federal grant-in-aid programs, we also selected a major city to examine the way the Reagan changes have affected local governments and state-local relations.

The sample was chosen to be representative in terms of size, location, and economic and social characteristics. All fourteen case studies cover the same time period, the first term of the Reagan administration; they were written according to a similar organizational plan. The case studies were initially presented at a conference on this research held at Princeton University in June 1984.

The nine case studies chosen for inclusion in this volume were selected on a somewhat different basis from the original sample. While we sought to preserve the representative character of this group on the bases indicated above, we also gave attention in the selection of the states to be included as the subject of case-study chapters in this volume to the degree and character of the response made to the cuts and changes in federal grants-in-aid during the Reagan first term.

As a first step, all fourteen states in the sample were classified according to the relative degree of their response to the Reagan changes as shown in table 1.3. Five states are classified as having made the *"most pronounced"* response to the Reagan changes. This classification was made on the basis of two criteria—fiscal and institutional. Specifically, the two criteria are: (1) the replacement out of state funds of federal aid cuts that were made or threatened under

Table 1.3. *Sample States Grouped by Degree of State Role Enhancement*

Most pronounced state response	Intermediate state response	Low state response
Florida	Mississippi	California
Massachusetts	Ohio	
New Jersey	Texas	
New York	Washington	
Oklahoma	Arizona	
	Illinois	
	Missouri	
	South Dakota	

NOTE: States included in the case-study chapters of this volume are shown in italics.

the Reagan administration; and (2) the actions taken by the sample state governments to play a stronger policy-making and administrative role in response to the changes made in federal grant-in-aid programs under Reagan. In effect, these two criteria can be thought of as *fiscal and institutional replacement* in the areas in which the federal role in domestic policy was reduced under the Reagan administration. The five states in the "most pronounced" response group, in alphabetical order, are Florida, Massachusetts, New Jersey, New York, and Oklahoma.

At the other end of the scale, California is classified as having made a minimal response to the Reagan changes, because according to the field researchers the enactment of major state referenda affecting state finances, and the debates about others, swamped the effect of the Reagan federal aid policy shifts.

The remaining eight states in the sample are classified in one category that we label the *"intermediate-response"* group, although we need to indicate important differences among these states. Three states in this group were found to have replaced some federal aid cuts (or threatened federal aid cuts) out of their own funds—Mississippi, Ohio, and Texas. In all three of these cases, there was both a fiscal-replacement and an institutional-replacement response to the Reagan cuts and changes in federal grants-in-aid; however, these responses were not as strong as in the case of the five states classified above in the "most pronounced" response category. One state in the sample, Washington, initially decided to replace anticipated cuts in federal aid, but then rescinded these replacement actions when its economic situation deteriorated sharply in 1981. Four states in this "intermediate-response" group were found not to have replaced federal aid cuts out of their own funds; however, they did take steps to exercise a stronger policy-making and administrative role in functional areas in which the devolutionary policies of the Reagan administration involved the assignment of greater discretion to state governments. The four states in this subgroup are Arizona, Illinois, Missouri, and South Dakota.

The nine states chosen for inclusion as the subjects of case-study chapters in this volume were selected to represent a cross section of the different types of responses just described. Three states from the "most pronounced" response group are included—Florida, Massachusetts, and New York. Two of the states in the "intermediate-response" group, which did take fiscal-replacement actions, are included—Mississippi and Ohio. The other three states in this group that are the subject of case-study chapters are Washington (which initially voted and later rescinded federal aid replacement actions), Arizona, and Illinois. All three of these states took steps to increase their policy or administrative role in areas in which Reagan's decentralization policies assigned a greater role to state governments. The ninth state included as the subject of a case-study chapter in this volume is California, which, as indicated above, is classified as having made a minimal response to the cuts and changes made in federal grants-in-aid during the Reagan first term.

These nine states reflect the substantial diversity that is customarily found in the policies, finances, and political values and behavior of state and local governments in American federalism. This diversity presents a formidable challenge to researchers. We have tried in this book to strike a balance. In the six overview chapters, we present generalizations about the responses to the Reagan policies; at the same time, a fuller picture of the intricacy and complexity of our subject matter is presented in the case studies included in this volume.

A major premise of the field network evaluation studies in this series, beginning with the study of the general revenue sharing program, is that our role as researchers should be to describe and analyze the effects of major changes in the federal grant-in-aid policies of the national government. Our concern in this research lies not with making a judgment about the wisdom of these policies, but rather in understanding how they played out in the diverse, complex, and fragmented real world of American government. Whether one views Reagan's policies as good, bad, or indifferent, successful or unsuccessful, depends on the values and preconceptions that each reader brings to the subject matter.

The remainder of this volume is divided into four main parts. The next two chapters describe the history of federal grants-in-aid to state and local governments. Chapter 2 considers the history of federal grants up to the turnaround that occurred in the middle of the Carter years. Chapter 3 describes the efforts made since then to curb federal aid spending and devolve federal government responsibilities. Chapters 4 and 5 present the overview analysis of the findings of the field researchers on the responses of the sample jurisdictions to the cuts and changes in federal grants made during the Reagan first term. Chapter 4 discusses how the responses differed on a *program-by-program* basis; chapter 5 summarizes the findings on a *state-by-state* basis. Chapters 6–14 are the case studies. Chapter 15 presents our concluding observations about the implications of the material presented in this volume for American federalism.

2

The Evolution of Federal Aid

*

*F*ederal grants-in-aid to state and local governments have played a crucial role in the development of U.S. federalism. According to Michael Reagan and John Sanzone, "the grant relationship is far and away the most decisive means of intergovernmental cooperation today."[1] Similarly, Kenneth N. Vines observes that grants-in-aid have become "a vital way in which the nation and the states relate to each other."[2]

It was during the time that the United States operated under the Articles of Confederation that the Continental Congress adopted the first grants-in-aid to the states, putting aside land for the support of public schools in the territory west of the Ohio River. Starting in 1802, when Ohio became the first state to be carved out of this territory, each new state was given sections of land to distribute to localities, which usually sold them and used the proceeds to support public schools.[3]

In the two centuries since the first land grants were made, intergovernmental transfers from the federal government to states and now also to localities have increased markedly in number, diversity, and magnitude. Along the way there have been many important shifts and permutations in federal policy, of which the Reagan cuts and changes of 1981 is but one, albeit important, example. As background for our consideration of the Reagan changes—what they were and

[1] Michael D. Reagan and John G. Sanzone, *The New Federalism* (New York: Oxford University Press, 1981), p. 75.

[2] Kenneth N. Vines, "The Federal Setting of State Policies," in Herbert Jacob and Kenneth N. Vines, eds., *Politics in the American States, A Comparative Analysis*, 3rd edition (Boston and Toronto: Little, Brown, 1976), p. 20.

[3] James A. Maxwell, *The Fiscal Impact of Federalism in the United States* (New York: Russell & Russell, 1970), pp. 67–69. Originally published by Harvard University Press in 1946.

how they affected the recipient jurisdictions—it is useful here to present a brief history of federal aid. This chapter reviews the evolution of federal grant policy from the pre-Constitution period through the mid-Carter years; chapter 3 describes the retrenchment in aid programs that began under Carter and accelerated under Reagan.

Early Forms of Federal Grants

Like early aid for public schools, other grants were given in the form of land during the nineteenth century. They included land grants to states to support the construction of roads, canals, railroads, colleges, river and harbor improvements, and other capital projects. Land was also granted to private companies formed to construct roads, canals, and railroads, and even directly to individuals, as in the case of the homestead program and land grants made by the Continental Congress to veterans of the Revolutionary War.

Land was used in these early programs because "land was plentiful and money was not," as Daniel Elazar has noted. Furthermore, politicians who were opposed to money grants on grounds that they were not authorized by the Constitution could rationalize land grants as "gifts by the federal government in its capacity as property owner rather than grants made in its governmental capacity."[4]

The earliest grant-in-aid programs had few strings. The first land grants specified the purposes for which proceeds from the sale of land were to be used, but they made little provision for checking on how states distributed the land or how localities used the proceeds, nor did they establish any sanctions for improper uses. Increasingly detailed specifications were written into grants of land to states that came into the Union later, as Congress determined the need for such controls and as the federal government gained strength in relation to state governments.[5]

[4] Daniel J. Elazar, *The American Partnership: Intergovernmental Co-operation in the Nineteenth-Century United States* (Chicago: University of Chicago Press, 1962), p. 143.

[5] James A. Maxwell notes, "It is a matter of common knowledge that this endowment was not always wisely used. . . . In most cases a permanent public-school fund was set up . . . but some states . . . diverted the funds to other uses. There is a temptation to lament the squandering of a magnificent endowment, and to wish that Congress had insisted upon strict conditions or had even kept control of the endowment in its own hands. . . . But pretty plans about what might have been do not take into account the temper of the times. Congress was in no mood up to the Civil War, and for several decades afterwards, to lay any conditions upon the states; and only an optimist can have a conviction that Congress, until nearly the twentieth century, would have been a better trustee than the states themselves." Maxwell, *The Fiscal Impact of Federalism,* p. 69.

The earliest money grant to states was made in 1837. For almost every year in the previous two decades, the federal government had enjoyed considerable surpluses—a circumstance that is almost unimaginable today. An overflowing treasury was not seen as a blessing, however, but as a "serious inconvenience."[6] The problem was that no one could agree on a way to reduce federal revenues, which came almost entirely from tariffs on imports and proceeds from the sale of federally owned land. Sectional rivalries between the commerce-oriented North and the agrarian South made it difficult to agree on changes in tariffs or land-sale arrangements. Nor was it felt that spending could be increased to take up the surpluses. The federal government was already spending as much as was thought desirable on the relatively small number of domestic functions it then served (which in terms of manpower consisted mostly of the postal service, customs collections, the Corps of Engineers, and administration of territorial governments).[7]

After long debate, Congress and President Andrew Jackson agreed on a compromise whereby surplus funds would be sent to states as bank deposits that, in theory, could be recalled by the federal government. In fact, one of the bill's prime supporters, Sen. Henry Clay of Kentucky, said he "did not believe a single member of either house imagined that a dollar would be recalled."[8] Congress placed no restrictions on the uses by the states of these funds, though many states passed laws allotting their shares to localities. A proponent of the legislation, Sen. Mahlon Dickerson of New Jersey, explained that "It is not proposed to restrict the states in the application of the funds to be assigned to them as the states may be safely trusted to make the best use of their own . . . as their exigencies or interests may require."[9]

A few months after the first payment to states was made, the speculative boom of the previous years suddenly collapsed. Many of the banks in which surplus revenue had been deposited closed their doors, at least temporarily, and the federal government's surplus vanished. A total of $28 million was distributed under the Surplus Distribution Act of 1837, but the fourth quarterly payment, scheduled for January 1838, was never made.

Political scientist Jane Perry Clark, writing in 1938, concluded that the 1837 surplus distribution accomplished little that was concrete and lasting. She observed, "There was no suggestion as to how the states were to spend the money,

---

[6] Ibid., p. 12.

[7] David B. Walker, *Toward a Functioning Federalism* (Cambridge, Mass.: Winthrop Publishers, 1981), p. 53.

[8] Edward G. Bourne, *The History of the Surplus Revenue of 1837* (New York: G. P. Putnam's Sons, 1885), p. 21.

[9] Elazar, *The American Partnership*, p. 204.

and they squandered their patrimony, or at best sold it for what many people think was a mess of pottage."[10]

The next major turning point in the development of federal grants came in 1862, when Congress passed the first Morrill Act. This legislation was important not only for the purpose it served—granting land to states to establish agricultural colleges, which later evolved into the "land-grant" colleges of today—but also for the terms of the grants. The act specified the purposes for which grants could be used: to support instruction focusing on "agriculture and the mechanical arts." It required colleges to make annual reports and required governors to account for the use of resources made available through the sale of land grants. "No longer were gifts to be scattered with an entirely prodigal hand," Clark has commented. Nevertheless, she points out, "the states were at liberty to fulfill in any way they chose the few obligations imposed on them."[11]

The slow pace of the development of grant programs in the nineteenth century reflects the considerable hesitation of federal officials about such developments. The Morrill Act, which was signed by Lincoln, was originally vetoed by James Buchanan on the grounds that it violated the then-widespread and quite rigid dual federalism view of the American system. "Should the time arrive," said Buchanan, "when the State governments shall look to the Federal Treasury for the means of supporting themselves and maintaining their systems of education and internal policy, the character of both Governments will be greatly deteriorated."[12]

The first money grant of the type familiar to us today was enacted in 1887 to support state agricultural experiment stations affiliated with the land-grant colleges. In 1890, Congress passed the second Morrill Act, which supplemented land-grant institutions' revenues with annual allotments of federal funds.[13]

Expansion of Purposes

Not until 1911 did Congress approve grant-in-aid programs for purposes other than agricultural research and education. In that year, Congress enacted a pro-

[10] Jane Perry Clark, *The Rise of a New Federalism* (New York: Russell & Russell, 1965), p. 142. Originally published by Columbia University Press in 1938.

[11] Clark, *The Rise of a New Federalism*, p. 141.

[12] As quoted in Maxwell, *The Fiscal Impact of Federalism*, pp. 20–21.

[13] Each state's allotment of $25,000 was to be secured by sale of public lands. In 1898, Congress began to make appropriations from the federal treasury when land sales no longer covered the grants. The 1890 act introduced some further controls over colleges' use of grant funds. See Maxwell, *The Fiscal Impact of Federalism*, p. 71, and Clark, *The Rise of a New Federalism*, p. 142.

gram of cooperation with the states for preventing forest fires.[14] The forest fire program required states to submit plans for prevention activities, which had to be approved by the secretary of agriculture before federal money was released. Also, the federal government inspected how states used the money. Clark has noted that this marked the first time federal aid programs specifically required states to conform to conditions before receiving aid and to "live up to a certain minimum of performance if they wished to continue the cooperative plan."[15]

Four important cash grant-in-aid programs had their start during the Woodrow Wilson administration. The first was the Smith-Lever Act of 1914, which authorized funds for land-grant colleges to set up "extension" programs that would offer instruction in agriculture and home economics outside the colleges. Although the purpose of this act was closely related to earlier aid for land-grant colleges, its funding provisions set it apart from past programs. Part of a state's allocation was a flat amount, but another part was allotted to states on the basis of rural population; states were to match the population-based part of the federal allocation. Past grant programs had made grants of the same amount to all states (though some were later amended to make grants of varying sizes), and none had a matching requirement.[16] The Smith-Lever Act also required advance approval of state plans for spending federal funds for agricultural extension. In these respects—its funding provisions and its control over state spending—it can be considered the first "categorical" federal grant program in the sense we now use that term.[17]

The second Wilson-era program was initiated in 1916 when Congress acceded to persistent demands for a federally aided highway construction program. Pressure had come both from farmers who needed local roads to get their crops to rail depots and from automobile drivers who wanted interstate highways. During the 1920s, the highway aid program was by far the largest federal program of grants to states, and even in the 1930s its expenditures were second only to those for emergency relief.[18] New highway aid legislation in 1921 added another element to federal influence over the states by requiring them to have highway departments that were "suitably equipped and organized" to carry out their duties under the aid program.[19]

In 1917, the federal government further expanded its reach in domestic af-

[14] Clark, *The Rise of a New Federalism*, p. 142.

[15] Ibid., pp. 142–43.

[16] See Maxwell, *The Fiscal Impact of Federalism*, pp. 77ff.

[17] See Martha Derthick, *The Influence of Federal Grants* (Cambridge, Mass.: Harvard University Press, 1970), p. 5.

[18] V. O. Key, Jr., *The Administration of Federal Grants to States* (New York: Johnson Reprint Corporation, 1972), pp. 6–16.

[19] Ibid., p. 30.

fairs with aid for vocational education. Labor unions, industrial organizations, and educational associations lobbied for this program, which expanded educational opportunities for those who sought neither a classical college education nor a career in agriculture. This program is an early example of the use of federal grants to respond to changes in the structure of the nation's economy, which by then was well on its way from a mainly agricultural base to an industrial base.

The fourth new grant program of the Wilson administration was spurred by public health problems associated with World War I. In 1918, Congress passed a rider to an army appropriations act providing funds to help states combat venereal disease. Although funding for this purpose ended after two years, Congress in 1921 renewed federal grants to states for public health with the Sheppard-Towner Act, which supported programs for mothers and children to help reduce infant mortality. "This modest pioneer legislation encountered virulent opposition from those who purported to see in it an invasion of the powers of the states," observed James A. Maxwell.[20] Although the Supreme Court in 1929 rejected a legal challenge to this program, Congress let it expire two years later. Federal grants to states for public health services were made permanent with passage of the Social Security Act in 1935.[21]

Enactment of these new grant-in-aid programs within a few years of each other in the early twentieth century may have been related not only to recognition of the needs to be met, but also to the availability of a new source of federal revenues—the income tax,[22] levied after the Sixteenth Amendment passed in 1913. Money was now more available than land; the western frontier had been closed by the turn of the century.

During the 1920s, the national government turned away from social concerns; new social initiatives were left to the states. Political scientist Virginia Gray, in her study of the diffusion of innovation among the states, notes that the social phase of the Progressive Movement "was by far the most important at the state level."[23] She cites the example of mothers' pension legislation, an outgrowth of the White House Conference on the Care of Dependent Children in 1909, as a prime illustration of this point. In this period several states, especially the most industrialized ones, adopted social legislation which President Franklin D. Roosevelt later used as a basis for new federal programs.

[20] Maxwell, *The Fiscal Impact of Federalism*, p. 204.

[21] Ibid.

[22] George E. Hale and Marian Lief Palley, *The Politics of Federal Grants* (Washington, D.C.: Congressional Quarterly Press, 1981), p. 8.

[23] Virginia Gray, "Innovation in the States: A Diffusion Study," *The American Political Science Review* 67 (December 1973):1174–85.

Explosion of Programs under the New Deal

Roosevelt's New Deal brought an enormous expansion of federal grant programs. Several major efforts to put people back to work and ease the poverty of the unemployed were undertaken.

Between 1933 and 1935, the Roosevelt administration, in characteristic fashion, tried several competing approaches for aiding the poor and unemployed, some direct and some channeled through state governments.[24] The first of these was the Federal Emergency Relief Administration, which provided grants to states for direct relief and work relief. The director of the relief administration was Harry L. Hopkins, who had headed a relief agency in New York State while Roosevelt was governor. State agencies varied widely in their ability to meet the challenge posed by their overwhelming needs and the influx of federal funds. According to Arthur M. Schlesinger, Jr., "Hopkins and a small field staff used their power to pump new life into the faltering state agencies. Where a local organization seemed hopelessly incompetent, Hopkins asked the governor to make the necessary changes. . . . In a few cases, FERA had to go into the state and appoint its own administration."[25]

The Public Works Administration had its start in 1933, under the National Industrial Recovery Act. Its task was to oversee construction of public buildings and other facilities, both for federal agencies and for local governments. It bypassed state governments. Partly because few localities had done any architectural and engineering planning and partly because Public Works Director Harold L. Ickes exercised tight control to avoid any hint of scandal, this new agency was slow in putting people to work. As a stopgap effort to create jobs during the bleak winter of 1933–34, Hopkins persuaded Roosevelt to issue an executive order creating the Civil Works Administration (CWA). Projects funded by this agency were administered directly by the federal government; workers on the projects were federal employees.[26] When the Civil Works Administration closed its doors in spring 1934, Hopkins's Emergency Relief Administration

[24] This tension between national solutions to the problems of the Depression and state interests was present through much of the New Deal. Samuel Beer recounts Roosevelt's call for the nationalization of politics and federal solutions to domestic problems. See Samuel H. Beer, "In Search of a New Public Philosophy," in Anthony King, ed., *The New American Political System* (Washington, D.C.: American Enterprise Institute for Public Policy Research, 1978), pp. 5–44. Even with Roosevelt's popularity, the states continued to have independent power in the federal system. See James Patterson, *New Deal and the States: Federalism in Transition* (Princeton, N.J.: Princeton University Press, 1969).

[25] Arthur M. Schlesinger, Jr., *The Coming of the New Deal* (New York: Houghton Mifflin, 1958), p. 267.

[26] William J. Tobin, *Public Works and Unemployment: A History of Federally Funded Programs* (Washington, D.C.: U.S. Department of Commerce, Economic Development Administration, April 1975).

again picked up the work relief function, reverting to the approach of making grants to states.

The task of screening applicants for public works jobs under the New Deal agencies was shouldered by employment service agencies. These had been started by the federal government during World War I and turned over to the states after the war ended. Many states let them lapse; by 1930 only twenty-four states still had such an agency, and many were very small. In New Hampshire, the Employment Service consisted of a single person who handled requests by mail order; if someone wrote seeking a job, his or her name was put on a card "and filed to await the possibility that an employer in the same locality might inquire for help."[27]

The Wagner-Peyser Act of 1933 set up the U.S. Employment Service and authorized grants to states that affiliated with the federal system. Some states were slow to establish functioning offices, however; not until 1938 did all states have active systems. Some states had statewide systems but many confined services to major cities. To fill the gap in service, the federal government for a time ran its own employment offices in states that did not have them and in areas of states that were not served by the state offices. Many of these federally operated offices were later absorbed by states as they set up or expanded their own systems.[28]

In 1935, the Roosevelt administration moved to rearrange the functions of the federal government, the states, and the local governments under the New Deal programs. The federalism theory underlying Roosevelt's efforts can best be described as *eclectic*; it changed rapidly and abruptly for different programs, agencies, and Roosevelt lieutenants. The federal government was to directly administer work relief for persons who would be able to work if jobs were available, while states were to run federally aided direct relief programs for those unable to work due to old age, disability, family responsibilities, or other reasons.

In April 1935, Congress approved a set of work relief programs that included several agencies, of which the Works Progress Administration (WPA) soon became the largest. WPA put workers on the federal payroll, though local governments had a role in initiating projects, and local and state relief agencies certified eligible workers.[29]

Direct relief programs for the unemployable were authorized by the Social Security Act of 1935. In addition to the federally administered insurance programs for retirees and survivors of workers, the act set up programs of grants to

[27] Raymond C. Atkinson, Louise C. Odencrantz, and Ben Deming, *Public Employment Service in the United States* (Chicago: Public Administration Service, 1938), p. 22.

[28] Ibid., pp. 22–27.

[29] Tobin, *Public Works and Unemployment*.

the states to provide financial assistance to low-income elderly persons, aid to families with dependent children, aid to the blind, services for crippled children, and child welfare services.[30] The act also set up a system of unemployment compensation, although administration was left to each state separately and no federal grants were made to provide benefits.[31] All of these grant program initiatives were based on programs previously established by states, with the older, more urban and progressive states usually taking the lead.[32]

Building on these state efforts, the permanent grant-in-aid programs initiated by the Social Security Act marked a major expansion of federal government activity and a distinct break with past practice, particularly in the social welfare field. Relief for the poor was a local function in colonial times to the extent it was provided at all. In the late nineteenth century some states began to build institutions for certain groups, such as the insane, the blind, and the deaf; after the turn of the century some states began to help localities provide financial assistance to mothers with children and to the aged. Social reformers had tried to involve the federal government in these activities as early as 1854, when Congress approved land grants to the states for the support of institutions for the indigent insane in response to pleas from Dorothea Dix. President Franklin Pierce vetoed the measure, arguing that "the fountains of charity would be dried up at home" and that the states would "become humble suppliants for the bounty of the federal government" rather than "bestowing their own means on the social wants of their people."[33]

Social workers began to renew the call for federal involvement in 1901, but Martha Derthick has observed that it was the Depression that was the big impetus to action.

> But for the Depression, the social work profession might have had to wait
> a long time for federal action. . . . The Depression exposed the political

---

[30] Aid to low-income elderly, blind, and disabled persons was taken over by the federal government in 1974 under the Supplemental Security Income (SSI) program.

[31] States continue to play the primary role in administering unemployment compensation, though the federal government plays a role as well. At present, state payroll taxes are used to pay unemployment benefits for up to twenty-six weeks. During periods of high unemployment, extended benefits are available for up to thirteen weeks after the regular benefits have been exhausted. The cost of the extended benefits is split evenly between the states and the federal government. Because some persons who held a job in one state later move to another state and apply for benefits, a central trust fund within the U. S. Department of Labor handles the flow of revenues and payments among the states; it keeps a separate account for each state. Each state sets its own rules for eligibility and level of benefits. For historical background, see Maxwell, *The Fiscal Impact of Federalism*, chapter 11.

[32] See Jack L. Walker, "The Diffusion of Innovations Among the American States," *The American Political Science Review* 63 (September 1969):880–99.

[33] *Congressional Globe*, 33d Congress, 1st sess., May 3, 1854, p. 1062, quoted in Walker, "The Diffusion of Innovations," p. 52.

and fiscal limits of state and local capacities. Although nearly all states had laws for aid to mothers and the aged, these were not necessarily backed with state funds, and they were not always mandatory for local governments. Only half the counties in the country were giving mothers' aid as of 1934, and the number was actually declining. Even where grants were given, the amounts were often tiny, and disparities among and within states were extreme. The average monthly old-age assistance grant in 1934 ranged from $0.69 in North Dakota to $26.08 in Massachusetts. . . .[34]

New Deal Forms of Federal Aid

The New Deal programs of grants to states generally shared a common structure. They all (1) defined what activities were to be aided; (2) were provided almost exclusively to states; (3) required states to submit plans for these activities in conformance with federal standards; (4) required states to match federal aid with state money; and (5) provided for the review and audit of federally aided programs by federal agencies. This structure had evolved from the increasingly specific programs of the previous two decades and was the model for most subsequent "categorical" grant-in-aid programs—that is, programs aiding a particular category of activities. This was the typical structure of grants until the 1970s, when the Nixon administration introduced general revenue sharing, which provided unrestricted grants, and "block grants," which consolidated closely related categorical grants into broad functional-area grants.

By the end of the New Deal period, three main types of categorical grant programs were extant:

1. *Entitlement grants* provide money or in-kind assistance to persons who meet certain requirements such as age or income, some of which are set by the states. Entitlement grants created during the New Deal include aid to families with dependent children; more recent entitlement programs include Medicaid, which was created in 1965.
2. *Operating grants* provide support for services administered directly by, or under contracts for, the recipient entity; examples are education, community development, health, employment and training, and other social services.
3. *Capital grants* are used to construct or renovate facilities or to buy major equipment. Highway construction and public works programs are

[34] Derthick, *The Influence of Federal Grants*, pp. 17–18.

prime examples; more recent examples include grants to public transportation systems for purchase of buses or the construction of subway
systems, and grants for construction of wastewater treatment plants.

This is the classification scheme we use in this volume. It needs to be noted,
however, that there are other ways of classifying grants. They can, for example,
be grouped by their structure (revenue sharing, block grants, categorical, etc.),
by type of recipient, by their financing provisions (open-ended, closed-ended,
matching, non-matching), by size, or by functional area.

Truman: Direct Aid to Localities

One of the most important shifts in federal grant-in-aid policy since the New
Deal was the provision of federal aid on a regular basis directly to local governments, bypassing the states. Prior to the administration of Harry S Truman, a
few "demonstration" grants for highways had been made to localities before the
highway aid program was enacted in 1916; federal funds for agricultural extension agents for a time went directly to counties, but this arrangement was ended
in 1914.[35] Public works funds and direct relief for the poor were channeled directly to localities in the first years of the Roosevelt administration, but this,
too, was a temporary arrangement.

The "foot in the door" for ongoing direct grants to localities was the Housing
Act of 1937. This legislation set up the U.S. Housing Authority, which made
grants to local governments for slum clearance and public housing. The act
aided only big cities, however, and public housing faced stiff opposition in
Congress for ideological reasons. The program was caught in a wave of budget
cutting, and received no new appropriations between 1939 and 1949.[36]

The door was opened wider for direct aid to localities in 1946, when Congress established grants for the construction of airports. But the big departure
during Truman's administration came with the passage of the Housing Act of
1949, which authorized grants directly to cities for housing and urban renewal.
Besides renewing appropriations for construction of public housing, the 1949
act provided grants for "urban redevelopment" projects. Legislation in 1954
and later years refined the "urban redevelopment" provisions of the 1949 act,
which eventually became known as "urban renewal." This was one of the largest federal grant programs to cities in the late fifties and early sixties.

[35] Key, *The Administration of Federal Grants to States*, pp. 228ff.
[36] See Mark I. Gelfand, *A Nation of Cities* (New York: Oxford University Press, 1975), pp.
64–65.

Eisenhower: Search for a "Logical Division"

Under President Dwight D. Eisenhower, the major development in grants-in-aid was not so much the initiation of new programs as the validation of what had gone before. The Eisenhower administration did not interrupt the growth in federal spending on grant programs. By fiscal 1961, total federal aid had increased to $7.3 billion, three times as much as in the last year of the Truman administration.

The new programs that were added under Eisenhower emphasized capital development. The largest was the start of a decades-long effort to build a new system of interstate highways, which Eisenhower supported on the ground that it was necessary for national defense. The financial basis of the new program was different from that of previous highway programs; funds were provided not from general federal revenues but from a highway trust fund financed by a federal excise tax on gasoline.

Although he did not roll back the level of federal grants, Eisenhower did try (without much success) to make changes in the scope and character of federal aid programs. Soon after he took office in 1953, Eisenhower appointed a Commission on Intergovernmental Relations headed by Meyer Kestnbaum, president of Hart, Schaffner, and Marx clothing company. Eisenhower gave the commission the task of finding "a logical division between the proper functions and responsibilities of the state and federal government."[37]

The Kestnbaum Commission's report, however, rejected Eisenhower's premise that there should be a clear division between state and federal responsibilities. Instead it put forth the principle that the two levels of government should be regarded as "cooperating with or complementing each other in meeting the growing demands on both." It continued: "In the light of recent Supreme Court decisions and in our highly interdependent society, there are few activities of government indeed in which there is not some degree of national interest, and in which the national government is without constitutional authority to participate in some manner."[38]

Eisenhower in 1957 tried again to find a formula for revising federal aid and rearranging governmental functions by creating a joint action committee with representatives from the federal government and from the governors to identify federal functions and revenue sources that might be shifted to the states. The committee came up with a program, though a very limited one: to eliminate

[37] Excerpts from President's Remarks at the Closing of the White House Conference of Governors, May 5, 1953, *Public Papers of the Presidents, 1953*, p. 260, as quoted in James L. Sundquist, *Making Federalism Work* (Washington, D.C.: The Brookings Institution, 1969), p. 8.

[38] "Final Report of the Commission on Intergovernmental Relations," H. Doc. 198, 84th Congress, 1st sess. (1955), pp. 2, 5, quoted in Sundquist, *Making Federalism Work*, p. 8.

federal grants-in-aid for vocational education and sewage treatment plants (then very small) in return for letting states share revenues of the federal tax on local telephone service. As Sundquist observes, "There was no considerable public support for these modest proposals, the interest groups that would have been affected mobilized against them, and they were rejected by a hostile Congress."[39]

The Great Society

The 1960s was another period of dramatic change in the scope of activity of the federal government. The decade began with the election of John F. Kennedy; the strengthening of the already existing movement to secure civil rights for blacks; and the "discovery" of poverty in the midst of a generally affluent economy. Although Kennedy supported the aspirations of blacks and the poor, only a few relatively minor pieces of civil rights and antipoverty legislation were passed before his assassination in 1963. The situation changed after Lyndon B. Johnson was elected in his own right in 1964 with a mandate from the voters in the form of a landslide victory and a large Democratic majority in Congress. Johnson's administration ushered in what Jesse Burkhead has called "a period of simply unprecedented social legislation with a major redefinition of 'the national interest.' "[40] Johnson's Great Society initiatives expanded the federal government's activities in many areas where programs had already operated, and extended governmental efforts into new areas. Grants-in-aid to state and local governments nearly doubled between 1965 and 1969, from $10.9 billion to $20.2 billion. As a percentage of gross national product, federal grants-in-aid rose from 1.7 percent in 1965 to 2.2 percent in 1969 (see table 2.1). The two fastest growing components of federal domestic aid were health programs and programs providing education, training, employment, and social services, as shown in table 2.2.

The largest new grant program was Medicaid, enacted in 1965.[41] Medicaid, which is similar in its structure to AFDC, is an open-ended entitlement program under which states have considerable leeway in setting eligibility rules and levels and types of benefits. Persons who receive AFDC are automatically eli-

[39] Sundquist, *Making Federalism Work*, p. 9.
[40] Jesse Burkhead, "Intergovernmental Administration: The Johnson Presidency," faculty essay, The Maxwell School, Syracuse University, Spring 1981, p. 2.
[41] Another large health program enacted in 1965 was Medicare, which extended the social security retirement insurance system to cover the medical costs of the elderly, both poor and nonpoor. Like other social security payments to the elderly, Medicare is administered directly by the federal government and is not a program of grants to states.

Table 2.1. Federal Grants-in-Aid to State and Local Government, 1940–84

Federal fiscal year	Total grants in current dollars (dollars in millions)	Total grants in constant dollars (fiscal year 1972 prices, dollars in billions)	Total grants as a percentage of gross national product
1940	871.5	3.3	0.9
1941	846.6	3.1	0.8
1942	892.0	3.0	0.6
1943	913.6	2.9	0.5
1944	910.6	2.7	0.5
1945	858.6	2.5	0.4
1946	819.0	2.2	0.4
1947	1,603.2	3.7	0.7
1948	1,612.0	3.4	0.7
1949	1,875.8	3.8	0.7
1950	2,253.3	4.6	0.8
1951	2,287.0	4.3	0.7
1952	2,433.0	4.4	0.7
1953	2,834.6	5.0	0.8
1954	3,055.8	5.4	0.8
1955	3,207.2	5.6	0.8
1956	3,560.6	6.2	0.9
1957	3,973.8	6.5	0.9
1958	4,904.7	7.8	1.1
1959	6,463.4	10.0	1.4
1960	7,019.4	10.8	1.4
1961	7,126.4	10.9	1.4
1962	7,926.1	11.9	1.4
1963	8,602.1	12.6	1.5
1964	10,164.2	14.7	1.6
1965	10,910.0	15.5	1.7
1966	12,887.1	17.9	1.8
1967	15,232.5	20.3	2.0
1968	18,550.9	23.6	2.2
1969	20,163.9	24.2	2.2
1970	24,065.2	27.0	2.5
1971	28,098.9	29.6	2.7
1972	34,374.6	34.4	3.0
1973	41,846.8	39.7	3.3
1974	43,357.4	37.9	3.1
1975	49,791.3	39.2	3.4
1976	59,093.8	43.5	3.6

Table 2.1, continued

Federal fiscal year	Total grants in current dollars (dollars in millions)	Total grants in constant dollars (fiscal year 1972 prices, dollars in billions)	Total grants as a percentage of gross national product
Transition quarter	15,920.5	11.6	3.9
1977	68,415.0	46.7	3.7
1978	77,889.4	49.4	3.7
1979	82,858.4	48.1	3.5
1980	91,451.0	48.2	3.6
1981	94,761.9	46.1	2.9
1982	88,194.9	40.4	2.9
1983	92,495.9	40.7	2.9
1984	97,577.3	41.3	2.7

SOURCE: Table 12.1, "Summary Comparisons of Total Federal Grants-in-Aid (Including Shared Revenue) to State and Local Governments, 1940–1990," Executive Office of the President, U.S. Office of Management and Budget, *Historical Tables, Budget of the United States Government, Fiscal Year 1986* (Washington, D.C.: Government Printing Office, 1985), pp. 12.1(1)–12.1(2).

Table 2.2.   Federal Spending for Education, Training, Employment, Social Services, and Health Programs, 1965 and 1969

Federal fiscal year	Expenditures (dollars in millions)		Percentage of total federal grant expenditures	
	1965	1969	1965	1969
Education, training, employment, and social services	1,049.8	5,085.0	9.6	25.2
Health programs	624.5	3,202.9	5.7	15.9

SOURCE: Table 12.3, "Federal Aid to State and Local Governments—By Function and Fund Group," Executive Office of the President, U.S. Office of Management and Budget, *Historical Tables, Budget of the United States Government, Fiscal Year 1986* (Washington, D.C.: Government Printing Office, 1985), p. 12.2(3).

gible for Medicaid, though states can provide Medicaid coverage for others as well.

For both AFDC and Medicaid, federal grants contribute varying percentages of a state's total benefit payments, depending on the state's per capita income in relation to the national average. Medicaid spending has far outstripped the projections made when it was enacted. By its tenth year of operation in 1975, federal spending on medical benefits had reached $6.5 billion, almost nine times the $741 million distributed in 1966; the federal share of benefits amounted to almost $19 billion in 1984.[42] Because states contribute part of these costs, the fast growth of Medicaid and AFDC during the late sixties and early seventies put great pressure on state budgets.

Other areas in which the Great Society brought about significant expansion of federal activity are described below:

1. *Education.* The largest new program was the Elementary and Secondary Education Act of 1965, which provided aid to school districts with large numbers of children from low-income families. Other new education grant programs adopted during the Great Society period included adult basic education and the Teacher Corps.

2. *Employment and Training.* New programs to combat unemployment were enacted under President Kennedy, notably the Area Redevelopment Act of 1961 and the Manpower Development and Training Act of 1962. Johnson expanded these efforts with the Economic Opportunity Act of 1964, which initiated a wide array of programs aimed at helping the most disadvantaged groups among the unemployed develop the skills needed to obtain jobs. Two training programs established in the Economic Opportunity Act of 1964 were targeted at youths—the Job Corps, which set up residential training centers, and the Neighborhood Youth Corps, which funded nonresidential programs in cities.

3. *Housing and Model Cities.* Johnson in 1965 persuaded Congress to create the Department of Housing and Urban Development, first proposed by Kennedy. A year later Johnson pushed through the model cities program, which was intended to coordinate federal urban programs, such as urban renewal, economic development, housing, and education and to focus them on the needs of the poor in selected, highly distressed urban areas. It was administered by HUD and was supposed to obtain cooperation with other federal departments, but this goal turned out to be elusive.[43]

4. *Community Action Agencies.* The most distinctive feature of the Great Society period was the "war on poverty," launched with passage of the Economic Opportunity Act in 1964. Though this act incorpo-

[42] Executive Office of the President, U.S. Office of Management and Budget, *Historical Tables: Budget of the United States Government, Fiscal Year 1986* (Washington, D.C.: Government Printing Office, 1985), table 11.3.

[43] See Bernard J. Frieden and Marshall Kaplan, *The Politics of Neglect* (Cambridge, Mass.: MIT Press, 1975) for a discussion of the history of the model cities program.

rated a number of specific programs, including the job training efforts mentioned earlier, its best known and most controversial legacy was organizational. It established a community action program, which in turn set up community action agencies that were specially created entities outside the traditional political structure. These agencies were intended to coordinate federal efforts and to give the poor a significant voice in the policies of the local programs that aided them. The underlying assumption was that a lack of political power had deprived the poor of a sense of control over their own destiny. Some of these local agencies believed that fighting local elected officials was part of their duty in fighting poverty, and mayors and other officials protested. Johnson instructed the Office of Economic Opportunity to rein in the community action agencies, and in fall 1965 he trimmed the antipoverty agency's budget request and assigned a team to overhaul its management.[44] Later, Congress also limited the role of community action agencies.

Block Grants and Nixon's New Federalism

Because the number of federal grant programs to state and local governments grew rapidly during the Great Society period—and because some of these programs were experiments in finding ways to deal with complex social issues—problems of management and coordination inevitably arose. Sometimes Congress responded to a problem by passing several programs, differing only in the particular segment of the population they were intended to assist or the particular technique they applied. Thus job training programs were created for in-school youths, out-of-school youths, elderly people in rural areas, welfare recipients, and other groups.

Moreover, grants for related purposes were operated by different federal agencies, each of which allocated funds to and had administrative relations with different state and local agencies and nonprofit organizations. In many cases a single state or local agency received funds for closely related purposes from several different federal agencies, each with its own rules and procedures. The same was true of programs assisting individuals and families. Mayor Henry W. Maier of Milwaukee commented that "a whole maze of some thirty possible agencies involving the city, the county, the state, and the federal government,

---

[44] Frieden and Kaplan, *The Politics of Neglect*, pp. 32–33.

and, yes, the private sector might be dealing with the welfare problems of a single family."[45]

The large number of programs sometimes made it difficult for local officials to keep track of the types of federal aid available. In 1966, when Robert F. Kennedy was a senator from New York, he asked the secretary of commerce at a hearing how local officials could learn about all the programs. The secretary described a new computerized information system, but Kennedy was not impressed. He replied that a mayor would probably tell the computer what he was looking for "and out of it would come something saying, 'Vote Republican.' "[46]

Concerns about the proliferation of grants, the need for state and local agencies to spend considerable time writing grant proposals and engaging in other forms of "grantsmanship," and the lack of coordination led to support for what came to be known as "block grants." This type of grant consolidated several categorical grants into one program. Block grants typically distribute funds according to a formula based on such statistical factors as population and income, rather than in the form of individual grants for particular projects (which are known as "project" grants). The concept of block grants generally was supported by Republicans and conservative Democrats. Members of both groups had gained seats in the House of Representatives in 1966. They saw block grants as a strategy for devolution of programs from the federal government—that is, as a way to return decision-making authority over the uses of grant funds to states and local governments.

The first block grants were actually enacted under Johnson. A small block grant in 1966 replaced several public health programs with a single comprehensive grant for a range of health services. In 1967, Johnson proposed a new grant program to help localities fight street crime. His proposal was for a categorical "project" grant in the mold of earlier Great Society initiatives. Arguing that federal money would inevitably lead to federal control of what had historically been a local function, Republicans and conservative Democrats in Congress led a successful effort to convert the program into a block grant to states, with funds allocated on the basis of population. States were required to pass on 75 percent of operating funds to localities.[47]

Two years later, the block grant approach became one of the key elements in President Richard M. Nixon's "New Federalism" program. Nixon's concept of

[45] Sundquist, Making Federalism Work, pp. 16–17.

[46] U.S. Senate, Committee on Governmental Operations, Subcommittee on Intergovernmental Relations, Creative Federalism, 89th Congress, 2d sess., November 16, 17, 18, and 21, 1966. Reprinted edition (New York: Arno Press Inc., 1978), p. 371.

[47] Kenneth T. Palmer, "The Evolution of Grant Policies," in Lawrence D. Brown, James W. Fossett, and Kenneth T. Palmer, The Changing Politics of Federal Grants (Washington, D.C.: The Brookings Institution, 1984), p. 20.

federalism was not only decentralist but also antibureaucratic. Nixon emphasized the goal of returning power to elected officials of states and localities. In
August 1969, he presented proposals designed to sort out the functions served
by the federal government and those served by state and local governments.[48]

The centerpiece of the Nixon "New Federalism" program was general revenue sharing, the most conspicuous legislative achievements of the Nixon
administration in domestic affairs. This proposal—to distribute funds to state
and local governments for them to use in any way they saw fit—is the modern
version of the surplus revenue distribution of 1837. Nixon first sent a relatively
small general revenue sharing proposal to Congress in 1968, but it aroused little
support. A second proposal submitted in 1971, which upped the ante tenfold,
was successful. As passed by Congress in October 1972, the program allocated
over $5 billion per year for five years. The revenue sharing program was never
a favorite of Reagan's, perhaps reflecting tensions between Nixon and Reagan.
As president, Reagan, as discussed in the next chapter, has taken a much harder
devolutionary line than Nixon. In 1985, he recommended elimination of the
revenue sharing program.

A second major element of Nixon's "New Federalism" program was the enactment of two new block grant programs. The first, which consolidated manpower training programs, was the Comprehensive Employment and Training
Act (CETA), another Nixon program terminated in the Reagan period. Under
CETA, funds were allocated on the basis of a formula to "prime sponsors,"
which could be a single local government, a consortium of such governments,
or, in some cases, the state government. These prime sponsors decided which
particular kinds of training programs would be operated in their area.

The second new block grant initiated under the Nixon administration—
though it was signed by President Gerald R. Ford on August 22, 1974, two
weeks after Nixon resigned—was the community development block grant
(CDBG) program. It consolidated seven categorical grants, the largest of which
were the urban renewal and model cities programs. To gain support from Democrats in Congress and from the interest groups that had benefited from the categorical programs, drafters of the legislation inserted language directing local
governments to use CDBG money for "activities which will benefit low- and
moderate-income families or aid in the prevention or elimination of slums and
blight. . . ."

On another major part of Nixon's domestic program, he was not as successful in winning congressional support as he had been in revenue sharing and

[48] See Richard P. Nathan, *The Administrative Presidency* (New York: John Wiley, 1983),
chapter 2.

block grants. Nixon was unable to secure passage of a proposal to replace the existing aid to families with dependent children program with a federally administered program called the "family assistance plan."[49] Although Nixon's family assistance plan was not enacted, Congress did enact his proposal for the Supplemental Security Income (SSI) program. It gave the federal government responsibility for aid to the low-income aged, blind, and disabled, which had previously been administered by the states and by local governments.

The changes made during the Nixon and Ford administrations had an important effect on the overall pattern of federal grant programs. By 1977, almost two-fifths of the nonwelfare grants distributed to state and local governments came in the form of "broad-based" grants—that is, block grants or general revenue sharing. (This excludes grants such as AFDC and Medicaid that are income transfers channeled through states to individuals.) Funding arrangements for the more traditional categorical programs moved away from "project" grants toward formula funding. The proportion of categorical grant programs funded through formulas rose from 26 percent in 1967 to 35 percent in 1978.[50]

Though the form of grants was changed under Nixon and Ford in ways intended to give local and state officials more discretion and authority, these Republican administrations did little to slow increases in the amount distributed by federal grants. In Nixon's first term, federal grants-in-aid grew from 2.2 percent of the gross national product in 1969 to 3.3 percent in 1973; by the end of the Nixon-Ford period in 1977, this figure had reached 3.7 percent.[51] Federal grants as a fraction of state and local government expenditures grew from 19.2 percent in 1970 to 25.9 percent in 1977.[52]

Carter: Economic Stimulus and Fiscal Stringency

Federal grants to states and localities during the presidency of Jimmy Carter went on a roller coaster ride. When Carter entered office in 1977, the nation

[49] See Vincent J. and Vee Burke, *Nixon's Good Deed: Welfare Reform* (New York: Columbia University Press, 1974), and Daniel P. Moynihan, *The Politics of A Guaranteed Income: The Nixon Administration and the Family Assistance Plan* (New York: Random House, 1973).

[50] Palmer, "The Evolution of Grant Policies," p. 30.

[51] Table 12.1, "Summary Comparisons of Total Federal Grants-in-Aid (Including Shared Revenue) to State and Local Governments, 1940–1990," Executive Office of the President, U.S. Office of Management and Budget, *Historical Tables, Budget of the United States Government, Fiscal Year 1986* (Washington, D.C.: Government Printing Office, 1985). The average annual increase between 1969 and 1973 was almost 20 percent each year, even faster than the comparable figure of 17 percent under Johnson between 1965 and 1969.

[52] Executive Office of the President, U.S. Office of Management and Budget, *Special Analyses: Budget of the United States Government, Fiscal Year 1986* (Washington, D.C.: Government Printing Office, 1985), table H-7, p. H-19.

was still feeling the effects of a recession that bottomed out in 1975. At his urging, Congress approved funding through fiscal year 1978 for three major elements of an "economic stimulus program": (1) a special program of "countercyclical" grants similar to revenue sharing to communities where unemployment was high; (2) grants for local public works projects that would create jobs; and (3) an expansion of the public service employment (PSE) component of the Comprehensive Employment and Training Act, providing subsidies for local government jobs that would be filled by the unemployed.

This attempt to counter the recession through increased domestic spending sent federal grants-in-aid sharply upward during 1977 and 1978. Then, in the spring of 1978, Carter proposed a new initiative that, in effect, would have put his countercyclical program on a permanent basis. This was his "national urban policy," which incorporated a variety of proposals, a number of them resembling the three main elements of his 1977 economic stimulus program. But events overtook the Carter plans.

As the economic stimulus appropriations were expiring, and a few months after Carter announced his "national urban policy," a new element appeared on the national scene that put a damper on proposals for spending increases. California voters approved Proposition 13, a ballot initiative that forced the state and local governments to limit property tax rates. Similar "tax revolt" efforts were soon mounted in other states. As the tax revolt movement spread, Carter's proposals languished in Congress, and in fact Carter himself and his administration pulled back from their own initiatives. Although Congress approved some programs with small price tags, it dragged its feet on Carter's major urban proposals. His urban program quietly died.

The most important new urban aid program successfully initiated under Carter was the urban development action grant (UDAG) program, which provided public funds in distressed cities as a means of attracting specific investments from private firms and developers. The UDAG program, which was authorized at $440 million, proved to be successful as a catalyst to development in many cities.[53] Yet UDAG was basically an afterthought. It was added to legislation extending the CDBG program in 1977 as Carter's way of putting his stamp on the extension.

In the second half of the Carter presidency, there was a decided shift in federal aid policy as the retrenchment mood of the country became more pronounced. This shift, plus the strong federal aid cutbacks enacted during the Reagan first term, are the subject of the next chapter. The slope of federal aid

[53] See Richard P. Nathan and Jerry A. Webman, *The Urban Development Action Grant Program* (Princeton, N.J.: Princeton Urban and Regional Research Center, 1980).

can be seen to have had a steady upward incline in the twentieth century, certainly during the modern presidencies from FDR through the middle Carter years. Grant concepts changed; purposes varied; new agencies came upon the scene. But the basic trend did not shift at the federal level until the late 1970s. The shift that began in the Carter years was accentuated under Reagan.

3

Changes during Reagan's First Term

✳

*I*n the first year of Ronald Reagan's first term as president, he presented two major sets of proposals that affected both the size and structure of federal grants-in-aid to other levels of government and the relative roles of the national, state, and local governments in American federalism. One was his economic program, announced in a speech to a joint session of Congress on February 18, 1981. It called for massive tax cuts plus reductions in domestic spending to shrink the size of the federal government in the domestic area. Although Reagan's 1981 economic program was aimed at basic economic goals, it had an important effect on grants and federalism. A second set of proposals, announced in the president's first year in office (in this case in the State of the Union message in January 1982), was focused exclusively on grant programs and issues and the structure of American federalism. This was his "swap and turnback" plan to realign responsibility between the federal government and the states for funding many domestic programs.

The two sets of proposals met very different fates. Although many governors favored the general idea of clarifying the division of program responsibility between the federal and state governments, the detailed "swap and turnback" proposals considered by the Reagan administration encountered resistance from governors. The proposals became tangled up in controversy over Reagan's requests for further spending cuts beyond the initial round, and eventually disappeared from view. By contrast, Congress gave the president much of the domestic spending cuts he asked for in his first-year cuts and even more than he asked for in tax cuts.

The 1981 economic program of large tax cuts and reductions in domestic spending, advanced under the banner of "supply-side economics," did not bring about growth in the economy sufficient to balance the federal budget. Instead, the desire to pay for increased defense programs (an essential part of the Reagan program), the refusal of Congress to accept all the domestic spending cuts requested by the administration, and lower than expected tax revenues due to the 1981–82 recession sent federal deficits soaring. The Federal Reserve Board, meanwhile, was restraining the money supply in an effort to hold down inflation; real interest rates rose sharply. More than anything else, the deep recession in 1981 and 1982 dampened congressional enthusiasm for the president's economic program and his domestic and social policies.

Reagan's efforts to obtain further domestic cutbacks in the fall of 1981, when it became clear that deeper budget cuts were necessary to "solve" his budget equation, were largely unsuccessful. In the following years Congress restored some domestic programs to previous spending levels (or levels close to them), added some new programs, and also took steps to raise federal taxes. These actions went against the administration's economic program and slowed the momentum of its conservative domestic policy realignment.

In light of the failure of the "swap and turnback" plan and the partial reversal of some domestic spending cuts, many observers wrote off federalism and social program changes as an important part of the Reagan program. However, our findings show that change in these terms has been consequential under Reagan. Fundamental changes in domestic policy were enacted that are likely to have a lasting impact. Many recipients of public assistance who can be described as the "working poor" lost welfare eligibility or substantial benefits, and in some cases became subject to new job-search and "workfare" requirements. We also found a decided shift of authority to the states during Reagan's first term, despite the unceremonious demise of his "swap and turnback" realignment plan and the partial rollback of some of his 1981 spending cuts. The role of state government was enhanced through (1) changes in the form of grant-in-aid programs which gave states more authority than they previously had, and (2) the signal sent by the federal retrenchment efforts of the administration that future initiatives in domestic policy would not come from the federal level. Each change focused greater attention and spending pressure on the states.

The following sections discuss the events of 1981 and the rest of the first Reagan term in more detail. After sketching the philosophical underpinnings of Reagan's approach to domestic policy and the broad outlines of his 1981 tax and spending changes, we describe what Congress and the president did in the years after 1981.

The 1981 Economic Policy

The three main themes of the Reagan administration embodied in the administration's 1981 economic policy that are most important for this analysis are:

1. A commitment to the idea that the public sector should be smaller and less intrusive, and that the private sector should be strengthened and made more influential.
2. A theory of federalism that involves reducing the role of the federal government by devolving federal responsibilities to state governments.
3. A concept of programs to aid the poor that consists of providing adequate benefits to the "truly needy" for whom public assistance is a last resort and removing from the welfare rolls working persons receiving assistance to supplement low wages.

All three themes can be traced to views that Reagan had held before becoming president. In 1964, while supporting Arizona Senator Barry Goldwater's campaign for the presidency, Reagan said; "The full power of centralized government was the very thing the Founding Fathers sought to minimize."[1] As governor, Reagan in much the same way had stressed his views on decentralization: "I am one who believes that government has tended to grow further from the people and more centralized in authority—on up from the local government to the state, from the state to the federal government."[2]

By the end of his second term as governor, three distinctive features of Reagan's views on federalism were clear. First, Reagan urged decentralization, but through what might be called the "governmental chain of command." The federal government should devolve responsibility and authority to the states. The states, in turn, had the responsibility to decide the proper role for local government. Direct federal-local relations did not fit into Reagan's ideas about intergovernmental relations.

Second, although Reagan favored the devolution of many public services in California to the local level, welfare was an exception. His welfare reform program in California increased state control over eligibility determination and benefit calculation by tightening state regulations governing county administration of the program.

Third, Reagan argued that domestic functions of the federal government should be reassigned. Many politicians were calling for a reallocation of do-

[1] Reported in Ronald Reagan with Richard Hubler, *Where's the Rest of Me?* (New York: Duell, Sloan, and Pearce, 1965), p. 266.
[2] *California Journal* 1, no. 12 (December 1970):332.

mestic governmental functions in the early 1970s. What distinguished Reagan was his ideas about welfare. Most state and local officials advocated a federal takeover of welfare. But not Reagan. He argued that welfare should continue to be primarily a responsibility of state governments. The federal government should reduce its control over welfare programs, freeing states governments to hold down fast-growing assistance costs. [3]

On leaving the governorship in 1974, Reagan continued to develop and argue for his concepts of American federalism. Decentralization became an important theme in his long campaign for the presidency. As a former governor of the country's largest state, he presented himself as a successful chief executive who had put his ideas into practice rather than simply theorizing. When Reagan challenged President Ford for the Republican nomination in 1976, his federalism views came under intense public scrutiny. In most instances he spoke in general terms about the need to trim, rearrange, and devolve domestic governmental functions. But in one ill-fated speech he moved beyond these generalities to offer a sweeping proposal:

> What I propose is nothing less than a systematic transfer of authority and resources to the states—a program of creative federalism for America's third century. Federal authority has clearly failed to do the job. Indeed, it has created more problems in welfare, education, housing, food stamps, Medicaid, community and regional development, and revenue sharing, to name a few. The sums involved and the potential savings to the taxpayer are large. Transfer of authority [to the states] in whole or in part in all of these areas would reduce the outlay of the federal government by more than $90 billion, using the spending levels of fiscal 1975. With such savings it would be possible to balance the federal budget, make an initial $5 billion payment on the national debt, and cut the federal personal income tax of every American by an average of 23 percent. [4]

Reagan, in this speech, presented to the Chicago Executive Club in September 1975, and in subsequent briefings and back-up documents, named some of the federal programs to be reassigned. But as the questioning increased, he was unable to provide a full and satisfactory accounting of his program. The reception accorded the proposal is suggested by the label the media soon attached to it: "The $90 Billion Misunderstanding." As journalists Rowland Evans and Robert Novak explained:

[3] Governor Ronald Reagan, *California's Blueprint for National Welfare Reform* (Sacramento: State of California, September 1974).

[4] See Lou Cannon, *Reagan* (New York: G. P. Putnam's Sons, 1982), chapter 14.

Functioning without the benefit of what later would become widely known as "supply-side" tax ideology, Reagan had stumbled over a scheme that posed more questions than it offered solutions: How would all these $90 billion worth of federal programs be transferred to the state level? How would they be paid for by the states, particularly the poorer states? How would tax reduction be coordinated with the massive transfer? Worse yet, the flaws would soon be compounded by Reagan's own blunders in explaining the program.[5]

Though economist Martin Anderson was called in on an emergency salvage mission to develop answers to questions raised by the press, this proposal continued to haunt Reagan throughout the campaign. Some political experts argue that this proposal cost Reagan the 1976 Republican nomination for president.

Despite this setback, Reagan's quest for the presidency continued, and federalism and decentralization remained a part of his platform. Learning from the disaster of 1976, Reagan in his 1980 campaign avoided grand designs for governmental reorganization. Instead, he concentrated on specific functional areas where he felt federal programs hindered solutions to problems and decentralization was the right approach. Criticizing the performance of federal urban renewal programs, for example, Reagan proclaimed:

> Billions of dollars, thousands of studies, hundreds of experts—this is the formidable array of weapons the federal bureaucrats brought to the struggle to revitalize the cities. And what did it all lead to? Failure. Failure so great, so costly, so devastating in its destruction of neighborhoods—all in the name of "urban renewal"—that it is all unbelievable. You don't need billions of taxpayers' dollars to save a city. You need a sense of purpose, some pride, some hope, and a capacity for work.[6]

By talking about selected examples of policy problems where federal programs were, in Reagan's view, a part of the problem rather than the solution, he continued to advance his argument for cuts in federal programs and decentralization. But this approach was less threatening, and allowed the candidate to concentrate on the issues where the election was to be won: inflation, economic stagnation, and foreign policy.

Shortly after Reagan's inauguration as president, he presented his "program for economic recovery" in a speech to a joint session of Congress on February 18, 1981. Reagan's speech wove together several strands of conservative eco-

[5] Rowland Evans and Robert Novak, *The Reagan Revolution* (New York: E. P. Dutton, 1981), p. 43.
[6] Quoted in Ronnie Dugger, *On Reagan: The Man and His Presidency* (New York: McGraw-Hill, 1983), p. 512.

nomic thinking and closely reflected his political philosophy. As Hugh Heclo and Rudolph Penner have written:

> Within the conservative movement two concerns, each identifying something real, had become inextricably linked: the problem of a malfunctioning economy and the problem of a malfunctioning big government. It was an act of political theory to link the latter as the chief cause of the former.[7]

The economic program had several elements. First, major reductions in taxes over three years were to give consumers more money to spend and firms more money to invest in new plants and equipment. Second, revisions in many types of regulations would free companies from what the administration saw as costly and unnecessary constraints. Third, federal spending was to be directed toward national defense and away from domestic activities that could be handled by other levels of government or private philanthropy. Programs that constituted a "social safety net" for the poor, however, were to be protected from major cuts. Fourth, monetary restraint was to hold down inflation.

The result, according to the president and his supporters, would be a spurt in noninflationary economic growth. The administration in March and July 1981 forecasted an average increase in gross national product (GNP) of 4.5 percent after inflation between 1981 and 1986, and an inflation rate of about 6 percent per year. Heclo and Penner reflect the views of many economists in pointing out that this forecast, involving growth in the money value of the GNP of almost 11 percent per year for five years, might have been possible with a rapid growth of the money supply but was "totally unreasonable given the monetary policy advocated by the administration."[8]

What Happened to Federal Aid?

In its proposals for trimming domestic spending, the Reagan program can be seen as an acceleration of trends present at the end of the Carter administration. Retrenchment percolated up through the federal system. The roots of retrenchment in domestic spending can be traced to local policy shifts in the mid-1970s, when a number of cities began to cut spending and reduce employment. These actions were taken to avoid the kind of fiscal crisis that befell New York City in 1975, when years of high spending and heavy borrowing collided with a dwin-

---

[7] Hugh Heclo and Rudolph G. Penner, "Fiscal and Political Strategy in the Reagan Administration," in Fred I. Greenstein, ed., *The Reagan Presidency: An Early Assessment* (Baltimore: The Johns Hopkins University Press, 1983), p. 28.

[8] Heclo and Penner, "Fiscal and Political Strategy in the Reagan Administration," p. 30.

Table 3.1.   *Federal Aid in Real Terms, 1978–84 (dollars in billions)*

Federal fiscal year	Total outlays	Entitlements	Capital	Operating
Carter Pulls Back Over Three Years, 1978–81				
1978	77.9	20.6	18.3	38.9
1981	73.1	23.9	17.0	32.1
Change	−4.8	+3.3	−1.3	−6.8
	(−6%)	(+16%)	(−7%)	(−18%)
Reagan Makes Sharp Cuts in 1981				
1981	73.1	23.9	17.0	32.1
1982	64.1	22.7	14.9	26.5
Change	−9.0	−1.2	−2.1	−5.6
	(−12%)	(−5%)	(−12%)	(−17%)
But Then the Cutting Stopped, 1982–84				
1982	64.1	22.7	14.9	26.5
1983	64.9	22.9	14.3	27.7
1984	65.1	23.2	15.2	27.0
1985 (est.)	68.9	24.3	16.6	28.0
Change	+4.8	+1.6	+1.7	+1.5
1982–85	(+7%)	(+7%)	(+11%)	(+6%)

SOURCE: Executive Office of the President, Office of Management and Budget, *Special Analyses: Budget of the United States Government* (various years).

NOTES: Entitlements include Medicaid, unemployment insurance administration, food stamp administration, child nutrition, Supplemental Security Income administration, AFDC, and refugee assistance. Adjustment for inflation is based on the GNP deflator.

dling tax base to bring the city government to the brink of default on the bonds it had floated to pay for current operating expenses.[9]

Table 3.1 shows the changes in federal aid since 1978. Grants are grouped here into entitlement grants, operating grants, and capital grants, as defined in chapter 2.

Between fiscal years 1978 and 1981, the latter part of the Carter presidency, spending in all categories grew in nominal terms, but rapid inflation converted nominal increases into a real decline of about 6 percent. The $4.8 billion countercyclical public service employment program under CETA took the heaviest cuts. But capital grant outlays also declined in real terms as the $3.1 billion countercyclical local public works program ended. Entitlement programs, by contrast, grew by 16 percent in nominal terms over this three-year period, with increases in Medicaid, food stamps, and public assistance leading the way.

[9] See Charles Morris, *The Cost of Good Intentions: New York City and the Liberal Experiment* (New York: W. W. Norton, 1980).

In his last budget message, delivered just before he left office in January 1981, President Carter said he was presenting a budget for fiscal year 1982 that would meet the nation's needs "while continuing a four-year policy of prudence and restraint." The budget called for increased spending for only a few social programs, such as a basic skills program for unemployed youths; most other social programs would be kept at their fiscal 1981 levels, and some would be reduced. Carter's proposal was a compromise resulting from a political struggle within his administration between those who wanted to call for large cuts and thus preempt Reagan's position and those who favored holding the line, and in some areas expanding, major social programs.

In the end, Carter's proposals were largely ignored when the new Republican administration came into office. Reagan's statements on his plans for domestic programs were quite different both in tone and substance from those of his predecessor. Not only would spending for domestic programs be constrained, it would be sharply cut in some areas. "Spending by government must be limited to those functions which are the proper province of government," Reagan told Congress as he presented his economic plan in February 1981. "We can no longer afford things simply because we think of them."[10]

In March, Reagan submitted detailed proposals for spending changes in the form of amendments to Carter's budget for fiscal year 1982. He asked that budget authority be reduced by $37 billion (4.6 percent) compared with what it would have been under Carter's budget.[11]

While Reagan's proposed fiscal year 1982 budget was smaller than Carter's budget for the same year, both showed increases over fiscal year 1981 levels. Compared with the budget resolution Congress had passed for fiscal year 1981 in the fall of 1980, Carter's 1982 proposals would have increased budget authority by $115 billion (16.6 percent) while Reagan's 1982 proposed budget would have raised it by $78 billion (11.2 percent).

Though he did not get all the domestic spending cuts he wanted in 1981, Reagan did get most of them. One reason for his success was the brilliant performance of his budget director, David Stockman, who showed his power of persuasion in innumerable congressional hearings. Another reason was that

---

[10] "Program for Economic Recovery" (Address before a joint session of Congress, February 18, 1981), *Weekly Compilation of Presidential Documents* 17, no. 8 (February 23, 1981):137.

[11] An alternative way to show the size of Reagan's proposed reductions is to compare them with the Congressional Budget Officer's estimates of what would be spent in fiscal year 1982 under "current policy"—that is, if the government had simply spent what was called for under laws already passed. This comparison shows a proposed reduction of $23.2 billion (2.9 percent) in budget authority and $43.4 billion (5.9 percent) in fiscal year 1982 outlays. See John William Ellwood, ed., *Reductions in U.S. Domestic Spending* (New Brunswick, N.J.: Transaction Books, 1982), chapter 4, for a discussion of alternative ways to calculate the magnitude of the budget changes and their distribution among budget functions.

Reagan and his staff persuaded each house of Congress to hold a single vote on a package that had been put together by his congressional allies, a strategy that enabled him to blunt opposition to cuts in individual programs. By keeping support from almost all Republicans (even those from northeastern states that were likely to be hurt by some of the budget cuts) and attracting support from a number of conservative Democrats, Reagan in August 1981 won passage of the Omnibus Budget Reconciliation Act. The overall effects of the act's changes are shown in the middle section of table 3.1.[12]

Table 3.2 shows how Reagan's proposals for selected programs compared with: (1) the Congressional Budget Office's calculation of what spending on each program would have been in fiscal year 1982 if previous policy had been left unchanged; and (2) the final spending levels approved by Congress for fiscal 1982, taking into account the appropriations acts adopted after the reconciliation act was passed.[13]

Where Were the 1981 Cuts Made?

The 1981 budget cuts were concentrated in two areas: entitlement programs that assist the poor and operating grants to state and local governments for a wide variety of programs. This focus arose in part from the Reagan administration's desire to implement conservative ideas and partly from the facts of budget making that would constrain any administration. The constraint referred to is that out of the hundreds of domestic programs the bulk of federal domestic spending is concentrated in a handful of programs, consisting mostly of entitlement programs, some of which are extremely difficult, if not politically impossible, to cut. The biggest of these, social security retirement benefits and Medicare, are federally administered programs that benefit the elderly, whose numbers and political allies in Washington give them considerable clout. Other entitlement programs, which are relatively smaller than social security and also politically more vulnerable include Medicaid, food stamps, and aid to families with dependent children (AFDC). These are programs administered by states and localities that provide benefits to those who pass a "means test"—that is, who have incomes and other sources of support under certain limits. Aside from entitlement programs, the only functions that could be cut once defense was exempted from reductions were those supporting federal activities and

[12] For a detailed discussion of the 1981 changes, see John W. Ellwood, ed., *Reductions in U.S. Domestic Spending.*
[13] Note that the dollar figures in table 3.1 are adjusted for inflation while figures in table 3.2 are for current dollars.

Table 3.2. *Comparison of Final Congressional Appropriation for Federal Fiscal Year 1982 with Congressional Budget Office (CBO) Baseline and with Reagan Budget Requests*

Program	CBO current policy baseline for 1982 (dollars in millions)	Reagan budget proposal (dollars in millions)	Final congressional appropriation (dollars in millions)	Percentage difference between appropriation and CBO baseline
Child Nutrition				
Budget authority	4,110	2,738	2,847	− 30.1
Outlays	4,032	2,588	2,662	− 33.9
Energy Conservation				
Budget authority	850	195	145	− 82.9
Outlays	874	498	741	− 15.2
Wastewater treatment grants				
Budget authority	3,600	2,400	2,400	− 33.3
Outlays	4,320	3,840	4,089	− 5.3
Federal aid to highways				
Budget authority	7,854	8,742	8,279	5.4
Outlays	8,285	8,110	8,065	− 2.7
Community development block grant				
Budget authority	3,960	3,666	3,456	− 12.7
Outlays	4,750	3,998	4,128	− 13.1
Urban development action grant				
Budget authority	675	500	440	− 34.8
Outlays	744	610	500	− 32.8
Education block grant				
Budget authority	764	589	470	− 38.5
Outlays	—	—	—	—
Social services block grant				
Budget authority	3,099	3,800	2,400	− 22.6
Outlays	3,086	3,500	2,387	− 22.7
Special milk program				
Budget authority	125	30	28	− 77.6
Outlays	124	27	27	− 78.2
Grants-in-aid to airports				
Budget authority	789	450	476	− 39.7
Outlays	674	485	485	− 28.0

SOURCE: John W. Ellwood, ed., *Reductions in U.S. Domestic Spending* (New Brunswick, N.J.: Transaction Books, 1982) and Executive Office of the President, U.S. Office of Management and Budget, *Special Analyses, Budget of the United States Government, Fiscal 1984* (Washington, D.C.: Government Printing Office, 1983).

grants to state and local governments for operating and capital programs in health, education, social services, community development, and transportation.

Reagan's original budget proposals avoided cuts in social security and Medicare benefits, though his administration did impose a system of cost containment on hospitals treating Medicare patients. The primary areas for Reagan's first round of domestic cuts were the means-tested entitlement programs operated by the states and a variety of operating grant-in-aid programs.[14]

CHANGES IN WELFARE PROGRAMS

Savings in the means-tested entitlement programs were to be achieved by tightening eligibility requirements for AFDC and food stamps and by capping state spending for Medicaid, although Reagan promised that the "basic social safety net" of assistance would be retained for the "truly needy." The effect of these changes was to exclude a sizable number of people who had incomes just above the new ceilings or otherwise failed to meet new rules.

Policy toward the Working Poor

This group—the "working poor"—is the group that Reagan has consistently believed should be weaned from the welfare system. It consists of able-bodied persons of working age who have some earnings from employment and also receive welfare benefits. Many conservatives agree with Martin Anderson, Reagan's first domestic policy adviser, that these programs establish "a 'poverty wall' that destroys the financial incentive to work for millions of Americans."[15]

There are essentially two approaches to reducing welfare dependency: rewards (i.e., incentives) and punishment (i.e., the imposition of additional program requirements). People who favor the former tend to support plans, such as the negative income tax, that provide a cash incentive to work by allowing welfare recipients to keep a portion of their assistance payments after they go to work. The second approach emphasizes policies like "workfare" that may deter people from ever getting on the welfare rolls. This is the approach favored by Reagan and his principal advisers on welfare issues.

The 1981 reconciliation act made three kinds of changes in programs affecting the working poor. First, the act put an income cap on eligibility for benefits.

---

[14] Later in 1981, Reagan suffered one of his biggest defeats when he proposed changes to cut social security spending.

[15] Martin Anderson, *Welfare: The Political Economy of Welfare Reform in the United States* (Stanford, Calif.: Hoover Institution Press, 1978), p. 43.

Households with gross earnings above 150 percent of the state's "standard of need" were no longer eligible for AFDC benefits. A similar ceiling of 130 percent of poverty-level income was set for the food stamps program.

Second, the character of the AFDC program was altered. Under the previous eligibility rules, which had been designed as an incentive to work, a family receiving AFDC benefits could keep thirty dollars per month of its earnings, plus one-third of the earnings above that amount. The 1981 reconciliation act removed this "30 and 1/3" exclusion after four months of eligibility. Both this provision and the 150 percent ceiling have the effect of removing families with earnings from the AFDC rolls.

A third change has to do with the "categorical eligibility" for Medicaid coverage of families receiving any AFDC benefits (even relatively small monthly amounts). In about half the states, only people who receive federally aided public assistance such as AFDC are eligible for Medicaid. Loss of AFDC eligibility means loss of Medicaid benefits. For many "working poor" households, medical and hospital insurance coverage under Medicaid is equal to, if not better than, the coverage these households could get in employment-related medical and hospital insurance programs. The loss of this protection for the parents and the children in a welfare family is in many cases more serious than the loss of the AFDC cash payment.

The reconciliation act contained still another important substantive change in welfare policy involving able-bodied welfare recipients of working age. Reagan has long supported the idea of "workfare," whereby a person is required to work off the value of his or her welfare check. Under most workfare arrangements, a welfare recipient works in some public agency, usually at the minimum wage, for the number of hours required to "earn" the welfare benefit for which the family or individual is eligible. The Reagan administration proposed that "workfare" be made mandatory for AFDC family heads on a comprehensive basis throughout the nation, with the stipulation that child-care arrangements be available or provided in all cases where this mandate is enforced. Congress balked at this comprehensive approach, and instead made workfare programs optional to the states on a demonstration basis.[16]

Reagan's 1981 victory in securing these changes in the reconciliation act made it a historic piece of social legislation. It was not just a money bill; it also contained a wide range of major substantive changes in national policies, in-

[16] As of 1984 about half the states had set up workfare programs, many of them demonstration programs in a few counties.

cluding the Reagan philosophy that a "safety net" should be established for those who cannot work, while those who can work are weaned from welfare.

Spending Restraints for Medicaid

Another Reagan goal was to redesign formulas for entitlement grants so that states would be encouraged to restrain spending under these programs. The most important such change was made in Medicaid, the largest and fastest-growing federal aid program. The federal government provides an open-ended grant to each state that covers a certain percentage of the costs of providing Medicaid services to eligible persons; the percentage for a particular state is based on the state's per capita income in relation to the national average. The percentage contributed by the federal government in the early 1980s ranged from 50 percent in thirteen states to 78 percent in Mississippi.

In 1981, seeking to restrain spending on welfare, Reagan proposed a ceiling on federal contributions to state Medicaid programs, so that the federal contribution for Medicaid to each state would be limited to no more than 105 percent of the federal payment in the previous year. This change moved strongly in the direction of converting Medicaid into a block grant—that is, a closed-ended grant for a predetermined amount of money. This was an approach that Reagan had also favored for AFDC during his 1980 campaign, although he did not advance this proposal in his package of budget cuts for fiscal year 1982. In one of the few defeats for the president on the fiscal year 1982 budget, House Democrats substituted their provisions reducing the federal matching rate for Medicaid for Reagan's proposal to cap this federal contribution. Under the House plan, the Medicaid program was still open-ended, but the matching percentages were in some cases reduced. States that kept expenditure growth under target rates or adopted specified cost-control reforms could avoid these reductions in the Medicaid matching rate.

At the urging of the National Governors' Association, Congress also increased the states' ability to control Medicaid spending by increasing their authority over the scope, coverage, and operations of their Medicaid program. States were given authority to design systems for reimbursing hospitals and other health care providers; to limit recipients' freedom to choose which provider they would use; and to define who would be served and what services would be provided under the "medically needy" portion of the program (the portion serving those who are not on the AFDC rolls and thus are not automatically eligible for Medicaid).

President Reagan also argued that administration of welfare programs was lax and that fraud control programs had to be improved. In response, Congress passed a series of Reagan proposals requiring states to monitor more closely the income and eligibility of welfare recipients.

Though the recession pushed up spending on public assistance programs during 1982 and early 1983, these changes had an important impact on federal welfare policy; growth in spending was less than it otherwise would have been. In AFDC, for example, case loads were cut by approximately 10 percent and spending in the years immediately following these changes was estimated to have been about 10 percent below what it would have been under previous policy.

Reversal of Some Welfare Changes

Some of the 1981 changes made in entitlement programs were later undone by Congress. In 1984, Congress passed the Deficit Reduction Assistance Act of 1984 (P.L. 98-369), which went into effect in fiscal year 1985. This act restored eligibility to some AFDC recipients with earnings by extending the duration of the $30 earning disregard to a year and raising the gross income ceiling to 185 percent of the standard of need. Congress allowed states to continue Medicaid if a family left AFDC (because a member took a low-paying job) for up to fifteen months after AFDC payments ended. Congress also ended the federal subsidy reductions in Medicaid and required states to provide Medicaid to certain needy non-AFDC women and children not covered by some states.

BLOCK GRANT PROGRAMS AND JOB TRAINING ACT

The most important changes in other grant-in-aid programs besides entitlements was the creation of new block grants and revisions to existing block grants, which were adopted as part of the 1981 budget act, and the passage in 1982 of a new program for job training. While the changes in entitlement programs had furthered the goal of concentrating welfare assistance on the "truly needy," the block grant initiatives and the job training act advanced Reagan's efforts to achieve two of the three other goals identified earlier: reducing the federal domestic role and shifting responsibility to the states.

In March 1981 Reagan proposed consolidating eighty-five categorical grant programs encompassing $16.5 billion into seven new block grants. Congress however gave him only part of what he asked for. The budget act of 1981 created or revised nine block grants that affected fifty-four existing programs with total budget authority for fiscal year 1982 of $7.2 billion. Some of these changes were not very important. Four of the nine block grants contained only one established categorical program (see table 3.3), while two of the "new" block programs—social services and community development—were already block grants. The budget act did, however, change some of the provisions of the previous programs.

In a number of cases, the block grant legislation helped Reagan shrink the federal role in domestic affairs by reducing the spending compared with fiscal year 1981 levels for the previous programs. Reagan's rationale for spending cuts under block grants was that the block grants would "reduce wasteful administrative overhead."[17] His budget proposals requested an average cut in spending of about 25 percent; Congress approved reductions averaging about 12 percent. Reductions from the fiscal year 1981 outlays ranged from nothing in the case of the energy assistance block grant for low-income persons to 34 percent for the community services block grant. (Appropriations for each block grant are detailed in chapter 4 where we discuss the state and local responses to the Reagan changes.) Although Reagan's block grant proposals were similar in many ways to the block grants enacted under Nixon, one of the ways they differed was that Nixon's proposals had come with "sweeteners" in the form of spending increases, while Reagan's came with the bitter pill of spending reductions.

There is another important difference between Nixon's and Reagan's block grants. In contrast to the block grants enacted under Nixon, which devolved authority to whatever level of authority Nixon was able to persuade Congress to

Table 3.3.   *New or Changed Block Grants Enacted in 1981*

Block grant	Number of programs consolidated	Final federal fiscal year 1982 budget authority (dollars in millions)
Social services	3	2,400
Low-income energy assistance	1	1,875
Small city community development	1	1,037
Elementary and secondary education	29	470
Alcohol, drug abuse, and mental health	3	432
Maternal and child health	7	348
Community services	1	348
Primary health care	1	248
Preventive health and health services	8	82
Total for nine block grants	54	7,240

SOURCE: John W. Ellwood, ed., *Reductions in U.S. Domestic Spending* (New Brunswick, N.J.: Transaction Books, 1982), p. 341.

[17] "Program for Economic Recovery" (Address before a joint session of Congress, February 18, 1981), *Weekly Compilation of Presidential Documents* 17, no. 8 (February 23, 1981):130–37.

devolve it to, Reagan's approach concentrated on shifting power to the states. Block grants enhanced state authority by giving them greater flexibility in administering these grants. Increased flexibility for the states also resulted from the removal or loosening of federal regulations governing such matters as how the states report their uses of federal grant-in-aid funds and the procedures they follow in procuring goods and services with these funds. By and large, the states were allowed to follow whatever reporting and accounting procedures they used for their own funds.[18]

In employment and training, the president achieved further successes in cutting spending and increasing the role of the states. One of the biggest cuts in domestic spending under Reagan was in the employment and training area in 1981, when Reagan rescinded unspent fiscal year 1981 budget authority for the component of CETA that had funded public service employment programs. This component of CETA subsidized positions in local governments and provided training for the people who held those positions. The public service employment program was terminated in the 1982 budget act.

In 1982, Congress enacted a program similar to the 1981 block grants, the Job Training Partnership Act (JTPA), which was fully in place in 1984. It was the federal government's new vehicle for training unemployed people and helping them find jobs. Compared with its predecessor, the Comprehensive Employment and Training Act (CETA), it increased the decision-making authority of state governments and decreased that of local governments. It also involved representatives of private firms to a greater degree in setting policy, both at the state and local levels.[19]

CHANGES IN OTHER GRANT PROGRAMS

Aside from the changes made through block grants and under the new job training program, the Reagan administration won congressional approval for spending cuts and program changes in a number of other grants-in-aid providing funds for operating purposes. Though these were spread among a wide variety

---

[18] See Catherine Lovell, "Effects of Regulatory Changes on States and Localities," in Richard P. Nathan, Fred C. Doolittle, and Associates, *The Consequences of Cuts* (Princeton, N.J.: Princeton Urban and Regional Research Center, 1983), chapter 6.

[19] Budget authorizations for CETA programs totaled nearly $7.6 billion in 1981. In 1982, Congress authorized slightly over $3 billion for CETA; the lower funding level reflected cuts in job training programs and the elimination of public service employment grants. For fiscal year 1983, Congress appropriated approximately $4 billion for job training and employment services. Fiscal 1984 appropriations exceeded $6.5 billion; however, the funding was for a 21-month period to facilitate transition of the new JTPA programs.

of programs, a number of changes affected programs with sizable proportions of low-income beneficiaries. The compensatory education program is an example. This program provides grants both to states and to local school districts; in 1981 much of the grant money was given in the form of "concentration grants" to districts with a high proportion of children from low-income families. The reconciliation act gave states the authority to allocate funds among local districts and provided more discretion in deciding what factors to use in making the allocations. These changes were expected to result in spreading funds more widely and thus decreasing aid to big-city school districts, which had received the bulk of such aid in the past.

Finally, revisions were made in several grant-in-aid programs for capital purposes. These cuts, however, tended to be smaller than in the case of entitlement and operating grants. In some cases, they involved changing the timing, rather than the level, of federal grants. The net effect was to make federal funding less certain for capital grants for such purposes as highways, mass transit, wastewater treatment, and airports.

The program most affected by policy changes in capital grants under Reagan is housing assistance. Section 8 of the Housing Act assists low-income families in two forms: (1) direct subsidies to renters, and (2) subsidies to builders who rent units to low-income families. The 1981 budget act sharply reduced the projected number of housing units to be added to the stock of subsidized units; increased the percentage of a family's income that it is required to devote to rent from 25 to 30 percent; and, for families receiving direct subsidies, reduced the percentage who could have incomes of more than half the median income, thus focusing the program on very low-income households.

Table 3.1 shows a reduction in capital outlays between fiscal years 1981 and 1982. However, this drop in large measure reflects the reluctance, and sometimes inability, of the states to borrow funds for capital projects in the recession period.

At the same time that the Reagan administration was trying to trim old capital programs, it did offer one new proposal to help economically distressed cities attract new capital investments. This was the urban enterprise zones proposal, which would provide tax breaks and some easing of federal regulations for firms that build plants and hire workers in specified zones of cities. This proposal does not involve new spending; however, it is estimated that it would reduce federal tax revenues by $800 million per year. Although Reagan repeatedly mentioned the proposal in speeches, the Congress did not give it serious consideration during his first term.

Slowdown in Budget Cuts

The Reagan administration's success in obtaining congressional approval for spending cuts in domestic programs reached its high point in August 1981 with passage of the reconciliation act. In September 1981, Reagan found Congress in a less receptive mood when he argued that the cuts in the budget reconciliation act had not been deep enough and sought $16 billion in additional spending reductions. After initially vetoing a supplemental appropriations bill, Reagan accepted one containing additional cuts of $4 billion. Later, in 1982 when Congress received Reagan's fiscal year 1983 budget, lawmakers paid relatively little attention to the president's requests for further spending cuts. Instead, they concentrated on trying to reduce the deficit by recapturing part of the revenues lost as a result of the 1981 tax cut, and on appropriating additional funds for programs designed to combat the effects of the recession that had begun in fall 1981 and was growing deeper in 1982.

The first antirecession spending legislation to be enacted was the Surface Transportation Assistance Act (STAA) of 1982, which increased the federal gasoline tax from four to nine cents a gallon and used the proceeds to increase spending for federal highway and mass transit programs (see table 3.4). Reagan opposed this bill at first but later accepted it as a way to rebuild infrastructure by means of user fees. Although both budget authority and outlays dropped for the affected transportation programs in 1982, budget authority jumped in 1983 and outlays followed.

In March 1983, Congress followed up with the emergency jobs act, which boosted fiscal year 1983 budget authority for a wide range of existing federal grants by $2.8 billion (see table 3.5). For operating grants, outlays rose immediately, while for capital grants the outlay effect was delayed.

The bottom rows of table 3.1 show the net effect on federal spending of these congressional initiatives. Total outlays increased slightly in real terms from 1982 through 1985 because of increases in operating and capital programs. Operating grant increases came primarily in 1983 with the jobs act, while capital program growth occurred in 1984. Total entitlements spending was roughly constant in real terms because of the recession, although Medicaid outlays continued to grow rapidly.

The "Swap and Turnback" Initiative

In January 1982, at about the time his proposals for further cuts in federal domestic spending were encountering stiff resistance in the Congress, President

Table 3.4.   *Federal Grant Funding for Transportation Programs by Federal*
Fiscal Year (dollars in millions)

Program	1981	1982	1983	1984	1985
Federal aid highways					
Budget authority	8,850	8,137	12,444	13,777	14,508
Outlays	8,641	7,590	8,529	10,641	12,741
Mass transit					
Budget authority	4,585	3,516	4,409	4,201	4,004
Outlays	3,832	3,847	3,658	3,788	3,851
Airports					
Budget authority	570	476	800	994	987
Outlays	469	339	453	800	810
Total for all transportation					
Budget authority	14,323	12,843	18,454	19,280	19,846
Outlays	13,462	12,171	13,248	15,931	17,893

SOURCE: Executive Office of the President, U.S. Office of Management and Budget, *Special Analyses,
Budget of the United States Government,* various fiscal years (Washington, D.C.: Government Printing
Office).

Reagan in his State of the Union message proposed a sweeping reform of the
entire federal aid system. Calling current patterns of federal aid "a distortion in
the vital functions of government," he proposed to "return" to the state and local governments about $47 billion in federally funded programs, together with
the means to finance them. The shift was to be implemented over a seven-year
period, from 1984 through 1991.

As the details of the proposal emerged in the following weeks, state and local
officials learned that the president wanted the federal government to assume
full control and financial responsibility for the fast-growing Medicaid program,
which is administered by state and local governments. In exchange, Reagan
proposed that states take over administrative and funding responsibility for food
stamps and AFDC.

These proposals were thought out better than the ill-fated proposals of 1976,
but in the final analysis they suffered from the same problem of vagueness in
critical areas. The "swap" proposal represented a fundamental shift not only for
American federalism but also for Ronald Reagan. In his budget proposals a year
earlier, and indeed for a long time before that, Reagan had advocated devolving
Medicaid to the states, in essence as a block grant. Now he was proposing that
it be taken over by the federal government.

The idea of devolving AFDC and food stamps would have reversed the tide

Table 3.5. *Estimated Increase in Grants-in-Aid from the Emergency Jobs Act of 1983, by Federal Fiscal Year (dollars in millions)*

Grant Program	Budget Authority 1983	Outlays 1983	Outlays 1985	Outlays 1985–88
Community development block grant	1,000	250	500	250
Social services block grant	225	169	56	0
Health resources and services	175	84	91	0
Training and employment	173	101	72	0
Energy conservation	150	30	100	20
Rural water/waste disposal	150	6	48	92
Urban mass transit	133	7	27	100
Economic Development Administration programs	100	1	30	69
Special supplemental food (women, infant, and child food program)	100	92	8	0
Watershed and flood prevention	100	26	54	25
Other	485	210	764	674
TOTAL	2,791	976	1,778	1,231

SOURCE: Unpublished estimates from the Executive Office of the President, U.S. Office of Management and Budget.

of increasing federal responsibility for these programs. Although AFDC had always been a joint responsibility of the states and the federal government, the federal government had taken over public assistance for the aged, blind, and disabled. The most radical change in Reagan's "swap and turnback" proposal was to shift the food stamp program to state control, since this program had always been primarily a federal responsibility. The food stamp program was dropped from the administration's "swap" list early in the negotiating sessions between administration officials and representatives of state and local governments.

Not surprisingly, discussion of Reagan's 1982 federalism reform proposals quickly turned from political theory to money. The administration claimed that the net effect of the swap would save states and local governments money, but officials of these governments pointed out that any savings would occur only if AFDC and food stamps costs were calculated under the assumption that the cuts proposed in the fiscal year 1983 budget were adopted.

The finances of the plan were further complicated by the fact that the "swap" was only part of the proposal. The plan also called for establishing a trust fund to temporarily finance the costs of operating programs that would be "turned back" to the states. The fiscal year 1983 budget listed forty-four programs as "illustrative" of programs that would be devolved to states; these programs included 125 separate grants. Besides general revenue sharing, the major functional areas affected were education, employment and training, social services, public health, transportation (though not interstate highways), and community development.

The trust fund that initially was to compensate the state for taking over these program areas was to be funded from the federal excise taxes on alcohol, tobacco, and telephone service; part of the excise tax on gasoline; and part of the "windfall profits" tax on energy resources that had been enacted under President Carter. Under the plan, the federal taxes assigned to this trust fund were to be phased down starting in 1987; the fund was to go out of existence in 1991. After that, each state would be left to its own devices to provide funds, if it chose to do so, to continue the services and activities funded under the programs "turned back" to the states. This feature of the Reagan plan to have the states fund the entire cost of the "turned back" programs out of their own funds after the transition period had ended was one of the most controversial features of the plan.

Despite extended negotiations between White House officials, governors, mayors, and congressional representatives, the president's plan was never able to attract much support. The governors called for a federal takeover of the AFDC rather than a pullout. Mayors feared that states would not pass through to local governments the funds received from the trust fund. Though Reagan administration officials made many changes in the plan, they never even came close to building a winning coalition for it.

Richard Williamson, the president's aide for intergovernmental affairs during this period and the leading White House negotiator on the plan, wrote an article that puts some of the blame on the controversy engendered by Budget Director Stockman's efforts to win more cuts in domestic spending. The "swap and turnback" plan, Williamson contended, came to be viewed by many as a backdoor way to cut the federal budget. Williamson wrote, "Most often, . . . we failed to get the proposed cuts and, in the process of making the ill-conceived budget cut proposals, lost a chance for meaningful structural reforms that would have provided long-term budget savings."[20]

Finally, in mid-1982 the administration announced that it would not submit legislation for its federalism reforms during that session of Congress. The plan was not heard of again.

[20] Richard S. Williamson, "The 1982 New Federalism Negotiations," *Publius* 13, no. 2 (Spring 1983):31.

The Net Effect of First-Term Changes

To summarize the discussion of the changes in spending for federal grants-in-aid during the Reagan first term, funding for federal aid dropped sharply with passage of the president's fiscal year 1982 budget. Federal grants-in-aid declined by $6.6 billion in current dollars from the previous year, the first annual drop in nominal terms in more than twenty-five years. (The decline amounted to $9 billion, or 12 percent, in real terms.) For the rest of the Reagan first term, however, overall federal aid funding was roughly constant in real terms. Congressional rejection of later Reagan budget proposals and restoration of some of the 1981 cuts during the recession, plus recession-induced increases in public assistance rolls, meant the federal aid outlays in real terms stayed on a plateau from 1982 through 1984, then increased somewhat in 1985. Aid outlays in these years were below the 1981 level but significantly above the level envisioned in the Reagan budgets.

Budget Director David Stockman, in unguarded comments to reporter William Greider, said he began the 1981 budget-cutting process with the intention of "curtailing weak claims rather than weak clients. . . . We have to show that we are willing to attack powerful clients with weak claims."[21] By the end of the 1981 budget process, however, many of the proposals for cutting spending on programs that benefited the middle class had been removed from the reconciliation act, and Stockman's hopes of ending or trimming tax breaks for corporations and investors had been dashed by a tax act that added new and larger tax advantages and tax incentives for many special interests. According to Greider, "Now, as the final balance was being struck, he [Stockman] was forced to concede in private that the claim of equity in shrinking the government was significantly compromised if not obliterated."[22]

In the final analysis, Reagan's cuts in federal aid came together in a way that fell disproportionately on one segment of the population: the poor. These effects are most dramatic in the case of the cuts and changes in entitlement grant-in-aid programs, but they can be seen in the cuts and changes made in other types of federal aid programs as well. Public service jobs for the poor were eliminated. Funding for community service programs and aid to large cities and community development aid were reduced. Aid to schools serving low-income students in large cities was reduced because of changes in the method of allocating funds under the elementary and secondary education block grant as well as reductions in outlays under the compensatory education program. Unem-

---

[21] William Greider, *The Education of David Stockman and Other Americans* (New York: E. P. Dutton, 1982), p. 13.
[22] Ibid., p. 55.

ployed people were no longer able to receive a stipend while receiving job train-ing. And persons needing assistance in finding affordable housing were affected by increased rents in public housing and by the prospect of fewer new subsi-dized units as a result of cutbacks in construction aid. The way these and other cuts and changes in federal aid affected state and local spending and programs is discussed in the next chapter.

State Responses by Program

✳

*T*hree major types of effects of changes in federal grants-in-aid are considered in this chapter—*fiscal, programmatic,* and *institutional.* Under the heading of *fiscal effects,* we are interested in whether cuts in federal aid resulted in service cuts in state and local programs or whether the cuts were in some way offset at the state and local levels. Under the heading of *programmatic effects,* we are interested in the ways in which cuts and changes in federal grants resulted in changes in the type and character of the services provided by states and localities, the mix of services, and their incidence. And finally, under the heading of *institutional effects,* our emphasis is on the way a given service is organized and administered. The Reagan changes in some cases caused state and local governments to shift responsibilities between them. In others, they affected the administrative system for providing services and the roles of different types of providers.

When we began this research in 1981, our main objective, as was true of other similar studies in this period, was to determine the extent to which states and localities used their own funds to replace federal aid cuts. We sought to identify the various types of actions taken by states and localities to replace federal aid cuts out of their own funds (presumably new funds as a result of tax increases or revenue growth) in order to contrast them with cases in which states and localities ratified federal aid cuts by simply passing them along to program recipients. As the research progressed, however, two things happened. The cuts themselves became less important as the Congress restored some federal aid funding cut in 1981 to combat the recession that began at the end of the year. Also, we experienced increasing difficulties in making determinations about the types of measures which states and localities took to stave off the effects of federal aid reductions. Although states and localities could (and did) use their own funds to replace federal aid cuts, they often had other options. Sometimes federal aid funds in the pipeline were used to delay the effects of cuts. In some of these cases, carryover funds were available for a long enough period so that by the time they ran out states and localities had new federal aid money from other sources, for example, the 1983 emergency jobs act. In other cases, new authority to transfer federal funds provided under Reagan's block grants permitted states and localities to stave off the effects of federal aid cuts. Furthermore, states could shift state funds to protect services. In still other cases, the opportunity existed to shift services from a federal aid program that was cut to one that was not, for example, in the case of the social services and health block grants where some funding cuts in these programs were offset by shifting the aided services to the Medicaid program.

This coping behavior—delaying, blunting, and in some cases preventing the impact of the 1981 cuts in federal grants—is a consistent theme of the case studies prepared in this final summary phase of our research. The Illinois case study refers to these tactics as "dodging the cuts with fiscal footwork." The author states, "Although there were indeed some service reductions, Illinois political leaders—and their often resourceful program managers—had many techniques for smoothing out federal aid reductions and blunting their impact."

As a result of the diversity of these coping tactics, we pulled back from our original aim of specifying the fiscal responses on the part of state and local governments to cuts in federal aid. Instead of trying to pin down the way in which states and localities responded to these cuts, we concentrate in this chapter on the basic distinction between those cases where cuts actually resulted in reductions in benefits and services and those where they did not.[1] Our purpose in this chapter is twofold: (1) to compare those program areas in which cuts had a discernible impact on benefits and services and those in which they did not; and (2) to identify the reasons why some programs were protected to a greater degree than others.

The sections of this chapter review the effects of the Reagan-period cuts and changes in federal grants under four headings—entitlement grants, block grants, other operating grants, and capital grants. This is a modification of the typology used earlier in classifying federal grant-in-aid programs. We use four types (rather than three) in this chapter to emphasize the new block grant programs created under Reagan. Thus, we subdivide operating grants into two groups, block grants and other operating grants. The chapter concludes with

[1] In chapter 5 on the responses by state governments to the Reagan cuts in federal grants, we do distinguish between federal aid replacement out of state funds and those cases in which some other strategy was used to stave off the effects of federal aid cuts.

our interpretation of these findings, attributing variations in the responses to cuts and changes in different grants to three factors: (1) the incidence of the benefits or services provided; (2) the strength of a grant's constituency and the level of its general public support and visibility; and (3) the structure of the grant program.

Entitlement Grants

Entitlement grants provide cash and in-kind benefits such as food subsidies and medical care to persons who have incomes below a certain level and meet certain other requirements. Despite the Reagan changes in entitlement programs described in chapter 3, total spending on aid to families with dependent children (AFDC) and Medicaid, the two largest entitlement programs that operate as grants-in-aid, grew from 1981 to 1983 because of the recession, which put many people out of work and thus increased the number of persons who were eligible for aid. Likewise, spending for food stamps and child nutrition (school lunches, school breakfasts, and day-care meals) dropped in fiscal year 1982, after the Reagan changes, but rose again in 1983, reflecting the increased need caused by the recession.

This growth in spending from 1981 to 1984 in most entitlement programs makes it hard to discern the effects of the 1981 Reagan changes. The field associates were in agreement that the cuts in entitlement programs, especially AFDC, Medicaid, and food stamps, were the most important Reagan changes made in 1981. Small percentage cuts in these programs below previous levels amounted to large cuts in absolute dollar amounts. Except for Medicaid, the state-local reactions to these changes suggested that the public—except in the most liberal states—perceived these programs to be decidedly "federal" (as opposed to state or state-local) programs.

As discussed in chapter 2, starting with the New Deal, and accelerating in the 1960s and 1970s, the provision of welfare benefits to needy persons became an important function of the federal government. Most local governments gradually withdrew from the financing of these programs. State governments also came to play a less important role in financing public assistance due to increases in the federal matching rates in federal aid programs; the creation of federal food and health in-kind assistance programs; and the federal takeover in 1974 of aid to low-income aged, blind, and disabled persons.

In the 1960s and 1970s, many state and local officials urged full (or nearly full) federal financing of public assistance as a way to shift the growing costs of these programs to the national level. They argued that these increases were in large measure due to national economic and social changes such as migration, changing patterns of family structure, and new attitudes toward government assistance. As governor of California, Ronald Reagan stood virtually alone in opposing an increased federal role in public assistance. In this context, there is an interesting irony in the way events worked out under President Reagan, particularly in the AFDC program. Reagan curbed AFDC spending by increasing, rather than decreasing, federal control over the program through the changes made in the 1981 budget act in eligibility requirements and benefit calculations. On the other hand, he has failed, at least up to now, in his efforts to convert these programs, notably AFDC and Medicaid, into closed-ended grants, which many conservatives believe would result in spending reduction for these income-transfer programs targeted on the poor.

AID TO FAMILIES WITH DEPENDENT CHILDREN

Of all of the Reagan policy changes made in 1981, the one with the clearest and most immediate effect on the states in the sample was the change in rules for AFDC. The associates for more than half the sample states reported a decline in expenditures and case loads in 1982 despite the recession. Oklahoma's AFDC case load dropped by about one-third in one year after the 1981 changes and spending dropped by the same proportion within two years. This drop, the largest percentage change of any state in the sample, occurred because Oklahoma's recipients before 1981 included a higher than average proportion of working recipients, the group most affected by the 1981 changes. The 1981 AFDC changes also had a big impact in Massachusetts and Texas, where AFDC spending declined in 1982 and then declined further in 1983.

In other sample states, the recession pushed up AFDC expenditures despite the 1981 changes. In Arizona, for example, two factors—the recession and the growth in the number of newly arrived job seekers—combined to push up AFDC spending by 5 percent in federal fiscal year 1982 and 20 percent more in 1983.

Even in states with little net change in the AFDC case load, the 1981 changes had a major effect on many recipients in the program. The Ohio associates, for example, reported that 28,000 recipients were dropped from the AFDC rolls because of tightened eligibility rules, but at the same time the severe impact of the 1981–82 recession on the state forced thousands of people to apply for assistance. The net result was that the AFDC case load was virtually unchanged in 1982. This 1981–82 experience is in sharp contrast to previous recessions, which pushed up AFDC case loads and spending. In the 1975 recession, for example, the national AFDC case load rose by 12 percent between the time the unemployment rate began to rise rapidly in late 1974 and the peak of the case load in early 1976. Monthly AFDC spending rose about 20 percent in real terms in this period.

One of the goals of the 1981 AFDC changes was to target benefits on those without other income, and the associates reported that the changes had this effect. In California, the proportion of AFDC recipients with earnings declined from nearly 19 percent of the total case load in July 1981 to 5.6 percent in April 1983. The Missouri associates reported that the working AFDC parent became a "fast-vanishing category" as such recipients dropped from 18 percent of the case load prior to October 1981 to 5 percent in October 1982. Although the deepening recession played a role in reducing earnings, most associates reported that the federal legislative changes appeared to be the major cause of these cuts and shifts in the case load.

Despite the perception that AFDC is a "federal" program, the states do make important policy decisions affecting AFDC. For example, states set the level of benefits and the standard of need for eligibility. Some sample states took steps that state officials explicitly described as efforts to counter the effects of the 1981 policy changes. New York chose to provide assistance under the home relief program—which is financed by the state and local governments—to three groups removed from AFDC by the 1981 changes. The groups were women pregnant with their first child, students aged eighteen to twenty-one, and strikers. In New York, home relief benefit levels are the same as those received under the AFDC program, so these families received as much as they had gotten under AFDC.

Though a few other states did pick up some families removed from the AFDC rolls on their general relief programs, benefit levels usually were much lower than under AFDC. This happened, for example, in California, where counties provided assistance to some families removed from AFDC under county-financed general relief programs. Associates in Ohio and Florida report a similar shift to local general assistance programs.

Other states raised their AFDC need standards in the study period, thus partly countering the effect of the legislative change made in 1981 limiting eligibility to families with a gross income less than 150 percent of the standard of need.[2] The Mississippi associates reported that state officials increased the state's standard of need by 30 percent, effective in 1983. Publicly they justified the increase as an adjustment to account for inflation. However, officials conceded that the move was also intended to restore eligibility to those cut from the

---

[2] In October 1984, Congress increased this cutoff to gross income in excess of 185 percent of the standard of need.

federal public assistance rolls. Mississippi state officials were more concerned about the loss of Medicaid eligibility for those removed from AFDC than about the loss of the AFDC cash benefits, which in Mississippi are quite low.

The Reagan administration argued that with the rolls pared of "high income" recipients, states would be moved to increase payments for the remaining "truly needy" recipients, just as California did after instituting similar reforms under Reagan as governor. Nine states in the sample did raise AFDC benefits between October 1981 and mid-1984.[3] In Texas, for example, where the field researchers noted a shift in the political mood toward a more liberal stance on social issues, the state increased its AFDC benefits in January 1983. This decision required an amendment to the state constitution, which, to the surprise of many observers, passed by a 2-to-1 margin. Missouri also raised benefits, effective July 1, 1982, the start of the state's 1982-83 fiscal year. The field associates reported that "state officials chose to use approximately $5.6 million in funds that had been saved from federal eligibility restrictions to increase benefits to those families who remained eligible for assistance rather than those who had been dropped from the AFDC rolls. As a result, the average payment per family rose from $211.82 in September 1981 to $234.98, a 10.0 percent increase." A similar response was observed by the Ohio associates, who wrote: "For those eligible for AFDC, the state initiated a 5 percent increase in benefits effective June 1984, with another 5 percent scheduled for 1985 but conditioned on the rate of increase in case loads and AFDC spending."

The field researchers reported that most of the increases were justified on other grounds, for example, as compensation for the effects of inflation since the last benefit increase. While the evidence is not compelling, there are grounds for interpreting some of part of these state increases as a response to the Reagan changes. A comparison of AFDC benefit levels adjusted for inflation in the sample states reveals that in the two years before the 1981 changes went into effect, the purchasing power of the average AFDC benefits for a family of four with no other income declined 15 percent. In the two years after the changes took effect, the purchasing power of benefits continued to decline but at a lower rate, in this case 5 percent.[4]

The 1981 AFDC amendments also offered the states the option of adopting

---

[3] U.S. Department of Health and Human Services, Social Security Administration, Office of Family Assistance, *Characteristics of State Plans for AFDC*, various years (Washington, D.C.: Government Printing Office, 1983, 1984, 1985, 1986).

[4] A study by Tim Smeeding of all states reports a similar finding. AFDC benefit levels have continued to decline in real terms during the first years of the 1980s, though at a somewhat slower rate than during the 1970s. See Timothy Smeeding, "Is the Safety Net Still Intact?" in D. Lee Bawden, ed., *The Social Contract Revisited: Aims and Outcomes of President Reagan's Social Welfare Policy* (Washington, D.C.: The Urban Institute, 1984), pp. 98–99.

new employment programs for AFDC recipients. "Workfare" (usually defined as compulsory employment at the minimum wage to "work off" the AFDC grant) was the most important of these options. Two states in the sample, Oklahoma and South Dakota, established statewide workfare programs, and the associates reported that state officials were enthusiastic about them. Other sample states were more cautious. Four states—California, Ohio, New York, and Washington—set up pilot AFDC job search and workfare projects in a portion of the state during the study period.

Some states, especially states with low-level AFDC benefits, were not interested in workfare. In Arizona and Mississippi, for example, the associates reported that state officials did not see workfare as cost effective. They explained that with their states' low AFDC benefits, the administrative costs per workfare participant would be too high to justify the effort expended because each recipient would end up working only a few hours a month to "work off" the AFDC grant. In addition, the Mississippi associates reported that in some poor counties, where 30 to 40 percent of all families received AFDC, the tax base was very small, which meant that few public services could be provided. Hence, there were relatively few agencies that could offer workfare jobs.

A number of sample states that did not adopt workfare increased employment services and job training for AFDC recipients. Associates in Florida, Massachusetts, New Jersey, New York, Missouri, and Washington reported states' efforts to increase their job placement and training activities for AFDC family heads.

What happened to the AFDC recipients cut off the rolls in 1981? Some welfare experts predicted that working recipients who were removed because of earnings would quit their jobs and return to AFDC. They reasoned that the financial incentive to work was reduced under the Reagan approach in a way that would be likely to produce this outcome. Studies examining the 1981 changes are consistent, however, in their conclusion that this did not happen.[5] Somewhere between 15 to 20 percent of the people cut off from AFDC after the 1981 changes were found to have returned to the AFDC rolls by a year later, a rate similar to the return rate for normal case terminations.

[5] For example, see Research Triangle Institute, "Final Report: Evaluation of the 1981 AFDC Amendments," submitted to the Office of Family Assistance, Social Security Administration, Department of Health and Human Services, under Task Order 1, Contract Number 600-82-0095, April 15, 1983; Mitchell Ginsberg and Alvin Mesnikoff, "Work, Welfare and the Family: The Consequences of AFDC Losses for New York City Working Mothers and Their Families," Columbia University School of Social Work, May 1984; U.S. General Accounting Office, "An Evaluation of the 1981 AFDC Changes: Initial Analysis," GAO Report PEMD-84-6 (Washington, D.C.: Government Accounting Office, April 2, 1984).

FOOD STAMPS

The 1981 changes in the food stamp program paralleled those in AFDC in tightening eligibility requirements.[6] Some people stopped receiving food stamps in 1982 because of new eligibility rules; others were terminated from the program because they had lost their AFDC eligibility and thus were no longer automatically eligible for food stamps. One of the 1981 changes postponed a cost-of-living adjustment for recipients.

The food stamp program is decidedly countercyclical; nationally, the number of recipients and benefit levels tend to rise during recession periods as larger numbers of unemployed workers and their families enter the program. At first, the 1981 Reagan changes in the food stamp program appeared to reduce the rolls and benefit levels, but as the recession deepened a turnaround occurred and there was a pronounced rise in spending under this program in the sample states. In Ohio, hit hard by the recession, food stamp spending was nearly 30 percent higher in 1982 and 1983 as compared with 1981. Associates in six other states (Illinois, Mississippi, Missouri, Oklahoma, South Dakota, and Texas) reported 1983 spending more than 15 percent above the 1981 level. A decline occurred only in Florida, but it appeared to have been the result of special circumstances in that state. The 1981 case load (the base year for comparison) was temporarily swelled by the recent arrival in Florida of large numbers of Cuban refugees. (Refugees are eligible for food stamps.) In 1982 and 1983, the refugees gradually left the food stamp rolls, causing a drop in outlays despite the recession.

Associates reported that state governments did not increase spending to compensate for food stamp cuts, although it must be noted that the basic structure of the food stamp program made it difficult to do so. What response there was came at the local level, primarily from nonprofit feeding and food distribution programs that served many more people in 1982 and 1983 than they had in 1981. The deepening recession was reportedly a more important reason for this increase than the food stamp cuts.

CHILD NUTRITION PROGRAMS

Spending for child nutrition (mainly for school lunches) programs dropped sharply in 1982 due to reductions in the subsidy rates for meals and tightened income eligibility standards. The Reagan policy in this area, similar to that in the case of AFDC, was to target aid on the "truly needy" by increasing the sub-

[6] Unlike AFDC, the federal government finances the entire cost of the food stamp benefits and sets the benefit levels.

sidy rates for the poorest recipients while reducing it for children from better-off families. Increases in meal prices in many places caused children in families with incomes above the new eligibility ceilings to drop out of the program. Oklahoma was the only state in the study sample where state aid increased to replace federal spending cutbacks in lunch subsidies. A more prevalent response was for states to pass along the cuts to local school districts, which in turn absorbed the reductions primarily by increasing the cost of school lunches.

MEDICAID

Both the rolls and the benefits under Medicaid, the largest federal grant-in-aid program, grew rapidly during the 1970s and 1980s, which sent state costs soaring and created pressures for cost control measures. The costs of Medicaid benefits are shared primarily by federal and state governments, although some states require local contributions. States have considerable discretion in setting eligibility and in determining the range and scope of benefits. The 1981 legislative changes in the Medicaid program permitted state governments to play an even stronger policy role under Medicaid. The changes incorporated a number of recommendations by the National Governors' Association to give the states greater authority over Medicaid. Among the most important changes were those that allowed states to negotiate hospital and doctors' fees instead of having to pay the "usual and customary" rates and changes that permitted states to assign patients to providers instead of giving them "freedom of choice."

The 1981 Medicaid changes also reduced the federal matching rate for states that failed to control costs.[7] In states with fast-growing Medicaid programs, however, the fiscal effects of these percentage reductions were much smaller than the potential cost to the state treasury of continued Medicaid growth; the threat of federal penalties was not the primary motivating force for efforts to contain costs under Medicaid. In Missouri, for example, where both state and federal costs rose by more than $40 million between 1980 and 1981, the potential drop in federal aid in 1982 would have been $7.6 million had the state not taken the necessary steps to prevent program growth.

[7] The main method used in 1981 to reduce federal Medicaid expenditures was a reduction in the federal government's matching share of Medicaid costs. The 1981 reconciliation act required the federal share to be reduced by 3 percent in fiscal year 1982, 4 percent in fiscal year 1983, and 4.5 percent in fiscal year 1984. States could avoid this loss in two ways. They could avoid up to three percentage points of the reduction if they had a qualifying hospital cost review program, had high unemployment, and reduced fraud by a certain amount. Second, if a state controlled spending so that federal Medicaid expenditures were below a specified target, the state was entitled to a dollar-for-dollar offset against the reduction up to the difference between the federal Medicaid expenditures and the target amount. Congress discontinued reductions in the federal matching rate when it passed new legislation in 1984.

The response of states in the study to the changes in Medicaid reveals different attitudes from those toward other welfare programs. Like the AFDC program, the main purposes of federal aid for Medicaid are to stimulate the provision of services and to compensate for differences in fiscal capacity among jurisdictions. However, there are important differences between the two programs, including the type of benefits provided and the programs' constituency. The Medicaid program—providing in-kind aid—has a dual constituency: beneficiaries and providers (hospitals, physicians, nursing homes). The latter group (the providers) often has political clout of a high order, and the recipients in this case are more predominantly the elderly, who also tend to have considerable political influence, certainly much more than in the case of the beneficiaries of the AFDC and food stamp programs.[8] In South Dakota, for example, the associate reported that despite federal policy changes that increased state costs "there has been no legislative resistance to the Medicaid program." The situation was similar in Mississippi, where the field associates offered several possible reasons for the special treatment of Medicaid:

> Several factors explain the apparent willingness of the state to replace federal funds in this program. First, the general population perceives this to be a joint federal-state program rather than exclusively federal. Second, the medical profession has provided indispensable support for the program. Third, over 40 percent of Medicaid funds directly aid the elderly. The threat of turning the aged poor into the streets has proven to be effective in obtaining additional funds.

The federal matching rate penalty provisions of Medicaid were a major focus of attention. The sample states did not passively accept these federal cuts. Most sample states avoided the full effect of the penalties in 1982 by putting in place fraud-control programs, implementing hospital cost-review programs, and in some cases taking action to hold the growth in total Medicaid spending below the target rate. Seven of the sample states avoided any reduction in federal assistance, and two other states avoided more than half the penalty. Some states expanded Medicaid coverage. In Ohio, for example, state officials extended Medicaid eligibility in an effort to reduce fiscal pressures on the state's general relief programs. New York health care administrators projected that the only

---

[8] Of the four groups of Medicaid participants—the aged, blind, disabled, and members of families with dependent children—the aged represents the most costly group of participants. The elderly accounted for 15 percent of Medicaid eligibles, and health care services provided on behalf of the elderly accounted for 37 percent of Medicaid expenditures. See John W. Ellwood, ed., *Reductions in U.S. Domestic Spending* (New Brunswick, N.J.: Transaction Books, 1982), p. 229.

way the state could stay below federal targets for Medicaid expenditures would be to cut services—something the state refused to do.

Despite the fiscal pressures on the states created by the 1981 budget act and the recession, the associates report surprisingly few major service cuts in Medicaid. Most states responded to the federal changes by working to cut costs rather than services.

In several states in the sample, however, fiscal stress and recent rapid growth led to substantial program cuts. In three states—Illinois, Missouri, and Washington—serious state fiscal problems were reported by the associates to have forced the state to cut back on Medicaid services. As the fiscal condition of Illinois deteriorated in 1982, Governor James Thompson became increasingly critical of Medicaid as a program "out of control." In 1982 and 1983, Illinois used the increased flexibility provided in the 1981 budget act to cut outpatient services and limit hospital and nursing home reimbursement. Likewise, the rapid growth in Medicaid spending in Missouri and the state's fiscal crisis of 1981 led state officials to cut Medicaid eligibility, adopt a prospective payment system for hospitals and nursing homes (paying for services based on rates set in advance for each particular diagnosed condition), and introduce patient co-payment requirements for a wide range of health services.

While most of the sample states moved to control Medicaid costs, some states chose to use the new flexibility in ways that actually increased Medicaid spending. They did this by shifting services that were previously fully state-financed into Medicaid (thereby getting a federal match) and by expanding home health care services. Missouri, for example, acted to obtain Medicaid funding for services to the mentally retarded and developmentally disabled persons in state-operated centers; in both cases these were services that were previously funded completely out of state revenue. The South Dakota associate also reported the state used Medicaid funds to finance services to the developmentally disabled that were previously paid for by local school districts. The New Jersey and Texas associates reported state initiatives to broaden home health care under Medicaid. New Jersey established a Medicaid program for the medically needy, while plans for a similar program in Mississippi were delayed by state fiscal pressures. This was easier to do under the 1981 budget act because it provided greater flexibility to the states to limit and specify the services offered under this program. Overall, cost shifting and the adoption of new Medicaid services were modest during the study period. However, these developments indicate that the states see the new flexibility under Medicaid as a way to *increase* federal costs as well as to *contain* them.

Summary on Entitlement Changes

The most important Reagan changes in 1981 were in the entitlement programs and tended to be concentrated on one group, the working poor. Moreover, with the exception of Medicaid, the general tendency we observed was for these cuts to be ratified, that is passed along to the recipients of benefits under AFDC, food stamps, and the school lunch program. There were exceptions to this generalization in some states for AFDC, where states changed the rules under their programs to continue benefits to some recipients affected by the 1981 Reagan changes, but they were not widespread.

The most interesting point that emerges from this analysis involves the differences in what happened in 1981 under two similar grant programs, AFDC and Medicaid. Both programs are open-ended matching grants for income transfers administered by states and in some cases state and county governments on a joint basis. Both at the national and state-local levels, however, the stronger constituencies of the Medicaid program appeared to moderate retrenchment pressures. The fact that the health care industry and the elderly have a special stake in Medicaid caused politicians to be chary of strong action. On the other hand, the working-age, able-bodied adults and their children aided under the AFDC program are lacking in political muscle. This group was the victim not only of the AFDC cuts, but also of reductions and changes made in other grant programs. In the entitlement category, the cuts in school lunches and food stamps hit hardest at this group, as did the new rules that increased rent levels for subsidized housing. As is shown in the sections which follow, this same group bore the brunt of the cuts that were made in operating programs in 1981. They were the chief victims of the elimination of the Comprehensive Employment and Training Act (CETA) public service employment program and, to the extent services were cut under block grants and other operating grants, it was often the services targeted on this group. This outcome no doubt reflects the public mood in a period of conservatism and retrenchment on social policy; this is the group that was most vulnerable to the backlash reaction to the social policy initiatives of the 1960s and 1970s.

Block Grants

The 1981 budget act created or revised nine block grants that affected fifty-four existing programs with total budget authority for fiscal year 1982 of $7.2 billion. Funding for two of these programs—the small cities portion of the community development block grant (CDBG) and the low-income energy assistance block grant—did not decline at all when compared with fiscal year 1981 outlays. Federal appropriations in the remaining programs dropped in 1982, but increased somewhat in 1983.

The coping behavior on the part of state and local governments described at the beginning of this chapter was most evident in the case of block grants. In fiscal year 1982, three factors—carryover funds in the pipeline, opportunities for states to shift federal aid funds between programs, and a small amount of state and local replacement funding out of own-source revenue—enabled state and local officials to maintain existing service levels in many (but not all) programs. In fiscal year 1983, new appropriations from the federal government coupled with a higher level of state and local replacement funding (especially in health and education) kept many services from falling to the levels envisioned in the 1981 budget act.

The sections that follow discuss major features of the block grants affected by the 1981 budget act and the responses to them in the sample jurisdictions, beginning with those in which the changes were the greatest.[9]

COMMUNITY SERVICES BLOCK GRANT

This block grant provides aid for community-based social service programs for health, nutrition, housing, employment, and other services for low-income persons. The community action agencies aided under this program were created under President Johnson's 1965 Economic Opportunity Act. The percentage cut in 1982 in community service funding was the largest of any block grant (34 percent). Funding continued to decline in 1983 despite the fact that a supplemental appropriation for this program was included in the 1983 emergency jobs act that provided special antirecession funds.

The major institutional effect of the changes made in 1981 in the community services block grant was to give state governments a new role in the finances and managerial oversight of community action agencies. Prior to the 1981 budget act, these agencies received financial assistance directly from the federal government. The change meant that states had a new administrative relationship with these agencies.

---

[9] The U.S. General Accounting Office conducted a series of studies evaluating the individual Reagan block grants. These studies confirm the finding we have made about delayed effects, and focus on the state role under these programs. See, for example, *State Rather Than Federal Policies Provided the Framework for Managing Block Grants*, GAO Report HRD-85-36 (Washington, D.C.: Government Accounting Office, March 15, 1985).

In this changed administrative environment, most community action agencies did not fare well. No state or local government in the sample replaced the federal cuts out of own-source revenues, although a few states transferred other federal funds temporarily to aid community action agencies. Texas drew upon the social services block grant, the low-income energy assistance block grant, and various health grants to help finance local community services. Washington shifted some low-income energy assistance to community services. Carry-over funds were an important source of support for community action agencies in Oklahoma and Mississippi. Florida combined the management of the community services and Head Start programs; this resulted in a reduction in education outlays for Head Start, but not for grants to operate community service agencies.

New state distribution decisions further reduced funding for some community services agencies; this was particularly the case in large cities. A number of the states in the sample spread the funds they received under this block grant more widely across the state, taking some funds away from big-city community action agencies that had done relatively well under direct federal administration of the program. This happened in Boston, Seattle, and Chicago. A reduced level of federal aid was spread among a greater number of jurisdictions. In two states, Illinois and Washington, community service funds were dispersed on a formula basis that considered poverty distribution. Local officials succeeded in convincing the states to provide temporary transition funding for community service programs in the larger urban centers. Even with the additional funds, however, poverty-fighting agencies in cities like Chicago and Seattle found that they had fared better prior to state implementation of the block grant, when federal aid had been distributed by the Community Services Administration.

The new state role in allocating community service funds was controversial in some sample states. In South Dakota, a legal battle erupted over this issue. Governor William Janklow's decision to eliminate funding for three of the six community action agencies was challenged in the courts. After losing an initial legal battle, the governor won the war.[10] In most of the other states in the study

[10] One of the agencies whose funding was cut off brought suit arguing that the state's plan for using block grant funds was invalid because the state had failed to comply with federal mandates for public hearings. The Eighth U.S. Circuit Court of Appeals in 1982 agreed and ruled the plan invalid, which meant that community services funds had to be distributed under provisions of the Economic Opportunity Act. The U.S. Department of Health and Human Services then awarded grants to all six community action agencies, as directed by the court, but the governor exercised his power under the Economic Opportunity Act to veto the grants. The same community action agency challenged this action, but this time the Federal Appeals Court upheld the governor (Southeastern Human Development Corp. v. Heckler, No. 83-1585, slip. op., 8th Court of Appeals, April 10, 1984).

sample, however, the tendency was to preserve the status quo: to continue funding those community action agencies that had received funding prior to the block grant. In large part, this was due to "hold-harmless" provisions in the 1981 budget act that limited state discretion over block grant funds, capping the amount of federal aid that could go to new agencies. However, it also reflected the ability of local officals to influence state administration. Community action leaders in California, for example, were especially effective in Sacramento; they drafted the legislation that was used by the state to distribute funds.

Funding cuts caused many community action agencies to adopt new service priorities, in general moving away from programs that have long-term payoffs such as vocational counseling and cost-intensive social services in favor of direct job search and training programs and emergency assistance.

COMMUNITY DEVELOPMENT BLOCK GRANT

Community development block grant (CDBG) funds for such purposes as infrastructure improvements, housing rehabilitation for low- and moderate-income families, and neighborhood economic development have been provided to all big cities and many smaller communities since 1974. The principal change made in 1981 was to give states more authority in allocating funds under the small-cities portion of this block grant.

CDBG funds are distributed in two segments. Cities with a population of more than 50,000 automatically receive funds under a formula, whereas under the law as originally enacted smaller cities applied to the U.S. Department of Housing and Urban Development for a share of their state's allocation of so-called small-cities CDBG funding. The 1981 reconciliation act gave states the option of taking over this small-cities portion of the program. Among the study states, all but New York did so.[11] The act also increased the proportion of total funds allocated to small cities from 25 percent to 30 percent.

Community development funding was cut by $220 million, or 6 percent, for fiscal year 1982, but the emergency jobs act of 1983 more than made up for this cut by adding $1 billion for the program. Out of the additional money provided in the 1983 jobs act, the large formula-funded cities (called "entitlement cities") received an additional $775.2 million; funding for the small-cities portion

[11] New York was one of the four states in the nation not administering the program by mid-1984. State officials initially feared that the state would be left holding the bag if the federal government reduced its assistance. In addition, over one-third of the state's 1982 appropriation was already committed to multi-year projects. Governor Mario Cuomo, who took office in January 1983, favored state assumption, but as of December 1986 the state has yet to assume the program.

increased by $222.8 million. Federal appropriations to HUD for the CDBG program totaled $3.468 billion in 1984 and $3.472 billion in 1985.

On the whole, small cities tended to fare better than large ones under CDBG in the Reagan period. This was partly because of the decline in the percentage of total funds (from approximately 75 percent to 70 percent) going to entitlement cities and partly because the number of entitlement cities increased when the 1980 census identified a larger number of cities with a population over 50,000. Funding for the small-cities portion of the program increased; the sample states received increases in funding in 1983 for small cities under the CDBG program ranging from 10 percent in Mississippi to 45 percent in Arizona.

Governors were the principal actors shaping the state administration of the small-cities block grant program. Associates noted several differences under the new state programs. States put their mark on the block grant program by identifying the types of projects to be funded and setting up procedures to distribute funds. Economic development and public works projects tended to receive top priority, instead of the housing and neighborhood rehabilitation programs, which had been favored when HUD administered the small-cities CDBG program. South Dakota used its small-cities CDBG money almost entirely to help localities finance water projects, a top development priority in the state. Missouri and Oklahoma instituted matching requirements under the small-cities program, with the objective being to leverage private funds for local development projects.

Most of the states in the sample distributed small-cities CDBG funds on a competitive basis. Funds tended to be spread more widely, with more cities getting smaller and shorter-term grants, than had previously been the case. Three sample states—Mississippi, Oklahoma, and Ohio—included automatic formula provisions in their system for distributing these funds. Mississippi localities had the option of joining regional districts that automatically received a portion of the state's small-cities allocation or competing on their own for individual project grants. In Oklahoma, funds were awarded on a competitive basis after program administrators allocated aid by region on a formula basis. In Ohio, the state distributed most of its 1982 small-city funds on a formula basis. More than 200 small cities and counties received aid in 1982, whereas in the previous year, when HUD distributed aid, approximately 50 localities in the state participated in the program. In 1983, the state adopted a dual distribution system, whereby a portion of small-city aid was dispersed on a formula basis to all eligible localities and a portion was awarded to selected communities on a project basis.

HEALTH BLOCK GRANTS

Three new health block grants were created by the 1981 budget act—(1) alcohol, drug abuse, and mental health; (2) maternal and child health; and (3) preventive health.[12] Fiscal year 1982 appropriations under each of these block grants were about 25 percent less than the funding received under the previous categorical health grant programs.

In two of the new block grants, the maternal and child health program and the alcohol, drug abuse, and mental health program, carryover funding from previous grants delayed the full impacts of the cuts.[13] These two programs also received additional funds under the emergency jobs act in 1983. Many associates reported in mid-1984 that the full service effects of the fiscal year 1982 funding cuts still had not yet been felt. These two programs also benefited from wide public support at the state and local levels, again underlining the importance of constituency factors in assessing the effects of changes in federal grant-in-aid policies. The state and local programs funded by these two block grants deal with easily dramatized problems of public concern, such as the need to treat alcoholics and the rehabilitation of crippled children.

By contrast, advocates of the services funded by the preventive health block grant (services such as rodent control, planning for emergency medical services, and unrestricted aid to state health programs) were unable to build politi-

[12] A fourth health block grant, the primary care block grant for community health centers, was to take effect in fiscal year 1983. States were not required to assume responsibility for the block grant and few states did. A substantial matching requirement and federal restrictions limiting state discretion over the program deterred states from assuming responsibility for the block grant. In most states, primary care funds continued to be distributed directly from the federal government to local community health centers. For this reason, we do not discuss the block grant here.

[13] Studies by the U.S. General Accounting Office also acknowledge the importance of carryover funds in preventing service reductions. During 1981 to 1983, maternal and child health expenditures increased in eight of eleven states viewed in a GAO study. According to the report, "a major reason most states did not experience expenditure reductions similar to the federal funding reductions was the availability of substantial federal categorical funds during the first year of block grant implementation." See *Maternal and Child Health Block Grant Program Changes Emerging Under State Administration*, GAO Report HRD-84-35 (Washington, D.C.: Government Accounting Office, May 7, 1984), p. 14. A similar observation was made by GAO in its study of the alcohol, drug abuse, and mental health block grant. In twelve of thirteen states under observation, GAO found that about 68 percent of the categorical grants awarded in 1981 "extended into fiscal year 1982; some continued into 1983." California, the thirteenth state in the GAO study, was excluded in the above observation, because the state did not accept the block grant until July 1, 1982. The GAO study also found that in the twelve states under observation, about 63 percent of total federal categorical and block grant aid used in 1982 was from categorical programs. See *States Have Made Few Changes In Implementing The Alcohol, Drug Abuse, and Mental Health Services Block Grant*, GAO Report HRD-84-52 (Washington, D.C.: Government Accounting Office, June 6, 1984), p. 15.

cal support for increased funding. Only four states out of the fourteen in the sample made any effort to protect these services.

SOCIAL SERVICES BLOCK GRANT

The funding cut in the social services block grants program was the largest in absolute amount among the block grants, although the changes made in the structure of the program were relatively minor. Before the 1981 changes, the states were already administering the predecessor program (known as title XX) which operated effectively as a block grant. The fiscal year 1982 cut in funding was partly restored for 1983 in most states by the emergency jobs act.

Coping behavior on the part of states and localities was a notable response in many of the sample states to the 1981 cut in funding in this program. Officials were able, at least in part, to protect social service levels by using three tactics: shifting other federal funds to finance social services; shifting some social service costs to Medicaid or AFDC; and securing state or local replacement funding for the most popular social services.

Field associates in nine of the fourteen states in this study reported instances where federal aid was transferred from the low-income energy assistance block grant to support social services and health care programs.[14] Four states were also able to offset federal reductions in social services by expanding the home health care activities funded by Medicaid. Other states absorbed social service cuts by shifting day-care expenditures for welfare recipients to the AFDC program.

More than half the states in the sample at least partly replaced federal aid cuts out of their own funds. Replacement was somewhat more common in 1983 than in 1982. Organized political support by elderly groups, protests by day-care operators, and publicity given to problems of child abuse played an important part in building political support for this program.

ELEMENTARY AND SECONDARY EDUCATION BLOCK GRANT

The elementary and secondary education block grant merged twenty-nine categorical programs. A little more than one-fifth of the total budget authority for these programs for fiscal year 1981 was for project grants for local school districts undergoing desegregation, most of which were big-city school districts.

[14] The U.S. General Accounting Office observed a similar pattern. Ten of thirteen states in the GAO study transferred energy assistance funds in 1982 or 1983. See *States Fund an Expanded Range of Activities Under Low-Income Home Energy Assistance Block Grant*, GAO Report HRD-84-64 (Washington, D.C.: Government Accounting Office, June 27, 1984), p. 11.

Funding for these programs had been dropping before 1982 as the level of federal desegregation aid declined.

The percentage decline in 1982 for the elementary and secondary education block grant was less than for other block grants. Furthermore, since this aid typically made up only a small part of the total revenue of local school districts, its character is quite different from that of the other block grants discussed in this section. In New Jersey, for example, funding under the programs consolidated into the education block grant fell by about $2 million during the Reagan first term, yet state aid to local school districts increased by about $500 million. The tail in this case (federal block grant funds) could not be expected to wag the dog (total state and local spending on elementary and secondary education). As a result, it would be hard to say that state and local spending "replaced" federal cuts. In other states in the sample, state aid for education was steadily rising in the study period. These state funds also were not a direct substitute for the previous categorical federal aid.

The net effect of the federal aid policy changes in this area was that school districts that had received substantial amounts of federal desegregation funds or large grants for other types of special projects lost money—sometimes relatively large amounts—while other school districts received increases in federal aid under the new state formulas for distributing these federal block grant funds. Most school districts, however, were not greatly affected by this change.

The main issue for the states under the education block grant was how to allocate the funds previously distributed under categorical grants, some of which went to the state and some to local school districts or nonprofit agencies. States are required to pass on at least 80 percent of their allocation under this block grant to local school districts. Distribution to school districts is based on a formula that considers student enrollment. The 1981 budget act specified broad guidelines by which states could make adjustments in their distribution so that federal aid could be concentrated in those school districts that had the greatest number of students "whose education imposes a higher than average cost per child."[15] Adjustments could be made for such factors as the number of students from low-income families, the number of students from sparsely populated areas, and the number of gifted and talented students.

In most states in the study, as noted above, state distributions resulted in a spreading of funds among many more school districts than had received funds under the previous categorical grants. Associates in Florida, Mississippi, Missouri, New York, Oklahoma, and Washington reported that the development of state distribution formulas was controversial, as is often the case in education

[15] *Omnibus Budget Reconciliation Act of 1981*, P.L. 97-35, 95 stat. 471, August 13, 1981.

allocation issues. The new federal block grant program in this way opened up issues of state school aid allocation that involve much larger amounts of funding than was at stake in the allocation of these federal aid funds.

Summary on Responses to Block Grants

Several factors combined to prevent large cutbacks in services under the 1981 Reagan block grant: carryover funds; federal restorations of funding in 1983; shifts of federal and state funds from other programs; and some state and local replacement funding.

Replacement of cuts under the block grants was greatest in programs that historically have been areas of greatest state and local activity and where organized and politically active local constituencies cared about the aided activities, as in the case of disease-focused public health services, social services for the elderly, child abuse services, and day-care services. Other broader and, in effect, more amorphous federal aid programs—the community services program is the best example among the block grants—fared poorly under the new block grants.

Some of the biggest effects of the 1981 Reagan block grants, especially in large cities, occurred because of state government grant allocation decisions rather than because of the federal aid cuts. In some programs, such as community services and education, large cities suffered more than their share of funding cuts due to state formula action to spread federal aid funds more widely among jurisdictions.

Other Operating Grants

Under this heading we discuss two programs, the Job Training Partnership Act and compensatory education.

JOB TRAINING PARTNERSHIP ACT (JTPA)

Programs funded under the Comprehensive Employment and Training Act (CETA) were big losers under Reagan. The public service job program under CETA was eliminated in 1981, and funding for training was reduced. In 1983 CETA was replaced by the Job Training Partnership Act (JTPA), a new block grant for training that reflected important purposes of the Reagan administration. The JTPA program highlights the role of state governments (CETA funds went almost entirely to localities) and assigns important responsibilities under the act to councils of private industry leaders.[16]

Almost all the sample states experienced a decline in training funds with the transition from CETA to JTPA. However, in most jurisdictions the percentage drop in the number of people receiving training was smaller than the percentage reduction in funding. This was because JTPA funds are concentrated on training; the act limits the proportion of funds that can be used for stipends to participants and for administration. Another change that tended to prevent a decline in the total number of people served was the shift by many local agencies away from training and toward efforts to help people search for work, which require shorter periods of service. The biggest impact of the 1981 changes fell on low-income persons who could no longer receive income under the public service employment component of CETA.

Few associates reported any state replacement of CETA funds, and there was no local government replacement of the cuts. In those few instances where state officials did increase state funding for training—California and New Jersey— they were careful to distinguish their initiatives from the CETA program, which had become very unpopular among politicians and with the public as a whole.

The nature and pace of administrative change under JTPA varied widely from state to state. Associates in some states, such as Oklahoma, reported that as of mid-1984 the state had not yet put its own stamp on the program. But others reported that governors saw the program as a chance to combine training with state economic development initiatives. Similar efforts were mentioned in Massachusetts, Missouri, New York, Ohio, and Washington.

As a general rule the transition from CETA to JTPA depended heavily on the governor's interest in the program. Changes at the local levels were slower in coming. Under both CETA and JTPA, federal funds could be provided either to a single local government (such as a large city) or a consortium of local governments. These entities were called "prime sponsors" under CETA and "service delivery areas" under JTPA. Many associates reported that as of 1983 the local service delivery agencies looked very much like the old CETA prime sponsor agencies; the former CETA administrators simply moved over to the new agency to run JTPA.

[16] The findings reported here on the implementation of JTPA are similar to, although less detailed than, those of other field evaluation studies on the implementation of this program. See Robert F. Cook et al., *Implementation of the Job Training Partnership Act: Final Report* (Rockville, Md.: Westat, Inc., November 1985). See also Gary Walker et al., *An Independent Assessment of JTPA; Phase II: Initial Implementation* (New York: Grinker, Walker, and Associates, January 1985).

The most noticeable institutional change under JTPA at the local level was the decline in the role of nonprofit, community-based organizations. In large part, this was due to the elimination of the CETA public service employment program.

While associates did not report major administrative changes at the local level in the transition from CETA to JTPA, there were changes in program priorities. JTPA's emphasis on private-sector placement—a heavily weighted factor under the new program evaluation system for JTPA—resulted in a preference for short-term, on-the-job training as opposed to classroom training. Associates reported that this emphasis on placement, at least in the short run, resulted in "creaming"—that is, selecting persons who could more easily be placed in jobs after receiving brief periods of service as opposed to serving persons who need long periods of intensive service to become employable. Even local programs that engaged in creaming, however, typically provided some services to the hard-to-employ.

COMPENSATORY EDUCATION

The other operating grant program considered in this section is the compensatory education program, which Reagan tried unsuccessfully in 1981 to merge into the elementary and secondary education block grant. Instead the program was maintained in essentially its existing form, and its name was changed from title I to chapter 1, in this case chapter 1 of an act that included the elementary and secondary education block grant as chapter 2. Federal appropriations for the compensatory education program were cut by less than 3 percent between 1981 and 1982 and increased in subsequent years. Funding for chapter 1 took a big leap forward in 1984 and since then has exceeded the 1981 level in nominal terms as shown in table 4.1.

Federal aid to education is distinctive in that most programs are "forward funded," that is, aid is appropriated each year for the year following in order to allow school districts to plan before the start of a school year. We observed wide variation in the impact and timing of the 1981 cut in federal aid for compensatory education. Some associates reported cuts in 1982; some said there was basically level funding for this program; and others noted a steady increase in funds.[17] While the changes in compensatory education were not great in rela-

---

[17] The pattern of federal cuts was different among the sample states. A major reason for these differences was a supplemental appropriation that was passed late in fiscal 1982, providing additional federal funds to about ten states that had sued the federal government in an attempt to get the U.S. Department of Education to distribute compensatory education funds on the basis of the

Table 4.1. *Budget Authorizations for Compensatory Education Programs, Federal Fiscal Years 1981–85*

Year	Dollars in millions
1981	3,098
1982	3,028
1983	3,196
1984	3,475
1985	3,683

SOURCE: Table H-11, "Federal Grants to State and Local Governments—Outlays and Budget Authority," Executive Office of the President, U.S. Office of Management and Budget, *Special Analysis to the Budget of the United States Government*, various years (Washington, D.C.: Government Printing Office, 1982, 1983, 1984, 1985, 1986).

tion to total school spending, the varied picture in the sample states again demonstrate the pitfalls of easy generalization in federal aid studies.

Capital Programs

The major federal capital grants to states and localities are for transportation (highways and mass transit),[18] the environment (the largest being wastewater treatment facilities), and subsidized housing.[19] The programs discussed in this section were less affected by cuts in funding during the first Reagan term than other programs, with the important exception of federal aid for housing.

HIGHWAY AID

The 1981 reconciliation act reduced the amount of federal highway trust fund money that could be used to finance highway aid programs. An initial fiscal

1980 census. The states argued that they had a greater number of disadvantaged (low-income) students, according to the latest census. These states lost the suit, but the federal supplemental spending bill was enacted for them. New Jersey received about $15 million in supplemental aid, while New York's allocation increased by $36 million. Another factor was budget rescissions, which affected 1981 spending.

[18] The categories here are not as neat and clear as one would like. Federal aid for mass transit includes support for operating purposes, which is treated in this section because it is easier to present the analysis in this way. In fact, the status of operating aid for mass transit, as shown in this section, was a major issue in the Reagan first term.

[19] Housing subsidies are also not easily classified. Some, but not all, housing programs produce new construction. All federal aid housing programs involve a shelter subsidy for the poor, hence they are similar to the income-transfer programs discussed in this chapter under the heading

1982 obligation ceiling of $8.2 billion had been set by the budget act. This was lowered to $8.07 billion by subsequent spending bills. The federal spending ceiling for 1981 had been $8.75 billion.

Federal spending for highway aid programs increased significantly, beginning in 1983, as a result of the Surface Transportation Assistance Act (STAA) of 1982. The emergency jobs act passed in 1983 also increased the amount of funds the Federal Highway Administration could obligate. Fiscal 1983 and 1984 obligation ceilings totaled $12.375 billion and $12.520 billion.

The resulting allocations for most of the states in the sample exceeded their 1982 apportionments by 30 to 70 percent. Ohio's 1983 allocation, for example, was $120 million higher than in 1982, a 57 percent increase. South Dakota received over $24 million in additional funds (a 40 percent increase), while Mississippi's highway aid rose $57 million (a 70 percent increase).

Most of the increase in highway aid went to the interstate highway program; the STAA also raised authorizations for primary highways, i.e., state highways, often major "feeder" roads in the interstate highway system. Spending for the bridge repair and replacement program was also increased substantially. Funding remained level for two other programs that are part of the federal highway aid programs—federal aid for urban roads and streets and aid for secondary (rural) highways.[20]

The highway aid increases caused states to raise their own spending for highway construction and maintenance programs in order to meet federal matching requirements. The field associates reported, however, that the federal aid increases were only one of several factors leading states to raise appropriations for transportation facilities. Other reasons included backlogs in construction or rehabilitation projects and the perception that road, bridge, and public transit facilities were essential to promote economic development.

Several states raised taxes to increase highway spending. For example, in Oklahoma the legislature approved an increase in the state motor fuel tax, while voters in New York approved a $1.25 billion bond authorization. State leadership in New Jersey established a transportation trust fund in 1984 after considering several proposals for financing infrastructure projects. Backed by state appropriations, revenue from the state's gasoline tax, and contributions from the state's toll-road authorities, the trust fund is expected to generate more than $3 billion in federal and state funds for highway, bridge, and mass transit projects.

---

of entitlement grants. Housing subsidies, however, are not automatic as in the case of "entitlement" programs where all eligible recipients receive benefits.

[20] President Reagan had recommended in 1982 that these two programs be turned back to the states.

MASS TRANSIT GRANTS

The federal program to provide aid for local mass transit systems includes both capital construction grants and operating subsidies. Although budget proposals presented by the Reagan administration during the president's first term called for major change and spending reductions in mass transit grants, federal spending remained relatively stable.

The big story for mass transit was the Reagan administration's effort to eliminate federal mass transit operating assistance (as opposed to capital grants). Federal aid for mass transit in 1981 was $4.7 billion, of which approximately $1.1 billion was for operating aid to local mass transit agencies. Although the administration was unsuccessful in its efforts to eliminate mass transit operating grants, it did cut operating assistance.[21] Between federal fiscal years 1981 and 1982 the transit agencies serving jurisdictions in the sample sustained reductions in federal operating subsidies that ranged from 5 to 13 percent. Associates reported further cutbacks in fiscal year 1983.

In many instances spending for mass transit increased at the state or local level during the study period. This was a response to actual, as well as anticipated cuts. Some of the replacement action came through increased state and local appropriations under existing programs, some through increased fares. The federal cuts were not the only factor causing increased fiscal pressure on transit agencies. New wage agreements and escalating operating costs were also important. Federal aid is generally a small part of the total revenue of local transit agencies. In Jackson, Mississippi, for example, city subsidies for transit doubled from the late 1970s to 1984. Likewise, city officials in Orlando, Florida, agreed in 1981 to pay 40 percent of the operating costs for the county bus service. Voters in the Los Angeles and Seattle areas also agreed to raise local taxes to supplement the revenues of local transit authorities. In New Jersey, one of only two states in the nation with a statewide transit authority,[22] the state increased aid for transit operating subsidies, a move justified in part by citing decreasing federal funding. Another and notable example of increased state involvement in transit operations occurred in New York. Before the 1981 reconciliation act was signed into law, the state gave the New York City transit authority the power to issue bonds, appropriated state funds for other local mass transit capital programs, and dedicated new state tax revenue to transit operations. Before Reagan took office, the regional transit authority serving the

---

[21] In 1982, mass transit aid totaled $3.53 billion, of which a little more than one billion dollars was for operating assistance. Mass transit grants amounted to $4.5 billion and $4.2 billion in 1983 and 1984, respectively. Federal operating subsidies in these two years totaled $875 million and $870 million.

[22] The other is Rhode Island.

Rochester area received approximately one-quarter of its revenue from the federal government; state aid accounted for 13 percent. For the agency's fiscal year ending March 1984, federal operating subsidies amounted to 14 percent and state aid had doubled as a proportion of total revenues, accounting for over 30 percent.

WASTEWATER TREATMENT CONSTRUCTION GRANTS

By far the largest capital grant program in the environmental field is for the construction of wastewater treatment facilities. This grant did not fare as well under Reagan as the more established federal aid programs, especially those for highway and bridge construction. Federal allotments for wastewater treatment facilities for 1982 in the sample states typically were 5 to 15 percent less than 1981 allotments. This 1981 level, it should be noted, had in many cases already been cut due to federal budget rescissions made by Reagan in 1981. The associates for Mississippi and Oklahoma reported year-to-year reductions in excess of 25 percent. Federal grant appropriations for the wastewater treatment construction program remained at about $2.4 billion per year from fiscal years 1982 through 1984. This funding level was much lower than in the peak years of this program in the late 1970s, when Environmental Protection Agency (EPA) budget authorizations for the program exceeded $4 billion.

In 1981 an important change in the requirements under this program was made that can be thought of as "stretching out" the effect of this federal grant. A new federal provision reduced the maximum federal grant awards for new construction costs from 75 percent to 55 percent beginning in fiscal year 1985.

State and local governments adopted a variety of measures in response to the slowdown and stretch-out of federal aid in this area. Among the sample sites, one of the more dramatic responses to the federal changes occurred in Orlando, Florida, where city and county officials raised user fees sharply because they anticipated that expansion of their waste treatment system would receive little federal support. Efforts were made in other jurisdictions to rearrange funding priorities, find new revenue sources for local projects, and use unobligated fund balances to offset cuts and delays in federal funding. In no case was a major project already underway cancelled in the sample sites during the study period due to federal aid policy changes, although the changed situation in Washington did appear to influence future plans involving the phasing and character of wastewater treatment facilities. Several states and localities stepped up their own efforts in this field, in part because of expected reductions in federal aid.

HOUSING

Two major types of federally aided public housing programs were in operation during the study period. One was the low-income public housing program created by the U.S. Housing Act of 1937. It was the primary vehicle for federal aid for low-income housing until the expansion of private-sector housing programs under section 8 of the Housing and Community Development Act of 1974. Through most of its history, section 8 had two main components—assistance for existing housing, whereby assistance is tied to the individual or household, and federal aid for new or substantially rehabilitated housing, where assistance is channelled through the builder or owner of the subsidized unit. Congressional debates in the latter part of the 1970s and the early 1980s focused on the mix of new and existing section 8 housing. The Reagan administration was largely successful in its efforts to shift federal assistance away from new construction in favor of aid for low-income residents in existing units. This shift, actually underway prior to Reagan, was accelerated during his administration. Reagan sought to stop all additions to the section 8 new and substantial rehabilitation programs. The end result of these efforts on the part of the Reagan administration was a sharp reduction in new and substantially rehabilitated section 8 units in 1983. New section 8 units dropped from 93,000 units in 1980 to 6,000 units in 1983. The public housing program also experienced a decline in new construction funds, although Congress would not go along with the much deeper cut sought by the administration. However, funds for modernization and for assisting troubled projects actually increased in the study period.

For the section 8 programs for the existing housing, the Reagan administration brought fewer changes. The number of new units under the section 8 existing housing program was modestly increased, and a new housing voucher program was enacted to test this approach as an alternative to the section 8 new construction program.

There is another important way in which Reagan changed the housing programs that affected the residents of publicly subsidized housing. As mentioned earlier, the 1981 budget act contained a provision that increased the rental contribution of the residents of federally subsidized housing units from 25 to 30 percent of their income. The new requirement applies to the residents of both new and existing subsidized housing. The important point demonstrated by this change is the concentration of the impact of Reagan's policies on the working poor; it was these residents of subsidized housing that tended to be hardest hit by the new rent requirement.

With the exception of the increase in the rent contribution of residents, there tends to be a long lag between changes in federal housing policies and observable effect at the local level. The changes made in the early period of the Reagan administration in subsidized housing were expected to have their greatest effects locally in 1984 and subsequent years. For this reason, few state or local governments were found to have responded to the changes in federally assisted housing policies. This is probably due in part to the fact that housing is an area in which the tradition has been one of a much stronger federal role relative to that of state and local governments. We did find some increased activity in this functional area in three of the sample states. Massachusetts, New York, and South Dakota expanded their housing programs: associates reported that this was partly in response to the reduction in federal subsidies for new construction, and in part it was justified as an effort to stimulate economic activity in the housing industry. Massachusetts increased its spending for its elderly housing and rental assistance programs, and in 1983 established a new subsidy program to provide incentives for developers of mixed-income housing. New York's effort to stimulate activity by home builders took the form of an acceleration in bond sales that enabled the state mortgage finance agency to provide $350 million to subsidize long-term borrowing costs for first-time home buyers. South Dakota initiated a rental subsidy program under which 20 percent of the units built in subsidized developments were to be rented to low-income families.

Most associates reported that housing authorities expected large and immediate cutbacks under the Reagan administration. As it turned out, however, the operations of most housing authorities in the sample were affected less and much more slowly than was initially expected.

Summary on Capital Programs

For the capital programs considered in this section, both the cuts and the responses varied appreciably. In the case of the federal highway aid programs, the initial federal cuts were minimal, and then in 1982 and 1983 the federal government added substantially to the spending stream for these programs. We found little tendency on the part of the sample jurisdictions to cut back highway spending due to the limited changes made in the highway program in 1981, which did involve holding back some highway spending authority. Highway spending is a long and well-established function of state and local government. The main influence on spending in this functional area in the period of the study appeared to be economic conditions. In particular, the recession and the level of interest rates were cited as major factors influencing the timing of state and local highway spending.

In the field of mass transit, federal aid policy changes in the Reagan period were more important than for the highway programs. Here, the most interesting finding is the degree to which the recipient jurisdictions (particularly local governments) took steps to replace threatened, as well as actual, federal aid cuts. In fact, some states and localities responded to the Reagan rhetoric and moved to increase their own efforts before Reagan's proposals were even voted on in the Congress. The end result in this case of the combination of greater state and local effort to provide funds for mass transit, plus the unwillingness of the Congress to go along with the Reagan effort to eliminate federal operating aid for this purpose, in some instances produced a higher level of spending than would have been the case in the absence of the Reagan program.

The reduction and stretch-out under Reagan of grants-in-aid for wastewater treatment plants had little effect on projects that were already underway or that had already received a commitment of federal funding. Still, state and local governments faced with a backlog of wastewater treatment needs began seeking alternative funds in anticipation of federal cutbacks.

The fourth capital grant program considered in this section, housing subsidies, has both a capital (shelter) and income-maintenance purpose (i.e., aid to the poor). At the state and local levels, this function is the least well established of those considered in this section. As it turned out, housing suffered the biggest hit among the capital programs in the Reagan period, and we noted less effort here than in the other capital grant areas to compensate for these cuts or in other ways to protect housing agencies and programs.

Conclusions

At the beginning of the Reagan period, federal aid cuts were at center stage, and, while Reagan did not get all he asked for, he made a major dent in grant programs and signalled a federal pullback in many functional and program areas in which federal grants are provided. Yet, in the federal aid field, things are not always what they appear to be from the Washington perspective. The cuts made in 1981 took time to materialize at the state and local levels. Furthermore, state and local governments had many ways to stave off the impact of the cuts that did occur. Often, they were able to delay the day of reckoning, and in some cases they were able to prevent it altogether. This is because two things happened. Congress restored some federal aid cuts. And, second, the strong recovery in 1983 and 1984 from the 1981–82 recession put state and local governments in a much better position to step up their own efforts in areas where the federal government under Reagan was pulling back or threatening to do so. Three factors appear to us to have been the most important in influencing the way state and local governments responded to federal aid cuts: (1) the incidence of the benefits or services provided; (2) the strength of a grant's constituency and the level of its general public support and visibility; and (3) the "identification" in the minds of state and/or local officials of the grant program as "federal" or state and local. State and local officials were more likely to label a program federal—and hence outside their political responsibility—if (1) federal rules gave grant recipients little flexibility in how they used the funds and (2) the program was outside an area of traditional state or local responsibility. The discussion of the way these factors influenced the responses of state and local governments under different programs is organized below by type of grant.

Among entitlement grants, the program that stands out in terms of the degree of effort made to protect, and even expand, service levels is Medicaid. It is particularly interesting to contrast the Medicaid and AFDC programs in this connection. Both are open-ended matching grants for income-transfer purposes; they are often administered by the same state and local agencies. Yet, states did much less to prevent the impact of the 1981 AFDC changes than they did in the case of Medicaid.

On all three of the factors listed above, there are important differences between Medicaid and AFDC. Medicaid is an in-kind, rather than a cash, transfer, and the providers of services (hospitals and medical practitioners) tend to be politically powerful. Medicaid also has a stronger constituency than AFDC in terms of the program's beneficiaries. A high proportion of Medicaid spending (approximately two-thirds) is for elderly and disabled persons. Older citizens as a group tend to be politically active. In addition, their families, often also better off and politically active, can also be seen as beneficiaries in this case.

These constituency factors tie in closely with the point in this analysis relating to the incidence of grants. For entitlement grants, and in fact as a general proposition, we found that the stronger the redistributive purpose of a given grant program (i.e., redistributive to the poor), the less likely was it to be protected by state and local governments from the effects of cuts made in federal aid. The AFDC program is more highly redistributive in terms of the ultimate beneficiaries of the program than Medicaid. This is especially so if one takes into account the fact that the elderly persons aided under Medicaid often were not poor until they required long-term nursing home services.

The third factor in this analysis, the "identification" of a grant as federal or state-local, also works in favor of Medicaid. Health care has traditionally been a state and local government function. In contrast, since the 1930s, the federal government has assumed primary responsibility for income maintenance. Furthermore, states have more control over the use of Medicaid than AFDC funds.

We saw that some states did raise their standard of need or benefits under AFDC to cover people dropped from the AFDC program as a result of the 1981 changes. But these efforts were much less pronounced and extensive than the efforts made to protect and even expand Medicaid services.

The other programs in the entitlement category are feeding programs (food stamps and school lunches). Like AFDC, they are more highly redistributive than Medicaid, and, although they do have provider constituencies, they appear to have less at stake and to be generally less powerful than the provider constituency of the Medicaid program. Similarly, the structure of these programs—especially food stamps—makes it difficult for state or local governments to directly replace the cuts in eligibility and benefit levels made in 1981. Food stamps is completely a federal program, with federally set benefits and eligibility rules and federal financing of assistance. As it turned out, there was some replacement of cuts in the feeding programs, but it was limited and it was achieved indirectly at the local level where governments and nonprofit organizations increased the size and scope of their food distribution and meal programs in a manner that can be viewed as offsetting the cuts made in the food stamp and child nutrition programs.

Turning next to operating programs, those with the strongest provider and beneficiary constituencies and with the broadest incidence pattern in terms of the groups affected tended to fare best at the state and local level. Services for the elderly, and public health programs for children, for example, received replacement funding. On the other hand, the notable lack of efforts to protect the services provided by community action agencies under the community services block grant is a case in which the providers of service tend to have very limited or no political clout and the benefits provided are highly redistributive. A similar point was made for preventive health services, in this case reflecting both the specialized character of the provider constituency (a limited group within the health professions) and the lack of visibility and emotional appeal of the services provided. For the most part, the operating programs support activities that—although not identical with state and local services—are very similar. Many of the programs supported by federal operating grants are already viewed as basic state or local services. There are some major exceptions to this: job training, education aid for desegregation purposes, and perhaps energy assistance.

The third category of grants, capital grants, provides a similar contrast to that between Medicaid and AFDC as a way of showing the influence of the factors we have identified. In this case, the interesting comparison is between the highway and housing programs. Highway grants have a strong and politically active constituency (contractors and highway users) and affect nearly everyone. Although assisted housing programs also have a strong provider constituency (builders and housing authorities), they are highly targeted on the poor. Furthermore, as in the case of AFDC, the structure of the federal aid housing programs is heavily influenced by the federal government. This factor (high-level federal control) is especially important; the recipient jurisdictions, in effect, cannot adopt policies to continue the federally aided services without having to pay for the entire service out of their own funds.

In the case of mass transit and wastewater treatment, both are important program responsibilities at the local level, although they are not as long-standing functions as highway and bridge construction and repairs. The benefits under these programs are provided on a broader basis than in the case of housing, although mass transit services often are redistributive. We found that activities in both of these program areas, mass transit and wastewater treatment, often were protected against federal aid cuts. Moreover, in both cases, as in the case of the highway program, we observed a tendency for states and localities to step up their efforts in anticipation of federal aid cuts.

In sum, it was the most redistributive programs that tended to be cut most heavily by the federal government in 1981. We found a parallel tendency, with Medicaid being the notable exception, for state and local governments to do less to protect these programs than in the case of other programs affected by federal aid cuts that have a broader incidence pattern. This is not surprising in a conservative period characterized by a backlash against previous large increases in spending for social programs targeted on the poor.

The degree and character of the actions taken to offset federal aid cuts were found to vary, not only by programs, but also by jurisdiction. This is the subject to which we turn next, focusing on the effect of Reagan's policies on the fourteen state governments in the sample for this study.

Variations in States' Responses

✳

*T*he previous chapter examined the responses to the Reagan cuts and changes in federal grants-in-aid on a program-by-program basis. This chapter shifts the focus to *the states as the unit of analysis*. We begin in this chapter by considering the differences in the character and degree of the responses of all fourteen states in the study sample.

Four aspects of the Reagan domestic program have influenced the role of state government: (1) the *"signal"* of a reduced federal role in social policy; (2) the *cuts* in grants-in-aid; (3) the enactment of *devolutionary* policies in the case of the block grants, Medicaid, and the Job Training Partnership Act; and (4) the administration's "hands off" approach to the *management* of non-welfare grant-in-aid programs.

As discussed in the introductory chapter, we classified the fourteen states in the sample for this study according to the character and degree of their response to the Reagan changes. These classifications were made on the basis of two factors: (1) the actions taken by the sample state governments to allocate new resources to replace federal aid cuts; and (2) the actions taken by these state governments to play a stronger policy-making and administrative role in response to the changes made in federal grant-in-aid programs under Reagan. These two responses can be thought of as *fiscal* and *institutional replacement*. The term "fiscal replacement" refers to cases in which state governments allocated new tax revenues, or additional funds received as a result of the growth in receipts from state or local sources, to replace federal aid cuts enacted under Reagan. The main distinction involved here is between cases in which states acted to replace federal aid funding cuts out of new revenues as opposed to the many ways described in the previous chapter in which states used various coping strategies to reallocate funds within a general program area, used carryover federal aid, or used new federal grant funds enacted during the 1981–82 recession as a way of delaying or staving off the effects of federal aid cuts.[1]

Five states are identified as having made the most pronounced response to the Reagan cuts and changes in federal grants-in-aid: Florida, Massachusetts, New Jersey, New York, and Oklahoma. Three of these states are the subjects of case studies included in this volume—Florida, Massachusetts, and New York.

In the "intermediate-response" group of eight states, three states—Mississippi, Ohio, and Texas—were found to have allocated some new or additional state funds to the areas affected by the Reagan federal aid cuts. Among the other states in this group, one state, Washington, initially acted to replace federal aid cuts, but later rescinded these actions. Four states in this "intermediate response" group were found not to have replaced federal aid cuts out of their own funds, although they did take steps to exercise a stronger policy-making and administrative role in the functional areas affected by the Reagan administration's budget cuts and devolutionary policies. These four states are: Arizona, Illinois, Missouri, and South Dakota. From this "intermediate-response" group, Mississippi, Ohio, Washington, Arizona, and Illinois are the subject of case-study chapters. The ninth case-study chapter is on California, which is classified as having made a minimal response to the Reagan federal aid change.

State Classifications

At the state and local levels, the field researchers drew on budget and program data and interview data from a cross section of respondents to conduct their analysis of the responses to the Reagan policies. The resulting case studies were reviewed by readers familiar with the subject matter and with the particular jurisdictions studied. The discussion in this section deals with the reasons for classifying the states in our overview analysis.

FLORIDA. Florida was in transition in the study period from a long and quite strong conservative political tradition to a more moderate position on the role of government in social programs. The authors of the Florida case study note that the Reagan program accentuated this political debate, with conservatives

---

[1] In his research George Peterson groups all these responses together under the term "replacement." Hence, he finds more "replacement" than we do in our study. See George Peterson, "Federalism and the States," in John Palmer and Isabel Sawhill, eds., *The Reagan Record* (Cambridge, Mass.: Ballinger, 1984).

favoring the Reagan policies and resisting a stronger state role in the areas in which the federal government was pulling back, and more moderate forces, including Governor Bob Graham, favoring some state action to replace cuts in federal aid. The state allocated money from its working capital funds for federal aid replacement, raised the sales tax by one cent in 1982 (in part to replenish this fund), and in 1984, increased AFDC benefits by 5 percent. The main program areas affected by federal aid replacement were social and public health services. The city of Orlando, also included in the sample, took major steps to replace lost federal aid in the capital grant areas, particularly for wastewater treatment and mass transit.

MASSACHUSETTS. The Reagan program was a political issue in Massachusetts, as in Florida. Governor Edward King, a conservative Democrat who served from January 1979 to January 1983, was supportive of the Reagan retrenchment efforts, but was opposed by the liberal state legislature, which sought to (and did) vote to replace substantial amounts of the 1981 federal aid cuts. In some areas—social services in 1981 and health services in the following year— the state actually increased its spending by more than was cut from federal grants, which we define as not only a fiscal replacement, but an *augmentation*, response to the Reagan cuts. In November 1982, Michael Dukakis, a liberal Democrat who had previously served as governor, unseated King. He took further action to increase the state role in areas of federal retrenchment. Fiscal replacement of the Reagan cuts occurred in Massachusetts in both operating and capital programs. The authors of this chapter attribute the state's decision to allocate additional funds to human service programs affected by the Reagan cutbacks to "a continued supportive climate of opinion in the Massachusetts electorate for programs that have apparently lost some of their national support."

NEW JERSEY. The third state in the "most pronounced" response group, New Jersey, is interesting since there was relatively little controversy about the response to the Reagan changes. Although the governor, Thomas H. Kean, is a Republican and the legislature is Democratic, the two branches were agreed on the desirability of stepping up state efforts in major domestic program areas. This, in fact, is a strong trend in New Jersey. Long a state with a limited state role in relation to that of localities, the New Jersey state government in recent years has taken stronger actions than any other state to centralize responsibility at the state level.[2] This trend has continued in the Reagan period. In some areas

[2] Empirical evidence of a rapidly growing state government vis-à-vis local governments in New

changes have been made without reference to the Reagan program. In other areas (social services, mental health, job training), recent actions to increase the state's policy-making and financial role have, at least in part, been in response to the retrenchment policies of the Reagan administration.[3]

NEW YORK. The authors of the New York case study emphasize the state's long and strong liberal tradition on domestic and social policy issues. Although the state in recent years has taken steps to cut back on its high-level state and local taxes to pay for these services, the basic ideology of the state has not changed. Both of the governors in the study period, particularly Mario Cuomo, have been strongly critical of the Reagan changes. At first the state resisted taking over the new block grants as a symbol of its resistance to the Reagan program. In several areas where the state could not delay the effects of federal aid cuts, replacement funds were provided. The state raised its AFDC standard of need to offset the effect of the Reagan changes in the program. It also transferred some welfare cases cut from the AFDC rolls to its "home relief" program, increased its own spending for social services, and took a strong leadership role in the job training field. The authors conclude that the Reagan domestic program in New York has been accompanied by greater centralization of policy making and financing at the state level and that the "efforts of the federal government to decentralize gave the state major new responsibilities in areas where its prior role had been secondary or non-existent."

OKLAHOMA. The fifth state in the "most pronounced" response group, Oklahoma, stands out in its region for its commitment to social programs. In the initial period of this study, which focused on federal fiscal year 1982, Oklahoma ranked first among the sample states in terms of the size and scope of the actions taken to replace federal aid cuts. The legislature played a strong role in forging a response to national domestic policy, relying on surplus state revenues to replace federal spending reductions in higher education tuition aid, mental

---

Jersey is provided by G. Ross Stephens. Stephens used his composite index of state centralization to examine public employment, financial responsibility, and delivery of public services in the fourteen states in the Princeton field evaluation study. According to the Stephens' measure, New Jersey showed the greatest level of state government centralization between 1957 and 1982. See G. Ross Stephens, "State Centralization Over the Last Quarter Century," unpublished paper prepared for the Princeton Urban and Regional Research Center's conference on the effects of the Reagan domestic program, June 1984.

[3] Richard W. Roper, John R. Lago, Nancy G. Beer, and Martin A. Bierbaum, *Federal Aid Cuts in New Jersey, 1981 to 1984,* Council on New Jersey Affairs working paper no. 9 (Princeton, N.J.: Princeton Urban and Regional Research Center, March 1986).

health, vocational education, and child nutrition programs.[4] By 1983, however, the state budget came under fiscal pressures from the 1981–82 recession and the decline in oil prices and production. The period of tax cutting and spending increases that had marked the late 1970s and early 1980s, quickly turned to a period of state spending cutbacks and tax increases, that curtailed, at least temporarily, state-replacement responses to the federal aid reductions.

Eight states in the sample for this study are classified as having made an "intermediate" response to the Reagan changes. Three of the states in this group were found to have made some measure of fiscal replacement in the areas in which federal aid was cut or threatened under Reagan.

MISSISSIPPI. Like Florida, Mississippi was seen in the period of the study as shifting from a conservative to a somewhat more moderate stance on social programs. It raised its AFDC standard of need to avoid some of the effects of the cuts in this program and to prevent people from losing their eligibility under Medicaid as a result of the Reagan changes in the AFDC program. Ironically, this action (i.e., raising the state standard of need by 30 percent) was made possible as a result of the estimate by the state's welfare department that in 1982 there would be "savings" in the AFDC and Medicaid accounts due to the federal policy changes. Small amounts of additional state funds were also provided for health services and education. The power of the governor's office in Mississippi was said to have been increased as a result of the strong role played by Governor William R. Winter in planning for the adjustments required by the Reagan changes. Governor Winter's successor, elected in November 1983, William Allain, is more conservative than his predecessor, who had spearheaded new state education programs. Governor Allain resisted an increase in state taxes, though the legislature had passed an increase. The authors in this case study conclude that the 1981 changes "did not result in fundamental changes in state-local relationships, but did somewhat enhance the role of state government. The formation of block grants from numerous categorical grants meant that certain program funds would flow to local governments from the state government rather than the federal government. The state government, often with a lack of direction from Washington, assumed a management role in several areas previously controlled by the federal government. The responsibilities in community development and community services demanded new expertise and program development."

[4] R. Lynn Rittenoure, Steve Steib, and Larkin Warner, "Oklahoma's Legislative Process in a Period of Fiscal Change," *Public Budgeting and Finance* 4, no. 2 (Summer 1984):42–57.

OHIO. State fiscal conditions in Ohio were already under severe pressure when the Reagan cuts hit in 1981. Although the incumbent governor at the time, James Rhodes, had little interest in compensating for these federal policy changes, his successor, Richard Celeste, moved in a number of areas to take advantage of the new opportunities provided to state governments. Celeste pushed through a major increase in state taxes, and although the fiscal pressures faced by the state continued to be formidable, there was a small amount of replacement funding for social services and in the health services areas for prenatal and infant programs. The most important response in this case to the Reagan changes was institutional. The state government moved under Governor Celeste to take advantage of the new authority to control Medicaid costs. Celeste also took steps to shape the new job training partnership program in a way that would advance the state's economic development aims. In other grant-in-aid programs where state discretion was increased, particularly under the new block grants, the policy-making and management role of the state was enhanced as a result of the Reagan changes. The authors of this case study note that while local control continues to be highly valued, the state role in federal grant programs "greatly increased." The authors note that "it is somewhat ironic that many aspects of the Reagan program have indirectly served the interests of the new governor, who is a liberal democrat."

TEXAS. Like Florida and Mississippi, Texas is described by the case-study authors as moving from a conservative to a politically more moderate stance on social programs in the study period. In November 1982, Democratic challenger Mark White defeated the conservative incumbent governor, William P. Clements, in a high-turnout election. The legislature, too, was shifting to a more moderate political philosophy. The areas in which fiscal replacement occurred in Texas involved welfare and social services. The state government used various coping strategies to delay and prevent the effects of other federal aid cuts, including a shift of persons receiving home-care services from the social services program to the open-ended Medicaid program, even though the latter requires an increase in state matching funds. The most notable policy change in a federally aided program area in Texas involved the steps taken to raise AFDC payment levels. In Texas, a limit on state spending for AFDC is included in the constitution. To the surprise of many observers, a constitutional amendment was adopted by a 2-to-1 margin in the fall of 1982 to raise this ceiling. The state also stepped up its efforts in the block grant areas and in the control of Medicaid spending, taking advantage of the new authority provided for this purpose in the 1981 budget act. The authors report that the new federal block grants caused "a shift in the location of the grantsmanship game." These changes are said to have been "well received" by both state and local officials despite the reduced funding levels.

WASHINGTON. The state planned to replace expected losses resulting from the 1981 federal budget act but rescinded these actions when the bottom fell out of the state's economy due to the precipitous decline in the wood products and aerospace industries.[5] At first, the state's response was both fiscal and institutional. Washington State's finances are particularly volatile due to its heavy dependence on the timber and aerospace industries. To a considerable degree, the efforts made by the state government to increase its managerial role in federally aided program areas was motivated by the need to control costs because of the state's sharp fiscal reversal in 1981. The state department of human services took a lead role in planning the response to the Reagan cuts in this environment of rising fiscal pressures at the state level. Another major effect of the Reagan changes in Washington was a decided tendency to spread out aid funds in taking advantage of the newly provided state discretion under block grants. The city of Seattle, included in the case study, was seen as having received a disproportionate share of the earlier funding, and as a result suffered losses in several areas in which state governments were given added authority to distribute federal grant funds.

Four states in the sample included in the "intermediate-response" group— Arizona, Illinois, Missouri, and South Dakota—did not replace federal aid cuts out of their own funds. They are classified in the intermediate-response category because of their efforts to take advantage of the added discretion allowed to state governments under Reagan. The authors of both the Illinois and Missouri case studies stress the fiscal problems faced by the states and the 1981–82 recession as the reasons for not replacing federal aid cuts. On the other hand, the authors of the Arizona and South Dakota case studies say that the conservative ideology of the states was the reason that fiscal replacement did not occur, but that in both cases there was strong support for the devolutionary aims of the Reagan policies.

ILLINOIS. The case-study author describes Illinois Governor James Thompson as "an enthusiastic supporter" of Reagan's new federalism who took advantage of the block grants, new job training partnership program, and Medicaid policy

[5] There appeared at a later time to have been a small amount of replacement of cuts in social services funding in Washington, although the authors are uncertain as to whether this is the proper classification for these expenditures.

changes to increase state policy and managerial control in these program areas on a basis that would aid the state's cost-containment efforts. The author concludes by saying, "the state's traditional role as political broker between Chicago, suburbs, and downstate was unchanged. But, the possibilities for a stronger state role in the future have been enhanced."

MISSOURI. Fiscal pressures in Missouri compounded the effect of the federal aid cuts. The state moved aggressively to control Medicaid costs and set some new priorities in health programs. Like Illinois, the state used federal jobs training aid to support economic development goals. Local sponsors under this program are required to reserve 10 percent of their job training allotment for customized training programs, which are used by the state to package incentives for business expansion and retention.

ARIZONA. In Arizona and South Dakota, the pattern is similar in terms of the way the states responded to the Reagan changes. The Arizona authors note that at the state level, Governor Bruce Babbitt took the lead role in setting federal aid policy. Although a Democrat, Babbitt was quoted approvingly by Reagan in his 1982 State of the Union message, which was devoted almost exclusively to federalism reforms. Babbitt was at the time a member of the U.S. Advisory Commission on Intergovernmental Relations; he played a strong role in developing the state's response to the Reagan block grants and the new job training partnership program. The authors of the Arizona chapter conclude by discussing forces for continuity and change in the federal aid relationship. They see the state role in their case as becoming more prominent in a system in which what they call the federal state "assistance relationship" frequently changes.

SOUTH DAKOTA. The South Dakota story reflects this same theme. The changes are not striking, but the attitude toward the state government is seen as having shifted. The state has taken a strong policy and administrative role in some of the areas of Reagan's block grants. The state, for example, used the alcohol, mental health, drug abuse prevention block grant as the basis for a major overhaul of its mental health programs. Likewise, the state government under Governor William Janklow took a major hand in changing the priorities under the small-cities community development block grant and the community services block grant. The aggressive action of the state in shifting the funding of the state's community action agencies resulted in lengthy court actions, in which the state ultimately prevailed. Looking broadly at the role of the state government, the author of the South Dakota case study concludes, "State priorities have been given an added boost. The state's administrative organization and managerial capacity have improved."[6]

CALIFORNIA. Tax cutting referenda passed in California in the late 1970s forced major spending cuts and fiscal and administrative reforms before the federal aid changes. The result was an important increase in the role of state government, but not because of the Reagan program. State reforms of Medicaid, education finance, and welfare are described in chapter 14 as being unrelated to federal aid changes.

Reasons for the Variation in State Responses

The next question to be considered in this chapter involves the reasons for the variations in state response to the Reagan changes. We found two main types of reasons to be most important in understanding the variations in state response: *political* reasons, here referring both to the political culture of the state and the role of its current political leaders, and *economic* reasons, referring to the economic climate in the state and the related fiscal condition of the state government.

POLITICAL REASONS

One of the clearest lessons of the past decade of field evaluation studies we have conducted of the effects of changes in federal grant-in-aid policies is the importance of political ideology in influencing state and local government responses to major changes in federal policies. We have found this factor to be especially important where a state's political mood is shifting. From conservative Arizona to liberal New York, the role of political ideology comes through strongly in the case studies. For example, the Arizona associates reported:

A conservative political and fiscal tradition is rooted in Arizona culture and has been a dominant theme of state politics, regardless of party and position. Populism, Arizona style, provides a somewhat negative image of government and expenditures for public services.

[6] William O. Farber, *The Impact of Reagan Federalism on South Dakota and South Dakota Government* (Vermillion, S.D.: Government Research Bureau, The University of South Dakota, December 1984).

The situation in New York is very different; among the state's political traditions is a:

> bipartisan commitment to high government expenditures, high taxes, and state mandated public services. This commitment flows from a liberal political culture, one that values the role of the public sector in aiding those in need.

Among the sample states, Florida provides a good example of the importance of shifts in political ideology in influencing responses to new federal aid policies. The Florida field researchers report that the political balance of power was changing from conservative to moderate in the late 1970s, and that this shift was one of the major reasons for the strong fiscal-replacement response on the part of the state government to the 1981 Reagan cuts in grants-in-aid. California also was in transition in the period of the study, although in this case from a liberal to a more conservative political mood. Although the legislature has remained under the control of liberal Democrats, California has not elected a traditional liberal as governor since 1962, and a number of tax and spending limits have been passed by the voters since the mid-1970s. The authors of the California case study emphasize these factors as the reason for the limited response by the state government to the Reagan cuts and changes in federal grants-in-aid.

In an earlier report on this study, we used census data on state government welfare spending per capita as a proxy for political ideology as shown in table 5.1. Of the five states in the "most pronounced" response group, two (New York and Massachusetts) are classified as liberal on this basis, two (New Jersey and Oklahoma) as moderate, and one (Florida) as conservative, although in the latter case we note above that political conditions were shifting in the period of the study.

It is interesting that the three other states in the sample that made a fiscal-replacement response to the Reagan cuts are classified as conservative (Mississippi and Texas) or moderate (Ohio). However, in all three cases, political conditions are described by the field researchers as shifting toward a more moderate stance in the study period and the amount of federal aid replacement was relatively small.

In a number of program areas, the case-study authors report that state responses to the federal aid changes under Reagan were significantly influenced by political leaders. Governors are most often cited as key actors in shaping the response to the Reagan changes. In particular, governors Babbitt of Arizona, Graham of Florida, and Dukakis of Massachusetts, Winters of Mississippi, Ce-

Table 5.1. *Political Data on Case-Study States*

State	State political ideology	Governor and party affiliation, 1984	Party split in state legislature Upper house D/R	Lower house D/R
Most pronounced state response				
Florida	Conservative	Bob Graham (D)	32/ 8	84/36
Massachusetts	Liberal	Michael S. Dukakis (D)	33/ 7	129/29
New Jersey	Moderate	Thomas H. Kean (R)	23/17	44/36
New York	Liberal	Mario M. Cuomo (D)	26/35	97/52
Oklahoma	Moderate	George Nigh (D)	34/14	76/25
Moderate state response				
Mississippi	Conservative	William A. Allain (D)	49/ 3	116/5
Ohio	Moderate	Richard F. Celeste (D)	17/16	62/37
Texas	Conservative	Mark White (D)	26/ 5	114/36
Washington	Moderate	John Spellman (R)	26/23	54/44
Arizona	Conservative	Bruce Babbitt (D)	12/18	21/39
Illinois	Moderate	James R. Thompson (R)	33/26	70/48
Missouri	Conservative	Christopher S. Bond (R)	22/12	110/53
South Dakota	Conservative	William J. Janklow (R)	9/26	16/54
Low state response				
California	Liberal	George Deukmejian (R)	25/14	48/32

SOURCES: Political ideology categories are based on per capita state and local government spending for public welfare programs 1980–81 as defined by the Bureau of the Census. States spending more than $300 per capita are defined as liberal. States where 1980–81 welfare spending is between $200 and $300 per capita are classified as moderate. Those where welfare spending is $200 or less per capita are classified as conservative. Data from U.S. Bureau of the Census, *Governmental Finances in 1980–81* (Washington, D.C.: U.S. Government Printing Office, 1982); *The Book of the States*, 1984–85, Table 1, "The Governors," pp. 49–50, Table 2, "The Legislators, Numbers, Terms, and Party Affiliations," p. 85. Party affiliations for Mississippi and New Jersey as of January 1984; all other states, party affiliations as of August 1983.

leste of Ohio, and Janklow of South Dakota are described as having played an important leadership role in shaping the state response to the Reagan changes. The Massachusetts case is particularly interesting. Massachusetts has a tradition of high-level spending for public services; however, it had a conservative Democratic governor, Edward King, in 1981 at the time the Reagan cuts were enacted. In 1982, the legislature pushed through spending increases to replace some federal aid cuts despite the governor's opposition. Coincident with Reagan's loss of momentum in 1982, King suffered an even worse setback, losing the primary election to his predecessor, Michael Dukakis. With the more liberal Dukakis back in the office, the controversy of how to respond to the Reagan cuts in social programs shifted from *whether* to replace federal aid to *how much* to replace.

ECONOMIC REASONS

All of the state governments in the sample were assigned a classification of their fiscal condition rating, which took into account current economic and budgetary trends. States were classified as facing extreme, moderate, or little fiscal pressure, and in each case the prevailing direction of change was noted.[7] Table 5.2 shows the sample states according to this analysis. A plus sign indicates that the fiscal condition of the state was improving during the period of the study; a minus sign indicates that it was worsening.

Of the eight states which are identified above as having made a fiscal-replacement response to the Reagan program, one (Ohio) is classified as facing extreme fiscal pressure, although in this case the state's fiscal-replacement response was small. Three states in this group (New Jersey, Oklahoma, and Texas), are classified as facing little fiscal pressure, and three states—Florida, Massachusetts, and New York—are classified as experiencing moderate fiscal pressure and improving fiscal conditions during the study period. Mississippi is classified as facing moderate but worsening fiscal conditions during the study period. Generally speaking, the northeastern states were not as hard hit by the 1981–82 recession as were states in other regions. This is reflected in the ratings for Massachusetts, New Jersey, and New York.

Among the states in the intermediate-response group that were found not to have replaced federal aid cuts in the Reagan period, Missouri stands out. It is

[7] The ratings for fiscal pressures are defined as follows:

EXTREME FISCAL PRESSURE. Own-source revenue and anticipated external sources of revenue are insufficient to meet the demands for essential services. Essential services are not defined as all existing services; this is a limited concept. Furthermore, there is no apparent and generally used revenue source available to increase own-raised revenue in the relative near term, on a one-year basis.

MODERATE FISCAL PRESSURE. Anticipated own-source revenue and external sources are insufficient to support the existing level of services. Therefore, the maintenance of the current level of services requires positive action (i.e., use of a new tax source, a significant increase in nominal tax rates) or the reduction of service levels.

LITTLE FISCAL PRESSURE. Anticipated internal and external revenues (using existing sources with possible small nominal rate increases) are expected to cover anticipated expenditure increases and even meet some new, but limited, service demands.

Table 5.2. Fiscal Data on Case-Study States

State	Degree of Fiscal Distress	Total General Revenue, 1980–81 (dollars in thousands)	Origin of Revenue, 1980–81			Total General Revenue, 1982–83 (dollars in thousands)	Origin of Revenue, 1982–83		
			Percentage Federal	Percentage State	Percentage Local		Percentage Federal	Percentage State	Percentage Local
Most pronounced state response									
Florida	Moderate +	14,857,900	19.9	41.0	39.1	17,890,200	15.5	39.7	44.8
Massachusetts	Moderate +	11,952,200	22.2	43.1	34.6	13,180,400	21.9	47.8	30.3
New Jersey	Little	13,790,900	16.8	45.3	37.9	16,675,300	15.1	48.5	36.4
New York	Moderate +	43,944,000	19.3	36.5	44.2	51,593,100	18.0	37.4	44.6
Oklahoma	Little –	5,339,200	19.5	54.2	26.3	6,111,300	17.6	54.6	27.8
Moderate state response									
Mississippi	Moderate –	3,714,000	28.3	46.5	25.2	4,140,800	23.9	46.7	29.4
Ohio	Extreme +	16,461,400	21.2	40.9	37.9	19,689,700	16.9	44.0	39.0
Texas	Little –	23,617,100	17.6	45.0	37.4	27,906,500	14.7	42.2	43.1
Washington	Extreme +	8,114,300	23.5	45.7	30.8	9,669,400	17.9	51.3	30.8
Arizona	Moderate –	4,657,200	18.4	47.2	34.5	5,630,500	13.3	45.0	41.7
Illinois	Moderate –	21,395,000	21.8	40.2	37.9	23,066,500	19.2	38.9	41.9
Missouri	Extreme +	6,903,700	24.3	37.7	37.9	7,861,800	19.6	42.0	38.4
South Dakota	Little –	1,180,000	27.8	39.1	33.1	1,311,400	24.7	41.9	33.4
Low state response									
California	Extreme +	51,561,300	21.5	46.6	31.9	56,966,200	18.9	45.8	35.3
U.S. TOTAL		423,403,700	21.3	44.3	34.4	486,877,700	18.5	44.7	36.8

SOURCE: Origin of Revenue, 1980–81: *Governmental Finances in 1980–81*, No. 5, U.S. Department of Commerce, Bureau of the Census, Table 8, "State and Local Government General Revenue by Origin and Allocation, and Level of Government: 1980–81," p. 29.

Origin of Revenue, 1982–83: *Governmental Finances in 1982–83*, No. 5, U.S. Department of Commerce, Bureau of the Census, Table 8, "State and Local Government General Revenue by Origin and Allocation, and Level of Government: 1982–83," p. 16.

NOTE: Revenue data are for state and local governments combined.

classified as facing extreme fiscal pressure and worsening fiscal conditions in the study period.

In sum, the main conclusion of this chapter is that the coming together of a supportive economic and political environment produced the strongest responses to the cuts and changes made in federal grant-in-aid programs in the Reagan period. By "supportive" in the case of economic conditions, we mean that the state's economy and its finances were strong enough to permit fiscal replacement efforts of the services and activities affected by federal aid cuts. In the case of a "supportive" political environment, we refer to two factors: (1) the existence of a liberal, pro-public spending ideology or a shift in this direction; and (2) an attitude on the part of key government officials favoring the kinds of devolutionary reforms Reagan has advanced as a means of strengthening the role of state governments in American federalism.

Case-Study Chapters

✳

Florida

LANCE DEHAVEN-SMITH AND ALLEN W. IMERSHEIN

*T*hree years after the 1981 federal budget reconciliation act, the net effects of this initiative on Florida state and local governments (particularly Orlando) would appear to have been minimal. For the most part, programs and services were maintained; some were even increased. This occurred because state and local governments took action to cushion or counter the effects of federal aid changes.

A conclusion of minimal change, however, overlooks the background of political changes and the underlying *forces* of population and economic growth driving those changes; and it ignores the serious opportunity costs incurred along the way. Further, to observe little programmatic change since the 1981 budget act is not to imply that federal changes have had minimal effects. For in a state where there has been continued growth, the lack of it in programs responding to and/or supporting that growth was itself significant. In addition, federal cutbacks, changes in federal regulations, the recession and resulting state budget rescissions, and the prospect of further federal and state retrenchment all generated an atmosphere of uncertainty and caution in government. Maintenance of programs and services therefore became the most opportune response in a highly charged and uncertain arena. Continued growth demanded no less; a conservative political mood in the state would allow no more.

The Setting

Florida's consistent growth has provided an expanding fiscal base for state government and has spurred the development of administrative capacity to respond

Authors have equal responsibility and are listed alphabetically.

to that growth. The state's fiscal capacity has consistently remained slightly above the national average, but its taxing effort has ranged between only 74 to 79 percent of the efforts of other states.[1] Florida has no personal income tax, a minimum inheritance tax, and in 1980 only a 4 percent sales tax. That Florida clearly has the fiscal capacity to assume major new responsibilities was significant in shaping the state's response to federal budget cuts.

Likewise, the management capacity of the state government has been strengthened steadily during the past fifteen years through a series of consolidations, reorganizations, and organizational innovations. In 1968 the state adopted a new constitution that consolidated 200 state agencies into 25. As a part of that process it established the Department of Health and Rehabilitative Services (HRS) to bring under one unit a broad range of health and social service programs and reorganized that department in 1975 into what is still the only integrated health and human service agency in the country.[2] Also, in 1979 an Office of Planning and Budgeting (OPB) was created statutorily in the governor's office to set goals, develop policies, and establish budgetary priorities. Given these changes, the state was well positioned administratively to take control of federal programs.

Political Constraints

Florida was in some respects an unlikely candidate to adopt willingly a larger role in federal domestic programs.[3] With a history of opposition to government expansion, Florida reflected its conservative political heritage as part of the South. Until the late 1960s both the legislative and executive branches were dominated by people with very conservative orientations. In the 1970s, however, under a new constitution and a newly reapportioned legislature, Florida's executive branch began to move to a more moderate and independent status. Two moderate governors—Reuben Askew (1970–78) and Bob Graham (1979–

[1] U.S. Advisory Commission on Intergovernmental Relations, *The Tax Capacity of the Fifty States: Methodology and Estimates* (Washington, D.C.: Government Printing Office, March 1982).

[2] See Laurence E. Lynn, *The State and Human Services* (Cambridge, Mass.: MIT Press, 1980) and Allen W. Imershein, "Integration of Health and Human Services in Florida," in Helen Darling, ed., *Health Services Integration: Lessons for the 1980s* (Washington, D.C.: National Academy of Sciences, 1982).

[3] See John M. DeGrove, "Strategic Planning, State Decision Making and Block Grants: The Case of Florida," unpublished paper prepared for the 1982 American Society for Public Administration meeting, March 21–25, 1982, Honolulu, Hawaii; and John DeGrove and Nancy Stroud, "State Government Reaction to the Reagan Budget Cuts, Block Grants, and Deregulation Initiatives: The Case of Florida," unpublished paper prepared for the 1982 American Society for Public Administration meeting, March 21–25, 1982, Honolulu, Hawaii.

present)—were elected, and they have pushed for greater commitment to human services and education. Their main problem was mobilizing political support in the legislature to raise taxes and follow through on their objectives. Thus, the traditional conservatism of the state, although waning somewhat, has remained an obstacle to Florida's taking an aggressive role in federal programs.

Florida also has a constitution that makes innovation difficult. Florida's executive branch is composed of a number of offices filled by statewide election for four-year terms, including the governor, attorney general, comptroller, treasurer, commissioner of agriculture, commissioner of education, and secretary of state. These officials form the cabinet, which presides over natural resource programs, certain fiscal and investment functions, and many other areas of policy. Florida's plural executive is a barrier to comprehensive planning and coordinated service delivery, despite bureaucratic organization to facilitate it.

Similarly, the organization of Florida's legislative branch makes concerted action difficult. The Florida legislature is a bicameral body consisting of a Senate with 40 members and a House with 120. Although the legislature is well staffed and active, turnover is high, and the top leadership—the president of the Senate and the speaker of the House—has not been allowed (with one exception) to serve more than 2 years in these leadership positions. Moreover, the House and Senate have often been in conflict with each other because the Senate has been dominated by agricultural interests in the northern part of the state while the House has had greater representation from the urban south. Consequently, it has been unusual for the House and Senate to form a partnership with the governor and cabinet to adopt fiscal and programmatic initiatives.

Fiscal Constraints

Florida's ability to take a larger role in federal programs was also constrained by fiscal limitations. The Florida Constitution restricts local government operating millage levies to ten mills each for city and county governments. (This restriction alone is almost equivalent to Proposition 2 1/2, the fiscal limitation in Massachusetts.) The state also has a homestead exemption that precludes ad valorem taxation on the first $25,000 of assessed value. Because of the exemption, almost one-third of the homesteads in Orange County, where Orlando is located, pay no property taxes whatsoever.

Another indication of the state's reluctance to raise taxes is a fiscal limitation proposal that was to appear on a November 1984 ballot but was removed by the Florida State Supreme Court prior to election because it violated constitutional initiative procedures. Known locally as Proposition 1, the amendment would have taken as a baseline state fiscal year 1980–81 total revenue from all sources (excluding the federal government and debt) and allowed that base to grow no more than two-thirds the rate of growth in the Consumer Price Index plus ad valorem revenues resulting from new construction. Proposition 1 was far more restrictive than any of the fiscal limitation amendments passed in other states.[4] Had the amendment been enacted, state revenues for 1985–86 would have had to have been cut by 23 percent from the anticipated level.[5] Though stricken from the ballot, Proposition 1 may reappear in a different form at a later date.

THE LOCAL CONTEXT

The local governments of Orange County and the city of Orlando are similar to state government in having the capacity to take over responsibilities for federal programs. Own-source revenues account for about 70 percent of total revenues for both the city and county. Neither government is highly dependent on property taxes. The millage rates for the city and county have remained roughly constant over the past ten years (at approximately 6 mills for the county and 8.5 mills for the city). The nonexempt value of the property tax base has grown steadily, and the general obligation debt burden has been quite low by national standards.

The city and county governments are also strong administratively. The county administers most federal aid programs aside from the entitlements, social services, and health programs run by the state. The city has a strong mayor form of government, in which the mayor appoints department heads, serves on many area-wide and regional boards, and has voting and veto power in the city council. Similarly, the government of Orange County, like all counties in Florida since the adoption of the 1968 State Constitution, operates under a grant of home-rule powers. The executive branch includes a county administrator and a number of elected administrators including the sheriff, property appraiser, tax collector, supervisor of elections, and controller. Because turnover among commissioners is high, the county administrator, who has been in office for over ten years, has a great degree of control over policy and administrative matters.

The city of Orlando and Orange County are rapidly growing. The city's population grew by almost 30 percent in the 1970s, from 99,000 in 1970 to 128,000 in 1980. During the same period, the county population grew by 37

    [4] James C. Nicholas, "Citizen's Choice on Government Revenue: Florida's Proposition 13," *Florida Environmental and Urban Issues* XI, no. 2 (January 1984):20–22.
    [5] James Zingale, "Fiscal Analysis of the Immediate Impact of Amendment 1 on State Revenues," *Florida Environmental and Urban Issues* XI, no. 2 (January 1984):23–26.

percent, from 344,300 to 471,000. Because this growth is expected to continue for the remainder of the century, Orlando and Orange County will be forced to provide such capital improvements as roads and expand utility systems. Therefore, the city and county were under pressure to replace with their own money any federal revenues lost in capital programs as a result of the Reagan budget cuts. The key questions were whether this replacement would serve the same objectives of capital programs administered by the federal government, and whether entitlements and operating programs could or would be supported as well.

THE RECESSION

The Reagan budget cuts and the national economic recession hit Florida at almost the same time. The economic slowdown reduced state revenues, nearly 60 percent of which comes from state income and sales taxes. When the economy continued its downturn into state fiscal year 1982–83, two sets of state rescissions were made. There was no rainy day fund to pick up any of the slack. Most state agencies were affected by the state cuts. The Department of Health and Rehabilitative Services was affected most seriously, receiving a 7.5 percent reduction in overall budget capacity by 1982–83.[6] Management of these reductions, and the uncertainty generated by them, became as important an issue for the state agency and had effects as serious in the short term as did any of the federal reductions.

Thus, the setting in Florida for the Reagan federal aid changes was both positive and negative. The state government's fiscal and administrative capacities could support additional responsibilities, and Florida's continued growth demanded a strong response. However, the state's constitution and political culture, combined with the economic recession, made a strong response to federal changes difficult.

Florida's Response to Federal Aid Changes:
Maintenance for Growth

Even if no recession had occurred, the Reagan budget cuts would have presented major problems for Florida's state and local governments. In 1980, over 10 percent of state and local revenues were federal dollars. The total loss to the

[6] Allen W. Imershein, James Max Fendrich, William J. Page, and Richard Chackerian, *Analysis of the Projected Impact of Federal Fiscal Changes on HRS Programs and Policy Alternatives*, 1982 report to the Department of Health and Rehabilitative Services, Tallahassee, Fla., 1982.

state government in federal fiscal year 1982 was approximately $120 million. This was about 1 percent of the state's budget and no less than 10 percent of the federal funds received by the state. Immediate impacts were experienced in all programs except primary care services, and community development. Hardest hit at both state and local levels were social and health services, employment and training, and highway construction programs (tables 6.1 and 6.2).

The pattern of cuts observed in 1982 generally did not continue in 1983 at either the state or local levels. Changes in state payment levels, the recession, and rising health care costs, for instance, actually raised total spending for aid to families with dependent children (AFDC) and Medicaid. In other cases, such as in maternal and child health, preventive health, and community development block grant programs, funding was fully or partially restored by the federal government.

In spite of the reinstatement of some federal funds, the last several years have been a period of uncertainty for many parts of state government—uncertainty

Table 6.1. *Federal Aid to Florida, Federal Fiscal Years 1981–83 (dollars in millions)*

Grant Program	1981	1982	1983
Aid to families with dependent children	118.4	116.0	136.9
Medicaid	295.8	334.7	406.7
Social services block grant	116.6	103.1	112.5[a]
Maternal and child health block grant	11.5	9.3	12.4[b]
Primary health care grants	19.4[c]	19.5	23.4
Alcohol, drug abuse, and mental health block grant	35.7	22.4	24.5[d]
Preventive health block grant	4.0	2.9	3.1
Community services block grant	14.2	9.3	10.3[e]
Small-cities community development block grant	21.1	23.1	30.8[f]
Education block grant	23.7	17.3	16.4
Wastewater treatment construction grants	96.4[g]	90.6	82.6
Section 8 housing	2.6	2.6	4.7
Highway aid	397.0	328.0	519.0
Food stamps	500.9	447.7	419.3

SOURCES: Florida Departments of Health and Rehabilitative Services, Community Affairs, Education, and Transportation.

NOTES: [a] Includes $7.8 million from the 1983 emergency jobs act.
[b] Includes $3.1 million from the 1983 emergency jobs act.
[c] Funding includes grants for community health centers and migrant programs.
[d] Includes $1.6 million from the 1983 emergency jobs act.
[e] Includes $700,000 from the 1983 emergency jobs act.
[f] Includes $4.8 million from the 1983 emergency jobs act.
[g] Funding after federal budget decision of $28.6 million.

Table 6.2. *Federal Aid to Orange County and the City of Orlando, Federal Fiscal Years 1981–83 (in dollars)*

Program	1981	1982	1983
Aid to families with dependent children	12,600,000	11,800,000	12,200,000
Food stamps	27,200,000	24,300,000	21,600,000
Medicaid	242,000	217,000	230,000
Family planning	203,944	231,000	207,000
Maternal and child health block grant	370,000	333,000	336,000
Education block grant	6,700,000	6,170,000	6,200,000
Community services block grant	481,000	365,000	368,000
Job training grants	12,451,000	6,410,000	5,841,000
Mass transit operating assistance	969,000	1,091,000	1,370,000
Mass transit planning grants	16,000	9,000	72,000
Revenue sharing (Orange County)	4,200,000	4,900,000	5,600,000
Community development block grant			
Orange County	4,263,000	3,784,000	4,190,000
Orlando	2,452,000	2,378,000	2,001,000
Section 8 housing (Orange County)	2,504,000	2,532,000	2,371,000

SOURCES: Personal interviews and data provided by: The Florida Department of Health and Rehabilitative Services; Orange County Health Department; Orange County service delivery area; the Metropolitan Planning Organization for Orange County, the Orange County Housing Authority; the Orange County School District; and the Orange County Department of Community Affairs.

both over future federal funding levels and over the threat of a potential tax revolt. The net effect of this uncertainty has been to divert organizational resources, especially staff, into monitoring changes at the federal level. It also resulted in an unwillingness on the part of the state to engage in new program development or to commit to any innovation that was likely to require funding at levels higher than presently available. What was once proposed as a boon in flexibility at the state level was accompanied by rising levels of uncertainty that restrained innovation.

For the Department of Health and Rehabilitative Services (HRS) in particular, the acceptance of the block grants at the beginning of 1982 roughly coincided with the first round of state-level rescissions. Thus, HRS received a combined cut of roughly $44 million in federal funds and $15 million in state funds. HRS's response set the overall pattern for management of further state and federal cuts during the following year. The agency chose to absorb budgetary cutbacks by reducing administration and training rather than services. In this respect the agency was successful; in the short term, few services were cut.

Uncertainty and administrative difficulties aside, the state consistently maintained service levels and replaced federal cuts. In fact, the continuation of

economic growth, to keep pace with ongoing population growth, all but demanded political commitments to replace federal monies in those areas supporting that growth. At the same time, the most significant political careers in
the making in Florida, especially that of the governor, were emerging on the
basis of moderate political rhetoric rather than "new right" politics. Thus, despite the strongly conservative political heritage of the state, a course that would
have simply passed through all of the changes and cuts was not the one chosen.
Moreover, some of the traditional conservative claims in the South, namely the
assertion of states' rights and the rejection of federal intervention, were evoked
as a basis for an increase in state involvement in programs and services being
cut back at the federal level.

The issue was not whether to respond, but in what areas, to what extent, and
at what cost. Capital programs most obviously demanded support in order not
to impede economic growth; for sustaining the tourist industry in particular,
highways were especially important. An increasing population in general and
an increasing elderly population in particular made visible the need for continued services. Health programs, most of them associated with public health, received support from a strong interest group, the Florida Medical Association.
Of the major areas suffering federal cuts, only those that were without organized state political support, namely entitlements, received a minimal state response (see table 6.3). Even there, given the already low baseline for those programs in Florida, entitlements could not be entirely ignored without
considerable political embarrassment to those making the decisions.

Table 6.3.   *State Funding by Program Area, State Fiscal Years 1981–83
(dollars in millions)*

Program	1981–82	1982–83	1983–84
Aid to families with dependent children	82.5	84.3	99.5
Medicaid	220.5	275.2	324.9
Social services block grant	54.8	57.7	30.5
Maternal and child health block grant	29.0	33.3	37.5
Alcohol, drug abuse, and mental health grant	35.6	42.3	49.3
Preventive health block grant	3.8	5.4	5.3
Highway aid			
Funding from motor fuel tax	194.5	206.9	268.2
Funding from license tag fees	147.2	170.1	198.1

SOURCES: Interviews with state officials at the Department of Health and Rehabilitative Services and the
Department of Transportation.

STATE REPLACEMENT

In federal fiscal year 1982, the state met a shortfall in own-source revenues by withdrawing $567 million from a $601 million working capital fund. This allowed state programs to continue operation, albeit under tight budgets. The effects of the federal cuts in 1982 were mitigated by several factors. First, some programs and services funded under the block grants continued to receive federal aid from 1981 appropriations to categorical programs. Second, many state agencies were able to carry forward unspent funds from one year to the next, giving them a buffer to some of the immediate impacts. Third, in the case of the education block grant and the compensatory education programs, federal aid is forward funded. Thus, the spending changes for 1982 did not take effect until July 1982.

Because the working capital fund had been reduced to $34 million in 1982 and the state expected further cuts in federal programs and a continued recession in 1983, the Florida Legislature in 1982 passed a one-cent increase in the state's sales tax. This amounted to a 25 percent increase in the state's largest revenue source, generating $677.3 million in additional revenue, and making up for lost revenues almost twice over. The proceeds were divided equally between the state and local governments. Local governments were required to use a substantial part of the funds for property tax relief. However, even the short-term revenue increase was not sufficient to stave off the immediate effects of the federal cuts or the need for state rescissions. Florida partially replaced some of the lost federal funding in AFDC and health care programs in 1982.

In 1983, the state government again raised taxes; the four-cents-per-gallon gasoline tax was repealed and a new five-cent sales tax was applied to all motor and diesel fuels. Additionally, counties were authorized to levy up to an additional four cents per gallon on motor vehicle fuels. All of these monies were earmarked for road construction. Finally, the legislature met again in special session in July 1983 to raise money for education programs by increasing corporate taxes. The willingness of the governor and legislature to raise taxes, especially the unpopular corporate unitary tax, is indicative of the political capital expended to maintain an image of commitment to services and growth.

LOCAL-LEVEL REPLACEMENT

Replacement of federal aid cuts in Orlando and Orange County occurred in a number of areas. Capital programs—specifically, wastewater treatment and mass transportation—were the only ones with significant replacement in state fiscal year 1982–83; replacement funds derived mostly from increased fees and sales tax revenue. In wastewater treatment, connection fees and sewer and water fees were at least doubled and in some cases more than doubled over the two-year period. In mass transit, a percentage of the city's revenue from the new five-cent sales tax was earmarked to support the county-operated bus service. The following year, replacement at the local level was spread beyond capital programs into social services, income support, and indigent health care.

City and county officials decided to fund social service programs with federal general revenue sharing grants. Increasing population in both the city and county resulted in increases in revenue sharing grants. In 1982 the social service council responsible for distributing social service funds among providers received $375,110 from the city and county. The council received $597,153 in 1983.

In the area of entitlement programs, the Orange County Division of Social Services increased total spending for emergency income payments. The increase in local expenditures occurred in spite of the county's decision to lower the maximum monthly benefit from $250 to $200 and reflected growing enrollment that resulted from the 1981–82 recession and federal policy that tightened AFDC eligibility rules. Expenditures rose from $350,000 in 1982 to $650,000 in 1983.

In health programs a fee structure was established to replace budget reductions in indigent health care. Recipients who fall below the threshold do not have to pay fees, but those who are above it now pay a fee based on their income and the services they receive. In 1982 fees amounted to 4 percent of the health department's revenues. In 1983 fees contributed 8 percent.

In sum, at the local level the decision principle in program cuts was to spread the cuts as thinly as possible. This approach appeared to stem from concern about maintaining service providers rather than from a conclusion that all programs are equally effective. The fact that Orange County and Orlando were in excellent fiscal health made this strategy relatively painless.

Program and Service Effects

ENTITLEMENT PROGRAMS

Those persons receiving AFDC, food stamps, and Medicaid were the hardest hit by the federal budget cuts. In each program area, a number of different economic, demographic, and political factors converged simultaneously, making it difficult to ascertain the precise effects of the Reagan initiative alone. It is clear, however, that each program was forced to eliminate a number of recipients from its case rolls. Florida's initial response was by and large to pass through the cuts in entitlements. There were two exceptions. The AFDC payment standard was raised, but only by $16 per month from a previous base that ranks near the bottom of states' per capita funding nationally. In addition, the standard of need was raised during the 1982 legislative session to counter the effect of the 150 percent rule implemented under the 1981 budget act; however, this change failed to compensate for other federal measures which eliminated recipients.

Aid to Families with Dependent Children

Florida officials implemented without delay the basic provisions of the reconciliation act, including the "150 percent rule," the capping of child-care deductions at $160 per month, and changes in the 30 and 1/3 work incentive disregard. The "150 percent rule" was immediately challenged in court, and a court injunction reinstated those persons eliminated from the rolls by imposition of that rule. Passage by the legislature of an increased standard of need the following spring may have been directly influenced by the presence of this suit (which is technically still open). However, as mentioned earlier, many of those who would have been eliminated under the "150 percent rule," were nonetheless eliminated by other provisions also implemented, notably the deduction caps. The net result was the elimination of approximately 20,000 persons (7.7 percent of the case load) from the AFDC rolls. Since welfare eligibility varies considerably from month to month, and given the added complication of the court case, it is difficult to estimate the effects of the 1981 budget act on AFDC enrollment.

The yearly budget totals for AFDC (see tables 6.1 and 6.3) do not reflect this decline in case load for two reasons. First, and most immediate, the payment standard was raised from $230 per month for a family of four to $246 per month effective in February 1982, five months after the 1981 budget act took effect. Second, there was a gradual increase in case loads during federal fiscal year 1983 because of the recession. The net effect was a slight decline in total federal funds from 1981 to 1982 and an increase in total funds from 1982 to 1983.

Workfare

Florida has been reluctant to make welfare payments contingent on work. As an alternative to workfare, the state passed the Public Assistance Productivity Act (PAPA), which requires Florida's Departments of HRS, Community Affairs, and Labor and Employment Security to pool their resources in an effort to move people off welfare and into gainful employment. PAPA programs provide intensive training and supportive services to individuals who have received welfare continuously for at least three years. Local agencies develop pilot projects, which are funded on a competitive basis.

Food Stamps

Unlike other southern states, Florida has shown an overall decline in food stamp recipients during the 1981 to 1983 period, going from a high of over one million recipients in October 1980 to 747,933 in September 1983. Funding levels have decreased accordingly (see table 6.1). This decrease cannot be attributed to any one factor. Enrollment declined by 29,000 in October 1981, with the implementation of the 1981 budget act, but this was not the biggest month-to-month decline (though one of the biggest) during the three-year period. Three other factors explain declining enrollment. First, food stamp case load in Florida had been unusually high prior to enactment of the 1981 federal budget act, due to the Cuban boat lift. A high of over one million recipients in October 1980 reflects the influx of "boat people." In the early 1980s there was a decline in food stamp enrollment as many of these people became settled and no longer needed benefits. Second, Florida's economy did not decline as much as and recovered somewhat sooner than that of other states. Third, during the study period, the economic services program of HRS, which administers food stamps, adopted more stringent verification requirements for food stamps eligibility. In sum, while there certainly were changes in the number of food stamp recipients from 1981 to 1983, case-load reductions are not directly attributable to the 1981 federal budget cuts *per se*.

Medicaid

Changes in Medicaid in Florida occurred primarily as a result of federal policy affecting AFDC enrollment. Medicaid case load declined; expenditures, however, increased sharply (see tables 6.1 and 6.3) by over $93 million from 1981 to 1982. Total federal and state spending increased by nearly $122 million from 1982 to 1983. Rising expenditures stemmed from the increase in health care costs, particularly those for hospital and for nursing home care. With an increase of 12,000 cases (3 percent) from 1981 to 1982, hospital costs rose from $146 million to $178 million; from 1982 to 1983, cases declined by 14,000 but costs increased to $199 million. For intermediate nursing home care, case load increased from 12,252 in 1981 to 14,951 in 1983. Costs grew even faster—47.5 percent during the same period, from $93 million to $137 million. Those two areas alone accounted for a significant portion of the rise in Medicaid expenditures. Thus, federal changes reduced Medicaid rolls, but expenditures rose nonetheless.

Local Effects

In Orange County, the average number of families served monthly by AFDC declined from 10,500 in fiscal year 1981 to 9,555 in 1982, to 9,345 in 1983. Similarly, during the same period the average number of persons receiving food stamps each month declined from 51,211 to 33,653. The decline in enrollment was due mainly to tighter eligibility requirements. In the AFDC program, two factors had the most significant effect on case loads: the inclusion of stepparent income in family income calculations, and the 150 percent ceiling on the state standard of need. The latter immediately eliminated about 350 cases from the AFDC rolls in Orange County. Although these cases were notified they might still be eligible when the 150 percent rule was challenged in the courts, very few returned to HRS for another eligibility determination. In spite of cuts, the city and county were able to shift revenue sharing monies into social programs and meet demands for emergency income support with general revenues; the resulting local perception is that new or different programs are not needed.

OPERATING PROGRAMS

Operating programs in Florida suffered some substantial cutbacks, but the state's responses to these cuts differed significantly from its reaction to losses in entitlement programs. In some cases, the state was able to maintain services by transferring funds from other areas or utilizing new revenue sources. In other cases, federal supplemental appropriations from the emergency jobs act of 1983 or carryover funds appropriated prior to the 1981 federal budget act reduced the impact of the 1982 cuts. Finally, the state replaced a large portion of federal cuts.

Florida's centralized Department of Health and Rehabilitative Services is unique in encompassing a wide range of services; of the eight new block grants, the five largest ones fall under HRS's jurisdiction, as do AFDC, Medicaid, and food stamps. Unlike most state human service umbrella agencies, Florida's HRS is not a loosely federated set of categorical divisions.[7] Instead, the array of programmatic areas over which the agency has responsibility are organized under a unified administrative hierarchy whose authority rests largely in a decentralized system of eleven districts. Each of the eleven districts, headed by a district administrator, provides the entire range of services in a highly integrated manner. Planning and development for each of the program areas at the state level occur in a set of program offices that have no direct line authority to the

[7] See Imershein, "Integration of Health and Human Services in Florida."

district offices. Budgets are prepared by program in respective districts and then pulled together from the districts and the state level. The net effect is to have an organizational structure which not only fosters, but really requires extensive co-ordination across categorical program areas for most phases of operation. Thus, the potential for handling the majority of block grants was already in place in Florida.

The fiscal and program review that was necessitated by block grants was con-ducted by an already existing administrative grouping within HRS: the Execu-tive Management Group (EMG). It was well suited not only to review federal changes and propose state level ones, but to carry out their implementation as well. The EMG umbrella was composed of all the top administrators from the agency including those from program areas and districts. HRS took advantage of the limited increase in flexibility within the block grants to shift funds and funded areas across grants.

Social Services Block Grant

Federal social services cuts amounted to roughly $13.5 million in 1982 (see table 6.1). State funding increased by $3 million from 1981 to 1982, but the economic downturn resulted in a reduction of over $27 million from 1982 to 1983 (see table 6.3). Social services were the major area of HRS affected by the state cuts; however, the effects of the cuts were not so drastic as they might seem at first glance. The state budget cut for state fiscal year 1982–83 was largely ex-pected and planned for by the agency because of the budget and program flex-ibility within this area. Overall the agency responded by shifting available funds from other areas and finding other sources of funds not previously tapped to continue existing services. Mental health services previously funded by the title XX program that was replaced by the social services block grant were covered by the overlap between categorical and block grant alcohol, drug abuse, and mental health funds. Medicaid reimbursements were used more extensively. Title XX training was eliminated, a hiring freeze was imposed, and vacant po-sitions were eliminated. Though some minor service reductions occurred (for aging and adult services), the clients served were shifted to other programs. The net result was few changes in the social service programs.

Maternal and Child Health Block Grant

Federal funding in this area was cut by over $2 million from 1981 to 1982 but maintained for the following year. State and local funding increased by $4.3 million and $2.4 million respectively the first year, and state funding increased by another $4 million the following year. Thus, the state more than made up the difference in federal funding cuts. The maternal and child health block grant program also received supplemental funds from the 1983 jobs act; Florida's share of the emergency appropriation was $3.1 million. The state continued to fund those programs previously supported by the federal government, and the block grant was assumed using already existing organizational procedures and capacities.

Preventive Health and Health Services Block Grant
Federal funding for preventive health services was cut roughly $1.1 million from 1981 to 1982 (see table 6.1). The state replaced the loss. Only one major program shift occurred. The emergency medical services program was eliminated during the second year of the block grant, and its funds were shifted to other areas. The most significant possible long-term change will be greater direct state control of county health units. Previously funded by federal, state, and local dollars, and backed on occasion by the Florida Medical Association, the county health units had maintained some considerable degree of independence from state direction. With federal dollars flowing increasingly through the state agency, HRS will be more able to assert its management direction if it so chooses. This prospect has already evoked a legislative response to county government pressuring for continued control of county health unit budgets.

Alcohol, Drug Abuse, and Mental Health Block Grant
Florida's federal alcohol, drug abuse, and mental health grant was cut by $13.3 million from 1981 to 1982. Categorical grants awarded in 1981 but extending into the period when the new block grant took effect helped reduce the effects of the federal cut. Thus, total federal funds used within the state remained roughly stable from 1981 to 1982 and declined by $10 million from 1982 to 1983. At the same time the state also increased its own spending by approximately $14 million over a two-year period for treatment and prevention. State replacement helped maintain major program and service areas funded by the ADAMH block grant and also helped maintain social services that had been supported by the title XX program.

With the shift of federal funding now coming through the state instead of directly to the local agencies, mental health programs, like those of public health, will be potentially subject to greater state scrutiny and direction than before. Though most local agencies were subject to state guidelines already, because they were receiving some state funds, the direct provision of federal funds had allowed considerable independence on the part of local mental health boards. These boards were in fact eliminated in the 1984 legislative session. The centers that had been under them may now also be under increasing pressures from the state-level HRS offices when policy differences arise.

Primary Care Services

The primary health care program was not assumed by the state and there is little indication that it will do so. Local community health centers and migrant programs continue to receive primary health grants directly from the federal government. There has been a $6 million increase in community health center funds and a $2 million decrease in migrant funds from 1981 to 1983. Estimates are that these figures would have been cut by 20 to 30 percent if the state had assumed the block grant. Thus, there was no necessity and no incentive for the state to do so.

Community Services Block Grant

This block grant was assumed by the state in July 1982 and is administered by Florida's Department of Community Affairs (DCA). Federal funds for community services were cut from $14.1 million in 1981 to $9.3 million in 1982. When DCA assumed the block grant the state agency instituted a local match requirement that had been in place in 1981 when the program was federally administered. Monies available in 1983 also included $700,000 from the jobs act, but otherwise were roughly the same as in the previous year. No significant changes occurred at the state level beyond the continued cutbacks that had begun in 1978.

Small-Cities Community Development Block Grant

The state's community affairs department also administers the small-cities portion of the community development block grant program. Florida's small-cities allocation increased by $2 million from 1981 to 1982 and by another $2.9 million the following year, when the state assumed the block grant. In addition, Florida received $4.8 million in small-cities aid from the 1983 jobs act. Again, at the state level there are no apparent changes, and no really direct comparisons can be made over this period in program differences, since the state had just assumed administration of the program. The state adopted a competitive application process between cities and counties, similar to the one previously administered by the U.S. Department of Housing and Urban Development.

Education Block Grant

Federal funds that came under block grant administration for education were significantly cut by $6.4 million from 1981 to 1982. No state replacement occurred. For a number of reasons the effects of the cutbacks are not clearly visible. The funds were distributed to the counties, and the majority went into hardware; thus there were few direct program effects. Also, these funds account for only a small percentage of the state's total education budget. The most visible result of the block grant was a more equitable distribution of funds across different counties, since the grantsmanship capabilities of larger counties were no longer significant. The net result was only minor cuts overall.

Local Level

In Orlando and Orange County, federal funding for the new block grant programs was cut substantially between 1981 and 1982. Major spending cuts occurred in education and community service programs. With the exception of Orlando's community development block grant, further reductions were not experienced in federal fiscal year 1983, and in some cases, notably the maternal and child health block grant and Orange County's community development block grant, much of the funding was restored. In fact, Orlando and Orange County received $66,000 and $1.15 million in community development aid from the emergency jobs act.

Only the community service and educational block grant experienced programmatic impacts as a result of the federal cuts. Because of the loss of desegregation assistance funds, the school district eliminated a program to promote parent involvement in schools where children are being bused. Similarly, the ceiling for the target group for compensatory education was lowered from students in the thirtieth to the twentieth percentile in achievement, a shift which hurt program performance because of the severity of the problems in the latter cohort.

The programmatic changes in the community services block grant were more complicated. Orange County's Department of Community Affairs responded to the budget cuts by combining the management of this block grant with the Head Start program, which it also handles and which did not experience a reduction in funding. Community service programs were maintained at previous levels by drawing on funds from the latter, and also by obtaining some operating funds from the Orange County community development block grant program. However, four of the nine Head Start centers in the county were placed on double sessions, and class sizes were increased. Thus, the community service budget cuts indirectly affected Orange County's Head Start program.

Job Training Partnership Act (JTPA)

Anticipating that the Comprehensive Employment and Training Act (CETA) would be fundamentally revised in 1982 when it came up for reauthorization, the governor's Office of Planning and Budgeting (OPB) in 1981 reviewed its economic development, employment, and training programs with an eye toward reorganization. As part of the study, OPB conducted a survey of program operators and employers. The survey indicated that one-third of the program operators perceived duplication between CETA and Employment Service programs and two-thirds supported laws mandating interagency coordination.[8]

In 1982, Florida reorganized the Department of Labor and Employment Security. Training, placement, and apprenticeship services were consolidated into a single structure organized locally into Employment, Placement, and Referral Districts. The creation of districts with unified planning procedures for economic development, employment, and training programs anticipated the service delivery areas mandated by JTPA.

Shortly after President Reagan signed JTPA, a Job Training Coordinating Council was created in Florida to guide the transition from CETA. The coordinating council decided to eliminate the balance-of-state operation which had served rural areas under CETA. The CETA balance-of-state and nineteen prime sponsors were replaced by twenty-four service delivery areas (SDAs); territory was added to seven prime sponsors and a number of SDAs were created from scratch.[9]

The budget data for CETA and JTPA require interpretation to be meaningful. Florida's total allocation under CETA in fiscal year 1981 was $93.6 million. In most jurisdictions, about half of this went to administration, supportive services, and stipends, leaving $46.8 million for training. The allocation under JTPA for October 1, 1983 through June 30, 1984—a nine-month period—was $65.9 million. Prorating the latter to cover a 12 month period comparable to fiscal year 1981 would make the allocation $87.9 million, of which at least 70 percent, or $61.5 million, must be used for training. Thus, there was a 6.1 percent reduction in the total allocations between 1981 and 1984, but there was a 31.4 percent *increase* in monies available for training because of JTPA's restrictions on expenditures for stipends, supportive services, and administration.

Because of JTPA's restrictions on expenditures for stipends and supportive services, the Orlando SDA has encountered problems in spending its training grant. The biggest problem is in the classroom training, where stipends were reduced from $3.35 per hour under CETA to $1.00 per hour under JTPA. Potential enrollees can easily find jobs in Orlando starting at $4.50 per hour, and, unless they have income from some other source, they are reluctant to participate in training at $1.00 an hour.

Selection of service providers has not been affected by the shift from CETA

[8] Pam Bennet et al., *Report 4: Profile of Florida Programs in Economic Development, Employment, and Training* (Executive Office of the Governor, Office of Planning and Budgeting, October 1982).

[9] An overview of the Job Training Coordinating Council in Florida is contained in *Employment and Training Alert* 2, no. 1 (April 1983), a publication of the Florida Training Institute.

to JTPA. However, significant changes are likely as the city's private industry council (PIC) develops expertise. The only organization selected to represent community-based organizations on the PIC is the Associated Building Contractors, hardly the type of community representative associated with CETA's Employment and Training Advisory Council. Additionally, enrollment problems in classroom training will probably push the Orlando SDA away from traditional providers and toward on-the-job training programs with employers. Whether the latter will be effective remains to be seen, but as it stands, the SDA also has enrollment problems in its on-the-job training programs.

CAPITAL PROGRAMS

Wastewater Construction

Grants to local government was one of the areas most seriously affected by federal funding cuts. However, these cuts are not apparent from an examination of budget figures for 1981 to 1983. The largest cuts were made in June 1981, and consisted of a $48.8 million rescission of funds that had been authorized for 1980 but not yet distributed. Florida also lost $28.6 million in wastewater treatment grants from a federal rescission of 1981 spending. Thus, the series of federal budget rescissions resulted in a $77.4 million cut to the state. Federal funds for federal fiscal years 1982 and 1983 were $8 million less each year than the previous one.

These cuts resulted in major changes in the state. The first result was the withdrawal of approval for fifty-four projects that had already been approved for funding. Second, a high demand for wastewater treatment services and federal cutbacks led the state to change the way it distributed construction grants among localities. The major features of the priority changes included the following: Where local governments had previously been able to get increases during ongoing projects this would no longer be possible. In particular, no more add-on projects were allowed, and since this was a fairly common practice among local governments, the change came as quite a jolt. Independent proposals now had to be made for all grant monies, and these monies were made available on a priority basis dependent upon the severity of existing pollution in the locale.

Most significantly, local governments could not get funds to build facilities based on projected growth. In stable population areas this is not a problem; but given the long-term process for building facilities, such restrictions could leave areas with rapid population growth without adequate facilities in the future. One final change of note was a shift from a 75 percent-25 percent federal-local match to a 55 percent-45 percent federal-local. This was scheduled to take effect nationally October 1, 1984, but the State of Florida implemented it two years earlier, in order to spread waning federal funds among a greater number of local projects. By and large, local governments were able to come up with the larger match.

Both the city of Orlando and Orange County planned to expand their treatment capacities with projects totaling $101 million; city and county officials expected about $75 million in federal support.

Anticipating that they might have to generate all of this money locally, in 1982 Orlando and Orange County raised fees substantially. Connection fees in the city increased from $120 to $1,400, and water charges doubled. Similarly, the county increased water fees by about 40 percent to cover a $28 million bond issue, and it increased connection fees from $600 to $1,000. The city and county also began to consider merging their utility systems into a single water and sewer authority to achieve economies of scale.

In 1983, when it became apparent that federal funding for wastewater treatment construction grants would continue, at least in the short term, plans to merge the city and county utilities were laid aside because of fears that consolidation might mean fewer federal dollars. However, additional fee increases were implemented. In August 1983, the county increased sewer fees by 24 percent and raised connection fees from $1,000 to $1,600. At about the same time, the city tacked a $1 charge onto monthly water bills to replace $600,000 in annual funding lost from the Environmental Protection Agency for leakage repair.

Mass Transit

A similar response was taken in mass transit. Anticipating cuts in operating subsidies, the city was persuaded by the county to assume 40 percent of the cost of operating the countywide bus service. Before the 1982 federal budget cuts, the city had provided no funding for the service. To fund the service, Orlando used a portion of its newly acquired sales tax receipts, which it received after the state elected to raise the sales tax and share half of the additional revenue with local governments.

Housing

Federal funding for housing (section 8 programs) was stable from 1981 to 1983 with an increase when the state received new funds under the moderate rehabilitation program. The stability, however, is misleading unless one looks closer at long-term trends in federal support for public housing needs. The number of federally subsidized new construction projects in Florida declined in 1981 to two new starts with no new starts in 1982 or 1983. Federal funds are provided for these projects on a five-, fifteen-, or thirty-year basis. Federal funds will continue to come into the state for a length of time for already existing projects, but since new commitments are not being made, federal funds will decline. Combined with the elimination of other federal funding that went directly to local programs, these changes are regarded at the state level as a full-fledged federal withdrawal from programs that it has supported for the last thirty years. The major effects of these changes will be felt in the long term.

Highway Aid

Both federal and state spending for highway programs increased during 1981 to 1983. At the federal level funding declined from $397 million in 1981 to $328 million in 1982 and then increased sharply to $519 million in 1983, after the April 1983 increase in federal excise taxes on gasoline from four cents to nine cents per gallon. During the same period state funding increased from $194.5 million in state fiscal year 1981–82 to $206.9 million in state fiscal year 1982–83 and to $286.2 million in 1983–84. As mentioned earlier, the increase in state highway aid was funded by revenues raised from the extension of Florida's 5 percent sales tax to motor and diesel fuels. In addition, state revenues for highway aid from license tag fees has increased from $147.2 million in 1981–82 to $170.1 million in 1982–83 and to $198.1 million in 1983–84. Highway projects which had been delayed during 1981 and 1982 were put back on track after the increased revenues started becoming available. Otherwise, no major changes occurred.

Conclusions

Florida's response to the cuts and changes in federal programs was significant, but the response had a high political price. The state and the local governments of Orlando and Orange County replaced much of the funding that was cut from federal operating and capital programs. They did not, however, replace much of the lost funding in entitlements, the area of heaviest federal funding. Moreover, the effort to maintain federally supported programs used up the political and financial resources needed by the state to increase its services in other areas.

Florida's politics historically have been conservative. State leaders are very reluctant to raise taxes. During the course of the 1981–82 recession, rainy day funds helped relieve some of the fiscal pressure on the state. State spending had to be cut and state taxes raised nonetheless. The legislature passed three new tax packages in a two-year period.

Florida was not unique in passing new taxes during this period. What makes Florida distinctive is that most other states were forced by circumstances to raise taxes or shut down services, and in some cases the latter was necessary even with new taxes. This was not the case in Florida. Florida's growth was at a point when new taxes might have been passed even without adversity forcing such action, and such taxes could have been used to expand the state's services to its residents. It is not clear that such political capital can be mustered again any time soon. In fact, with a tax rollback initiative still looming in the background, it seems highly unlikely.

Fiscal capacity was drawn upon significantly to meet the immediate needs of the state. Gasoline taxes were raised to fund state road building that had fallen behind—and this in a state that depends especially on its roads for the tourists that supply a major source of its revenue. The sales tax was raised from four to five cents, but the state-level portion of these funds was used to maintain existing commitments and replenish in a very limited way the state's so-called rainy day fund. And corporate taxes were raised to increase education funding. However, given low levels of funding in previous years and the baseline starting level, such funding was only a minimal start toward the governor's goal of putting Florida in the top quartile of state spending for education and did nothing to raise other programs, especially those for the poor, above minimum levels. In short, the fiscal capacity was there, and it was used for maintenance.

The character of Florida's response to the cuts and changes in federal aid has been accounted for in large part by the state's need to respond to rapid population growth and related economic development. Capital investment is required for roads, schools, utility systems, and other services to meet the needs of new residents. Hence, Florida's state and local governments replaced most of the federal cuts in capital programs.

Thus, many of the fiscal adjustments made by Florida in response to cuts in federal aid were consistent with the adjustments that might have been made at some point anyway. Sales taxes were increased, property taxes were reduced, and user fees associated with construction (water and sewer connection fees) were raised dramatically. The cuts in federal aid generated these adjustments sooner than would otherwise have been expected. At the same time and of greater significance, they diverted new revenues into maintaining federal programs rather than expanding state and local services in other areas.

The shift of power from local to state government, although fostered by the new block grants, was also already in motion because of population growth and the fiscal and administrative adjustments it requires. The consolidation of state agencies in the 1960s and 1970s and the creation of HRS and a state Office of Planning and Budgeting are examples of an existing trend toward centralization. Likewise, greater reliance on sales taxes and less reliance on property taxes entail a shift of power from local to state government. Thus, authority had been flowing to the state government for some time, and the changes required by the block grants were minimal.

Because many of the changes that were stimulated by the cuts in federal aid were consistent with preexisting trends, most likely they will persist indefinitely. In fact, state control over local programs will probably increase as state offices develop expertise in their new areas of authority. Whether community-based organizations will be able to exert greater influence over state decisions in the future remains to be seen, but many of the changes in local decision making promise a further reduction in their influence locally. More significantly, it is not clear how state or local programs and agencies will fare in the face of further potential cuts and the renewed uncertainty in the second term of the Reagan administration.

7

Massachusetts

ARNOLD M. HOWITT AND R. CLIFFORD LEFTWICH

*P*resident Reagan's new federalism policies—set by the Omnibus Budget Reconciliation Act of 1981 and several other legislative and administrative initiatives—have had important but not dramatic impacts on Massachusetts state and local governments.

One set of effects involves the allocation of funds to programs supported by federal intergovernmental aid. The state largely accepted federal reductions in *entitlement* programs (aid to families with dependent children, Medicaid, and food stamps)—reflected either in absolute cutbacks or in lower than anticipated growth—that resulted from changes in federal eligibility requirements. The *operating* grants, however, were a different story: Massachusetts has at least partially replaced federal reductions for a number of these programs. And for *capital* programs, where the original federal cutbacks were less severe and some federal appropriations were restored or increased in subsequent years, Massachusetts has replaced and even augmented funds for some programs. More than most states, therefore, Massachusetts has chosen to cushion the impact of federal grant reductions by replacing them with state funds; but this response has varied by grant type.

A second set of impacts involves policy influence and decision-making authority over federal grants. Massachusetts state government has achieved an en-

The authors gratefully acknowledge help without which this study could not have been completed. Peter H. Henderson, David Hulse, and Thomas Montvel-Cohen served as research assistants. Many other individuals generously helped by agreeing to interviews or otherwise providing information. They are not cited by name because many were promised anonymity in return for their candor. The authors have also benefited from the work of an earlier research team in Massachusetts that worked on the first round of the Reagan domestic program study. Headed by Fred Doolittle, then at Harvard, the team included Kathryn Haslanger, Kenton Rose, Eve Sternberg, and Pam Wessling. Their field notes have been enormously valuable to the current research team.

hanced role in managing these programs and in its relationship with local governments. This is the *direct* result of federal policy changes mainly for the new block grants, which have given the state more authority to allocate funds among localities and to set policy for the use of funds. But state government has also increased its influence in other program areas—partly as an *indirect* result of federal policy, and partly because of Proposition 2 1/2, the state's tax limitation initiative, and subsequent increases in state aid to localities. As the state's fiscal commitment has increased, whether to replace federal grants or to boost local aid, its influence on program content has also expanded.

The Setting: Massachusetts and Boston

Massachusetts, the largest state in New England, has a proud colonial heritage, a currently robust economy, and a government that has steadily modernized in the past several decades. After long years of growth, the state's population has essentially stabilized—it was 5,689,000 in 1970 and 5,737,000 in 1980—but its rank among the states slipped from 10 to 11.

The Massachusetts economy has been quite healthy since the late 1970s, and this has certainly facilitated the state's activism and replacement efforts. In the recessions of 1969–70 and 1973–75, the state had been hit harder than the United States as a whole—in the first instance because of defense cutbacks and in the second because of the state's dependence on petroleum for 80 percent of its energy needs. But its high technology sector has led an economic expansion, and the state has growing service and financial sectors as well. The high technology picture is particularly favorable. Massachusetts has the highest concentration of high-tech industry in the nation and trails only California and Texas in absolute numbers. This growth has been supported by the state's vigorous venture capital industry and by the concentration of educational institutions in the state. (The Boston region alone has sixty-five colleges and universities.) As a result, Massachusetts has fared better during the most recent recession, with unemployment rates consistently below the national average.[1]

Boston, the state's and New England's largest city, is the capital of Massachusetts. The Boston region in eastern Massachusetts is the population, economic, educational, and cultural center of New England. The population of the Boston primary metropolitan statistical area (PMSA), like the state's, has been stable—declining slightly from 2,887,000 in 1970 to 2,806,000 in 1980.

[1] Helen F. Ladd, "The Experience of Massachusetts," unpublished paper presented at the Conference on the Present Condition and Future Prospects of State-Local Finances, University of California, Santa Cruz (April 1983), pp. 4–5.

The city itself, however, has experienced a decrease in population—from 641,000 to 563,000 during those years. The state's high-tech industry is concentrated in Boston's suburbs. The city's own economy has been healthy in recent years, evidenced most dramatically by a downtown building boom. The city has vigorous service and financial sectors but has not shared equally in the region's industrial growth. A significant proportion of the city's higher paying jobs, moreover, are held by suburbanites. The city's own residents have quite low per capita incomes.

GOVERNMENT AND PUBLIC FINANCE

Both Massachusetts and Boston governments have expanded and modernized in recent decades; but the state is currently fiscally healthy, while the city struggles with severe fiscal problems.

In recent decades, Massachusetts state government has steadily expanded the scope of its direct services—most notably in 1968 by the assumption of full responsibility for the state welfare system, which had previously been a local government function. State and local welfare expenditures are among the highest in the country.[2] The state has also taken major steps to modernize its government structure, particularly with the introduction of a cabinet system in the early 1970s which has strengthened the governor's ability to manage state agencies. State tax revenue has grown more easily than local government's. The state has been able to take advantage of tax sources that are relatively responsive to economic expansion: personal income, sales, and various business taxes. These provide 82 percent of its total revenues.[3] Consequently, total state tax revenues have increased from $3.209 billion in state fiscal year 1978 to an estimated $5.424 billion in state fiscal year 1984.[4] Local governments, in contrast, are exceptionally dependent on a relatively inflexible revenue source— the property tax—which traditionally has accounted for well over 70 percent of their own-source revenues. Several campaigns to overhaul the state's tax structure have failed to generate a consensus sufficient to move the state legislature. Localities, however, have had better luck persuading the legislature to increase state aid, as will be described below.

In the late 1970s, the fiscal pressure on local government was exacerbated by inflation, which kept property tax rates climbing. As a consequence, Massa-

[2] Massachusetts ranked fifth in per capita state-local public welfare spending in 1981–82.

[3] Ladd, "The Experience of Massachusetts," p. 5.

[4] Information through state fiscal year 1982 comes from Richard M. Kobayashi and Marilyn Contreas, "The Potential for Partnership: A Working Paper on the Future of State-Local Relations" (Commonwealth of Massachusetts: Executive Office of Communities and Development, December 1982), p. 5. Additional data supplied by Massachusetts Department of Revenue.

chusetts was a leader in the national "tax revolt." In November 1980, an initiative referendum, dubbed Proposition 2 1/2, swept to approval. This required high-tax communities to reduce property taxes by 15 percent annually until they had reached a rate no higher than 2 1/2 percent of full and fair valuation of real property. In 1982, the first year in which Proposition 2 1/2 was in effect, 182 of the state's 351 communities (comprising 80 percent of its population) were required to cut their property taxes. In 1983, 40 communities had to make another round of cuts; and 11 were required to make a third round of reductions in the following year. Once communities had reached the 2 1/2 percent level, moreover, they were permitted no more than a 2 1/2 percent increase per year. (Proposition 2 1/2 also reduced the state motor vehicle excise tax, which goes to local governments, from a 6.6 percent rate to 2.5 percent.)[5]

Boston was among the cities most severely affected by Proposition 2 1/2. It was forced to make cuts in its property tax rate for three years. At about the same time as the initial tax reductions, the city was hit by a court judgment that required it to refund $120 million in property taxes that businesses claimed had been overcharged over a period of years. The loss of revenue in the first year was substantial enough to make Mayor Kevin White lay off police and firemen and to force the school committee to lay off teachers. Political controversy swirled.[6]

Enormous pressure was placed on the state to use some of its revenues to increase state aid to localities. Governor Edward King initially resisted this idea, but legislative leaders pressed him to propose spending cuts in state government and to increase state aid. Massachusetts' budget for state fiscal year 1982 imposed cuts on many state programs, including personnel layoffs, and added to the state's local aid funds.

As noted above, the state had been increasing aid to localities already. Total direct state aid had gone up from $871 million in state fiscal year 1978 to $1.288 billion in state fiscal year 1981. In the wake of Proposition 2 1/2, the amount continued to rise: to $1.539 billion in the following year. In the 1982 gubernatorial campaign, former Governor Michael Dukakis, seeking to return to office, made a major campaign pledge to allocate 40 percent of state tax growth to local aid—a pledge that he has kept in office. State aid has continued to increase: to $1.696 billion in 1983 and $1.827 billion in 1984.[7]

In Massachusetts, therefore, the Reagan cutbacks in federal grant-in-aid programs have come against a backdrop of significant change in the state's public

[5] Ladd, "The Experience of Massachusetts," p. 9.

[6] Katherine L. Bradbury and John Yinger, "Adjusting to the 1980s: Boston's Fiscal Condition in the Years Ahead" (Cambridge, Mass.: MIT-Harvard Joint Center for Urban Studies, September 1983).

[7] Kobayashi and Contreas, "The Potential for Partnership," p. 5; additional data from Massachusetts Department of Revenue.

economy. Local government, which perennially has been pressed by the in-
flexibility of its major revenue source—the property tax—was squeezed even
more by the limitations of Proposition 2 1/2. State government, with more ample tax resources, chose to make moderate reductions in its own programs and
to share an increased amount of its revenue with localities. Given this background, it is appropriate to ask how the federal aid cuts affected Massachusetts
and how these impacts related to other changes going on.

ENTITLEMENT PROGRAMS

The reconciliation act sought to reduce federal expenditures and the number
of recipients for three large intergovernmental grant programs—aid to families
with dependent children (AFDC), Medicaid, and food stamps—under which
eligible low-income citizens are "entitled" to receive cash or in-kind benefits if
they apply for assistance. In Massachusetts, as will be described below, the act
has had substantial effects. AFDC and Medicaid case loads declined by 27 and
20 percent, respectively, between 1982 and 1983. As a result, expenditures for
AFDC dropped by more than 16 percent. Medicaid spending still climbed by
14 percent; but some of the costs were shifted from the federal government to
the state, and the overall increase was smaller than otherwise would have been
expected. During this period, the food stamp case load actually increased, but
this was wholly the result of a change in state law that made Supplemental Security Income (SSI) recipients eligible for food stamps. The 1981 "base" case
load declined by 19 percent. Thus, even though food stamps spending increased by 3 percent, it was significantly lower than it would have been without
the reconciliation act's changes. Table 7.1 shows the changes in federal funding
for federal fiscal years 1981–84.

To a substantial degree, Massachusetts has "ratified" these federal cuts under
the three major entitlement grant programs. It is true that increases in the
AFDC standard of need and in clothing allowances have given beneficiaries
more funds than they would otherwise have had, and some families are on the
AFDC and Medicaid rolls who would not have been; but the overall effects of
these state actions are small relative to the federal policy impacts.

The state has made significant responses in other ways, however. Programmatically, the state has begun an ambitious counseling and training program
for AFDC recipients as a substitute for "workfare," and it has launched a "managed care" program to help reduce Medicaid costs. Administratively, the state
has experienced difficulty keeping its AFDC error rate within acceptable limits;
but it has tightened administration of the food stamps program and has developed an innovative hospital cost control program.

Table 7.1. *Entitlement Program Budget Trends in Massachusetts, Federal Fiscal Years 1981–84 (dollars in millions)*

Funding Levels	1981	1982	1983	1984
Aid to families with dependent children[a]	502.0	463.0	419.0	417.0[b]
Medicaid[a]	919.7	983.0	1,050.0	1,070.0[b]
Food stamps	190.5	188.4	197.1	190.2[b]
Funding Changes	1981–82	1982–83	1983–84	1981–84
Aid to families with dependent children	−39.0 (−8%)	−44.0 (−10%)	−2.0 (−0.5%)	−85.0 (−17%)
Medicaid	63.3 (7%)	67.0 (7%)	20.0 (2%)	150.3 (16%)
Food stamps	−2.1 (−1%)	8.7 (5%)	−6.9 (−4%)	−0.3 (−0.1%)

SOURCES: Commonwealth of Massachusetts, *Analysis of the Proposed Fiscal 1985 Budget of the USA*, and the Massachusetts Department of Public Welfare's budget request, state fiscal year 1985.

NOTES: [a] Includes 50 percent state funds for AFDC and varying percentages of state funds for Medicaid as described in the text.
[b] Projected funding levels.

Aid to Families with Dependent Children (AFDC)

The reconciliation act had immediate and dramatic effects on the Massachusetts AFDC program.[8] In August 1981, the AFDC case load totaled 120,548 families. By August 1982, it had dropped nearly 22 percent to 94,544 cases. State officials estimate, moreover, that benefit levels were reduced for an additional 11,374 cases. The case-load decline continued, but at a slower pace, during the second year. In December 1983, the AFDC rolls stood at 87,604—an overall reduction of 27 percent.

To a large degree, therefore, Massachusetts has ratified federal cuts in the AFDC program by allowing federal regulatory changes to cut the case load and affect recipients' benefit levels. The federal restrictions on AFDC eligibility resulted in a savings to the state, which pays approximately half of the cost of welfare benefits. The state, however, has taken some steps to mitigate the reconciliation act's impacts.

The reconciliation act's effects have been more sweeping in Massachusetts than elsewhere. A forty-seven-state survey conducted by the state Department of Public Welfare showed that only two other states cut their AFDC rolls by a higher percentage than Massachusetts did during the first year. To a large extent this occurred because the federal eligibility changes disproportionately affected AFDC families with earned income, of which Massachusetts had a relatively high number. About 16,000 such families were among the 26,000 cases re-

[8] "Budget Request, FY 85" (Commonwealth of Massachusetts: Department of Public Welfare, 1984), pp. 17–20, 109–22. [Hereafter cited as DPW 85.]

moved from the Massachusetts AFDC rolls in the first year, and more were dropped in the second. The proportion of the total Massachusetts AFDC case load with earned income declined from 18.9 percent in 1981 to 9.8 percent in September 1983.

Although most of the case-load impacts were felt during the first year, the 16.5 percent expenditure reduction took effect over a two-year period because the case-load and payment reductions came in the midst of a state fiscal year. The percentage of overall AFDC savings is smaller than the percentage of case reductions mainly because the families cut from the AFDC rolls, especially the working poor, received lower than average benefits; however, the state legislature also increased the standard of need by 5 percent, which raised benefits by about $5 million.

Governors Edward King and Michael Dukakis have differed significantly in dealing with the AFDC program. This is reflected, first, in their attitudes toward benefit levels. When the reconciliation act was passed in 1981, Governor King, a conservative on social welfare issues, pressed the state welfare department to implement the cutbacks promptly. Nonetheless, at the state legislature's initiative, Massachusetts raised the AFDC standard of need by 5 percent for state fiscal year 1983 (which made more families eligible for benefits and increased benefit levels for many recipients) and authorized a $50 per child increase in clothing allowances. In contrast, when Governor Dukakis returned to the statehouse in January 1983, elected in part because of strong support from social welfare liberals, he took the lead in seeking increased benefits for AFDC recipients. Another 5 percent increase in the standard of need and a $75 boost in the clothing allowance were enacted in state fiscal year 1984; and for state fiscal year 1985 the Dukakis administration proposed another 5 percent standard of need increase, a $125 clothing allowance and a 5 percent increase in the maximum allowable AFDC grant.

The Dukakis administration has also been concerned about the homeless. Among measures adopted to deal with this general problem are several aimed at AFDC families. The administration sponsored legislation which removed the dollar cap from emergency assistance grants (which pay for rent arrearages, housing deposits, and emergency shelter). It also increased funding for community-based family shelters from $2.2 million in state fiscal year 1983 to $3.8 million in 1984, which permitted an increase from five to fifteen such shelters.

The King and Dukakis administrations have also taken different positions on AFDC work requirements. The King administration had been planning a work program even before the reconciliation act was passed, but the act permitted a broader scale effort than otherwise would have been possible. The state applied for and was granted demonstration status to administer a comprehensive federal work incentive program in 1982. After some delay by political controversy, a watered down "workfare" program was implemented in April 1982. It required all AFDC recipients whose children were over six to spend six weeks as members of a "job club" looking for work. If they did not find a job, they were obliged to participate in a training program or accept a nonpaying community service job to remain AFDC-eligible. Subsequently, the welfare department, encountering resistance to the program from case workers, issued a directive that ordered them to stop trying to match recipients with "suitable" jobs but to assign them to any "available" position.

When the Dukakis administration took office in 1983, it made revision of this program a high priority. Enlisting welfare-rights advocates and former recipients to help plan the program, the state sought to emphasize the counseling and training dimensions of the program so that participants could eventually find permanent employment. The administration won a federal waiver to make only program registration, but not acceptance of a job, mandatory for recipients. During its first nine months, state officials claim, the program will have placed 5,000 AFDC recipients into jobs at average pay levels 175 percent above the AFDC benefit level. The program has still encountered opposition from advocacy groups who contend that its registration requirement is coercive, and many AFDC recipients are reluctant to accept jobs if that entails losing Medicaid benefits.[9]

Administratively, the King administration was experimenting with monthly income reporting even before the reconciliation act required it. With other federal policy changes and new methods of calculating error rates, however, the state had difficulty keeping its error rate at acceptable levels. The final three error rate estimates during the King administration were 5.6, 9.5, and 10.4 percent—the last of which exposed Massachusetts to federal sanctions. The Dukakis administration has therefore developed a correction plan targeted on specific error sources.[10]

Medicaid

The reconciliation act affected the Massachusetts Medicaid program by reducing both eligibility for benefits and the percentage of program costs paid by the federal government. As a result of changes in eligibility, the Medicaid case load has declined significantly—approximately 20 percent between 1981 and 1983 (from 557,000 people to 445,000). A substantial percentage of this decrease is attributable to the reconciliation act's mandated reductions in AFDC case load. AFDC recipients, who are automatically eligible for Medicaid, account for

[9] DPW 85, pp. 69–80; Boston *Globe*, May 6, 1984, p. A28.
[10] DPW 85, p. iv.

about 60 percent of the program case load. Not all of the terminated AFDC cases lost Medicaid benefits, however, because some became eligible for Medicaid-only status.

Despite the case-load reductions imposed by the reconciliation act, Massachusetts' Medicaid program—the largest item in the state budget—increased its cost by 14 percent from 1981 to 1983. This anomaly is explained mainly by inflation and the distribution of expenditures within the case load. Although 66 percent of Medicaid recipients are families with children (primarily AFDC cases), these beneficiaries account for only 27 percent of Medicaid expenditures. The elderly and disabled, who are more likely to require hospitalization or nursing home care and other expensive services, constitute only 34 percent of the case load but consume 73 percent of the program's financial resources. Cuts in the AFDC-Medicaid case load therefore did not proportionately reduce the amount of services that were consumed and that therefore were subject to cost inflation.[11] Moreover, the inflation rate for medical services was between 9 and 10 percent during these years. Furthermore, about $60 million in costs have been shifted from the federal to the state budget as a result of reconciliation act changes.

The costs of the Medicaid program have been a major state budgetary concern. Beginning in state fiscal year 1982, therefore, the state welfare department developed an annual cost savings agenda which seeks to cut expenditures by changing methods of benefit calculation, assuring that services are necessary and provided in cost-effective ways, developing new health care delivery methods, and maximizing private third-party coverage of medical care bills.

A key initiative has been a "managed care" system in which recipients are initially treated by a personal primary care team attached to a health plan. Care is paid for by contract. To encourage cost savings, the department shares with providers any savings from what a fee-for-service system would cost. This program, which had 7,800 enrolled at the end of state fiscal year 1982, is expected to have an enrollment of 25,000 by the end of state fiscal year 1985.

Administratively, the state has also tried to improve its eligibility determination process by assuring that such determinations are prompt and accurate, that cases are regularly redetermined, and that errors are reduced. But as a result of a recent successful suit that prevents AFDC and SSI recipients from being automatically eliminated from the Medicaid rolls if they lose benefits from those programs, the state has been plagued by a backlog of redetermination actions.

To control hospital costs, the King administration, with a federal waiver, in-

[11] DPW 85, pp. 177–230.

itiated an experimental "prospective reimbursement" program that creates for the first time an acute care hospital reimbursement program uniform across all payers—Medicaid, Medicare, Blue Cross, and other private insurers. This plan is designed to give hospitals financial incentives for cost cutting. Implementation of this program has continued under Governor Dukakis.[12]

Food Stamps

In Massachusetts, the impact of the reconciliation act changes on the food stamps case load was complicated by a simultaneous state policy change. Until amended by the legislature in 1981, state law had prohibited recipients of SSI benefits from also receiving food stamps. (The SSI program is federally financed and administered; state funds supplement monthly cash payments from the federal government to low-income elderly, blind, and disabled persons.) This change in Massachusetts law made it possible for SSI recipients to apply for food stamps in 1982—in effect substantially increasing the pool of potential food stamp recipients by about 36,500 new cases. But there were about 29,320 fewer non-SSI cases as a result of the reconciliation act eligibility changes (and changing economic conditions). Overall, therefore, there was a small net increase in the number of food stamp recipients.

Under the King administration, only partly in response to federal changes, the state moved to tighten the administration of the food stamps program. To reduce fraud, replacement of lost coupons, and mail theft, the state inaugurated a photo ID system (nationally, it was the first to have a statewide program) and eliminated mail delivery of coupons. Recipients must now come to a distribution site and show their ID cards to receive food stamps. The Dukakis administration has retained these administrative changes.

In late 1983, in response to a Department of Public Health nutrition survey that showed hunger problems in the state, the Dukakis administration sponsored supplemental nutrition programs. This included efforts to expand the distribution of food stamps by an outreach program to identify and eliminate barriers to participation, especially for malnourished children and the elderly. In addition, the state appropriated about $3 million for supplemental nutrition programs.

OPERATING PROGRAMS

The reconciliation act made sweeping changes in programs that financed health, social service, education, and employment and training programs in

[12] DPW 85, pp. 179–207.

state and local governments. One key effect was the consolidation of a number of previously existing categorical grant-in-aid programs into seven new block grants. This change was intended to give states more discretion over the use of federal funds, reduce federal regulation, and reduce program costs.

A second key effect was to cut back the federal funds allocated to these programs, except in education. In Massachusetts, funding for the new health block grants in federal fiscal year 1982 declined by between 10 and 36 percent; two new block grants for social services were reduced by 28 and 23 percent; and employment and training funds were cut by 46 percent. Only the new education block grant and a revised compensatory education program received stable or marginally increased funding levels. In federal fiscal years 1983 and 1984, funds were restored to some of these programs, but virtually all were receiving significantly less federal money than before. Three of the four health block grants were receiving 20 to 25 percent less, while one had almost returned to its pre-reconciliation act funding level. The two social services programs were still at 26 and 15 percent below their pre-reconciliation act levels. Employment and training programs had dropped still further—to only 50 percent of their previous levels. Again, the education programs were an exception: Massachusetts' allotment of federal aid from the education block grant remained stable, while the state's allotment of compensatory education aid increased by 12 percent. See table 7.2 for a summary of these changes.

State Government's Role

Overall, state government's decision-making authority and administrative responsibility have increased significantly in most of the operating programs studied.

Given the opportunity, the state took charge administratively of three of the four health block grants, the community services block grant, the elementary and secondary education block grant, and the new Job Training Partnership Act (JTPA) programs. Generally, this resulted in more centralized authority than had been the case under the predecessor categorical programs, either because the state acquired control over programs that had previously gone directly to local governments or nonprofit organizations, or because the state consolidated control over previously separate categorical programs, which it already managed.

Administratively, responsibility for the maternal and child health and preventive health block grants was assigned to divisions of the public health department. Management of the alcohol, drug abuse, and mental health block grant was parceled out so that responsibility for alcoholism and drug abuse programs was given to two units in the public health department. The education

Table 7.2. *Operating Program Budget Trends in Massachusetts and Boston, Federal Fiscal Years 1981–84 (dollars in millions)*

	MASSACHUSETTS			
Funding Levels	1981	1982	1983	1984
Alcohol, drug abuse, and mental health block grant	24.6	17.0	18.5	18.2
Maternal and child health block grant	7.9	7.1	9.5[a]	7.7
Preventive health block grant	3.1	2.3	2.5	2.5[b]
Primary health care block grant	5.6	3.6	4.8	4.6
Community services block grant	11.2	8.1	8.1[c]	8.3
Social services block grant	78.9	60.4	61.1[d]	67.0
Education block grant	10.0	10.3	10.1	10.2
Compensatory education	68.2	69.8	69.2	63.3
Job training	126.8	68.3	69.2	63.3
Funding Changes	1981–82	1982–83	1983–84	1981–84
Alcohol, drug abuse, and mental health block grant	−7.6 (−31%)	1.5 (9%)	−0.3 (−2%)	−6.4 (−26%)
Maternal and child health block grant	−0.8 (−10%)	2.4 (34%)	−1.8 (−19%)	−0.2 (−3%)
Preventive health block grant	−0.8 (−26%)	0.2 (9%)	0 (0%)	−0.6 (−19%)
Primary health care block grant	−2.0 (−36%)	1.2 (33%)	−0.2 (−4%)	−1.0 (−18%)
Community services block grant	−3.1 (−28%)	0 (0%)	0.2 (2%)	−2.9 (−26%)
Social services block grant	−18.5 (−23%)	5.7 (9%)	0.9 (1%)	−11.9 (−15%)
Education block grant	0.3 (0%)	−0.2 (0%)	0.1 (0%)	0.2 (0%)
Compensatory education	1.6 (2%)	0 (0%)	8.5 (12%)	10.1 (15%)
Job training	−58.5 (−46%)	0.9 (1%)	−5.9 (−9%)	−63.5 (−50%)

	BOSTON			
Funding Levels	1981	1982	1983	1984
Education block grant	0.7	1.4	1.4	—
Compensatory education	11.3	10.2	12.0	—
Job training	24.8	12.1	10.2	8.7[b]
Funding Changes	1981–82	1982–83	1983–84	1981–84
Education block grant	0.7 (100%)	0 (0%)	—	—
Compensatory education	−1.1 (−10%)	1.8 (18%)	—	—
Job training	−12.7 (−51%)	−1.9 (−16%)	−1.5 (−15%)	−16.1 (−65%)

SOURCES: Commonwealth of Massachusetts, *Analysis of the Proposed Fiscal 1985 Budget of the USA* and interviews with state and local officials.

NOTES: [a] Includes $2.4 million in jobs act funds.
[b] Projected funding levels.
[c] Includes $500,000 in jobs act funds.
[d] Includes $4.4 million in jobs act funds.

block grant—only a few of whose categorical ancestors had been state-run—was lodged in the department of education. To run the community services block grant, whose predecessor programs the state generally had not managed before, the state established and staffed a new Office of Community Action in the Executive Office of Communities and Development (EOCD).

Although the state already had responsibility for the title I program, its authority became stronger under the new chapter 1 compensatory education program.

Massachusetts chose not to assume responsibility for the primary care block grant. The Massachusetts League of Community Health Centers lobbied against state control, in part because it was wary of the state as an unknown "master" and in part because state control would have meant switching from an advance-funding system to a reimbursement basis. The state, for its part, was concerned that the reconciliation act had fuzzy language about state matching funds; and the public health department felt no urgent need to control the program because it had a very cooperative relationship with the Bureau of Community Health Services in the U.S. Department of Health and Human Services' regional office.

Replacement of Federal Funds

The state's new responsibilities exposed it to pleas from program administrators and constituency groups to find resources to diminish the impact of the federal budget cuts. In several cases, the state offset cutbacks in federal fiscal year 1982 by carrying over federal funds appropriated in the previous fiscal year. This was possible because some of the categorical grants operated on administrative calendars different from the federal fiscal year. Therefore, they had finished only part of their current program year when the 1982 federal fiscal year began. As a result, carryover funds were available for the alcoholism, mental health, maternal and child health, preventive health, and community services programs.

With its own funds, Massachusetts chose to replace a larger proportion of federal cuts in these operating programs than it did in the entitlement programs. Massachusetts' budget response came slowly, though. State fiscal year 1982 had started on July 1, 1981, about two months before the reconciliation act was passed, so the next state budget-making round did not come until well into the first year of federal cuts. State government, however, did choose to use its own funds to make up a portion of the lost federal money. It did not do so in all cases, and was unable to replace *all* of the cuts, but new state money was appropriated for a number of the affected programs.

The most significant replacement (and, indeed, augmentation) was for so-cial service programs. The political-administrative situation here was complex. Unlike most other federal grants, the state intermingled title XX/social services block grant funds with state appropriations and treated the federal money as a reimbursement for state program expenditures. Most eligible services were de-livered by the state Department of Social Services (DSS), which had been split off from the welfare department as a separate agency only a few years earlier to give its mission more prominence. DSS had strong legislative support, and this was reinforced by the fact that several suits had resulted in court orders man-dating improved social services—e.g., in child abuse cases. Consequently, the legislature supported increasingly large appropriations for DSS. The depart-ment's total budget in state fiscal year 1981, including federal funds, had been $175.3 million. In the following year, despite impending federal cuts, the leg-islature appropriated $194.0 million. Given the ultimate reduction imposed by the reconciliation act ($18.5 million), this would have been a net increase of $37.2 million in state funds. Governor King impounded $10 million of the leg-islature's appropriation. Nonetheless, despite this impoundment, the state still replaced all of the federal fiscal year 1982 cutback and added $8.7 million more. Moreover, the state fiscal year 1983 appropriation again increased the overall level of DSS spending to $197.7 million, a hike of $17.7 million over the previous year. Taking account of $5.7 million in additional federal funds that the state would receive in federal fiscal year 1983, the state increased its net contribution to the DSS budget by $12 million. Massachusetts expected to spend about $224 million in 1984, with less than $1 million of that increase coming from the federal government.

The only other replacement in state fiscal year 1982 came in education. To make up for the loss of targeted desegregation funds which were absorbed in the education block grant, the state increased its own desegregation aid program by $500,000.

There was somewhat more state replacement and augmentation of federal funds in state fiscal year 1983. Besides the new funds for social services, the state also appropriated $1.5 million to replace lost federal money for maternal and child health programs, and it augmented funds in this policy area by starting a new early health intervention program. To replace money cut from the primary care block grant, the state approved $1.0 million extra for community health centers; but it spread this money out to thirty-six centers—not just to the sixteen receiving federal funds. There were also small increases in drug, alcoholism, and mental health spending. However, there was no replacement of lost funds in either the community services and preventive health block grants or employ-ment and training programs.

Fiscal year 1984 saw little additional replacement of federal budget cuts in these programs, although the previous year's spending levels were maintained. There was some additional money available for maternal and child health, drug and alcoholism programs, and social services.

Reallocation of Federal Grant Money

Beyond its ability to replace federal funds, Massachusetts exerted increased influence over the operating programs by changing the allocation of federal grants-in-aid. In 1982, it began to use the new authority that resulted from the reconciliation act in two main ways. First, the state instituted a competitive request-for-proposals (RFP) system to distribute certain discretionary grants to local governments and nonprofit service providers. This decision gave state administrators control over the criteria for and process of selecting recipients for alcoholism and drug abuse grants, for some mental health projects, and for maternal and child health and preventive health care projects. Second, for other grant programs, the state developed new formulas to distribute money to recipients. This was done for a portion of mental health funds, for the community services and elementary and secondary education block grants, and for the compensatory education and JTPA programs.

Two important consequences resulted: Boston tended to lose funds relative to the rest of the state, and money generally was spread more widely. This came about because, under some of the categorical predecessors of the new block grants, large cities like Boston had occupied a privileged status—partly because policy makers in Washington believed their problems were more severe and partly because big cities had considerable strength in congressional and executive branch politics. The transfer of authority from Washington to state agencies meant that a different balance of political power shaped policy. (Boston also lost some funds because its population was declining relative to the rest of the state).

In the RFP process, grant recipients were chosen on a competitive basis. Boston sustained cuts in alcoholism, drug rehabilitation, and maternal and child health programs because state administrators felt that other localities had higher priority needs. For example, the state chose to give money to Worcester to start up a new minority-oriented alcoholism prevention program; previously, Boston had been the only city to get such funds from the federal government. At the same time, some other Boston programs were dropped, with their functions supposedly assumed by the remaining facilities in the city. Boston's officials saw such decisions as unwarranted. Typically, they felt that the state's policies overlooked the seriousness of their problems. For example, they saw drug abuse money being redirected to suburban communities whose problems involved softer drugs.

Formula reallocations also tended to divert money from Boston. In the case of the community services block grant, for example, the state used its new authority to adopt a distribution formula that gave primary weight to the percentage of poor people living within a particular service area. Under the federal distribution system, Boston had received about 45 percent of the state's funds even though it had only about 25 percent of its impoverished people. Of the twenty-five community action agencies (CAAs) in the state, sixteen got a higher percentage of available funds under the new formula. For Boston, the new formula meant $1 million less for Action for Boston Community Development (ABCD), the local CAA. (To ease the transition to the new block grant, the state gave the "losers" a one-time only special grant from federal carryover funds. ABCD's share was $410,000.)

Devising the new formula for community services was a politically controversial process. The CAAs, acting through the Massachusetts Community Action Program Association, their lobbying organization, had to fend off efforts to divert part of the new block grant to community development corporations (CDCs), another type of community-based group that had similarities with the CAAs but did not share their history as part of the old federal antipoverty program. The CAAs naturally did not wish to share their now shrinking source of federal funds with competitors. Although successful in that endeavor, the CAAs were split in angry wrangling over the distribution formula, with Boston's ABCD, which got about one-third of funds statewide, on one side, and a number of smaller CAAs on the other. It is possible that these political battles prevented the CAAs from effectively lobbying for any state replacement of lost federal funds.

When the state adopted a formula allocation system to replace distribution by individual project grants, communities that had been aggressive and successful at grantsmanship tended to lose substantial proportions of their federal funds. Boston was often in this position, but other local governments suffered from the same problem. In the case of the elementary and secondary education block grant, Cambridge, which had received aid under several of the predecessor categoricals, lost 85 percent of its federal money. Eight other cities in the state were also losers.

At the same time, however, communities that had not been aggressive in seeking federal project grants received new money from the block grant. Only 20 percent of the communities in the state had previously gotten funds from the categoricals folded into the education block grants, so many additional towns now received assistance. Given the wide dispersion of money, though, the amounts were small. Many new recipients received only token grants of $1,000–$1,400.

Changing allocation formulas was a method for apportioning budget cuts without necessarily eliminating any grant recipients. When the RFP method was used to distribute project grant funds, however, the necessary cutting was typically done by a combination of selective project terminations and across-the-board fund reductions for the remaining grant recipients.

That arrangement applied to the health block grants. For the maternal and child health block grant in 1982, the state public health department eliminated funding for a program at a teaching hospital in Boston, contending it would have been terminated for underutilization and ineffective outreach even if federal cuts had not been made. The department then imposed an 8 percent reduction across the board on other aid recipients. For the alcohol, drug abuse, and mental health block grant in 1982, several dozen drug programs were dropped, and a 4 percent cut was spread equally among other recipients. For the preventive health care grant, congressional strictures about distribution of funds among the former categorical program areas actually led to program expansions for rape prevention projects; but cuts in other areas were apportioned across the board.

In a few cases, the beneficiaries of arrangements under the categorical programs were able to resist efforts to reallocate resources. State mental health officials wanted to use the new alcohol, drug abuse, and mental health block grant to assert more control over the highly independent community mental health centers. They sought to place all mental health funds into a single competitive RFP process rather than distribute the money as operations grants to the community mental health centers. The centers thwarted this plan by mobilizing their political supporters. As a result, only one-third of the funds were distributed on a competitive basis.

Other Effects

Aside from distribution questions, Massachusetts has made relatively few changes in these grant programs. In some cases, the reconciliation act limited potential change by protecting former categorical purposes with programmatic distribution requirements. That was true, for example, of the preventive health block grant. However, the state chose to continue programs with relatively little modification even when it had more latitude to institute change. In the case of the community services block grant, for example, the state adopted program regulations very similar to those imposed by the federal government. What programmatic change did occur tended to be fairly modest: in drug programs, a shift away from hot lines and outpatient/drug-free treatment to more inpatient treatment.

Administratively, the most important effect came in the method of financing alcohol, drug abuse, mental health operations, and some other programs. Instead of the advance-funding system used by the federal government, local governments and nonprofit grant recipients had to use their own money up front and seek reimbursement from the state.

CAPITAL PROGRAMS

The reconciliation act and several subsequent pieces of legislation had mixed effects on grants which contribute to the construction and operation of capital facilities. Most suffered cuts in federal fiscal year 1982, but since then several have seen these cuts restored. Overall, recent changes in federal policy have not hit capital program budgets as hard as they did entitlement or operating programs (see table 7.3).

In Massachusetts, subsidized housing programs were the most adversely affected by federal budget cuts: the amount of section 8 funds available shrank by 46 percent in federal fiscal year 1982 and in 1983 stayed 39 percent below their pre-reconciliation act level. The wastewater treatment construction program was also significantly affected: statewide, its budget dropped by 25 percent in federal fiscal year 1982 and remains 11 percent below the state's 1981 allocation. Highway and transit construction programs were both cut in 1982, but in the two subsequent years increased as a result of the Surface Transportation Assistance Act of 1982. By 1984, total highway aid increased by 29 percent compared to 1981. Federal capital grants for mass transit have fluctuated: allocations under the basic capital program have gone up, but interstate transfer funds have declined dramatically. The small-cities community development block grant, which the reconciliation act turned over to state administration, has received a 3 percent boost in funding.

The picture is more mixed for Boston and its transit authority, which receive some capital grants directly. Boston's community development entitlement grant declined steadily and stands 12 percent lower in federal fiscal year 1984 than in 1981. The drastic cutbacks in federal Economic Development Administration (EDA) funds have largely cut off new project commitments to the city. Urban development action grants (UDAGs)—made on a project-by-project basis—are lower than before and have fluctuated substantially (but city officials contend that city policy rather than federal changes has affected this program). Basic transit capital grants have increased, but the transit authority has seen its allocation of interstate transfer money decrease dramatically. Moreover, transit operating grants have been cut by 27 percent.

The Boston Housing Authority (BHA) is the largest public housing agency in Massachusetts. Since 1980 it has been under court receivership because of

Table 7.3. Capital Program Budget Trends in Massachusetts and Boston, Federal Fiscal Years 1981–84 (dollars in millions)

MASSACHUSETTS			
Funding Levels	1981	1982	1983	1984
---	---	---	---	---
Wastewater treatment	93.0	70.0	83.0	83.0[a]
Interstate highway aid[b]	88.4	92.2	124.9	126.8
Other highway aid[c]	83.4	67.0	91.9	94.3
Mass transit capital grants[d]	81.1	88.9	74.1	106.0[e]
Mass transit interstate state transfer funds	192.0	132.0	106.9	40.0
Assisted housing	38.1	20.6	26.2	30.2
Small-cities community development block grant	26.5	27.3	31.3[f]	27.3

Funding Changes	1981–82	1982–83	1983–84	1981–84
Wastewater treatment	−23.0 (−25%)	13.0 (19%)	0 (0%)	−10.0 (−11%)
Interstate highway aid	3.8 (4%)	32.7 (35%)	1.9 (1.5%)	38.4 (43.4%)
Other highway aid	−16.4 (−20%)	24.9 (37%)	2.4 (2.6%)	10.9 (13.1%)
Mass transit capital grants	7.8 (10%)	−14.8 (−17%)	31.9 (43%)	24.9 (31%)
Mass transit interstate transfer funds	−60.0 (−31%)	−25.1 (−19%)	−66.9 (−63%)	−152.9 (−79%)
Small-cities community development block grant	0.8 (3%)	4.0 (15%)	−4.0 (−13%)	0.8 (3%)

BOSTON			
Funding Levels	1981	1982	1983	1984
---	---	---	---	---
Massachusetts Bay Transportation Authority				
Capital grants	77.0	84.5	80.2	95.0
Interstate transfers	190.0	121.0	107.0	40.0
Operating assistance[g]	29.3	26.2	23.2	21.3
Assisted housing				
Modernization grants	9.0	15.2	17.7	7–10[a]
Operating subsidies	—	17.9	21.4	23.1
Community development block grant	26.1	25.8	23.3	22.9
Urban development action grants	21.6	13.6	3.9	25.3[a]

Funding Changes	1981–82	1982–83	1983–84	1981–84
Massachusetts Bay Transportation Authority				
Capital grants	−7.5 (−10%)	−4.3 (−5%)	14.8 (19%)	18.0 (23%)
Interstate transfers	−69.0 (−36%)	−14.0 (−12%)	−67.0 (−63%)	−150.0 (−80%)
Operating assistance	−3.1 (−11%)	−3.0 (−11%)	−1.9 (−8%)	−8.0 (−27%)
Assisted housing				
Modernization grants	6.2 (69%)	2.5 (−16%)	−10.7 (−60%)	−2.0 (−22%)
Community development block grant	−0.3 (−1%)	−2.5 (−10%)	−0.4 (−2%)	−3.2 (−12%)
Urban development action grants	−8.0 (−37%)	−9.7 (−71%)	21.4 (549%)	3.7 (17%)

its previous failure to maintain adequate living conditions for its tenants. The receiver's administration has enjoyed excellent relations with HUD. It has been given substantial amounts of discretionary "modernization" funds to renovate its buildings—$9.0 million in 1981, $15.2 million in 1982, $17.7 million in 1983, and an anticipated $7–$10 million in 1984. The BHA has also enjoyed increasing amounts of operating subsidies; its allocation has gone from $17.9 million in 1982, to $21.4 million in 1983, to about $23 million in 1984. (Data on operating subsidies for 1981 are unavailable.)

Replacement

In several key capital grant programs—wastewater treatment, highways, transit, and assisted housing—Massachusetts has chosen to replace or augment federal funds. Because of its weak fiscal condition, however, Boston generally has not been able to replace lost federal aid for capital programs.

For the wastewater treatment construction program, the state has approved an increase in its share of project financing from 15 to 35 percent to eliminate any disincentives that might arise from the reduction of the federal matching rate from 75 to 55 percent. Since the federal government, moreover, will no longer pay planning and design expenses on an advance basis, the state has approved a program that finances those costs, subject to reimbursement if and when federal funding for construction is secured.

Although the state did not initially replace funds for highway programs, it decided to piggyback an increase in its own gasoline tax when the federal tax increased as a result of the Surface Transportation Assistance Act of 1982. This money went to the state's highway trust fund, which finances road construction in much the same way as its federal counterpart.

In the mass transit field, federal cuts were not the only problem confronting the state's regional transit authorities. Rising costs were increasing the authori-

---

SOURCES FOR TABLE 7.3: Commonwealth of Massachusetts, *Analysis of the Proposed Fiscal 1985 Budget of the USA* and interviews with state and local officials.

NOTES FOR TABLE 7.3: [a] Projected funding.
[b] Includes interstate highway construction, as well as repair, replacement, and maintenance grants.
[c] Includes federal highway aid for primary, secondary, and urban highways, and grants for bridge construction, hazard elimination, and railroad crossings.
[d] Section 3 mass transit grants.
[e] Includes $65 million of section 3 funds and approximately $41 million from the capital portion of section 9 funds.
[f] Includes $4 million in jobs act funds.
[g] Section 5 funds for federal fiscal years 1981–83 and section 9 operating funds for federal fiscal year 1984.

ties' deficits at the same time that the state's Proposition 2 1/2 had greatly constrained the ability of cities and towns to subsidize service. The Massachusetts
Bay Transit Authority (MBTA), as usual, was in the deepest trouble—with
an escalating deficit, labor troubles, and service cuts. Under legislation adopted
in the early 1970s, the state already paid 50 percent of the MBTA's operating
deficit. The governor and legislature now chose to assume a larger proportion
of the deficit (58 percent in state fiscal year 1983 and 67 percent in state fiscal
year 1984) for all of its regional transit authorities. As part of the deal, the
MBTA adopted a fare increase.

Massachusetts also took steps to replace and augment federal funding for assisted housing. It increased spending for its own elderly housing program from
$7.2 million in state fiscal year 1982, to $9.4 million in state fiscal year 1983,
with additional money available in the following year. Its rental assistance
spending increased from $14.8 million in federal fiscal year 1982, to $18.4 million in federal fiscal year 1983, to an expected $21.5 million in 1984. More-
over, late in 1983, in response to the federal housing and urban-rural recovery
act's change in the section 8 construction programs, the state launched a new
"shallow" subsidy program to provide production incentives to developers of
mixed-income housing. To finance many of these housing programs, the state
authorized a $197 million bond issue in 1983, to be used over several years.
This bond issue was larger than the $178 million authorized in 1980.

Boston's precarious fiscal condition as a result of Proposition 2 1/2 precluded
replacing lost community development or EDA funds. In the initial years, in
fact, the city's own budget slashing often had the effect of compounding the federal cuts. Funds for street resurfacing and reconstruction, for example, were
drastically reduced. Such fiscal stringency had political impacts, though. During the 1983 mayoral campaign, the major candidates to succeed outgoing
Mayor Kevin H. White, including Raymond Flynn, the ultimate winner,
pledged to redirect city priorities toward neighborhood development. Proposals
for "linkage," by which developers would contribute to a fund for neighborhood
projects as a condition of being permitted to engage in downtown development,
were widely debated during the campaign by both mayoral and city council
candidates. The Flynn administration is seeking a framework for implementing a linkage policy, despite claims that it will merely discourage downtown
development.

To compensate for the loss of housing subsidy funds, the city's Neighborhood Development and Employment Agency (NDEA) joined with several private civic organizations in 1982 to form the Boston Housing Partnership, which
has raised $2.5 million to subsidize low-income housing.

Administrative, Policy, and Regulatory Issues

At the state level, capital grants have been connected to several major administrative and policy questions: management and allocation of the small-cities portion of the community development block grant program (CDBG), creation of Massbank and a regional water and sewer agency, and financing for two massive transportation projects in Boston. In Boston government, major change has come in management of the CDBG and UDAG programs and of the public housing authority.

At the state level, the principal administrative innovation associated with capital programs has come in the small cities community development block grant, a program for which state government has had no previous responsibility. Making use of its new authority, the state partially reshaped the program to suit its own sense of development priorities. Change was not abrupt, however.

Officials in the state Executive Office of Communities and Development, who were given authority over the program, sought out communities that had never participated in the community development program. To encourage communities with few grantsmanship skills, the state instituted a very simple pre-application procedure aimed at eliciting indications of need rather than well-developed project proposals. Where need seemed most pressing, the state provided technical assistance in preparing full-scale proposals. Programmatically, the state established four categories of general community development projects: housing and neighborhood revitalization; economic and commercial revitalization; comprehensive community development; and critical community needs. A few further changes were made in the second year.

The Dukakis administration gave high priority during 1984 to improving the state's ability to maintain its physical infrastructure. Two institutional initiatives were central to its plans. The key element was a proposal for a Massachusetts Development Bank—or "Massbank"—which the administration expected to help finance infrastructure projects, many of which would also be supported by federal capital grants. In the governor's proposal, Massbank's bonds would be repaid by new business taxes; some current business taxes would be reformed in compensation. The other proposal was to make an independent agency out of the water and sewer division of the Metropolitan District Commission (MDC), a state agency that provides various services for communities in the Boston region. This arrangement would make it easier to finance and manage needed water supply and wastewater treatment projects.

Because of opposition from some business sectors, especially high-tech firms, Massbank ran into political trouble; but the water and sewer authority was created by the legislature.

Another highly visible political battle—in this case between Massachusetts and the Reagan administration—was waged over federal financing of two massive transportation projects. During the first Dukakis administration (1975–78), the state sought federal funds to make the Central Artery, a key stretch of elevated highway through downtown Boston, into an underground route—a plan that would open prime land for development near the business district, make waterfront property more accessible and hence more valuable, and improve the city's aesthetics. Opponents attacked this project as frightfully wasteful because of its high costs. The King administration (1979–83) sought to kill the Central Artery proposal in favor of a plan that the Dukakis administration had vehemently opposed—a third tunnel under the Boston harbor. This project was intended to reduce traffic congestion and contribute to the region's economic development but was opposed by many neighborhood groups near the construction sites.

Each plan was priced at more than $1 billion and was supposed to be financed from the same pool of interstate highway funds. Each plan had enthusiastic partisans and vigorous opponents. When the second Dukakis administration took office in 1983, it proposed a compromise: construction of both projects, assuming that federal funds could be secured. The Reagan administration opposed funding, partly on procedural grounds raised by the Department of Transportation and partly because the congressional godfather of the request for additional funds was the administration's nemesis, Speaker of the House Thomas P. O'Neill, who represents most of Boston and Cambridge. The resulting controversy tied up the federal fiscal year 1985 highway authorization in congressional wrangling.

In Boston, there have been substantial changes in several major capital program areas; but while federal funding and policy changes have contributed to these developments, city policy and other pressures have also been significant causal factors.

The most sweeping change came in conjunction with slashes in employment and training funds. When federal job training and community development programs were at their peak funding, Boston had two agencies to run these programs: the Employment and Economic Policy Administration (EEPA) and the Neighborhood Development Agency (NDA). With sharp cutbacks in federal manpower funds and scandal in NDA over corruption and patronage appointments, Mayor White merged the two agencies in 1982 into a new Neighborhood Development and Employment Agency (NDEA) under a nonpolitical administrator with great experience in federal programs. With 173 employees, the new agency had almost 100 fewer staff than its two predecessors combined. In 1983, the Office of Housing, which had functioned as an arm of the mayor's office, was also brought into NDEA. This office had already dropped from a peak of 200 employees to 100 before the merger—and only 70 were brought into NDEA.

Several regulatory issues between HUD and the city have affected the community development block grant program in recent years. In 1981, HUD withheld $13 million of Boston's community development allocation because the city failed to meet fair housing guidelines. The city council, which balked at passing fair housing legislation, ultimately approved such an ordinance in 1982, which won the release of half of the impounded funds. The rest was released later after a report was completed on minority groups' neighborhood-by-neighborhood housing needs and possible solutions to their problems.

Another regulatory question was tied up with the battle between Mayor White and the city council over how much community development money would be used for human services. The administration wanted to commit only $1.5 million, while the council wanted to spend $3.5 million and designate the recipients. Partly in connection with this dispute, HUD granted Boston a waiver from the 10 percent limit on service spending for federal fiscal years 1982 and 1983.

National regulatory changes in the community development program have had mixed effects in Boston. In 1982, when under HUD's simplified application procedures the city produced a basic statement of objectives for the community development block grant program, rather than the former detailed application, city council members suspected the White administration of trying to conceal political tricks. The city administration has exceeded the minimal citizen participation requirements, holding a single citywide hearing and then a half dozen neighborhood hearings in conjunction with the city council. NDEA staff acknowledged the diminished paperwork and increased flexibility that has resulted from the relaxation of targeting requirements. As a policy matter, however, NDEA continues to target funds on low-income areas of the city.

Among Boston's other capital grants, the urban development action grant (UDAG) program has taken a sharp turn in policy in recent years. Initially, the city had used UDAGs almost exclusively for economic development. Beginning in 1982, however, the city began to use UDAGs for housing projects. At that time, officials developed a package of nine housing proposals, which has been the UDAG agenda since then. Four of these have been approved and the last five housing UDAGs, including a massive $21 million project for the Columbia Point section, have been submitted to HUD in 1984. Administratively, Boston's success in securing UDAGs has led HUD to insist on a "uniform management policy," which subjects the city to more detailed administrative requirements than previously.

At the Boston Housing Authority (BHA), the court-appointed receiver/administrator (who has been on the job since 1980) had made major strides in improving conditions in the physically deteriorating and poorly administered public housing agency. His reformist management team has had several goals: physical reconstruction and improved physical maintenance, development of BHA management capacity, and creation of strong tenant groups to build a sense of community in BHA developments. Both the federal and state governments have committed substantial amounts of discretionary capital funds to the BHA's reconstruction efforts. Moreover, the BHA's receiver/administrator has secured a number of significant regulatory concessions from HUD, to which he assigns much credit for making change possible. HUD has permitted the BHA to hire additional staff for construction management and to use some new construction money for making improvements in existing structures. Overall, the receiver/administrator has had excellent access to top policymakers in HUD and feels that they have given strong support to BHA reform.

New Program Initiatives

JOB TRAINING PARTNERSHIP ACT

The Dukakis administration, having made a strong campaign pledge to promote economic development, took office three months into federal fiscal year 1983, the transition year for job training programs authorized by the Job Training Partnership Act (JTPA). The new administration was quite comfortable with the changes in federal manpower programs, although definitely not with the level of appropriations. To guide the state's JTPA program, the governor appointed as associate secretary of economic affairs the executive director of the Boston Private Industry Council (PIC) who had earned a favorable reputation for working with both government and industry groups in managing the private-sector job training programs that had been authorized by the Comprehensive Employment and Training Act (CETA).

State implementation of JTPA required several steps. First, state officials, continuing a process begun in the waning months of the King administration, worked on state policy guidelines for JTPA, including interpretations of federal law and state decisions about planning processes, eligibility, and participant cost levels.

An early step was the governor's appointment of a state Job Training Coordinating Council (JTCC), prescribed by the national legislation, to advise the governor on employment and training policy and to work toward coordinating job training efforts with the diverse range of public manpower activities, including the employment service, public assistance, vocational education, and economic development programs.

The JTCC actively advised the governor about delineating the service delivery areas (SDAs) that would run the JTPA program. Under CETA, the state had twenty-two prime sponsors, plus the balance-of-state program with twelve subgrantees. Massachusetts ultimately created fifteen SDAs, after consultations with local government and business leaders. Deciding which communities ought to be placed together in an SDA proved a delicate task because of political rivalries, disagreements about what constituted relevant job markets, and the inevitable economic and social heterogeneity of some SDAs.

Another key task was the naming of each SDA's private industry council. With the chairperson and majority representation from the private sector, the PICs were intended to be the principal vehicle for business community involvement in JTPA. Members could also come from educational institutions, the employment service, community-based organizations, rehabilitation centers, and economic development agencies. At the state level, the Dukakis administration developed criteria for naming the local officials who, in turn, nominated PIC members.

By federal law, PICs are independent from local government and have their own budget of federal funds. (In the transition year, however, they got only $40,000—half the expected amount.)

The PICs and local governments have joint responsibility for developing a job training plan in each jurisdiction and submitting it to the governor for approval. The actual staff work of developing this plan may be done by local government, the PIC, both together, or a third party. These plans must identify organizations and agencies that will deliver job training services, identify the pool of potential service recipients, develop procedures and criteria for selecting participants, and prepare budgets.

In Massachusetts, early relationships between the PICs and local governments in the SDA were sometimes rocky—with confusion and conflict resulting from uncertainty about the working division of power under JTPA and the difficulty of jointly planning new operating programs. State officials sought to play a mediating role, so that effective collaborations could develop, but they ultimately had the governor's authority to intervene as an inducement to the parties to cooperate.

The number of people enrolled in programs under JTPA is far fewer than had been served by CETA. Planned enrollments for 1984 (12,750) were 81 percent less than the number enrolled in 1980 (67,541)—and 42 percent less than the 1983 estimated enrollment (22,000). State officials believe that the profile of JTPA participants is roughly similar to that under CETA, but suspect that some "creaming"—enrollment of a less disadvantaged eligible population— has taken place as a result of JTPA's emphasis on on-the-job training and elimination of participant stipends.

The regulatory relationship between the state and federal government has generally been smooth because the state has far greater latitude to develop policy for JTPA than it did for CETA. However, given its minimal oversight and monitoring role, the U.S. Department of Labor has been reluctant to provide direction to or even answer questions from the state about statutory interpretations. In a few instances, the state has issued policy directives only to have these subsequently contradicted by DOL's regional office. State officials expect that federal regulation will increase as time passes.

Conclusion

Massachusetts' responses to the Reagan domestic program varies among the three categories of grants. In the entitlement programs, Massachusetts has largely ratified federal cuts—permitting individuals to be dropped from the AFDC, Medicaid, and food stamp rolls, accepting altered eligibility regulations, and calculating benefits less generously. Nonetheless, the state continued to maintain a generous level of welfare benefits relative to most other states. The constituencies supporting generous social welfare benefits have been strong enough—in the legislature and in supporting the candidacy of Governor Dukakis—to secure some partial replacement funding. Thus, the state has increased its AFDC standard of need, increased clothing allowances, and accepted shifts in Medicaid costs from the federal government to the state.

In the operating programs, which mainly support human services programs, Massachusetts has chosen to replace greater proportions of federal budget cuts. It has replaced and augmented federal funds for social services and maternal and child health and has partially replaced money for school desegregation aid, community health centers, and drug, alcoholism, and mental health programs.

To some degree, this reflects a continued supportive climate of opinion in the Massachusetts electorate for programs that have apparently lost some of their national support. It also reflects, however, the effective organization and political mobilization of program constituencies in Massachusetts. These constituencies include service recipients, but also, even more importantly, service *providers*: doctors, social workers, mental health workers, schoolteachers, and the like have been extremely effective in lobbying the state legislature, where a

strong structure of party leadership facilitates interest group bargaining over legislation and budgets. The executive branch has been quite responsive, too,
even under Governor King, a fiscal and social conservative, and especially under Governor Dukakis, who was returned to office with the strong backing of
these interest groups. It is not insignificant that one of the few operating grants
not partially replaced by the state was the community services block grant,
where political conflict among different potential recipients apparently prevented an effective defense against the impact of the federal cuts.

The greatest degree of replacement, however, has come in capital programs.
Massachusetts has made major new commitments in several areas. It has increased from 15 to 35 percent the state match for wastewater treatment construction grants, so that the municipal share would not go up. It also has provided up-front financing for project planning and design so that the federal
policy of reimbursing such expenditures out of construction funds would not
create disincentives for municipalities to undertake projects. In highway programs, the state has piggybacked an increase in its own gasoline tax to raise
money for the state's highway trust fund. In support of regional mass transit
agencies, which were stung by rising costs and declining federal operating subsidies, the state has increased its share of deficit financing from 50 to 65 percent.
And, to make up for cuts in assisted housing programs, the state has expanded
several of its own programs and floated a major new bond issue.

An explanation for this commitment to capital programs must take account
of several factors. In Massachusetts, as is apparently true more widely, the public is more receptive to such expenditures than to most other kinds of government spending. Many of these programs can be publicly promoted and justified
as economic development investments; and the national press has transformed
the dreary subject of "public works" into the politically sexy "infrastructure" issue. But the climate of opinion is only one factor supporting capital programs.
They also enjoy significant interest group backing. Whenever potential construction projects are involved, there is tangible support from a politically powerful industry—contractors and suppliers, on one side, and construction trades
unions, on the other. Municipal governments, which pay substantial sums annually to support regional transit and water and sewer authorities, have also lobbied in favor of the state's commitment to capital programs. And various environmental groups have supported expenditures for transit and wastewater
treatment. Investments in assisted housing have a different character from other
capital programs, but they have long been a priority concern of the state's so-
cial-welfare constituencies.

Boston's response to federal cuts has been dictated primarily by its continuing fiscal woes. The reductions in property taxation mandated by Proposition

2 1/2 have left the city with insufficient resources even to maintain the previous level of city-supported services, let alone to replace federal grant cuts. Boston was left with no alternative but to ratify federal cuts—and, in some circumstances, it has compounded the cuts with reductions of its own.

FEDERAL-STATE RELATIONS

Block Grants

It is in the policy areas covered by new block grants that federal-state relations have changed most profoundly as a result of the Reagan administration's domestic program. In nearly every case, the block grants have enhanced state influence relative to the federal government's over the distribution of grant funds and policy formation.

The state's increased influence derives from several sources. First, some categorical grants that previously went directly from the federal government to local governments or nonprofit agencies have been folded into block grants that the state controls. In these instances—for example, the community service and small-cities community development block grant programs—the state has established new administrative staffs and developed procedures to give it the management capacity to run them. Second, some categorical grants that had been restricted to relatively narrow purposes, such as those incorporated into the elementary and secondary education block grant, have become part of the general pool of funds in the new block grants. Third, the state has acquired greater authority to determine who receives federal funds and how much they get. This is accomplished either by the state's discretionary distribution of project-grant funds (e.g., through a competitive RFP process as in the case of the maternal and child health or the alcohol, drug abuse, and mental health block grants) or by the state's writing of an allocation formula to govern distribution, as in the case of the education and community services block grants. Fourth, the state has been given authority to write regulations for some of these programs. And, finally, the state has enhanced responsibility for program monitoring and evaluation.

Massachusetts' state government has taken varying degrees of advantage of these sources of influence. Where necessary, it has quickly established the bureaucratic capacity to assume new management responsibilities, as it did in creating new offices to run the small-cities community development block grant (CDBG) and community services block grant programs. The state has also asserted its new influence over fund distribution by setting up RFP processes or writing allocation formulas. In practice, however, the state has used this authority sparingly. It has redistributed federal aid geographically (away from Boston, more widely among other communities) in several instances—but not radically. It has been even less inclined to redistribute funds programmatically (although several grants had statutory restrictions on such redistribution). For example, the small-cities CDBG program and the maternal and child health program have been altered in relatively minor ways. Similarly, the state has made relatively few changes in program regulations, despite its enhanced freedom to do so. Moreover, new program monitoring authority generally has not been used aggressively.

Such restraint reflects several facts. First, the state's new authority is not unlimited. In some cases, the reconciliation act phased in state discretion over several years as a way to protect preexisting program priorities. Second, the change of state administrations after a bitter 1982 campaign has probably slowed state government's assertion of authority over some programs. The new administration has taken time to put its policy makers in place and to familiarize them with the issues facing their departments. Third, the state has moved slowly in some instances so that it can establish orderly management processes before attempting to alter policy in major ways. And, fourth, the state has been cautious in asserting its policy-making influence in order to see whether Washington will issue statutory interpretations that might overturn state decisions.

Other Programs

The state's influence relative to the federal government's has not been equally strengthened in some other program areas. For the entitlement programs, relations in the AFDC and food stamps programs remain more or less as they were; program changes were achieved by a traditional style of federal regulation. In the Medicaid program, the state has become a more active manager and architect of cost control strategies; but its influence relative to the federal government's remains roughly the same.

The story is similar for the capital programs. Except for the small-cities community development block grant program, where the administrative role of the state and its potential program influence are greatly enhanced, the state has not secured significant new authority over program operations.

STATE-LOCAL RELATIONS

The Reagan domestic program has had mixed effects on the relations between the Massachusetts state government and its municipalities and special authorities. The impacts are least significant in the entitlement programs. Because all of these programs are state administered, local government has had no direct involvement in the changes. (It is possible that federal aid cutbacks have increased demands for human services on local governments and nonprofit providers.) The impacts are most significant in the block grant policy areas (which involve most of the operating programs, plus the small-cities grants). State authority and influence have increased, which means that local governments must now orient their policy processes at least somewhat more to take account of the state's preferences and priorities. That has been painfully apparent to Boston, which has lost program funds as a result of the state's distribution of health and community service funds. The effect is also apparent where small communities that had no federal links (at least for these programs) are being drawn into the grant system—for example, in the small-cities program and the elementary and secondary education block grant. Nonetheless, this effect must be measured against the fact that these communities already have extensive administrative and regulatory relations with state government in other policy areas.

Although the capital grant programs have not enhanced state authority directly, the fact that state government has chosen to replace substantial portions of lost federal funds has increased the state's influence with local governments and special agencies. For instance, the state extracted significant changes in management practices from the MBTA in return for its pledge of payment for a higher percentage of the transit system's operating deficit. The potential for greater state influence is also present in the wastewater construction grant program since the state now provides planning and design grants and pays 35 (instead of 15) percent of project costs.

One may reasonably conclude, therefore, that the Reagan domestic program has strengthened the state's policy relations to local governments in Massachusetts. These effects are significant, if not dramatic.

But such facts must be placed in perspective if one wishes to understand the larger context of state-local relations in Massachusetts. Forces other than federal grant programs have been making Massachusetts government relatively stronger. The reorganization of state agencies implemented in the early 1970s, and particularly the adoption of a strong cabinet secretary system, continues to have ramifications for state-local relations. More recently, the restrictions on local finances imposed by Proposition 2 1/2 have reinforced the relative advantages that state government has always had in raising money. It has used that money to expand local aid substantially in recent years—a fact that increases its leverage over local policy processes. The dynamics of state-local relations in Massachusetts are affected, but not dominated, by changing federal aid policies.

New York

SARAH F. LIEBSCHUTZ AND IRENE LURIE

ew York, virtually from its colonial origins, has represented the "composite nationality"[1] characteristic of the nation: "a pluralistic political system, a diversified economy, and a heterogeneous society."[2] However, New York's generosity to its "huddled masses"[3]—captured in the poetry inscribed on the Statue of Liberty in New York Harbor—has long made it distinctive among states. These traits of politics, economics, demography, and attitude form the framework within which New York has responded to changes in federal aid initiated by the Reagan administration.

Long a leader in the nation's industry and commerce, New York—the most populous state until 1960—has commanded much attention for its political institutions and traditions. Among them is a bipartisan commitment to high government expenditures, high taxes, and state-mandated public service programs. This commitment flows from a liberal political culture, one that values the role of the public sector in aiding those in need.

New York is known also for its political institutions, particularly the tradition since the 1920s of a powerful governor, dominant in the areas of fiscal planning and control. Although the role of the legislature has been changing in important ways in recent years, it is still secondary to that of the governor.

The authors would like to acknowledge the valuable assistance of Karen A. Reixach and Richard W. Small in the preparation of this chapter. They would also like to express their gratitude to the many officials in Albany, New York City, and Rochester who generously shared their information and insights. Finally, they would like to acknowledge the ongoing personal support and encouragement of Sanford J. Liebschutz and Thad W. Mirer.
    [1] David M. Ellis, *New York: State and City* (Ithaca, N.Y.: Cornell University Press, 1979), p. 50.
    [2] Ibid.
    [3] Emma Lazarus, "The New Colossus," in Ann Stanford, ed., *The Women Poets in English* (New York: McGraw-Hill, 1972), p. 141.

The state's relationship with its local governments is another important factor in the framework of federalism. Although there are important differences among them—whether labeled as upstate/downstate or urban/rural divisions—Albany's role is clearly central in constraining (or aiding) policy making, administration, and financing in the state's cities, towns, villages, counties, and school districts.

Finally, New York's difficult adjustment during the 1970s from high taxing, high spending policies to those designed to regain the state's competitive economic advantage must be noted. While the severe fiscal pressure on New York has ameliorated in recent years, it is not yet clear that the loss of population and jobs documented in the 1980 census has abated.

The following sections discuss in detail the major effects on New York State and the city of Rochester of federal policy to reduce resources and devolve decision making and program administration. The case study demonstrates how changes in federalism induced by the 1981 reconciliation act have buttressed the *activist interventionist* traditions of the New York State government. Decentralization of decision making from Washington to Albany has not resulted in decentralization from Albany to local governments. The pattern has been quite the reverse: Reductions in federal funding under Reagan have resulted in greater state centralization in the Empire State.

The Setting for the Reagan Domestic Program

THE GOVERNOR

The governor of New York is widely perceived as a powerful state executive, both because of the formal powers conferred on him by the state constitution and the exercise of those powers by such formidable incumbents as Al Smith, Franklin Roosevelt, Herbert Lehman, Thomas Dewey, Averill Harriman, and Nelson Rockefeller. The governor's formal powers derive from amendments in the 1920s establishing an executive budget system, providing for a four-year term with no restrictions on the number of terms, and for the item veto over budget legislation. The governor's authority and appointive power extend to all but three departments in the executive branch.

Although state budget processes have become slightly more complicated in recent years, budget policy in New York is still largely controlled by the governor and monitored by the Division of the Budget (DOB) in the governor's office. DOB has evolved since the late 1950s as the most powerful agency in the state bureaucracy, engaging in sophisticated economic forecasting, monitoring national economic and federal budget trends, and exercising day-to-day control over expenditures and fiscal affairs in every state agency. The Omnibus Budget Reconciliation Act of 1981 was enacted at a time when Governor Hugh Carey, a Democrat, was openly hostile to the domestic policies of the Reagan administration. Thus, the tradition of strong executive control was important in that the governor's DOB was in a central position to assess the early effects on New York of the changes in federal policy, and to delay implementation of those programs that were viewed as detrimental to the state.[4]

THE LEGISLATURE

The New York Legislature—a bicameral body of 150 Assembly members and 61 senators—has been described as "dominated by the governor."[5] While the governor's formal budget prerogatives and history itself would seem to support that assertion, the legislature has become more assertive since 1981 as a consequence of both statutory and judicial actions.

Since 1846, the state constitution has stipulated that "[n]o money shall ever be paid out of the State Treasury or any of its funds, or any of the funds under its managements, except in pursuance of an appropriation by law (Article VII, Section 7)." However, because the term "State Treasury" was never defined and because federal aid was not a prominent revenue source for New York until the 1970s, the legislature played a very limited role in appropriating federal aid. That has changed as a result of a court challenge initiated by Warren Anderson and John Marchi, majority leader and finance committee chairman, respectively, of the State Senate, against the state comptroller, Edward Regan. In July 1981, the state's highest court ruled in *Anderson v. Regan* that the legislature was empowered to appropriate all federal aid to the state. While the legislature exercised its newly affirmed power cautiously at first—deferring almost entirely to Governor Carey's policies on the cuts and block grants contained in the reconciliation act—it did begin to assert its own priorities over new or increased federal funds to New York.[6]

At the same time that *Anderson v. Regan* was concluded, the legislature enacted legislation creating a new accounting and financial reporting system for the state. Known as GAAP (generally accepted accounting principles), the leg-

[4] For elaboration of this point, see Sarah F. Liebschutz, Irene Lurie, and Richard W. Small, "How State Responses Confound Federal Policy," *Publius* 13, no. 2 (1983):51–63.

[5] Eugene J. Gleason and Joseph F. Zimmerman, "New York," *Public Administration Review* 36, no. 6 (1976):92.

[6] Sarah F. Liebschutz and Irene Lurie, "Evolution in Federalism: The Reagan Program and Legislative Appropriation of Federal Grants in New York," *Journal of Public Budgeting and Finance* 4, no. 2 (Summer 1984):24–41.

islation is expected to assist the legislature in its oversight of all state expenditures, including those funded with federal revenues.[7]

Political Culture

New York's political culture is basically liberal, demonstrating compassion through state spending and state mandating policies. Spending for the needy remains, at great cost to the state, among the most generous in the nation. The multibillion dollar public higher education system "still stands as a monument to Republican Governor Nelson Rockefeller and continues to receive strong support in budget battles from the conservative Republican Senate Majority Leader, Warren Anderson."[8] Laws mandating special education services, preventive mental health services to families in crisis, protective and health care services for children and the elderly are, in most cases, more comprehensive than their federal counterparts. Equity has also always been a priority concern in New York. Distributional equity ("something for everyone") is evident, for instance, in debates over resource and program allocation between upstate and downstate. Redistributional equity is seen in efforts to target state aid on the neediest individual or areas. While equity is not, of course, a concern unique to New York public officials, the state's diversity of population and geographical areas does complicate the decisionmaking process.

Current manifestations of big state government had their beginning in the early years of the twentieth century, when the

> trend [toward regulation] was felt in New York State, in the daily workings of the state government, earlier than in most places and long before price ceilings or commodity and business controls were thought to be within the power of the federal government. New York has had the most effective . . . public-utility regulation of any state in the Union; it was a leader in setting up factory inspection and tenement-house laws, in fixing mandatory workmen's compensation for injuries. These things led inevitably to big government in New York before it was established in the nation."[9]

FISCAL SETTING

New York's liberal political culture is reflected in the level of state and local expenditures and taxes. Three decades ago, before the rapid growth in the size of

---

[7] Ibid.

[8] Liebschutz, Lurie, and Small, "How State Responses Confound Federal Policy," p. 53.

[9] Warren Moscow, *Politics in the Empire State* (New York: Knopf, 1984), pp. 8–9.

the state-local sector, New York governments' expenditures and taxes per capita were the highest in the nation.[10] But income in the state was also high; the tax burden as measured by the ratio of revenues to personal income was lower than in many states, exceeding the national average by only 16 percent.[11] Beginning in the mid-1960s, growth in spending, especially for assistance to low-income people and areas, exceeded the growth of the state's depressed economy. By 1975, not only were taxes per capita the highest in the nation, but the tax burden was also the highest, 36 percent above the national average.[12]

For the state government, the era of rising spending in the face of a stagnant economy came to a close in the fiscal crisis of 1975, which began in New York City and soon cast doubt on the state's financial solvency as well. "The days of wine and roses are over," declared Governor Hugh Carey in his 1975 inaugural address. The new governor argued that high taxes were driving business out of the state, thereby contributing to the deterioration in the tax base and the state's financial difficulties, and urged the legislature to provide relief. Hence the fiscal crisis served the same function as the constitutional and statutory tax and expenditure limitations instituted by many other states. It encouraged New York to lower income tax rates and to cut back the growth of its spending, and heralded a new concern for economy in government.

The reduction in personal and business taxes, combined with the slow growth in the tax base, meant that revenues rose by less than the rate of inflation between 1975 and 1981. Expenditure remained essentially unchanged in real terms, producing deficits and the need for over $3 billion in short-term borrowing in 1981. Thus the budget was extremely tight as the state planned its response to the reconciliation act in mid-1981. The governor reluctantly proposed an increase in the sales tax and some smaller taxes to correct some long-standing problems facing the state. Compensating for the federal cuts would have required increases in income tax rates, and a reversal of efforts to lower a tax burden that remained the highest of any state, 40 percent above the national average in 1981.[13] The option of raising broad-based taxes, including the sales tax, had few supporters in the legislature and was rejected.

[10] U.S. Advisory Commission on Intergovernmental Relations, *Significant Features of Fiscal Federalism*, 1981–82 edition (Washington, D.C.: Government Printing Office, April 1983), table 23.

[11] U.S. Advisory Commission on Intergovernmental Relations, *Significant Features*, 1981–82, table 22.2.

[12] U.S. Advisory Commission on Intergovernmental Relations, *Significant Features*, 1981–82, Table 22.2. Taxes are high by other measures as well. Tax effort, as measured by the ACIR's Representative Tax System Method, was the highest in the country in 1980. Table 29.

[13] U.S. Advisory Commission on Intergovernmental Relations, *Significant Features*, 1981–

By rejecting most of Carey's proposed tax increases, while adding to his proposed expenditures, the legislature compounded the effect of the recession and left his successor, Mario Cuomo, with the worst fiscal crisis since 1975. The deficit for the 1982–83 state fiscal year, combined with the deficit for state fiscal year 1983–84, beginning April 1983, was estimated at $1.8 billion, the largest in state history. Governor Cuomo's first task after taking office in January 1983 was to prepare an austerity budget, one that called for a 14,000 person reduction in the state workforce, few inflation adjustments, and deferred maintenance of capital. Cuts in federal aid received little attention; they were cited neither as a major cause of the deficit nor as a gap that needed to be filled with state funds.

New York's economic outlook grew considerably brighter during the latter part of 1983. While New York's recovery began later and was somewhat weaker than in the country as a whole, it gave Cuomo funds for proposing initiatives that would express his own mission as governor.

Changes in Federal Aid

While the Reagan domestic program has been hailed as stemming the growth of big government, and criticized for dismantling the New Deal, neither conclusion can be reached without close scrutiny of the changes it has produced in both federal spending and the authority accorded each level of government. The changes in spending are examined in this section, as well as the outlines of the accompanying institutional changes. The more subtle question of how much authority was in fact transferred from one level of government to another is addressed in the next section.

In state fiscal year 1980–81, just prior to the Reagan initiatives, federal grants to the New York State government amounted to $6.7 billion, financing 24 percent of state expenditures. Federal grants directly to localities amounted to $1.8 billion, or 5 percent of their expenditures.[14] These grants financed a slightly smaller share of total state and local spending than the average for all states, 20.0 compared with 22.3 percent, reflecting both the structure of federal matching formulas and the liberality of state and local unmatched spending. But the absolute level of grants per capita was $2,419 compared to the national

---

82, Table 22.2. The ratio is higher in Alaska, but most of the burden is not borne by state residents.

[14] U.S. Department of Commerce, Bureau of the Census, *Governmental Finances in 1980–81*, series GF81, no. 5 (Washington, D.C.: Government Printing Office, 1982), tables 5 and 13.

average of $1,790, reflecting in large part the needs of the state's low-income residents and state choices affecting the generosity of programs financed with federal assistance.[15]

AID TO NEW YORK STATE

The most significant changes in federal grants to the New York State government are listed in table 8.1. For a meaningful measure of these changes, actual grants should be compared to what they would have been without the Reagan program. While it is impossible to know this with certainty, grants would have had to grow by 6.1 percent between 1981 and 1982, and by 3.2 percent the following year, just to keep pace with inflation. Programs alleviating poverty would have had to grow by more to compensate for the 11 percent increase in poor persons in New York State between 1981 and 1983. With this perspective, how significant were the changes in federal aid over the 1981–84 period?

Looking across programs, some clear patterns emerge. Smaller programs—the new block grants—were generally cut by larger percentages than bigger programs. The greatest cuts occurred in 1982, with many programs receiving stable or increased funding in the following years. By 1983, funding increases exceeded decreases so that total federal grants in these programs were 7 percent greater than in 1981. The inflation rate was over 9 percent for these two years, implying that federal grants in real terms declined a little over 2 percent.

Another unmistakable pattern is that programs serving the poor, disadvantaged, and unemployed suffered the greatest real cuts. Despite the recession, which raised the need for cash and in-kind assistance, aid to families with dependent children (AFDC) grants declined in real terms while food stamp and Medicaid grants just kept pace with the rise in prices of food and medical care. Hence in all three programs, federal grants met a smaller share of the needs of the poor and near-poor. All of the block grants are designed to improve the plight of the disadvantaged, and they were cut substantially. The biggest cut, both absolutely and relatively, was for unemployed workers participating in job training programs authorized by the Comprehensive Employment and Training Act (CETA). Funds for programs whose benefits are spread more evenly among the entire population—highways, mass transit, and wastewater treatment—were either not cut significantly or were increased.

For the state government, the major institutional impact of the federal changes was its new role in administering the block grants and job training pro-

---

[15] U.S. Advisory Commission on Intergovernmental Relations, *Significant Features*, 1981–82, pp. 85 and 118.

Table 8.1. *Federal Aid to New York State, Federal Fiscal Years 1981–84 (dollars in millions)*

Program	1981	1982	1983	1984 est.
Entitlement Programs				
Aid to families with dependent children[a]	1,053.3	1,062.5	1,016.3	965.8
Medicaid	2,637.0	3,000.0	3,227.0	3,400.0
Food stamps	929.3	878.4	986.7	982.0
Operating Programs				
Low-income energy assistance block grant	223.1	237.8	250.6[b]	263.2[c]
Alcohol, drug abuse, mental health block grant	55.4	36.4	28.5[b]	28.5
Preventive health block grant	6.5	5.8	6.1	6.1
Maternal and child health block grant	28.8	23.8	31.1[b]	75.0
Education block grant[d]	54.6	31.2	31.6	31.6
Compensatory education[d]	261.4	273.7	313.6	349.8
Social services block grant	236.0	184.9	202.0[b]	209.0
Community services block grant	46.7	30.4	30.2[b]	28.6
Job training	489.0	252.0	230.3	194.9[e]
Capital Programs				
Highways	515.9	404.2	596.3	749.4
Mass transit				
Operating grants	199.4	171.6	138.9	138.9
Capital grants	520.7	353.7	640.1	568.0
Housing				
Public housing	165.4[f]	144.2[f]	243.8[g]	—[h]
Section 8	63.9	25.9	38.0	—[h]
Wastewater treatment[i]	268.1	252.7	271.4	281.4

NOTES: [a] Calendar year.
[b] Includes emergency jobs act supplement:
   Low-income energy assistance block grant: $12.8 million
   Alcohol, drug abuse, mental health block grant: $2.6 million
   Maternal and child health block grant: $7.7 million
   Social services block grant: $13.1 million
   Community services block grant: $1.6 million
[c] Includes mid-1984 supplement of $25.4 million.
[d] Rescission in 1981 cut federal funds below 1980 levels of $73.9 million for programs consolidated into the block grant and $255.0 million for compensatory education.
[e] October 1–June 30 transition year.
[f] Comprehensive Improvement Assistance Program (CIAP) funds only.
[g] CIAP and operating subsidy funds.
[h] Not available.
[i] Allocation to New York.

grams authorized by the Job Training Partnership Act (JTPA). In assuming responsibility for the block grants, the state moved with circumspection. Only three block grants were assumed in October 1981: the alcohol, drug abuse, and mental health block yielded a temporary financial advantage and was assumed voluntarily; the social services and low-income energy blocks, which required no immediate institutional rearrangements, were assumed mandatorily. The maternal and child health, preventive health, and education blocks were assumed in July 1982 and the community services block when it became mandatory in October 1982. New York has still not assumed the small-cities community development and primary care blocks.

AID TO ROCHESTER

For Rochester, the state's third largest city, federal changes created effects that varied according to whether aid was for entitlements, operating, or capital programs. Entitlement aid, as shown in table 8.2, increased after 1981, in reflection of growing numbers of local residents affected by the recession. But the increases in AFDC, food stamps, and Medicaid would have been even larger if not for reconciliation act changes, which made more than 1,000 of the city's near-poor ineligible for these entitlements. Federal aid for operating programs decreased after 1981, principally because of significant cuts in CETA and urban education assistance. Capital grants were larger two years after the reconciliation act, reflecting Rochester's success in obtaining urban development action grants (UDAG).

Rochester is typical of New York's central cities—except for New York City[16]—in its reliance on other local governments for provision of many basic services to city residents. Monroe County assumes sole responsibility for income maintenance, social services, and health care. Three special districts— the fiscally dependent city school district, Rochester Housing Authority, and Rochester Genesee Regional Transportation Authority, provide public education, public housing, and public transportation, respectively. Federal grants to Rochester and the four other governments, as shown in table 8.2, reflect these divisions of functional responsibility. Monroe County, in fact, accounted for

[16] For an analysis of the reliance of Rochester on other local governments for provision of services in a context of the city's fiscal stress, see Sarah F. Liebschutz, *Federal Aid to Rochester* (Washington, D.C.: The Brookings Institution, 1984), pp. 1–14. New York City, unlike other cities in the state and in the nation, directly administers and assumes the local costs for a wide range of welfare, health, social and education services. For an analysis of the contribution of these responsibilities to the New York City fiscal crisis in 1974–75, see Peter D. McClelland and Alan L. Magdovitz, *Crisis in the Making: The Political Economy of New York State Since 1945* (New York: Cambridge University Press, 1981), pp. 310–316.

Table 8.2. *Federal Aid to Rochester, Federal Fiscal Years 1981–84 (dollars in thousands)*

Program	1981	1982	1983	1984	Service Provider
Entitlement Programs					
Aid to families with dependent children[a]	20,504	24,342	23,917	22,163	Monroe County
Medicaid[a]	47,278	66,616	67,776	77,256	Monroe County
Food stamps[a]	17,529	17,304	22,692	—[b]	Monroe County
Operating Programs					
Low-income energy assistance block grant[a]	3,096	3,796	5,393	6,156	Monroe County
Alcohol, drug abuse, and mental health block grant	488[c]	252[c]	—[b]	—[b]	Monroe County
Preventive health block grant[a]	99	210	178	160	Monroe County
Maternal and child health block grant	326	212	202	167	Monroe County
Education block grant[d]	3,650	3,260	910	710	City School district
Compensatory education[d]	5,330	4,170	4,710	5,270	City School district
Social services block grant[a]	5,944	5,602	5,710	6,105[e]	Monroe County
Community services block grant[f]	1,389	1,208	813[e]	750	Action for a Better Community[g]
Job training	5,142	3,940	3,586	3,072[h]	Rochester[h]
Capital Programs					
Highway aid	310	1,356	1,180	—	Rochester
Mass transit					
Operating grants[i]	4,756	4,313	2,169	2,979	Regional Transit
Capital grants[i]	2,715	6,205	2,738	3,200	Authority
Housing					
Public housing	3,925[j]	5,744[j]	3,459[j]	2,350[k]	Rochester Housing
Section 8	4,578	4,527	4,697	5,035	Authority
Community development block grant	12,972	12,512	12,921[e]	10,870	Rochester
Urban development action block grants[a]	4,256	1,390	20,360	995[l]	Rochester

NOTES:
[a] Calendar year.
[b] Not available.
[c] Drug abuse grant only received.
[d] September 1–August 31 school year.
[e] Includes emergency jobs act supplement:
Community development block grant: $2,366,000
Community services block grant: $30,000
Social services block grant: $395,000
[f] Agency program year, February 1–January 31.
[g] Community action agency.
[h] Transition year, October 1–June 30.
[i] Authority fiscal year, April 1–March 31.
[j] Operating subsidy and community improvement assistance funds.
[k] Operating subsidy only.
[l] Awards for January to April only.

more than two-thirds of all federal aid allocated to these five local governments between 1981 and 1984.

The city school district was most severely hurt by the federal changes; its block grant allocation in 1984 was only one-fifth of the categorical aid it had received in 1981. Transportation and housing authorities both experienced decreases in federal operating subsidies.

Monroe County actually administered more federal aid in 1983 than in 1981. The major increase occurred in Medicaid (see table 8.2), reflecting the federal government's share of escalating costs associated with New York's generous coverage of benefits and clients. However, as counties are mandated by New York to share with the state the nonfederal costs of Medicaid and AFDC, county spending also increased.

The city government in Rochester was least directly affected by the reconciliation act changes. Federal aid under the Job Training Partnership Act was about $2 million less in 1984 than in 1982 under CETA, but funds for community development, through the block grant and UDAG, remained a solid source of support for the city's neighborhood conservation and economic development programs.

The State-Local Response and the Effects of the Grant Changes

President Reagan reduced financial aid with the promise that states would also be relieved from the burden of regulation and would thus be free to manage the cuts in the best interest of their citizens. The following section traces the experience in the state and the Rochester area with a selection of the programs affected by the Reagan changes, namely those that provide the clearest insights into the issues raised. The analysis covers the period in which most of the adjustments to these changes occurred, fall 1981 through spring 1984. While some of the programs that are not analyzed involve large amounts of federal funds, such as food stamps, low-income energy assistance, highway assistance, mass transit assistance, and wastewater treatment grants, the changes in their funding levels and structure raise issues that are peripheral to those of interest here.

Because we focus on intergovernmental relations, attention is limited to changes in federal grants to New York State governments. Excluded from the analysis are federal programs that make direct payments to individuals, such as Social Security and student loans, and federal expenditures in the state for wages, salaries, and procurement. Since New Yorkers were disproportionately burdened by cuts in direct federal payments, but benefited less than residents of many other states from the increase in defense spending, our focus on intergovernmental grants understates the negative impact of the Reagan program on state residents.[17]

AID TO FAMILIES WITH DEPENDENT CHILDREN

New York has earned a reputation for income maintenance programs that are generous in terms of both eligibility and benefit levels. The state's constitution, as interpreted by the courts, gives state government an affirmative duty to aid the needy.[18] All groups are eligible for assistance, with the state-local home relief program (HR) providing aid for the needy who are ineligible for a federally funded program. AFDC and HR benefits equal the full difference between countable income and a need standard that varies only by family size, plus actual shelter costs up to a maximum. The need standard, which is set by state legislation, and the maximum shelter allowance, which is set by state regulation, are the same for both programs. Furthermore, eligibility requirements and benefits are uniform throughout the state, with the exception of the shelter allowance maximum, which the state varies by county.

Until the 1975 fiscal crisis put a brake on the growth in benefit levels, New York's were among the highest in the country. In an effort to balance the budgets of the state and New York City, the need standard and shelter maximums were frozen despite the rapid rate of inflation. By 1981, benefits had fallen relative to several other states, but remained well above the national average.

Although AFDC and HR are administered by counties, both administration and financing have been increasingly centralized in recent years. Localities no longer have a role in setting policy concerning eligibility and benefit levels, and are permitted no discretion in applying state rules and regulations. Since 1982, all upstate counties have determined eligibility and benefits using computers located in Albany, further centralizing administration. A somewhat separate computerized management system is scheduled to be introduced into New York beginning in 1984. The state has historically shared the nonfederal cost of income maintenance programs equally with the counties, but it has assumed a greater financial role in the late 1970s and the 1980s.[19]

---

[17] U.S. Department of Commerce, Bureau of the Census, *Federal Expenditures by State for Fiscal Year 1981* (Washington, D.C.: Government Printing Office, February 1983).

[18] See *Tucker v. Toia* (1977) (400 N.Y.S. 2d 728) and cases cited therein.

[19] In state fiscal year 1978–79, the state granted fiscal relief to the counties by assuming the full cost of state supplementation to Supplemental Security Income (SSI), at an estimated cost of $110 million by state fiscal year 1983–84. In 1981, just prior to passage of the reconciliation act, AFDC benefits were increased by 15 percent of the need standard to adjust for inflation since the last increase in 1974. The nonfederal cost of this increase, estimated at $100 million in 1983–84, is also

New York's response to the reconciliation act is consistent with its tradition of liberal support for the poor. Despite Governor Carey's public statements that New York would not increase its own spending to compensate for the federal cuts, he took steps to protect three of the four groups removed from AFDC by the narrowing of categorical eligibility: students eighteen to twenty-one years of age; women three to six months pregnant with their first child; and families in need because a parent is on strike.[20] These three groups were picked up on state/local-funded home relief.

No other public assistance legislation has been enacted to compensate for the reconciliation act, and its mandatory provisions have been implemented with only minor delay. However, public advocates have succeeded in softening the impact of the federal changes somewhat through court action. *Ram v. Blum* liberalized regulations on earnings, and *Powers and Kipp v. Perales* ensured that monthly benefits always meet the full standard of need in that month (thus compensating for retrospective budgeting procedures that delay a grant increase for a month or two after a recipient suffers a wage cut).

The workfare provision of the reconciliation act—the option to mandate participation in a Community Work Experience Program (CWEP)—has not been embraced by New York. Since 1971, the state has had a workfare program for employable HR recipients, which assigns them to public or nonprofit agencies to work off the amount of their grant at the minimum or prevailing wage. But extending workfare to AFDC has met with both ideological opposition and administrative difficulties. It is viewed by state administrators and the Democratic-controlled Assembly as a punitive case-load control device and is opposed by labor unions concerned about the potential displacement of regular workers. The $25 limit on work-related expenses limits participation in the workfare program. Some county welfare departments have been reluctant to administer the program. Even in the counties that do offer the demonstration program, participation is limited primarily to two-parent welfare families or to female-headed families with older children, who do not require day care. The state's role has so far been limited to supervising a demonstration CWEP in those counties that want one, twenty-one so far.

While workfare is not state policy, the Cuomo administration recognizes that public support for welfare requires some effort to encourage recipients to work. The administration proposed, and the legislature enacted, a "comprehensive employment program" to enable more AFDC and HR recipients to

---

financed entirely by the state. New York State also increased its share of Medicaid costs, as described later in this chapter.

[20] New York restricted assistance to two-parent families deprived of the support of the "principal earner."

join the labor force. The program is an administrative mechanism to tap and coordinate the full range of employment services available to recipients. These services are pulled together under one planning umbrella so that a program can be developed to help each recipient achieve unsubsidized employment. A recipient may be placed in a work experience job, but only as a last resort if a private job, training program, or educational opportunity is unsuitable.

Effects on the Poor

Estimating the impact of all these changes on welfare dependency and costs, and on the poor themselves, is complicated by the increased need for welfare resulting from the recession. Between 1981 and 1983, the number of AFDC cases declined from 370,971 to an estimated 361,930, or by only 2.4 percent. Costs declined an estimated 3.5 percent. If not for the recession and a 15 percent benefit increase in July 1981, these declines would have been greater. In 1984, as the recession ended, costs dropped by about 5 percent. Outside of New York City, 4,599 cases or 4 percent were closed by the 150 percent gross income limit during its first seven months. Some unknown number were denied assistance due to the income limit. About 1 percent of the cases closed returned to the program in these initial seven months. [21]

A follow-up survey in Monroe County found that families who became ineligible for AFDC lost an average of $128 in monthly benefits, almost a fifth of their total money income, and that many lost food stamps and Medicaid as well. Fourteen months after termination, 82 percent of the former recipients were employed, nearly all full time, and their incomes were just slightly above the poverty line. But 25 percent of families terminated had received welfare at some time during the fourteen months and 15 percent were active cases at the end of the period. Nearly two-thirds of families said they experienced more hunger, nearly 40 percent said their children had lacked appropriate clothes, and an equal number said they had untreated medical problems. [22]

With the recovery, and the consequent rise in tax revenues, Governor Cuomo had resources for putting his own stamp on the state's welfare programs. His concern about homelessness and the quality of housing for the poor led to two steps. By administrative regulation he increased the maximum public assistance shelter allowance by an average of 25 percent, effective 1984. Shelter grants were thereby increased by $230 million, benefiting more than two-thirds

[21] New York State Department of Social Services, "Effects of Selected Program Changes on Public Assistance and Food Stamp Cases from January through July 1982," March 1983.

[22] Center for Governmental Research (CGR), *Cutting Welfare Benefits to Working Mothers* (Rochester, N.Y.: CGR, 1983).

of public assistance recipients, at a state-local cost of about $145 million. Cuomo also amended regulations to provide more liberal shelter allowances for families facing emergency housing situations, to facilitate the provisions of emergency housing for homeless people, and to improve the conditions of hotels and motels in which the homeless are temporarily housed.

The governor increased the shelter allowance maximum without involving counties in the decision-making process, even though they must finance over a quarter of the cost. While many counties were sympathetic to the increase, they complained that they were not asked for input and were not given details in advance. The increase was announced just after they had completed their budgets for 1984, immediately throwing them out of balance.

MEDICAID

New York maintains one of the most generous and comprehensive Medicaid programs in the nation, providing every optional benefit with the exception of chiropractic services. Like AFDC, eligibility and benefits are determined by the state, while until recently the nonfederal share of Medicaid costs has been divided almost equally between the state and the counties. As Medicaid costs ballooned during the 1970s, and became the largest single expense of county governments, the state came under increasing pressure to grant fiscal relief to the counties and to control costs. Hence, the stage was set for a greater state role even in the absence of the reconciliation act.

Fiscal relief was provided by two pieces of legislation. The Human Services Overburden Bill, passed in 1982, shifted roughly 25 percent of local Medicaid costs to the state. While Governor Carey supported this legislation in part as a way of helping localities deal with the Reagan cuts in human services programs, the issue of the state assuming part or all of the county Medicaid costs had been hotly debated for years prior to 1981. Under legislation passed in 1983, the state will eventually assume 80 percent of the nonfederal share of the cost of long-term care services (including services in nursing homes, personal care, home health, and home nursing). The nonfederal share of eligible costs of long-term care to the mentally disabled will be fully financed by the state. The impact of these changes has already been felt: the state share of nonfederal Medicaid costs grew from 50.7 percent in state fiscal year 1981–82 to an estimated 62.7 percent in 1984–85.

When New York and its counties assumed the full cost of cash assistance for the three groups terminated from AFDC, but picked up on state-local home relief, the full cost of their Medicaid was assumed as well. Consistent with this, the state has not taken advantage of its new discretion to limit services or the eligibility of the medically needy.

Efforts to control Medicaid costs have been made not by restricting eligibility and benefits, but as part of a comprehensive program to contain hospital reimbursements under all state and private health financing systems. After several years of deliberation and negotiation, legislation was passed in 1982 instituting a three-year experimental prospective payment system for allocating hospital costs among third-party payers including Medicaid. A new "ratio-of-costs-to-charges" approach allocates hospital cost to payers in proportion to the services actually provided, rather than as a flat-rate average per diem cost. Since Blue Cross patients tend to have shorter hospital stays than Medicaid patients while utilizing more expensive medical services, this new methodology is considered fairer and is expected to reduce Medicaid costs by $75 to $100 million yearly. Also under this methodology, the state established a pool of funds, including Medicaid funds, to maintain a bad debt and charity care pool. This initiative is aimed at supporting financially distressed hospitals, but also at utilizing combined third-party payer funds to increase the real availability of hospital care to the indigent and working poor.

In January 1984, Governor Cuomo recommended Medicaid reforms to improve the delivery of health services by facilitating alternatives to the episodic care often received by the poor. Legislation was passed to promote the use of capitation and physician-care case management programs, thereby encouraging more comprehensive and cost efficient services. The state has also made a concerted effort to reduce fraud and abuse. Like the other recent state initiatives, these reforms stem from the state's fiscal crisis and the rapid growth of Medicaid costs. However, at least one senior Medicaid official credits the Reagan initiatives with creating the political context for turning planning into action.

Because of New York's successful efforts to contain costs and control fraud and abuse, the federal matching formula was reduced by only 1 percent in federal fiscal year 1982, 2 percent in 1983, and 2.5 percent in 1984. Economic conditions contributing to high case loads and rising health care costs have increased the total cost of Medicaid in each year since 1981, with the result that federal funding has grown by an estimated 29 percent from 1981 to 1984 or has remained essentially constant after adjusting for inflation. The net impact of the Reagan initiatives has therefore been to reinforce arguments for greater state financing, control over hospitals, and efficient delivery systems, rather than reduce actual costs or the generosity of the benefits for the needy.

EDUCATION: DISPARATE EFFECTS

Changes in the two chapters of the Education Consolidation and Improvement Act of 1981 (ECIA) had markedly contrasting effects on New York and its local school districts. Cuts in title I/chapter 1 funds for compensatory education were largely restored at both federal and state levels; the effects, if any, were nominal. Cuts in chapter 2, the education block grant, which consolidated twenty-nine small programs targeted at urban school districts, were not restored and have had serious consequences for these districts. The New York story illustrates the interplay between liberal values and state centralization for both chapters of ECIA.

Resistible Cuts: Chapter 1

Federal cuts in aid to compensatory education came in two waves—a federal fiscal year 1981 across-the-board cut and a federal fiscal year 1982 cut, which was accompanied by a revision in the laws governing compensatory education. The 1982 reductions eliminated concentration aid, resulting in deeper cuts to largely urban districts. However, because this form of aid is forward funded, both school districts and the state had time to plan to buffer the cuts. Both carried over large proportions of previous allocations in order to smooth the decline and, in addition, used other tactics to fight the cuts.

New York's commissioner of education and certain urban districts sued the U.S. secretary of education to prevent the use of 1970 census figures in distributing chapter 1 funds, since that would mean $40 million less for New York State than the 1980 figures. Although the suit was not successful, it did contribute to the drive to obtain a supplemental appropriation from Congress. As a result, New York received $31.1 million in additional funds for the 1982–83 school year in September 1982. In federal fiscal year 1983 New York's chapter 1 allocation increased $40 million over the supplemental federal fiscal year 1982 allocation—an increase of 14 percent[23] (see table 8.1). Title I/chapter 1 changes in program, institution, or politics were not fundamental either at the state or local level. The forces that preserve title I from being folded into the block grant at the federal level have equally resisted change at the state and local levels.

[23] It is important to note that personnel costs account for a high percentage of chapter 1 expenditures, and built into these costs are wage increases promised by union contract. Thus, in Rochester the $500,000 increase in chapter 1 funds in 1983–84 was almost entirely swallowed by increased compensation—with virtually the same size staff as the year before. To maintain a program, therefore, requires increased funding.

Irresistible Cuts: Chapter 2

By contrast, in chapter 2, the education block grant, aggregate cuts have been substantial and important structural changes have ensued. All antecedent programs for the education block grant were funded at $73.9 million for New York in 1980–81; after the block grant was instituted, those funds to New York dropped to $31.3 million—a decrease of 58 percent. Particularly severe losses in funding were sustained by the state education department, and by urban districts, especially those with large magnet school programs funded by the Emergency School Assistance Act (ESAA).[24] The cuts were intensified by redistribution of funds away from public school to private and parochial schools, and away from districts successful in prior competitive programs (largely urban and suburban ones) to smaller districts who benefited from the formula-based distribution system. The effects of funding cuts and redistribution largely swamped the greater flexibility, consolidated paperwork, and other positive features of the block grant.

Effects on Urban Districts

With the advent of chapter 2, revenues to local districts fell from almost $43 million to $25 million between federal fiscal years 1980 and 1982—a 42 percent decrease. This loss of funds especially strained the already tight finances of urban districts.[25] Rochester, for example, lost 75 percent of its funding during this period. Cuts were too deep to permit local districts to replace federal losses entirely, although New York City did allocate $31 million of its own tax revenue to compensate for losses in all its federal funds to education.[26]

The effort to counteract the cuts to urban districts involved active lobbying at the state and federal levels. Unlike chapter 1, where this effort was largely successful in Congress,[27] the state has been the arena for lobbying on chapter 2 cuts—both at the executive and legislative levels.[28]

[24] Magnet schools offer distinctive curricula which enable secondary school students to concentrate in such subject areas as the arts, math and science, and government and law.

[25] Education was hard hit by New York City's financial crisis during the mid-1970s: between 1975 and 1976 the city Board of Education lost 11 percent of its personnel and another 16 percent between 1976 and 1980. Meanwhile, special education requirements raised that part of the budget by 60 percent and staffing by 81 percent in 1981–82 alone. (See Trude W. Lash et al., *Public Expenditures for Children, 1980–1983, New York City: The Impact of Federal Policies on Services for Children* [New York: Foundation for Child Development, November 1983], pp. 157–58.) Rochester experienced a similar squeeze, albeit somewhat later than New York City. In 1981–82 Rochester cut over $8 million from its proposed school budget; the following year, over $4 million was trimmed, and in 1983–84 the Board actually presented a budget with a $6 million deficit for approval by the City Council. Like New York City, Rochester's special education expenses were increasing rapidly.

[26] Lash et al., *Public Expenditures*, p. 158.

[27] The state education department publishes an annual brochure "Federal Legislation and Ed-

Although the distribution of funds was largely determined by federal legislation—80 percent of chapter 2 was to go to local districts by formula and 20 percent was reserved for the state—the state chapter 2 advisory committee to the state Department of Education used its limited discretion to help urban districts. It set aside part of the formula funds for distribution to districts most hurt by the cuts, those with magnet schools,[29] and allocated part of the state's 20 percent share for a competitive grant program to local districts. Given the magnitude of the losses, however, replacing the cuts completely by tinkering with internal redistribution was impossible. Therefore, the state legislature became the focus of lobbying to replace ESAA cuts. Although state funds were not immediately approved in 1982, the legislature did appropriate $7 million in 1983 funds and $11.7 million in 1984 funds for magnet schools.

Effects on Rochester

The effects of these various measures can be seen by examining the Rochester City School District, which in 1980–81 received $3.7 million in ESAA funding and other categorical programs folded into the block grant. The ESAA funds supported enriched programs in elementary schools and magnet schools at the secondary level. Under chapter 2, the district received less than $1 million and responded by paring back its elementary program and focusing federal funds there, while investing local money in magnet schools in order to keep them in place until state magnet funding could be obtained. In 1983–84 Roch-

---

ucation in New York State" on its federal legislative agenda. The 1982, 1983, and 1984 editions do not mention chapter 1 as a focus whereas the restoration of ESAA is a goal in each of these editions. This omission suggests that New York was more confident about chapter 1 than chapter 2, and was seeking more limited goals.

[28] See "Progress on ESAA Slight," *Education Week*, March 14, 1984, p. 12. Rochester's commitment to lobbying in Albany has increased as well. From the superintendent to the school board president to district staff all attest to the growing importance of spending time in Albany not only on chapter 2 but as a general strategy. Whereas the district had in the past simply accepted state aid funds, now the thrust is both to go after state categoricals and to increase the size and number through pressure on the state legislature. Rochester's school board established its legislative committee in 1982 and funded its work using impact aid formerly devoted to title I programs.

[29] When the formula was devised, it was originally rejected by the U.S. Department of Education because it provided funds to the districts with magnet schools under a hold-harmless provision; when this was changed to a set-aside for high-cost pupils, the formula was approved. The set-aside had been 8 percent of the 80 percent, to be distributed according to the percentage of the district in magnets. In subsequent years the set-aside was to be phased out. In 1983–84 the set-aside fell to 6 percent and the basis was changed to the ratio of a district's magnet population to the statewide magnet population, a change that helped Buffalo (which is understandable since the chancellor of the board of regents is from Buffalo). Buffalo is under court order to desegregate, and has by far the largest magnet program. For 1984–85, the original plan was to have the set-aside fall to 4 percent, but the state chapter 2 advisory committee voted, instead, to retain the 6 percent set-aside with the current method of distribution. That arrangement continued through the 1985–86 school year.

ester continued to lose funding under the block grant, but this decrease was more than made up for by $1.75 million in state magnet funding. Rochester's experience suggests that local discretion consists in the main of deciding how to target greatly reduced funds.

Effects on the State Education Department

Federal funds have been critical in maintaining the state education department staff. Whereas less than 10 percent of all expenditures for elementary and secondary education in New York State come from the federal government, on the average more than half of the education department's budget for its own operations is federally funded. While the Reagan program invested more responsibility in the state, it offset this centralizing tendency by cutting administrative funds and providing for greater local discretion. So far, the state has fairly successfully resisted decentralization and erosion of authority.

Under chapter 1, the education department lost $1.5 million in administrative funds—a 35 percent decrease. However, carefully husbanded carryovers enabled the state to stave off staff cuts until 1983–84, when twenty-nine out of ninety positions were finally eliminated. Even then, most of the employees either retired under special incentives or were shifted to other functions, rather than being laid off. The chapter 2 reductions resulted in an 80 percent administrative cut. Despite this, staff decreased only 20 percent, as the state contracted services, travel, and other nonpersonnel costs first.

COMMUNITY SERVICES BLOCK GRANT

The community services block grant transferred responsibility for community action agencies from the federal government to the states, and gave New York the opportunity to exert greater control over these local agencies. But because the essential purpose of the agencies is to foster local initiative, the state took a hands-off approach, continuing the decentralization permitted under prior federal administration.

Because Democratic governors have been supportive of the disadvantaged, and in turn need their political support, the most difficult decisions regarding the block grant involved its distribution among community action agencies (CAAs) and other potential recipients. In order to postpone this sensitive task, Governor Carey deferred assumption of the block until the mandatory pickup date of October 1, 1982. Meanwhile, the legislature placed several restrictions on the distribution of funds, thereby deviating from its early policy of noninvolvement with the block grants. It required that funds for existing CAAs—at least 90 percent of the total block according to federal law—be distributed in proportion to each agency's 1981 funding, thereby extending federal protection of existing CAAs one step further. No more than 5 percent of funds could be distributed on a discretionary basis, with preference given to counties without a CAA in 1981. Amendments were added the following year permitting funds to be given to Indian tribes and effectively prohibiting the transfer of funds out of the block.

Criticisms of the distribution of block grant funds came from several quarters, including the Department of State, which administers the program. The department argued that funds would be better targeted on low-income people if allocations were based on current social and economic statistics, for example the number of people in poverty, instead of the level of 1981 funding. But since some agencies would lose, it recommended revision of the distribution formula be considered only "in the context of the availability of additional funding."[30]

Transition to the block, and the purely administrative task of substituting state procedures for federal, occupied much of the attention of the department for 1983. New York has not yet formally attempted to alter the activities of the state's forty-seven CAAs, giving them the same flexibility to meet local priorities that they had previously. The department gives agencies guidance, technical assistance, and occasional encouragement to develop an alternative program, but has basically left the existing program intact. Whether this policy will continue as the state becomes familiar with the individual programs remains to be seen, but the department's stance as advocate for the disadvantaged suggests that it will give the local agencies considerable freedom.

SOCIAL SERVICES BLOCK GRANT

The passage of the reconciliation act was widely hailed in New York State as a disaster for social services and social service recipients.[31] In fact, as table 8.1 indicates, New York's 1982 allocation of social services funds was $51 million less than the previous year's allocation. While this reduction was clearly a shock to the social services system in the state, simply looking at block grant funding totals does not tell the whole story.

To a considerable extent New York State was able to cushion the impact of the federal cuts so that, with a few exceptions, the full range of services was maintained at the local level. Two important structural characteristics of the state's political economy permitted this overall cushioning effect. First, at least

[30] New York State Department of State, *Report to the Governor and the Legislature*, January 15, 1984.

[31] See New York State, Governor's Task Force on the Federal Human Services Budget, *Impact of Federal Budget Reductions in Health and Human Services*, August 1981.

since the fiscal crisis of the mid-1970s in New York, cost-containment and management efficiency have been a major concern of the powerful Division of the Budget (DOB) directly under the control of the governor's office. By demanding administrative and program efficiency DOB played an important part in softening the impact of the cuts in the social services block grant.

Second, an even more important structural characteristic shaping New York's response to the reconciliation act was the state's long-standing tradition of maintaining comprehensive social services with generous benefit levels, broad eligibility, and high program standards. State law predating the Reagan administration mandates considerable state and county fiscal support of social services regardless of federal participation. By far the most significant piece of legislation in this regard is the New York State Child Welfare Reform Act of 1979 (CWRA). In brief, the CWRA is a set of amendments to the state social services law aimed at reducing out-of-home placement of children and offering fiscal and regulatory incentives to do so. The state requires that six core services be provided to clients for whom high priority has been assigned under CWRA: day care, parent aid or parent training, homemaker, clinical services, transportation, and twenty-four-hour access to emergency services. Although passed in 1979, CWRA has been phased in over five years, with new state funding becoming available in 1981 and final regulations issued in October 1984. In April 1981, counties were able to begin claiming services to prevent the need for foster care placement, hasten family reunification, or assist adoption under an open-ended state match.

From a state fiscal standpoint, the 75 percent open-ended state match for mandated services opens the door for an expanding commitment of state funds no matter how much is recovered from federal sources. From the local standpoint, counties realize significant benefits because of the large increase in the state share for mandated services, but at the same time lose flexibility because mandated services must be provided regardless of any other fiscal pressures. The impact of this extraordinarily comprehensive state social services legislation seems clear: While New York is substantially dependent on federal funds to provide supportive social services, the system is not driven by federal initiatives. Political and fiscal commitments to high levels of services at the state and local level are not simply matters of policy in contradiction to the Reagan program, but fixed, structural features of the system as a whole.

Fiscal Effects

The overall fiscal impact of the reconciliation act on social services in New York was somewhat complicated. The governor publicly refused to request new state funds to offset the shortfall, but at the same time was able to offset some of the decreased block grant allocations. This was done by shifting funds from other federal sources, taking advantage of carryovers from categorical funds allocated in previous years, and making a conscious administrative effort to make the largest cuts in the state operations in order to keep aid to localities at the highest possible levels.

In addition, as table 8.3 indicates, the reduction of federal title XX funds was also partially offset by significant increases in state and (to some extent) local spending for services which might otherwise have been cut given the decline of federal participation. In effect, New York's own legislative mandates for services acted to some degree as a "fail safe" buffer which has so far enabled the existing service structure to remain intact. Nonetheless, there were some reductions in services at the local level, particularly those services not mandated by the state.

Local Effects

New York's fifty-eight social services districts—fifty-seven counties plus New York City—are mandated by the state to meet one-half of the nonfederal share of block grant expenditures up to the federally preestablished limit. The districts, as we have just noted, are also able to take advantage of other sources of state (CWRA) and federal (AFDC and Medicaid) funds where the state shares the costs at varying rates of reimbursement to localities.

Thus, the reductions in the title XX/social services block grant ceiling for Monroe County (which administers such services for Rochester residents) do not tell the full story of local fiscal effects in social services spending. In fact, as is seen in tables 8.4 and 8.5, Monroe County surpassed its block grant share in 1982 and 1983 by utilizing and matching other revenue sources. Local spending, however, was lower in 1982 and 1983 than prior to the 1981 federal budget

Table 8.3. *Total Federal, State, and County Allocations for Title XX Social Services, Federal Fiscal Years 1981–84 (dollars in millions)*

Program	1981	1982	1983	1984 est.
Federal title XX allocation	236	185	189	209[a]
All federal sources[a]	257	207	222	209
State[b]	68	75	86	96
County[c]	68	64	69	77

NOTES: [a] Combined funding, including title XX allocations, transfers from other sources of federal revenue, and emergency jobs act funds in federal fiscal year 1983.
[b] Combined funding, including matching funds as required by the block grant and spending mandated by New York State law.
[c] Combined funding, including matching funds and spending mandated by New York State law.

Table 8.4. *Revenue for All Social Services Spending in Monroe County (dollars in thousands)*

	Revenues		
Year [a]	Federal [b]	State [c]	County
1981	9,210	1,670	1,670
1982	8,862	1,475	1,475
1983	9,314	1,552	1,552
1984 est.	11,144	1,857	1,857

SOURCE: Monroe County Department of Social Services.
NOTES: [a] January 1–December 31.
[b] Revenues are from title XX, Medicaid, and AFDC.
[c] Revenues are from the Child Welfare Reform Act of 1979.

Table 8.5. *Revenue for Title XX and Social Services Block Grant Spending in Monroe County (dollars in thousands)*

	Revenues		
Year [a]	Federal	State	County
1981	5,944	990	990
1982	5,602	933	933
1983	5,710	951	951
1984 est.	6,105[b]	951	951

SOURCE: Monroe County Department of Social Services.
NOTES: [a] January 1–December 31.
[b] This includes $5.71 million in social services block grant funds and $395,000 in jobs act money.

act. The decreases were largely the result of the elimination of day-care subsidies (not mandated by the state) to low-income, non-AFDC, employed families; these subsidies were reinstated in the 1984 budget.

Day-Care Cuts and Reinstatement

Day care, aside from that provided for preventive or protective purposes, is especially vulnerable to cuts because it is the largest nonmandated expenditure of all title XX services.

In New York City day care consumes 45 percent of all title XX funds and 83 percent of title XX optional services. The differential reimbursement rates between title XX (12.5 percent local) and state streams (25–50 percent local) available for certain mandated services when a district exceeds its title XX ceiling, encourage counties to use title XX funds for mandated services and reduce optional services, particularly day care. Reductions are made by entirely eliminating day care for the working poor funded out of title XX or by reducing eligibility levels. In FFY 1983, 34 out of 58 social services districts no longer offer[ed] income eligible day care.[32]

Monroe County's cuts in title XX day care actually predated the reconciliation act. "Beginning in the spring of 1980 . . . in anticipation of a county Department of Social Services (DSS) deficit of $2 million . . . DSS income eligibility for non-mandated [that is, not protective or preventive] day care was reduced from 70 to 62 percent of the state median income."[33] In July 1981, in anticipation of both continuing title XX shortfalls and a funding decrease of $800,000 (13 percent) for 1982, the Monroe County Legislature discontinued all income-eligible day care. (An income-eligible family of four, at that time, for example, was defined as a non-AFDC household with annual earnings up to $15,000.) A total of 328 families with 473 children—12 percent of the 4,000 children receiving day-care subsidies—were affected. Although some families became eligible for day-care aid from the United Way, the remaining 130 families were eliminated completely from service.

Monroe County was not alone in choosing to eliminate day-care subsidies for income-eligible families: eight other counties took the same step between federal fiscal years 1980 and 1983. In fact, with the exception of the Long Island counties of Nassau and Suffolk, and New York City, all of New York's urban counties cut their own spending for day-care subsidies by reducing income eligibility limits, raising parents' fees, or eliminating the program altogether.[34]

Monroe County's decision, however, had a short tenure. A coalition of groups led by Statewide Youth Advocacy Inc., a children's lobby based in Rochester, and including local day-care center directors, formed quickly in response to the cuts. The coalition argued that "many poor women [would be] forced to choose between jobs or child-care arrangements—or to compromise both" and attracted media attention for their cause.[35] The legislature established a special committee in late 1982 to investigate county services for children; the committee proved to be sympathetic to restoration of the subsidies.

A local survey of the effects of the day-care cuts also influenced the decision to restore the subsidies. Data from interviews conducted one and a half years

[32] Statewide Youth Advocacy (SYA), *Where Have All The Children Gone?* (Rochester, N.Y.: SYA, 1983), p. viii.
[33] Center for Governmental Research (CGR), *Effects of Cutting Day Care Subsidies to Low Income Families* (Rochester, N.Y.: CGR, 1983), p. 2.
[34] Statewide Youth Advocacy, *Where Have All the Children Gone?* pp. 35–46.
[35] Carol Eisenberg, "Study Backs Day Care Aid," *Rochester Times Union*, January 17, 1984.

after the subsidy cut with 38 percent of the affected families—overwhelmingly single parent, working mothers—revealed that 66 percent of those families lived in the city of Rochester. Twenty percent had become newly dependent on welfare since the cut, while another 10 percent had applied for but had not received welfare. Four-fifths reported that they were unable to pay bills on time, or to adequately feed and clothe their children or purchase medicines, or had to borrow money. One-half of the respondents were less satisfied with child-care arrangements since loss of their subsidy, while 40 percent felt less able to handle both child care and work responsibilities. Finally, 31 percent felt that their children's behavior was negatively affected by changes in day-care arrangements.[36] The study clearly substantiated the contention of day-care advocates that life had been made much more difficult for struggling single parents.

Monroe County reinstated the subsidies in September 1983—two years after their termination—to employed families with income at or below 58 percent of the state median. In January 1984, eligibility was expanded to families with incomes up to 65 percent of the median.[37] Total spending in 1984 for subsidies to about 500 income-eligible children is budgeted to increase by $1.3 million over 1983 spending; $400,000 will come from emergency jobs aid, and the remainder, equally from the state and county governments.

Future Implications

Despite efforts at state and local levels to cushion the social services cuts, it is not sufficient to say simply that no significant reductions in program services occurred. Even slight reductions of funding local social services need to be put in the context of three factors:

1. the reversal of a ten-year trend toward expansion of social services in New York;
2. the increase in the number of persons officially designated below the poverty level in New York in the last few years; and
3. the continuing emphasis on deinstitutionalization of the state's mental patients, which, in effect, creates a growing pool of clients with potential need for community-based services.

In this context, it is easier to understand the view taken by some state social services officials that the reduction in federal support for social services is a serious abdication of responsibility, with potentially disastrous consequences for the

[36] Center for Governmental Research, *Effects of Cutting Day Care Subsidies.*
[37] Hence, a family of four with income up to $15,395 was eligible for the subsidy.

most needy in New York. The fairest conclusion might be that the major program effect of the Reagan initiatives on social services in New York has been to shift an already extremely comprehensive system from a preventive/expansion-of-services mode to a no-growth, maintenance-of-effort mode. In the future, available resources may be directed to supporting mandated services only. Any such shift away from state and local support for "optional" services means that the population most affected by change will be the working poor and those marginally eligible for supportive services.

THE JOB TRAINING PARTNERSHIP ACT

The Job Training Partnership Act (JTPA) has given the state government broader responsibilities than it hitherto exercised. Whereas under the Comprehensive Employment and Training Act, New York's role in job training programs was largely limited to administration of funds for thirty rural, "balance-of-state" counties, its prerogatives extend under JTPA to the entire state. The transition from CETA to JTPA has been marked by complex institutional dynamics at the state level, as the governor has sought to centralize administration of this program; as powerful agencies have jockeyed to retain or enhance prerogatives over job training programs and funds; and as the legislature has asserted its discretion in the use of JTPA funds. At the same time, New York has chosen to decentralize decision making to local service delivery areas (SDAs). The net effect of this two-pronged approach has been to change policy-making procedures at the state level, but to promote continuity from CETA in the SDAs.

Prior to JTPA, employment and training programs in New York had been fragmented among ten different state agencies, including the labor, social services, and education departments, and the office for aging and division for youth. The Department of Labor had been preeminent under CETA in setting policy and administering all the grants that came to the state government, including the balance-of-state funds. However, legislative hearings in 1982 found a great deal of overlap and lack of coordination and communication among the other agencies also involved.

JTPA greatly enhanced the power of the governor; Cuomo was given authority to designate local service delivery areas (SDAs), distribute funds to localities, approve locally developed plans, monitor the performance of programs, establish a new statewide dislocated workers program, and create a state job training partnership council (JTPC). The state legislation that authorized the JTPC vested it with "significant new program responsibilities and . . . opportunities for addressing the lack of coordination among vocational, occupational and job training programs, through the planning, coordinating, governance and service delivery requirements it establishes" (Laws of 1983, Chapter 618).

Although the New York Department of Labor remains a key actor in implementing JTPA, the JTPC, with its broad policy-setting prerogatives, has served as a clear counterweight. The centrality of the labor department under CETA has been further challenged by representation on the JTPC of the departments of education and social services (along with labor), and their participation, together with the youth and aging agencies, on the interagency team, which reviews local SDA plans. While its state power has been reduced, the labor department can now exert wider influence at local levels than it did under CETA. Whereas it provided technical assistance to only 30 CETA balance-of-state counties, it now does so for the thirty-four SDAs which encompass the entire state.

The legislature is another key institutional actor at the state level. Besides enacting legislation to establish the JTPC, it was assertive in determining the state's use of emergency jobs funds for dislocated workers.

Governor Cuomo, as part of his general initiative to enhance the state's economic position, proposed in January 1983 to target $1.8 million in emergency jobs funds for dislocated workers to Erie County which overlies Buffalo, the state's most chronically distressed, heavily Democratic area, and five other counties. The Republican Senate leadership, wishing to expand eligibility to other upstate, mainly rural counties—the traditional base for the Republican party—proposed reducing the eligibility threshold for the funds from 133 to 125 percent of the state unemployment rate. The Democrat-led Assembly, concerned that community-based training organizations might fare much worse under JTPA than they had under CETA, wished to prohibit local governments from delivering services themselves with these funds. As the Senate and Assembly positions were not mutually exclusive, the two chambers negotiated an alternative to the governor's proposal. The result was legislation combining the jobs funds with $5 million in state funds and allocating $6.8 million to sixteen counties which, after negotiating for delivery of services with community-based organizations and other nongovernmental entities, had to apply for predetermined allocations. The effect was that Erie County was entitled to $3.2 million, 47 percent of the total. However, the executive's discretion was reduced in that fifteen other counties were also entitled to funds pending approval of their applications.

Local Factors

Whereas JTPA was the vehicle for the governor to centralize job training decisions at the state level, it appears, paradoxically, also to be promoting decentralization from the state to the local SDAs. To be sure, policy making at the local level is constrained by both national and state priorities. Nonetheless, the thirty-four local SDAs in New York have considerable discretion over endorsement of training programs, choice of service providers, and selection of target populations.

Decisions about programs and providers by Rochester during the 1983–84 transition period illustrate both the exercise of local discretion and the importance of the CETA experience. The decline of job training funds for Rochester in recent years has been dramatic—from $17 million in 1978 to $3 million in 1984. In 1978, CETA funds supported nearly 1,000 public service jobs in city government and nonprofit agencies, as well as a staff of forty-three full-time CETA program administrators. By 1984 public service employment positions had been completely eliminated and the staff had decreased to twenty-four.[38]

The key institutional change at the local level was the establishment of a private industry council (PIC), vested under the act with responsibilities for determining the training plan. Rochester's PIC, which has responsibility for the Monroe County SDA, is one of only two multijurisdictional PICs in New York.[39] While the Rochester City Council must approve PIC recommendations before they are forwarded to Albany for final action, the council is no longer the sole or even primary decision making body for manpower policy, as was the case under CETA. In fact, during the October 1983–June 1984 transition period, the council played a pro forma role of ratifying all of the PIC actions.

The Rochester/Monroe County PIC, whose twenty-five members were appointed in August 1983, immediately faced the task of preparing a plan for the transition year and selecting local programs and service providers. Both the plan and the program choices had to be accomplished quickly by the PIC, many of whose private sector members were unfamiliar with public manpower policy.

---

[38] An even greater decrease in JTPA administrative staff was prevented by the reassumption by the city government of the intake function, which, until 1982, had been contracted out to the state Job Service.

[39] From 1973 to 1976, Rochester and Monroe County had composed a single prime sponsor consortium to administer CETA funds. The consortium foundered on administrative and program disagreements, and after 1976, each jurisdiction reverted to the status of separate prime sponsor. While they were unable to agree to form a single SDA under JTPA, they did agree, with some urging from the governor's staff, to form a single PIC. For background on the CETA experience, see Sarah F. Liebschutz, *Federal Aid to Rochester*, p. 12.

Such circumstances favored continuity of past programs. The Rochester PIC opted to continue awarding program contracts to former CETA service vendors with a proven track record, rather than delay implementation and use new service providers. Thus, in Rochester, JTPA—despite its decentralizing features—did not look very different from CETA.

Continuity with CETA, however, may not be the typical future course for JTPA at the local level. The private sector majority of the Rochester/Monroe County PIC was unhappy with their passivity in the transition year although not necessarily with the final program choices, and moved to develop a more comprehensive strategic framework within which program proposals and provider performance can be more systematically evaluated. Such efforts were not confined to Rochester as the transition year concluded, but were common throughout the state, as the PICs—the act's principal vehicles for private-public partnership—began to assert themselves in setting local job training policy.

ASSISTED HOUSING

New York has long had its own programs to stimulate the availability of housing for low-income people. Since the mid-1970s, such programs were regarded as secondary in importance compared to those of the federal government. Thus, federal cuts in housing were of considerable concern to state officials and led to replacement initiatives by both the Carey and Cuomo administrations.

New York's prior experience with its own housing programs generated two distinct kinds of responses to the federal cuts: ratification of cuts in section 8 rental subsidy and moderate rehabilitation programs, and in public housing; and replacement, in part, of cuts in section 8 new construction funds. Separate from these responses, New York initiated a new program for a special population, the homeless. New York also retained its own assisted housing programs; these included 100,000 units of moderate- to middle-income housing under the Mitchell-Lama program and 66,000 units of state low-income public housing. The state also continued to make residential mortgages available, in part to lower-income families through the issuance of tax-exempt bonds for multi- and single-family mortgages by the Housing Finance Agency (HFA) and the State of New York Mortgage Agency (SONYMA).

The state's unwillingness to replace the rental subsidies (section 8 "existing") or public housing cuts stemmed from preexisting fiscal demands associated with the precarious financial position of many Mitchell-Lama projects, and insufficient revenues for the state's public housing units. In fact, long before the advent of the Reagan administration, New York had been seeking to have the federal government assume its public housing program.

On the other hand, New York's desire to stimulate the home building industry was reflected in 1982 legislation, supported by Governor Carey, which appropriated $7.6 million in state funds to leverage $40 million in federal Farmer's Home mortgages for 1,000 rural housing units—a kind of rural substitute for the section 8 construction cuts. In addition, SONYMA accelerated its bond sales so that proceeds from $350 million in offerings were used to generate low-interest mortgages for first-time homeowners and moderate-income families. Twenty percent of these loans were made in lower-income target areas.

Governor Cuomo, linking the "availability of adequate and affordable housing to decisions on business locations" in his 1983 budget message, proposed expanded bond authority of $500 million for HFA—subsequently approved by the legislature. In 1984, he recommended further increases in bonding capacity for SONYMA to produce 8,000 units of owner occupied housing, and for HFA to produce 20,000 units—20 percent of them for lower-income households.

The Homeless

The other major housing initiative of the governor involved the homeless, a subpopulation whose plight has become a major political issue at both state and local levels.

The homeless problem is most severe in New York City, where a Department of Social Services (DSS) survey in June 1983 found almost 2,000 families in temporary or emergency housing arranged by the welfare department. Many of these families remain in these shelters for five months or more. For the state as a whole, official estimates in 1983 of the homeless population ranged from 60,000 to 150,000 persons, of whom 60 percent were believed to be residents of New York City.[40]

In 1983, New York began to respond to the plight of the homeless by providing funds to local governments and private agencies for capital and operating programs. At Governor Cuomo's request, the legislature committed $50 million for capital projects over four years in the homeless housing and assistance program of 1983 (HHAP). Additional state funds were appropriated to reimburse local governments for 50 percent of the cost of emergency shelter programs, and 60 percent of the cost of selected shelter and services for runaway and homeless youth under the age of 16. In state fiscal year 1983–84, the operating subsidy programs cost over $30 million; for state fiscal year 1984–85, expenditures are anticipated at more than $40 million. If all sources of state funds

[40] Robert Pear, "$20 Million Private Projects to Aid Homeless," *New York Times*, December 4, 1983, p. 35.

for the homeless, including mental health and demonstration rehabilitation projects, are included, it appears that New York may spend over $87 million in state fiscal year 1984–85—an increase of almost 80 percent over 1983–84.[41]

The approaches used thus far by the state to address the homeless problem have been aimed at alleviating immediate crises. Both the governor and the legislature see the need for more comprehensive, longer-term planning; the legislature, in fact, mandated a statewide plan and periodic reports on the state's homeless population when it extended HHAP and increased appropriations in 1984.

These state efforts dwarf federal aid received by New York to assist the homeless. In 1983, the state received only $4.5 million in emergency jobs funds for this purpose. However, for state residents who are not homeless, but whose ability to find adequate and affordable housing is limited, the state's efforts, while commendable, replace only a small part of the total federal housing cuts.

The Local Story

In Rochester, the federal government, not the state, is the source of subsidies for low-income housing. Changes in federal housing funding and policies have not had damaging impacts on the operating side of public housing and section 8 programs, but they have reduced the expansion of subsidized low-income housing to a trickle. Between 1981 and 1984 the public housing authority in Rochester added about 230 units of conventional public housing, much of it for the elderly, 325 units of section 8 existing, and 168 units of moderate rehabilitation. But most of those units were already in the pipeline before President Reagan took office.

As the expansion slowed, waiting lists increased. As of May 1984, the Rochester Housing Authority (RHA) had waiting lists of over 1,000 for both two-bedroom and three-bedroom apartments in conventional public housing, the highest the list has ever been. The exception was in housing for the elderly, where the authority developed a campaign to publicize vacancies in its elderly projects.

Existing public housing units have been maintained and made more energy efficient with a combination of operating funds, comprehensive improvement assistance program (CIAP) funds, and weatherization monies. By using weatherization funds to make its buildings more energy efficient, RHA has lowered utility increases. RHA is not applying for more weatherization or CIAP funds for federal fiscal year 1984 because its staff cannot adequately manage any more projects than those already under way.

[41] Statewide Youth Advocacy (SYA), *Preliminary Children's Budget Report* (Rochester, N.Y.: SYA, 1984), pp. 2–13.

On the operating side, the major sources of revenue were both increased—federal subsidies from the Department of Housing and Urban Development increased by 21 percent and rental income by over 25 percent between 1981 and 1983. For tenants not on public assistance, the maximum proportion of their income devoted to rent is being gradually raised from 25 to 30 percent; for new tenants the 30 percent rule has applied since September 1982.[42] In 1984 public assistance rent levels were raised as well: rents for families on public assistance (about 400 units) will be raised 10 percent in every twelve-month period until the rents reach the public assistance shelter maximum.[43]

Despite the increases in subsidies and rents, uncertainty about the direction of federal housing policy contributed to RHA's efforts to manage more efficiently. Although most of the regulatory changes apart from the rent schedules were minor irritations, RHA in 1984 was waiting with trepidation for the arrival of vouchers and battening down for the blow that had not yet come.

COMMUNITY DEVELOPMENT BLOCK GRANT

Federal funds for community development are still federal-local in character in New York. Unlike most other states, New York elected not to assume administrative responsibility for the small-cities portion of the community development block grant (CDBG) program and the state has only a minor role in the entitlement portion of the CDBG program.[44]

At the state level, executive and legislative factors have precluded New York's participation in the small-cities program. At the local level, in Rochester, CDBG continues to play an important role—albeit with decreasing funds—in undergirding the implementation of neighborhood conservation and

[42] Although the increases have reduced tenants' disposable income, it does not appear to have increased the turnover rate in public housing since comparable housing is not available in the private market for less. Only in the case of high-income tenants does there appear to be any incentive to leave public housing because of the rent increases; this may be positive since it vacates units for needier families.

[43] This rent increase will not affect public assistance recipients since their grant will increase to meet the added cost. Instead, the increase will affect human services budgets at state, county, and federal level. Although the amounts in question are nominal ($5–$10 per family per month, or perhaps a total of $50,000 for an entire year), Monroe County contends that it was not notified and did not make provision in its 1984 budget to cover the increases.

[44] States, under the A-95 review process, are asked to review and comment on CDBG program submissions to HUD by entitlement cities. Their involvement in this process—even before its more narrow definition under the Reagan administration—was not an important factor in the CDBG process. See Paul R. Dommel et al., *Decentralizing Community Development: A Brookings Report* (Washington, D.C.: U.S. Department of Housing and Urban Development, 1978), pp. 64–65.

economic development priorities and affording city officials flexibility, free from state mandates.

Small-Cities Program

New York was one of only four states where small-city funds were administered by the U.S. Department of Housing and Urban Development (HUD) during federal fiscal year 1984.[45] New York's decision against assuming the program in 1982 resulted from a cost-benefit assessment of state assumption, which Governor Carey requested. The budget division and the Office of Development Planning cited as advantages to state assumption the enhanced ability of the state to implement its own economic development goals, the opportunity for the state to direct funds to currently underfunded areas, and the chance to nurture a more positive state-local relationship. However, disadvantages appeared to outweigh the advantages. State officials felt the federal government did not provide enough funding to cover the cost of administering the new block grant. In addition, state officials elected not to administer the program because they were reluctant to incur political and financial responsibility for continuing the program should the federal government continue to cut appropriations. A high percentage (36 percent) of small-cities funds were already committed by HUD for multi-year contracts, decreasing the scope of state discretion. Finally, New York State Association of Housing and Rehabilitation officials preferred the federal government to continue administration of the program.

Governor Cuomo favored state assumption, and the State Assembly passed a bill in 1983, specifying that the state use the same criteria for determining need as used currently by HUD. This stipulation was clearly intended to restrict discretion over the small-cities funds by the state administering agency. The Republican Senate majority declined to act on this block grant bill, precisely because of perceived negative effects on the state's small, rural communities. Without the assurance that the legislature will appropriate the funds, the governor has not yet assumed the small-cities block grant.

Community and Economic Development in Rochester

The community development block grant (CDBG) program, established in 1974 as part of the Housing and Community Development Act, remains the single most important source of federal aid to Rochester city government. Their program is important for several reasons. First, although CDBG entitlement grants to the city have decreased by 16 percent annually since federal fiscal year 1981 from nearly $13 million to $10.9 million in federal fiscal year 1984 (see

[45] The other states that did not administer the program in 1984 were Maryland, Kansas, and Hawaii.

table 8.2)—the entitlement grant still constitutes one of the larger sources of federal aid to the city. Second, CDBG funds still are appropriated directly to Rochester from the federal government, and the city, because of its entitlement status under this program, has independence from state mandates and state funding. Rochester's relationship with HUD, which predates the Housing and Community Development Act, has continued smoothly under the Reagan administration. Third and most important, CDBG provides the financial undergirding for implementation of Rochester's neighborhood revitalization and economic development priorities. Urban Development Action Grant (UDAG) funds, successfully garnered by Rochester since establishment of this program in 1977, have also been an important source of federal economic aid to the city and have been used to supplement CDBG funds.

Between 1981 and 1984, Rochester was able to temper the effects of cuts in its CDBG entitlement grants with the use of UDAG loan repayments and emergency jobs act aid. Prospects, however, for local replacement of lost funds beyond 1984 are not bright. Consequently, Rochester's future efforts to stem blight and promote investment may be slowed.

CBDG Background

At its outset in 1974, the block grant for community development was viewed by city officials as an incentive to redefining Rochester's development priorities and move away from exclusive preoccupation with urban renewal. The city, which had the thirteenth largest urban renewal program in the United States, had become disillusioned with its massive clearance projects, which resulted in large, vacant tracts of land in the central part of the city and also seemed to contribute to the steady decline of its middle-class population. Because of the latitude that CDBG allowed them, city officials saw an opportunity to shift away from the large-scale acquisition associated with traditional renewal and clearance activities in blighted areas to conservation and rehabilitation of marginal neighborhoods, and to investment in economic development.

City Council members were deeply involved with the city manager and staff in shaping the early policy outlines and program details of CDBG, and were instrumental in establishing a framework into which citizen comments were channeled which emphasized neighborhood reinvestment and economic development. For more than nine years that strategy has been translated into allocations of CDBG funds to a large primary target area, containing the vast majority of the city's black, Spanish-speaking, poor residents, for street and recreation improvements, demolition of abandoned structures, housing and small business rehabilitation loans and grants, and various downtown projects.

Conflicts over CDBG

Two kinds of conflicts have persisted throughout the nine years of CDBG in Rochester: neighborhoods versus downtown; and new development versus maintenance of city services. Both conflicts have been exacerbated by decreases in CDBG funds since federal fiscal year 1981. City officials were able to placate both neighborhood advocates and central business district supporters by carefully delineating target areas, judiciously applying almost $2 million in UDAG loan repayments, and utilizing $2.3 million in emergency jobs aid in 1983. CDBG funds have also continued to fund both new developmental projects and regular capital programs.

The conflict between the use of CDBG funds for development and for traditional capital projects has been played out against the backdrop of Rochester's severe fiscal pressure, continuous since the early 1970s.[46] In the effort to gain more direct influence over CDBG funds, so as to make greater use of them to carry out regular city capital programs, the city manager reorganized the community development function in 1981. He created a separate department of economic development and appointed a new commissioner of community development. While the lion's share of spending under the block grant has remained developmental in character there is evidence that CDBG is being used more and more to fund activities that Rochester—if it were under less fiscal pressure—would otherwise fund out of its own-source revenues.

As Rochester began planning for its tenth CDBG program year, 1984–85, it was clear that the effects of the cuts could no longer be ameliorated. Available UDAG repayment funds of $115,000 were not adequate to bridge the gap between $11.9 million allocated for community development in 1983–84 and $10.9 million in entitlement funds for 1984–85. Controversy erupted between neighborhood and downtown advocates, and between supporters of new development and service maintenance; these disputes remain unresolved. Clearly, three years after the reconciliation act, Rochester was feeling the effects of cuts in CDBG.

UDAGs for Rochester's Development Goals

The UDAG program has been a singular bright spot in a picture of decreasing federal funds available locally. Rochester, in fact, has been extremely successful in securing these funds to promote investment in industrial and commercial, and, to a lesser degree, housing developments. Awards of $27 million were made between 1981 and 1984 to leverage more than $125 million from private

[46] See Sarah F. Liebschutz, *Federal Aid to Rochester*, for discussion of Rochester's fiscal pressure since 1960.

sources and to create 3,400 permanent jobs in the city. These nineteen separate UDAG projects are demonstrable evidence of the city administration's grantsmanship with HUD and its ability to "package" the financing needs of developers with public and private funds.

Fifty-eight percent of the UDAG funds were for eight commercial developments in the central business district, with 36 percent for ten industrial projects, and 6 percent for three housing projects. Rochester's emphasis on revitalizing its downtown has been greatly aided by two multimillion dollar UDAGs for extensive rehabilitation of an existing hotel and for construction of a new $42 million Hyatt Hotel. The ten industrial UDAGs for plant modernization and expansion have generated considerable short-term construction activity and will help Rochester remain economically competitive in the long run.

Thus, UDAG grants have been useful to Rochester in two ways: stimulating new investment in the city's industrial and commercial enterprises, and then providing revenues from repayments where UDAGs were loaned at below market rate interest to developers. As discussed above, such repayment funds helped mitigate recent decreases in CDBG funds to Rochester.

Conclusion

"We are not cutting the budget simply for the sake of sounder financial management," President Reagan asserted in 1981.[47] "This is only a first step toward returning power to states and communities, only a first step toward reordering the relationship between citizen and government."[48]

For the federal government, that first step, embodied in the reconciliation act, did indeed represent a new thrust toward decentralization. For New York, it created opportunities for the state government to reinforce traditional policies as well as more recent economic development goals, and, in the process, to enhance its central role in policy making and financing vis-à-vis localities. The efforts of the federal government to decentralize gave the state major new responsibilities in areas where its prior role had been secondary or nonexistent. The community services and health block grants, whose consolidated categorical programs had directly linked Washington with localities, vested new authority in state government. Similarly, CETA had been primarily federal-local

[47] "Conservative Political Action Conference" (Remarks at the conference dinner, March 20, 1981). *Weekly Compilation of Presidential Documents* 17, no. 2 (March 23, 1981):329.
[48] Ibid.

in character; JTPA gave the state government authority to influence the nature of programs and the distribution of funds throughout the state.

New York's financing role also grew during the Reagan years, continuing a trend begun in the mid-1970s. Compensating for the social services block grant cut resulted in an increase in the state's share of nonfederal costs from 50 to 55 percent. Counties were partially relieved of their share of Medicaid costs by legislation enacted in 1982 and 1983. While pressure for the state to absorb a greater share of Medicaid costs was building prior to the reconciliation act, the federal initiative contributed to final legislative action.

The structure of existing state programs helped determine how much New York itself compensated for the federal cuts. Compensation tended to occur in programs structured to automatically fill gaps left by the contraction of federal support, as in the case of AFDC and compensatory education aid. Compensation also occurred in programs offering mechanisms for replacing federal cuts without enacting special legislation. Such mechanisms were crucial in replacing cuts in the social services block grant, where state mandates permitted the state and localities to finance services after block grant funds were exhausted. In Medicaid, New York was able to avoid the full cut in the federal matching share because it was already instituting a plan to control hospital costs.

A program's revenue source was also an important determinant of the degree to which the state increased its own spending to compensate for federal cuts. As might have been expected, compensation was greater in those programs financed by bonds and dedicated taxes than those funded out of general revenues. Some of the cuts in federal housing assistance were offset by increased bonding authority for the State of New York Mortgage Authority and the Housing Finance Agency.

Despite these examples of state centralization in policy making and financing, such actions were not always easily or successfully undertaken. The controversy surrounding the distribution of funds under the community services block grant and the failure of New York to assume the small-cities block grant together demonstrate the difficulties inherent in state assumptions of former federal programs that are basically redistributive.

Perceptions of the Reagan domestic program by New York officials and bureaucrats changed over time. Whereas in 1981 the reconciliation act appeared as a tidal wave threatening serious erosion of the structure of social programs, that perception moderated considerably three years later. By 1984, the act was seen as one of the series of waves emanating from Washington that changes the contours of programs but leaves most of their foundations intact. State officials, after choosing and implementing policies to adopt or to temper the act's provisions, were drawn to other issues. A new governor shifted the focus of concern away from the reconciliation act to new federal legislation, notably the Job Training Partnership Act, and, most importantly, to his own agenda.

Nonetheless, the legacy of the 1981 federal reconciliation act is important to note, not so much for its ability to reorder intergovernmental relationships within New York, but rather for its ability to reinforce those characteristics of big state government and liberalism that had long existed in the state.

9

Mississippi

LEWIS H. SMITH AND ROBERT S. HERREN

The population of Mississippi, perhaps more than that of any other state, is vulnerable to cuts in federal domestic programs. Mississippi for several decades has experienced the lowest per capita income and the highest poverty rate of any state. In 1980, over 23 percent of the population lived in poverty households; 44 percent of all households received social security or federal public assistance, primarily aid to families with dependent children (AFDC) or Supplemental Security Income (SSI) benefits. Twenty-one percent of the state's population received food stamps.[1] In addition, 14 percent of the state's population was eligible for Medicaid, while in twenty-three of Mississippi's eighty-two counties, over 20 percent of the population was eligible for Medicaid.[2] Other federal programs in areas such as health and nutrition obviously are important to a large segment of Mississippi's population. The figures cited above explain why changes in eligility and funding reductions in federal programs significantly affect the low-income population in Mississippi.

Reagan's conservative social and political philosophy struck a kindred note with attitudes prevailing in state and local governments in Mississippi, as well as with a large segment of the population. However, in a state where federal transfer payments were a major component of personal income, where internal revenue sources for state and local government were already strained, and

[1] U.S. Department of Commerce, the Bureau of the Census, *1980 Census of Population Volume 1, chapter C, General Social and Economic Characteristics, Part 26, Mississippi* (Washington, D.C.: Government Printing Office, July 1983), p. 51.

[2] Ibid. See also Mississippi Department of Public Welfare, *Annual Report Fiscal Year 1981–1982* (Jackson, Miss.: Department of Public Welfare, 1982), pp. 22–25, and Mississippi Medicaid Commission, *Eleventh Annual Report* (Jackson, Miss.: Mississippi Medicaid Commission, 1980), pp. 10–11.

where the recession was especially harsh, the loss of federal funds could be expected to evoke a pragmatic response regardless of philosophy. This conflict between fiscal reality and philosophy made anticipating the impact of the Reagan program difficult.

The most immediate, direct, and severe impact of Reagan's cuts was felt by the low-income portion of the state's population, particularly the working poor. However, the state was both unable and unwilling to replace any reduction in federal funding for entitlement programs such as food stamps or AFDC or for any programs perceived as "federal" rather than "state." In fact, the greater control given to state officials in some areas resulted in movement away from programs in which benefits were targeted to special (often poor) groups and toward programs which benefited a majority of the population and consequently a broader political constituency.

The tension between a conservative philosophical attitude and the need for federal aid was not as great for local officials as for state officials because most local governments in Mississippi (including Jackson, the case-study city) have avoided excessive feeding at the federal trough, except for general revenue sharing and capital projects. The reluctance to become heavily involved with federal funds in operating programs, coupled with the longer-term nature of the funding-expenditure relationship in most capital programs, meant that the impact of the Reagan domestic program was less drastic on local than on state government.

In addition to fiscal and programmatic impacts, the Reagan changes provided an opportunity for political jockeying. Transferring the control of several programs, most notably the block grant, from federal to state control enabled the governor to utilize the changes to expand the power of his office.

Fiscal and Institutional Setting

From 1981 to 1984, the Mississippi state government found it difficult to maintain the real level of services in the face of increasing fiscal difficulties. Fiscal stress resulted from recession-induced revenue shortfalls and continued increases in demand for government-provided services. Mississippi's budget problems also resulted from fiscal decisions preceding the 1981 federal budget act.

In 1979, an election year, end-of-year surplus moved the legislature to increase exemptions under the state's personal income tax code. Although the exemptions were initially designed to reduce revenue by $80 million over three years, members of the state's budgeting and accounting commission later estimated that the new state tax bill actually reduced revenues by over $180 million during the three-year period.

To compound matters, in 1981 the legislature passed a budget that spent down $77 million from an end-of-year balance that totaled $79 million. When the full impact of the recession hit Mississippi in 1982, the state government had little surplus to cushion fiscal problems caused by rapidly falling tax revenues. By late summer 1982 (early in state fiscal year 1983), the state faced a projected deficit, and was forced to freeze capital projects, hiring, travel, and purchases of equipment; in addition, the state transferred money from special funds to the general fund.

In November 1982, in the midst of the budget problems, Governor William R. Winter convened a special session of the legislature to discuss his recommendations for new educational programs. The result was enactment of the Mississippi Education Reform Act of 1982. Funding for the act was to come from increased taxes of $107 million in state fiscal year 1984 and $112 million in 1985, with 55 percent of additional funds coming from a sales tax increase and the remainder from an increase in individual and corporate taxes. All new taxes were to take effect January 1, 1984.[3]

During the regular 1983 legislative session, an election year, the legislators avoided imposing either a tax increase or budget reductions through utilization of optimistic estimates of tax revenues for state fiscal year 1984. The tax commission and state legislators publicly insisted that the recession in Mississippi would not continue much longer; however, the state's economy continued to lag several months behind the national economy. Tax revenues were $14 million below projections in July and $16 million below projections in August. On August 30, the governor and budget commission director slashed projected outlays by $53 million through a 5 percent budget reduction for all agencies and a complete hiring freeze.[4]

By November 1983, revenue estimates for state fiscal year 1984 were $122 million below earlier projections, forcing Governor Winter to convene another special legislative session. The legislature enacted an increase in the state sales tax from 5 to 6 percent effective December 1, 1983. Included in this bill was a phase-out provision for one-half of the increase on June 30, 1984, with the other half remaining in effect through December 1986 as a funding source for the Education Reform Act.

[3] Task Force for Educational Excellence in Mississippi, *An Opportunity for Excellence: The Mississippi Education Reform Act of 1982* (Jackson, Miss.: Office of the Governor, July 1983), p. 55.

[4] As discussed in the political structure section below, the governor usually has very limited impact on the making of fiscal decisions. In this instance, however, the legislators were more than happy to allow Governor Winter to lead the efforts to reduce budgetary authority.

The 1984 legislative session opened in an atmosphere of extreme fiscal stress. Legislators faced the unpleasant prospect of not only a new tax increase but also of cancelling the scheduled phase out of a previous increase. Moreover, the health agencies mounted a strong sustained effort to convince legislators that a major decline in health services would occur without additional state funds. Newly elected governor William Allain opposed a major tax increase. Instead, he suggested that agencies reduce spending while a task force appointed by the governor studied how best to modify the tax structure. The state legislature considered tax hikes during the 1984 session. However, disagreements between the House and the Senate over specific proposals, along with the threat of a veto from the governor, prevented passage of tax increases during the regular 1984 legislative session.

LONGER-TERM FISCAL PROBLEMS

The recession was a major and uncontrollable contributor to Mississippi's fiscal problems between 1981 and 1984. However, even without the recession state government in 1984 was constrained by several continuing fiscal difficulties, including: (1) limitations of the current tax structure; (2) problems with forecasting tax revenues; (3) financing the Education Reform Act; and (4) funding school construction.

According to the U.S. Advisory Council on Intergovernmental Relationships (ACIR), Mississippi has the lowest tax capacity in the nation (76 percent of the national average), while its tax effort is 96 percent of the national average.[5] Despite its difficulty meeting even existing funding needs, the state had committed in 1982 an 8 percent increase in tax revenue for new educational programs. The task of finding additional revenue for other programs, therefore, proved to be very difficult.

In their search for additional revenue, legislators considered and ultimately rejected new sources such as legalized horse racing and a state lottery. In the end, they returned to traditional revenue sources: sales taxes (accounting for about 45 percent of total tax revenue) and personal income taxes (accounting for 15 percent). Revenue from oil and gas severance taxes increased from $33 million in 1979 (or 3 percent of tax revenues) to $115 million in 1983 (over 7 percent); however, weakness in the petroleum market threatened the growth of this source of revenue.

Another important budgetary problem centered around the state's inaccu-

[5] U.S. Advisory Commission on Intergovernmental Relations, *The Capacity of the Fifty States: Methodology and Estimates* (Washington, D.C.: Government Printing Office, March 1982), p. 106.

rate revenue forecasts. Mississippi's tax commission projects revenues based on historical evidence, while the state's research and development center relies on an econometric (Wharton) model. Both agencies tend to revise estimates periodically throughout the year. Since 1980, both forecasts have been poor in predicting personal income tax revenues, usually missing by 30 to 50 percent. Such uncertainty makes it difficult to adhere to the balanced budget required by the state constitution and often forces the legislature or governor to make budget decisions in a crisis atmosphere.

Another long-term fiscal problem involved funding the Education Reform Act and financing school construction. In 1983, the state used revenues which were supposed to finance new educational programs in the current operating budget. Moreover, the 1984 legislature proved reluctant to fund studies by the Department of Education important to implementing the programs. On April 23, 1984, Mississippi's secretary of state, Dick Molpus, issued a report that revenues for education would fall short by about $85 million because the legislature was dipping into the new revenues generated by the educational reform taxes.[6] Molpus wanted to form a trust fund to "safeguard" those revenues; Governor Allain supported this plan. However, the speaker of the House and the House ways and means committee chairman opposed this concept in part because they believed all programs should compete each year for available funds. Not only education reform programs, but also the new construction of educational facilities suffered funding shortfalls. Since 1981, the state Educational Finance Commission (EFC) has advocated (so far unsuccessfully) a four mill state property tax to replace local bond financing, since most attempts to obtain voter approval of new bond issues at the local level have failed.

GOVERNMENTAL STRUCTURE AND RELATIONSHIPS

The structure of state government is an important factor in analyzing the impact of federal fund reductions, in part because some state agencies had better access to the legislature than others. Mississippi is a weak governor-strong legislature state.[7] At least three factors contribute to the governor's lack of power. First, the state constitution does not allow a governor to succeed himself.[8] Second, the governor has little input in the budgetary process, although he possesses veto power over legislative acts. Third, many key agency heads are

[6] Coleman Warner, "Molpus Seeks Trust Fund," *The Clarion-Ledger*, April 24, 1984, p. 1.

[7] David B. Ogle, *Strengthening the Mississippi Legislature* (New Brunswick, N.J.: Rutgers University Press, 1971), pp. 3–9.

[8] In the fall of 1986, Mississippi voters approved a constitutional amendment that allows governors to serve two successive terms.

elected, including the attorney general, commissioner of agriculture, superintendent of education, and highway commissioner. Historically, the governor has not had much impact on such agencies. In addition, the heads of many important state agencies such as the Medicaid commission, are appointed by boards controlled by members of the legislature.[9] What power the governor of Mississippi does possess is derived from four sources: the governor's ability to marshal public support for a policy or program, the governor's rapport with the legislature, the federal funds over which the governor has control, and a line-item veto.

The reconciliation act gave the governor an opportunity to expand his power by increasing the funds, primarily through the block grants, over which he had direct control. Consequently, the governor was very active in determining the state's reaction to the reconciliation act changes and funding reductions.

LOCAL GOVERNMENTS

The state's local governments were largely unaffected by and unconcerned with changes in federal aid in the Reagan years, in part because of their limited financial dependence on federal aid. Cities do rely on general revenue sharing funds but those changed little during the Reagan first term. Cities have no involvement in entitlement and little in most operating programs other than education. They do not in general replace lost federal education funds with local revenues but instead look to the state for additional funding. Indeed, some cities such as Jackson have transferred ad valorem taxes from the school district to the general fund.

The fiscal situation facing local governments in 1981 varied substantially by jurisdiction. In general, the larger municipalities such as Jackson were pushing the limits of local tax capacity, while smaller municipalities such as Tupelo had sufficient unused capacity to allow some degree of fiscal flexibility.

A closer examination of the fiscal difficulties of Jackson provides insights into the role of federal funds at the local level. From 1976 to 1980 city revenues in Jackson grew by more than 10 percent per year. Intergovernmental grants accounted for approximately 70 percent of the increase in revenues during this period. About half of the city's intergovernmental grants came from the federal government. Almost the entire growth of federal funds during this period occurred in capital grants, such as wastewater treatment, urban highways, and urban development.

[9] In 1983, the Mississippi State Supreme Court ruled that allowing legislators to serve on executive boards and commissions was unconstitutional. *Alexander v. State* (1983, Mississippi), *Southern Reporter*, 441, 2nd edition, p. 1329.

In 1981, Jackson began to feel growing pressure on its operating budget. City officials faced a $2 million deficit in the general fund revenues supported primarily by sales tax receipts. City officials projected a $6 million deficit by September 1981. Overestimation of sales tax revenue significantly contributed to this shortfall as the 10 to 12 percent annual increase in sales tax revenues dropped to a 2 to 3 percent increase in state fiscal year 1981. The city responded by freezing wages and reducing employment. Throughout 1982 and 1983, Jackson's regional economy continued to be depressed; sales tax revenues grew very slowly. City officials elected to increase the assessment rate on general property to raise additional revenue.

Thus, reduced federal aid was not a major cause of the city of Jackson's fiscal problems. However, the cutbacks compounded the city's problems. City officials have maintained a policy of not funding staff with federal grants. The major employment cuts that occurred in 1982 were unrelated to federal reductions because the portion of the operating budget dependent on federal funds was small and capital funding was set several years in advance.

However, local government faced funding losses through state administration of federal grant programs. The larger cities, which had been successful in obtaining discretionary federal funds, particularly in education, lost out when federal programs were transferred to state control and funding distribution practices changed. In addition, in its search to find funding for state programs, the state reduced transfers to local government. Thus, intergovernmental relationships were important in determining the impact of federal cuts on local government.

STATE-LOCAL RELATIONSHIPS

Local governments are the weak partner in the state-local relationship. Often, the relative position of a given locality is based upon individual political relationships between local officials and state legislators. Even the largest municipality in the state has relatively little political muscle.

State government is both a direct provider of services at the local level and a major source of funds for services provided by local governments. Approximately 40 percent of state revenue receipts is transferred to counties and cities.[10] The major flow of funds from state government to local units comes in education. Of the $677 million in state funds that went to local education authorities in state fiscal year 1983, about $150 million was a pass-through of federal

[10] Revenue figures cited in this and the following paragraph are taken from Mississippi Department of Public Accountants, *Annual State Financial Reports* for the years 1981 to 1983 (Jackson, Miss.: Department of Public Accounts, 1981, 1982, and 1983).

funds, including $67 million for school lunches. Another $67 million of state funds supported community junior colleges. The remaining state funds provided over 55 percent of local elementary and secondary school budgets. In other words, the state has fiscal responsibility for elementary and secondary education while the actual services are provided at the local level. In addition to education, the state provides funds for general assistance and public works for cities and counties ($120 million in 1981).

The $98 million of sales tax revenue remitted to cities in 1981, although only 12 percent of state transfers, normally accounts for 30 to 40 percent of a typical municipality's general fund budget. The state thus has a major role in establishing the fiscal well-being of local governments by determining the proportion of sales tax remitted. From 1968 to 1979, 19 percent of local gross sales taxes collected within a municipality was returned. After 1979, the rate increased to 20.5 percent, allowing cities to somewhat reduce dependence on property taxes.

Beginning in 1982, the Mississippi Municipal Association attempted to acquire additional funding. The strength of this organization was enhanced when the city of Jackson, under the leadership of Mayor Dale Danks, took a more active role in the association. The Mississippi Municipal Association requested permission from the state legislature to allow cities to impose additional sales taxes. With state-imposed limits on property tax increases, the most obvious source of additional revenue was a local option sales tax. During the 1984 legislative session, the association also lobbied for full home rule; without it, localities can only undertake activities which the legislature has specified. As might be expected, several legislators contended that the state's 292 municipalities just wanted to go on a "tax rampage" and delayed home-rule studies until after the 1984 session. Neither the local option sales tax nor home rule passed the legislature. Local governments remain highly dependent on state government's actions for their fiscal well-being.

General Fiscal Responses

Mississippi's state legislature did not become addicted to replacing lost federal funds during 1982 and 1983. Even if legislators had wanted to replace lost federal funds, the state lacked the capability to do so. The severe and long lasting recession prevented any substantial increase in nominal tax revenues. The unemployment rate remained above 10 percent through 1983 thus indicating that Mississippi's economy was not part of the booming sunbelt. The tax base within the state remained depressed throughout 1982 and 1983.

State revenues from the major tax increases approved during the study period were committed primarily to general educational programs enacted by the 1982 Education Reform Act. Thus, the state was not able to replace federal cuts in most programs because of budget decisions made prior to 1981, the recession, and its commitment of new taxes to general education.

The federal cuts had little effect on the size of state government. It is true that, with few exceptions, state agencies in Mississippi were providing services with smaller staffs in 1983 than in 1980. However, this was not a result of cuts in federal aid, but rather of state budgetary problems and the drive by Governor Winter for improved efficiency in state government. The five major state agencies affected by the 1981 federal budget act had reached their lowest employee level by October 1981, and by January 1982 had started a gradual increase.[11] Rather than adding to staff reductions, changes such as the assumption by the state of the small-cities community development block grant program actually contributed to an increase in state staffing.

The fiscal problems caused by the 1981 federal budget cuts in Mississippi may have seemed minor to the state legislature given the existing situation in 1982 and 1983. Nevertheless, by late 1983 it became apparent that at least some of the impacts of the cuts could not be ignored. State agencies affected began to mount pressure on the legislature for budgetary assistance. The extent of their success depended in large measure on the nature of federal aid changes involved and on the program affected.

ENTITLEMENT GRANTS

Changes in federal funds for entitlement programs in Mississippi reflect three major influences. First, changes in the eligibility requirements embodied in the reconciliation act reduced the eligible population in each program. Second, and counter to the first factor, the deepening recession increased the proportion of the population that met the new eligibility criteria. Finally, there was flexibility at the state level in determining eligibility requirements, available services and, to a limited extent, individual payment levels in AFDC and Medicaid.

In federal fiscal year 1982, federal funds for the food stamp program dropped from the 1981 level of $241.3 million to $236.4 million, a decline of 2 percent, while funds for AFDC fell from $48.2 million to $42.1 million, a 12.6 percent decline. In federal fiscal year 1983, however, funding for both programs increased. The state's food stamp allotment grew by 16 percent compared with the

---

[11] These agencies are: the departments of Health, Mental Health, Welfare, Education, and the governor's Office of Federal-State Programs.

previous year, to a level of $280 million. Federal spending for AFDC benefits increased by less than 1 percent.

The decline in funding levels in AFDC and food stamps in 1982 reflects a reduction in the number of recipients caused by the reconciliation act's eligibility changes. The average number of persons receiving food stamps declined from 505,175 per month in 1981 to 493,875 per month in 1982. Although there were several changes in food stamp eligibility requirements, the most important change arising from the reconciliation act was the new household definition, which stated that parents and children who live together are not to be considered separate households unless one of the parents is sixty years of age or older. Eligibility for AFDC was reduced by the application of the 150 percent needs standards and the inclusion of a stepparent's income in the determination of family income. The case load fell by 17 percent in fiscal year 1982.

The recession had the opposite effect of increasing food stamp and AFDC case loads. The state welfare department estimated that the decline in the number of persons receiving food stamps would have been 3 to 4 percent greater in 1982 had it not been for the recession. In 1983, the effects of the deepening recession became more apparent. The food stamp program average monthly rolls were 7.8 percent above the 1982 average and 3.3 percent above the 1981 average. There is little doubt that the recession also kept the size of the AFDC and Medicaid eligible population from falling further than it did. However, still other events made the magnitude impossible to estimate.

In the summer of 1982, the state Department of Welfare raised the AFDC standard of need by 30 percent. Mississippi had not adjusted the standard of need since 1977, and officially considered this revision to be an "inflation adjustment." Due to the case-load reduction in 1982, there was a potential surplus of state funds allocated for AFDC, so the standard of need revision did not require a controversial request for additional funding from the legislature. The case load after the revised standard went into effect remained 11 percent lower than prior to the reconciliation act although several welfare officials had contended that the new standards would restore eligibility to the majority of families cut. However, the case load did average 7 percent above the federal fiscal year 1982 average and the change may have prevented further reductions from 1981 levels.

Medicaid funding rose by 5.5 percent in federal fiscal year 1982 over the 1981 level of $209 million and by another 13.2 percent from 1982 to federal fiscal year 1983. The 1983 federal funding level of $247.4 million was thus almost 20 percent above the level existing when the reconciliation act was passed. Some of the increase reflects the rapidly rising cost of medical services rather than a change in the amount of services or the number of eligibles served.

In fact, changes in eligibility requirements which eliminated some AFDC recipients actually placed a downward pressure on the Medicaid case load and outlays. The 1982 monthly averages of AFDC children and adults eligible for Medicaid were less than the 1981 monthly averages by 26,641 and 5,570, respectively. An additional factor which reduced federal funds going to Medicaid was the reconciliation act's requirement that the federal share be reduced by 3 percent in federal fiscal year 1982, 4 percent in 1983, and 4.5 percent in 1984. State officials estimated that this requirement cost Mississippi between $30 million and $40 million each year.

The change in the AFDC standard of need was one of several actions by the state which also contributed to increased Medicaid funding in 1982 and 1983. In federal fiscal year 1982, the state expanded available services. For example, the maximum annual physician visits increased from twelve to eighteen and maximum annual hospital days increased from twenty to thirty. Equally important, the state did not adopt cost containment practices so that its reimbursement rates continued to reflect a high rate of increase in the cost of medical care.

Unlike the AFDC changes at the state level, the Medicaid changes required additional state funds. Several factors explain the apparent willingness of the state to replace funds in this program. First, there is a general perception in Mississippi that this program is a joint federal-state program rather than exclusively federal. Second, the medical profession has provided indispensable support for this program. Experts in the state say this support was a crucial factor in the legislature's agreeing to add a medically needy program in 1984. Third, over 40 percent of Medicaid funds directly aid the elderly. Medicaid officials argued that without enough state funds, benefits to the elderly would be reduced. The threat of turning the aged poor into the street proved to be effective in obtaining additional funds from the state legislature.

Outside of Medicaid both the private and public sectors in Mississippi showed scant initiative and little interest in replacing lost or reduced entitlement services. The state government did not begin any new food programs for the poor, nor was there pressure on state legislators to provide supplemental funding for food stamps—seen as a totally federal program. Nor was there any help for this or any entitlement programs from local governments. In Mississippi, local governments have not historically been involved with general welfare programs; they did not initiate new programs in 1982 and 1983. Existing nonprofit organizations reported an increased demand for their services but there are no accurate figures available which reflect the magnitude of nonprofit agencies' service to the state's low-income population. Moreover, the rural nature of Mississippi makes major private sector efforts to offset the impact of entitlement cuts difficult if not impossible. The agencies are concentrated in the larger urban areas with a disproportionate number in Jackson. Nonprofit agencies apparently were not a factor in reducing the overall impact of entitlement reductions in Mississippi.

OPERATING PROGRAMS

The number of operating programs and the diversity of their objectives make generalization concerning the impacts of the reconciliation act more tenuous than was the case for entitlement programs. Nevertheless, several broad conclusions are justifiable. For most operating programs, state officials were able to spread the effects of the reconciliation act across several years through the use of carryover funds and increased efficiencies. These efforts were enhanced by the additional aid appropriated under the emergency jobs act of 1983, which allowed some state agencies to postpone significant expenditure reductions until federal fiscal year 1984 or 1985. Institutional changes were limited by the existing structure of state government. However, some change did occur in mental health, education and community services, and in the governor's power. Local governments were largely unaffected by cuts in operating programs. Finally, state agencies utilized additional programmatic flexibility to spread funds throughout the state.

Table 9.1 shows the diverse ways in which the 1981 reconciliation act affected operating programs. Reductions in the allocation of funds to operating programs was most pronounced in 1982. This was a year of reaction and patchwork for state and local agencies administering operating grants. For example,

Table 9.1. *State Expenditures of Federal Operating Grants, Federal Fiscal Years 1981–84 (dollars in millions)*

Program	1981	1982	1983
Social services block grant	24.3	24.4	25.1
Community services block grant	5.9	3.1	5.2
Job training	74.7	36.2	33.9
Maternal and child health block grant	6.6	3.8	5.9
Preventive health block grant	1.6	0.6	1.7
Alcohol, drug abuse, and mental health block grant[a]	5.9	4.4	4.3
Education block grant	11.1	11.4	5.3
Compensatory education	71.0	70.3	65.5

SOURCE: Governor's Office of Federal-State Programs, and the state's health, education, mental health, and welfare departments.

NOTE: [a] Funding level.

funding for the three state-administered health block grants declined by 20 to 40 percent in federal fiscal year 1982 and remained at a reduced level. However, reductions in health *expenditures* were in general less dramatic than in other operating programs, although they varied more across programs. Expenditures for maternal and child health care programs declined by only 11 percent between 1981 and 1983, while spending for alcohol, drug abuse, and mental health declined by 25 percent. Preventive health expenditures experienced the most severe decline, falling over 62 percent between 1981 and 1982, but, as table 9.1 indicates, expenditures were restored by 1983. Expenditures for maternal and child health increased in 1983 and further spending increases were anticipated for all three health block grant programs in 1984. Both the Department of Mental Health, which administers the alcohol, drug abuse, and mental health block grant and the Department of Health, which administers the other health blocks, combined carryover funds from 1981 with 1982 appropriations. This smoothed implementation of the cuts. Efforts to offset 1982 spending cutbacks were further aided by emergency jobs act funds. In the middle of federal fiscal year 1983, the state received an additional $1.9 million in maternal and child health aid from the jobs act. The state's 1983 allocation of $4.3 million in alcohol, drug abuse, and mental health block grant aid was supplemented by an additional $291,000 from the jobs act. In 1983, the Department of Health spent less than 5 percent of its jobs act allocation, while the Department of Mental Health did not spend any of its emergency supplemental funds.

The state's Department of Human Development operated the community services block grant program in a similar manner. The federal fiscal year 1982 allocation was $4.0 million, a 20 percent drop from the previous year; expenditures decreased by 50 percent. However, Mississippi's 1983 allotment rose by 10 percent ($400,000), while carryover funds permitted expenditures to rise by 60 percent ($2 million). In both federal fiscal year 1982 and 1983, community action agencies (CAAs) returned funds to the state.

Both compensatory education assistance (chapter 1) and the elementary and secondary education block grant (chapter 2) are forward funded. Consequently, the full effects of the spending cuts in 1982 did not take effect until the 1982–83 school year. Nevertheless, Mississippi lost $1 million in compensatory education funding in 1982. In federal fiscal year 1983, there was a 7 percent reduction in funding with further reductions of 5 percent the following year.[12]

Actual expenditures for the educational block grant, which had been constant for the previous two years, dropped over 50 percent in federal fiscal year

---

[12] The federal fiscal year 1982 reductions and part of the reductions in subsequent years resulted from a change in the elementary and secondary school enrollment upon which allocations were founded.

1983 from $11.4 million to $5.3 million. The impact of the cuts fell exclusively on a few school districts—those that had aggressively pursued categorical grants that were replaced by the new block grant. The city of Jackson accounted for 60 percent of the 1982 reduction; many other school districts that had not actively pursued federal education aid under the former categorical programs received an "increase" in federal funding under the state's formula distribution of the block grant.

Federal social service grants increased slightly in federal fiscal year 1982 over the $24.8 million level of the previous year. With the addition of jobs act monies, 1983 allocations rose again by almost 12 percent. Nevertheless, miscalculation by the state Department of Welfare of the new funding level created a "mini-crisis" in the department and substantial reductions in the latter half of federal fiscal year 1982 as the welfare department spread budget reductions across service providers, forcing many to make difficult adjustments. The department had no carryover from fiscal year 1981 and their efforts to obtain aid from the state legislature were unsuccessful.

The one program which could not utilize carryover funds to cushion a dramatic reduction in funds was job training. The total expenditures for all job training and employment programs authorized under the Comprehensive Employment and Training Act (CETA) in Mississippi in federal fiscal year 1982 were less than half the 1981 level, falling from $74.7 million to $36.2 million. Over 70 percent of the reduction resulted from the termination of public service employment (PSE) grants and the completion of a youth demonstration project. The remaining reduction was due to the reconciliation act cuts in adult and youth job training. Federal job training grants to Mississippi for federal fiscal year 1983 declined by 6 percent from the 1982 level. Projected expenditures for 1984 indicated that funding had stabilized at the state level but that the state would fund the urban consortiums at a level almost 10 percent below that of the previous year.[13]

In general, the state did not replace the federal cutbacks in job training grants. In fact, Mississippi had a statute specifically prohibiting such an occurrence. However, Mississippi did appear to favor some long-term replacement in programs that serve broad constituencies, such as health and education. In 1982 and 1983, the state increased spending for alcohol, drug abuse, and mental health programs; a further major increase occurred in state fiscal year 1985. In addition, the 1984 state budget contained an increase of almost $1 million for maternal and child health programs. Unlike other agencies affected by the

---

[13] The majority of CETA funds (over 80 percent) were administered at the state level with the remainder administered by two urban consortiums—Jackson and the Gulf Coast.

acts, these programs were already receiving substantial state funding. More-over, they tended to provide services for a relatively broad segment of the state's population. Similarly, even though funding for compensatory education and the education block grant dropped from 1981, the state indicated a willingness to increase support for elementary education through its enactment of the 1982 Education Reform Act. The new programs provide services to all children in kindergarten and grades one through three, whereas the lost federal funds were targeted for low-income children.

Local governments were most directly affected by cuts in education pro-grams. Although replacement in education was not commonplace at the local level, a few instances did occur. For example, in 1983, the city of Jackson re-placed a portion of lost title XX funds in the day care program by picking up the salaries of four administrators and four tenured supervisors; this was in line with the city's general policy of not using federal funds for staff positions. However, local replacement was the exception rather than the rule. In part, because many school districts were already at the maximum millage, localities were not able to offset federal reductions. It may also be the case that the lost funding was seen as too rigidly targeted on specific groups, so that localities were reluctant to re-place it. On the whole, local governments continued to look to the state for ad-ditional funding.

INSTITUTIONAL IMPACTS

The state governmental structure in Mississippi limited the range of possible in-stitutional changes that could result from the provisions of the reconciliation act. The only major change was stimulated by Mississippi's assumption of the block grants—by 1983 the state had assumed administration of all blocks except primary care. Governor Winter's initiative in the block grant area allowed him to expand the power of the governor's office. His personal popularity and rela-tively good relationship with the state legislature accounted for the legislature's lack of involvement with the implementation of block grants. Additional strength in the governor's office derived from expanded input by the governor in state agencies administering block grants—agencies which were previously almost autonomous.

Governor Winter took a leadership role in the block grant planning process from the beginning. To assure uniform planning, coordination, and public in-put, he established a block grant task force, a planning group to advise the task force, and an education advisory board. The task force included directors of public health, mental health, public welfare, federal-state programs, and the budget commission and established joint eligibility criteria, a format for public hearings, and uniform cost categories.

Some direct shifting of power and responsibility among government agencies occurred. For example, the welfare department requested that social services funds be redistributed away from other agencies and concentrated more on welfare services. The task force, with the full approval of the governor, agreed to a redistribution of funds—but not one that favored the welfare department. In fact, the task force created "mini-blocks" within the social services block grant funds and transferred block grant funding away from welfare services to public and mental health services, as well as to social services for the elderly. Thirty-three percent of the state's social services block grant allotment was passed through as "mini-blocks"—18 percent to mental health, 12 percent to the governor's council on aging, and 3 percent to the health department. By depriving the welfare department of its administrative control of funds, the governor's office shifted all social services fund reductions to programs that the Department of Public Welfare was directly operating.[14]

The governor's Office of Federal-State Programs, which is directly under the governor's control, experienced an expansion of its role and responsibilities. In addition to the planning work involved with the block grant task force, this office undertook administration of the community services block grant. The state office accepted responsibility for supervision, contracting, technical analysis, and monitoring. In this case, state officials had to develop a new, more authoritative relationship with community action agencies.

The remaining block grants had very little political or institutional impact. Because public health has been centralized for many years, the health blocks did not alter state-local government relations. Little institutional impact from implementation of the education block grant occurred even though it replaced categorical grants which had gone directly from the federal government to local schools. Because the amount of funding involved in chapter 2 is so minuscule compared with the regular state aid to local school districts, the new block grant did not significantly increase the state's control over local districts.

The Job Training Partnership Act (JTPA) presented the possibility for expansion of the governor's influence. In the end, however, major institutional relationships remained unchanged, although the governor's office did gain some additional control. Implementation of JTPA in Mississippi is a study in political survival. Under the CETA program, there were three designated prime spon-

---

[14] In fall 1984, the governor's office assumed total administrative control over the social services block grant.

sors in the state. The Jackson Consortium and the Gulf Coast Consortium were urban prime sponsors each containing three counties. The remaining seventy-six counties in Mississippi were part of the balance of state administered by the governor's Office of Job Development and Training. The governor desired to have the entire state designated as a single service delivery area (SDA). In the end, the two urban prime sponsors under CETA were able to exert sufficient political muscle to forestall the governor's plan. As a result, Mississippi has three service delivery areas, which are essentially the old prime sponsors.

Even though the two former urban CETA prime sponsors managed to obtain SDA designation, their relationship with the state changed. The state now approves all local expenditure plans. More importantly, the two SDAs are assured only proportional funding under title IIA. Furthermore, most of the federal funds earmarked for training dislocated workers has been retained by the state, rather than redistributed to local service delivery areas. Thus, although funding for state-administered job training programs remained virtually unchanged, the combined funding of the urban SDAs was half what it was in federal fiscal years 1983 and 1984.

When all changes since 1981 are reviewed, the most remarkable conclusion concerning JTPA is that relatively little changed. Prime sponsors became SDAs covering the same geographical areas with essentially the same personnel. The primary actors in JTPA were the primary actors in CETA and had provided the same or similar services. The governor's office gained strength relative to the local SDAs but in general JTPA is a scaled-down CETA with no public service employment.

PROGRAMMATIC IMPACTS

As already discussed, the state replaced lost federal funds only in programs that served a broad segment of the population. For the same political reason, there were attempts within programs to spread available funds across the state rather than targeting specific groups whenever possible. For example, the health department replaced the local categorical grants with statewide grants. Similarly, most projects approved by the state Department of Education utilizing chapter 2 funds affected the entire student population of a local district. This reflected not only state but local officials' attitudes as well.

The state's ratification of all cuts in operating programs oriented toward low-income individuals and its acceptance of changed institutional and administrative relationships caused some other specific programmatic changes, most notably those funded under the social services block grant, the community services block grant, and JTPA. The Department of Welfare increased "in-house" utilization of social services block grant funds in 1982 and exempted these from budget reductions. This change allowed the state agency to minimize personnel reductions. The state agency directly provided such services as adoption, counseling, foster care, and protective services for children. The state welfare department also maintained outlays for day-care services provided by contractors; however, it reduced spending for such purchased services as family planning, maternity home care, and transportation.

In the community services block grant program, the state Department of Human Development imposed a 25 percent administrative expenditure maximum on all CAAs. The state also defined administrative costs. At first, CAAs contended that they were forced to operate with smaller, less qualified staffs. However, the director of the state Department of Human Development maintained that the agencies are now more efficient and are providing the same level of client services as they did under federal direction. In general, the state forced the CAAs to become "leaner" and to stop being a source of "subsidized" employment.

JTPA officials stressed more programs which are of relatively short duration and result in high placement rates. Moreover, the governor's office responsible for administering job training grants "re-discovered" on-the-job training. The reduced level of federal aid for training, 15 percent below the federal fiscal year 1981 level, coupled with the emphasis on performance-based evaluation which came with JTPA, was largely responsible for this change; the preference of private sector representatives for on-the-job training might also have been a factor.

While changes in already existing programs like community services block grant and job training programs were substantial, Mississippi did not begin new or innovative programs, even with the infusion of jobs act funds. Unlike other states, where the executive might control "new" money that comes into the jurisdiction "off-cycle," with very little competition from the state legislature, in Mississippi this control was limited. The pivotal role of the budget commission (and therefore the state legislature) in the budgetary process prevented the governor from automatically controlling the new or off-cycle funds. Also, the fact that key agency heads were not gubernatorial appointees reduced the governor's influence over the utilization of new funds. Although the governor controlled programs administered by the office of federal-state programs, even here the legislature limited the governor's flexibility. Thus, the state did not change the types of programs which it funded; nor was the governor able to use this new money to significantly increase his influence over the types of programs funded.

CAPITAL PROGRAMS

It is difficult, if not impossible, to draw any generalized conclusions regarding the impact of funding cuts in capital programs on state or local governments in Mississippi. Changes in funding for capital projects tend to have a delayed impact because of the lumpy nature of many projects and because of lags between appropriations and expenditures. As a result, federal funding reductions in 1982 and 1983 had a relatively small effect on state and local expenditures for capital projects. Table 9.2 shows federal allocations and expenditures for federal fiscal years 1981–83.

In 1983, new funding initiatives offset federal fiscal year 1982 losses in several areas. Relatively small reductions in community development block grant funds were more than offset by jobs act funds. Federal allocations for Mississippi highways were approximately 50 percent higher in 1983 than in 1981, and have been in the range of $100 to $108 million.

Mississippi's allocation of wastewater treatment funds fell by 32 percent from federal fiscal year 1981 to 1982 but remained stable at $23 million from 1982 to 1983. The initial impact of this reduction was probably uneven across the

Table 9.2. *Selected Capital Grant Allocations and Expenditures, Federal Fiscal Years 1981–84 (dollars in millions)*

Program	1981	1982	1983
Small-cities community development block grant			
allocation to state	31.3	33.9	30.3
expenditures	31.2[a]	0.1	11.6
Community development block grant—entitlement			
allocation to Jackson	5.2	5.0	4.4
expenditures by Jackson	6.1	5.6	3.0
Wastewater treatment			
allocation to state	34.0	22.9	23.0
expenditures by Jackson	12.4	4.4	1.2
Urban development action grants			
expenditures by Jackson	3.5	0.4	0.3
Economic Development Administration			
grants to state	7.7	4.7	4.7
expenditures by Jackson	0.2	0.6	0.7

SOURCE: Governor's Office of Federal-State Programs, and the city of Jackson's *Comprehensive Annual Financial Report* (1981–83).

NOTE: [a] Amounts drawn down in 1981, 1982, and 1983.

state and will be increasingly so in the future. In part, because of ecological problems, the Gulf Coast will receive about 50 percent of the state's future allocations. Some localities had already begun to look for other sources of funding in federal fiscal year 1983; some replacement of federal funds with local funds may occur as well.

Most other capital programs have never been a major source of funds in Mississippi; moreover, the reluctance of local officials to deal with the federal government makes it difficult to identify projects that had to be sacrificed as a result of Reagan's cuts. For example, in 1982, Jackson completed its last major urban development action grant—a three-year, $6 million grant to build a parking garage. City officials claimed that the Reagan program did not prevent them from applying for or receiving new grants; instead they contended that they had no projects which were appropriate for this program.

INSTITUTIONAL AND PROGRAMMATIC IMPACTS

Among capital programs, only the small-cities portion of the community development block grant presented an opportunity for institutional and programmatic changes. The small-cities program enabled the governor to expand the power and responsibilities of his office. In June 1983, Governor Winter created within the governor's Office of Federal-State Programs the Department of Community Development as the administrative unit for the small-cities block grant. Federal small-cities funds to the state increased by about 6 percent in 1982 compared with the previous year. In 1983, Mississippi received $37.2 million in small-cities aid, of which $6.9 million was appropriated by the jobs act.

The state developed a comprehensive plan to award grants on an "objective" basis, in which it established program categories and set up rating factors within each category. State officials believed their extensive system of rating factors minimized the perception that political factors were crucial in obtaining grants. The 1983 annual report states: "The selection system developed by the task force is mostly objective rather than subjective, thus mathematically allowing the best project to be funded. . . . Mississippi's selection system avoids any possibility of politicalization because the applications are numerically rated against each other."[15] The state set aside 10 percent of the allocation for a special opportunities program (to meet urgent needs) and prior federal multi-year commitments; otherwise, state allocations were unrestricted, depending on the number of applications and on the amount of funds requested. Localities either

---

[15] State of Mississippi, Governor's Office of Federal-State Programs, Department of Community Development, *1982 Community Development Block Grant Annual Performance Report* (Jackson, Miss.: Office of the Governor, December 1983), p. 3.

competed directly for funds or formed regional entitlement areas, which were then guaranteed a portion of community development block grant funds. Mississippi's distribution of small-cities funds has resulted in an increased emphasis on public facilities and economic development projects and less emphasis on housing projects. In federal fiscal year 1982, 70 percent of the new grants went toward public facilities, 22 percent fell in the economic development category, and only 8 percent represented new housing projects. Local officials favored this programmatic shift.

While the governor gained more authority under changes in the small-cities program, there was no institutional change in the entitlement portion of the community development program. Regulatory changes, however, provided local officials with greater programmatic flexibility. The funds for entitlement cities fell in Mississippi in both 1982 and 1983. The allocation to the city of Jackson (which receives over 70 percent of the community development entitlement grants in Mississippi) declined by approximately 4 percent in 1983, but the addition of jobs act funds resulted in a total 1983 allocation 25 percent above the 1981 level. Jackson's use of supplemental community development entitlement funds provided by the emergency jobs act in 1983 demonstrated the reluctance of city officials to use federal funds for permanent, administrative staff. City officials used jobs act money in fiscal year 1983 to hire 400 previously unemployed people for temporary, labor-intensive projects. The city plans to hire forty or fifty workers with the remaining jobs act money and to use regular community development funds for infrastructure repairs. Jackson was therefore able to avoid increasing regular staff positions which later would have to be eliminated. Jackson's actions also resulted in two programmatic changes: the intermingling of jobs act funds with regular funding, and the shift away from housing and toward infrastructure projects that benefit a wider group of recipients.

Conclusions

The national recession played a much more important role than did the new federalism of Ronald Reagan, in determining both the health of the Mississippi state economy and the financial strength of the state government. The recession in the state was severe, and more importantly, was long lasting. It swelled the rolls of entitlement programs despite restrictions in eligibility requirements and made significant replacement of lost federal funds by state and local governments difficult, even had they been so inclined. By spring 1984, as the recession subsided in Mississippi, the impacts of the reconciliation act on the state became clearer.

Although critics of Mississippi's state government have often charged that no systematic policy is ever followed, by late 1983 several strands of a discernible response to the challenges imposed by the reconciliation act emerged. The state possessed neither the will nor the financial resources to undertake major replacement in income maintenance programs. With the exception of the minor action of the Department of Welfare in altering the AFDC standard of need, no action in this area occurred. Clearly, the low-income population was adversely affected. Changes in other programs intensified the effects on the low-income population; where possible, categorical programs were dropped in favor of programs which addressed the needs of large constituencies rather than those targeted on a specific group. State and local officials appreciated the freedom that came with the broader-based block grants; however, they did not enjoy working with fewer funds.

The state government's response was strongest in the health area and differed to a large extent from its actions regarding other programs. The state, partially through transfer of social services block grant funds, attempted to maintain services in mental health and public health programs. In addition, the state continued to increase its funding for Medicaid, in part because of the political strength of organized health care groups. However, after 1984 the legislature will probably tie additional funding increases for Medicaid to some cost containment effort.

The impact of funding reductions in capital programs was minor in federal fiscal years 1982 and 1983, although some effects will certainly occur in the future. While capital programs have a broad-based constituency, no discernible state or local strategy toward funding reductions in these programs had emerged by mid-1984. As a result, both the actual and perceived impacts of Reagan's domestic program on local governments was small.

Governor Winter made a clear attempt to use the transfer of federal control to state government to expand the power of the office of governor. The situation was complicated when the State Supreme Court ruled that legislators could not serve on a board of a state agency simultaneously. While there are indications that the reconciliation act enhanced the governor's power, reorganization in the executive branch and the political maneuvering that occurred between the governor's office and the state legislature following the court's ruling overwhelmed impacts of the reconciliation act.

The reconciliation act did not result in fundamental changes in state-local relationships but did somewhat enhance the role of state government. The formation of block grants from numerous categorical programs meant that in certain programs funds would flow to local government from state government rather than from the federal government. The state government, often with a lack of direction from Washington, assumed a management role in several areas previously controlled by the federal government. The responsibilities in community development and community services demanded new expertise and program development. Although some would prefer the traditional housing projects, to date, local governments appear to be very satisfied with the operation and direction of the state's community development program; they probably would not welcome a reintroduction of federal interference. In most programs and for most people, however, the state role did not change.

Most of the institutional changes will persist, unless federal policy reverses itself. Organizationally, the governor's Office of Federal-State Programs has always been responsive to changes in federal initiative although usually to more, not less, federal aid. Local education officials prefer dealing with the state education department but could easily become reacquainted with the airlines' schedules to Washington. What will persist is the realization of government officials in Mississippi that federal programs can contract as well as expand—something almost forgotten during the 1970s. Although the state as well as local governments always attempted to isolate federal funds from general operating funds, they nevertheless expected federal fund increases. In 1982, for the first time, many managers of operating programs were forced to shoulder monitoring and auditing responsibilities; agencies became more cost conscious and in some cases even more efficient. The reconciliation act forced state and local governments to acknowledge the tenuous nature of federal aid; this lesson may cease to be such a constant concern if funding levels are restored at either the federal or state level, but it will not soon be forgotten.

Ohio

CHARLES F. ADAMS, JR., JOSEPH M. DAVIS,

AND MARILYN T. DAVIS

*O*ver the period from 1981 through 1983, the effects of the domestic policy initiatives enacted during the first term of the Reagan administration were monitored and analyzed for the state of Ohio and the city of Cleveland. Focusing primarily on those initiatives affecting entitlement, operating, and capital programs, the field analysis sought to clarify the fiscal and programmatic consequences of the Reagan policies, as well as the impact on people, politics, and institutions. The results of this three-year study are reported in this chapter. Briefly summarized, the key findings and insights derived from the field research in Ohio are as follows:

1. The *fiscal impact* of the program changes were, on balance, minor for both the state and the city. For the state, a precarious fiscal environment was thrown into complete turmoil as a result of the 1981–82 recession, the consequences of which totally overshadowed the effects of federal aid cuts. In the entitlement area, various program changes affecting eligibility and payment levels actually resulted in a net savings to the state, related increases in state-funded general relief spending notwithstanding. In various operating programs, carryover balances and the subsequent infusion of emergency jobs act money largely made up for funding cuts. And in the case of capital programs, little fiscal hardship was observed, especially in light of new funding provided under the Surface Transportation Assistance Act of 1982.

2. *Programmatically*, significant effects were observed in the employment and training area with the shift from the Comprehensive Employment and

The authors would like to acknowledge the assistance of their colleague, Professor Frederick D. Stocker, and to thank the many state and local administrators and officials for their cooperation and help.

Training Act (CETA) programs to Job Training Partnership Act (JTPA) programs. In the case of Medicaid, a number of major changes were initiated by the state. Otherwise, there is little to report by way of program shifts, although there is evidence of increased efficiency in the technical control aspects of a variety of state programs.

3. As to the *effects on people*, the Reagan cuts had dramatic consequences, especially for those dependent on entitlement programs, such as aid to families with dependent children (AFDC), Medicaid, and food stamps. Among various operating programs, the termination of CETA, and especially its public service employment components, had a similar impact. Again, however, these cuts, while significant in terms of the needs and circumstances of individuals, did not translate into significant consequences for the state or city. In general, despite a major change in state leadership and a significant expansion in the state's tax system, the attitude toward the federal cuts expressed early on in the field research persisted over time; namely, "It's not our problem." While there was some replacement, as in the case of increased spending on general relief due to cutbacks in AFDC and Medicaid, such replacement was essentially passive and did not reflect a deliberate effort by the state to fill the gap created by federal funding cuts.

4. There were a number of significant *political and institutional effects* from the Reagan initiatives. These included attempts by county government in Ohio to gain increased control over local service delivery systems operated under the auspices of community action organizations. The state generally assumed a larger role in local affairs in response to the block grant initiatives, the switch from CETA to JTPA, and with various entitlement programs. Within state government, the block grant initiatives were a catalyst to increased legislative involvement in state and local programs affected by federal aid. Even more significantly and quite ironically, the increased discretion afforded states in connection with the block grant, Medicaid, and JTPA initiatives worked very much to the advantage of Ohio's new, proactive Democratic governor.

Additional information and analysis of these and other findings are presented in this paper. In the following section there is a detailed discussion of the fiscal and political environments that shaped the state and city responses to the Reagan initiatives. This is followed by a review of the major program changes in entitlement, operating, and capital areas, with more in-depth analysis of the consequences of these changes along the dimensions noted above. The paper concludes with further consideration of the main findings from this field study.

The Setting for the Reagan Federal Changes in Ohio

Over the 1980–83 period, Ohio went through some troubled fiscal waters, buffeted by a severe economic recession, political stalemates over fiscal actions, and a threat of a taxpayer revolt.[1] The state weathered these storms, but not without some damage to public services and facilities. By early 1984, however, the worst seemed to be over. The state was operating for the first time in years with a realistic budget in the sense that no one expected that emergency cutbacks or "temporary" revenue measures would be necessary to avoid a constitutionally prohibited deficit.

The deterioration during 1980–83 in Ohio's economic and fiscal condition largely reflected the national recession. Because of the concentration of heavy manufacturing in the state, and because so much of Ohio's industrial plant is relatively old, the recession hit Ohio especially hard, with unemployment running far above the national average. Accentuating the problem was the fact that the extent and duration of the Ohio recession were much worse than anticipated. This fact, combined with a tendency, shared by both legislature and executive, to estimate revenues on the most optimistic assumptions, put the state in a fiscal crisis situation.

Over the period of three years, the state required five separate budget bills, $1.3 billion in spending cuts, and four rounds of temporary tax increases to remain solvent. In spite of these measures, the new governor, Dick Celeste, announced in February 1983 that the budget for the current biennium was out of balance by $528 million. He ordered spending cuts of $282 million and requested emergency tax increases of $300 million, the latter consisting primarily of extending, increasing, and making permanent the temporary taxes enacted in the previous year. This legislation increased by 40 percent a previously enacted "temporary" personal income tax surcharge. This gave Ohioans an income tax rate 90 percent higher than a year earlier, though it represented itself only as a 26.8 percent hike. Nevertheless, it was the 90 percent figure that was stressed in the press, and by critics, and which became the focal point of the subsequent tax repeal effort.

Governor Celeste's budget for the 1984–86 biennium retained the increased personal income tax rates, along with increases in several other taxes, including the state's corporate income tax. At the same time, it provided a number of revenue reducing changes (from the emergency tax program of February), concen-

[1] A detailed account of the economic and fiscal circumstances in Ohio during this period is provided in "Review and Status of Ohio's Economy and Finances for FY 1982 and FY 1983," Informational Memorandum, no. 76, January 25, 1982, Ohio Legislative Budget Office.

trating primarily on personal income tax payers. The governor stressed the importance of enacting taxes on a *permanent* basis, in order to provide stability and predictability both for taxpayers and for agencies of state government. The budget, as adopted, included tax increases essentially as requested by the governor. It provided for increases in general fund spending of 14.3 percent for state fiscal year 1984 and 8.9 percent for 1985. With tax revenue in the first eight months of the new biennium running close to projections and the state paying its bills on time, agencies of state government were able for the first time in several years to think of matters other than how to remain afloat.

POLITICAL SETTING

The 1982 election of Governor Celeste represented a sharp change in leadership at the state level—a shift from the conservative Republican ideology of Governor Rhodes to a liberal Democrat ideology. However, it would be wrong to infer that there was a dramatic shift in fiscal philosophy. While Celeste acted quickly to shore up the state's fiscal structure, the fiscal attitude in Ohio remained quite conservative, with no major spending initiatives in sight.

A more significant departure from the Rhodes era was the emphasis on improved planning and management in state government. This was reflected in efforts to upgrade management information systems and to staff up policy analysis units within various program areas, as well as efforts to achieve increased coordination among agencies in the pursuit of more broadly defined goals. Examples of the latter included the formation of "cabinet clusters" to deal with strategic-level issues in economic development and human services. From this perspective, it can be argued that the Reagan domestic policy initiatives, by giving greater responsibility to the states, were well suited to the proactive approach to planning and management taken by the new governor.

MAJOR ISSUES

Among the major issues facing state government in Ohio over the 1981–83 period, school funding continued to loom most significantly. With a ten-mill limit on local unvoted property taxes, schools are heavily dependent on voter-approved operating levies. To make matters worse, Ohio allows no revenue growth from voted levies when existing properties are revalued, as they are every third year. The resulting fiscal squeeze on local school districts places constant pressure on the state general fund for increased school appropriations.

Other major concerns during this period included efforts to shore up the economic base in Ohio and to control welfare costs, particularly the growth in

Medicaid outlays. Again, the increased discretion given to states in connection with the Job Training Partnership Act and Medicaid fit well with the new governor's approach to these issues.

INVOLVEMENT IN FEDERAL AID

Policy making and budgeting in relation to federal grants have traditionally been conducted in a very decentralized manner under the general purview of the executive branch of state government in Ohio. Within the budget itself, federal aid is included in three funds; one for Medicaid and AFDC, one for highways, and one for all other federal aid. Even before Reagan there had been a growing concern about whether there was adequate control over the federal aid portions of the budget outside of AFDC and Medicaid; for example, agencies low balling their federal aid estimates in order to get a larger share of general fund revenue. However, efforts to achieve improved control had been hampered by a lack of good accounting information to track individual programs.

In the case of the legislature, there has traditionally been little concerted effort to direct policy related to federal grant programs. With the Reagan initiatives, however, legislative activity increased and a joint committee was created to monitor the implementation of the various block grant programs.[2] Although having limited impact on policy during the period of observation, the subsequent appointment of a new committee chair, who also chaired the House Finance Committee, suggested a continuing concern within the leadership of the legislature to gain greater control over federal aid programs.

In the case of the new governor, there was a more concerted effort to incorporate federal grant programs, such as JTPA and the social services block grant program, into state policy initiatives in the area of employment and job training. Also, in the entitlements area, the new governor took an aggressive approach in exercising the increased discretion permitted states in restructuring the Medicaid program.

The City of Cleveland

An aging industrial core city surrounded by generally middle-class and a scattering of very prosperous suburbs, Cleveland has been the prototypical urban area in distress: racial conflicts, dwindling population, city-suburban conflicts,

[2] Made up of five members each from the House and Senate, the Joint Legislative Committee on Federal Funds was created in 1981 under House Joint Resolution no. 39. The chair of the committee alternates from session to session between the Senate and the House.

deteriorating industrial base, confrontation politics, and finally the ignominity of default and bankruptcy in late 1979.

With the election of George Voinovich, a Republican, the city began the process of restoring its credibility and credit. The new mayor galvanized business leadership and some of the city neighborhoods, forged an uneasy alliance with the powerful and long-term City Council president, instituted aggressive and far more competent city management, and led the fight for tax increases and an increased emphasis on planning, including greater leveraging of federal funds to rebuild the city.

The city itself is a rather limited general-purpose government. The county of Cuyahoga operates the bulk of the welfare and human services programs. A separately elected school board runs the public schools and there are a host of special-purpose, largely independent, boards: a regional sewer board, a mental health board, a mental retardation board, a regional planning board, a public housing board, and a regional transit authority. The state has more impact on Cleveland and its citizens through these special-purpose boards and the county than directly through the city government.

Within this institutional framework, federal grants have relatively little direct impact on city employment, a situation which contrasts sharply with that of the mid-1970s when over one-half of the city's work force was paid for out of federal funds. During the period of the field study, by comparison, such funds entered importantly only in the areas of community development and, to a lesser extent, health. Moreover, where the city once comingled all funds and was said to have unauditable books, federal funds were now carefully segregated.

In terms of fiscal conditions, both the city and county were under moderate fiscal pressure by the end of state fiscal year 1983. Faced with increasing pressure from the recession, the financial security derived from earlier tax increases was eroded and despite a small end-of-year surplus, layoffs and concerns about potential deficits were the order of the day for the city in 1983. The fiscal situation for the county also grew more tenuous during this period, although a windfall of $19 million in social services overpayments returned by the federal government to the state and, in turn, to the county provided some protection.

Changes in Federal Aid

AID TO FAMILIES WITH DEPENDENT CHILDREN

The greatest and most lasting impact of Reagan policy occurred in the entitlement programs. Thousands of people lost current or potential benefits. In the case of the AFDC program, for example, for the period October 1981 through February 1982 a total of 39,797 cases were affected by the AFDC changes with 4,449 denials, 23,729 terminations, and 11,619 cases where benefits were reduced.[3] About 28 percent of these cases related to changes in the treatment of stepparent income. Changes involving the 30 and 1/3 rule, the 150 percent limit on gross income, age limit on dependent children, and earned income disregards, each accounted for between 8 and 11 percent of the total cases affected by the rule changes.

During this same period there was a sharp increase in cases covered under the state's general relief program. While much of the increase was due to the worsening state economy, there was also evidence of some spillover effect from the AFDC rule changes. For the period October 1981 through February 1982 approximately 12 percent of approved general relief applications were related to the AFDC rule changes and, of these, about three-fifths were traced to rule changes associated with pregnancy status and the definition of principal wage earner.[4] Despite the increase in general relief case loads, however, the state is estimated to have realized net savings in total monthly cash assistance payments of between $1.5 and $3 million in 1982 as a result of the AFDC rule changes.

From 1982 to 1983, there was a slight increase in AFDC case loads (see table 10.1), while general relief case loads showed another dramatic year-to-year increase of over 40 percent. Although the state's economy improved steadily in 1983, with unemployment declining from a high of over 14 percent at the beginning of the year to around 11 percent at the end of the year, there is typically a lag before such improvements show up in AFDC case loads. The growth in general relief case loads in this period, however, runs contrary to historical patterns and raises the question of whether this reflects a further adjustment to the eligibility changes associated with AFDC. Unfortunately, state efforts to track general relief case loads in relation to AFDC terminations or denials were discontinued. Hence, it is not possible to make any systematic analysis of the relationship between general relief case-load increases during 1983 and the AFDC rule changes. There was, however, a general sense among those interviewed that these rule changes were a contributing factor. The specific change which reduced from twenty-one to nineteen the age at which children in school would no longer be eligible for AFDC payments, for example, was believed to have increased general relief case loads. There was also anecdotal evidence that

[3] As reported in "Federal ADC Changes Aggravate General Relief Program," *Budget Footnotes* 5, no. 5 (May 21, 1982), Ohio Legislative Budget Office. The estimates themselves were based on a review by county welfare departments of all AFDC cases for this period.

[4] Estimates taken from an unpublished analysis provided by the Ohio Department of Human Services.

Table 10.1. *Case-Load and Expenditure Data for Selected Entitlement Programs, State Fiscal Years 1981–83*

Program	1981	1982	1983
Aid to families with dependent children			
case load	199,898	201,710	205,993
outlays (dollars in millions)	601.4	620.5	645.3
Medicaid			
case load (AFDC)	199,898	201,710	205,993
case load (adults)	148,532	144,326	140,780
outlays (dollars in millions)	1,008.4	1,273.8	1,445.4
General relief			
case load	58,311	83,317	118,974
outlays—payments (dollars in millions)	77.3	103.1	114.8
outlays—medical benefits (dollars in millions)	62.2	87.3	130.7
Food stamps[a]			
case load[b]	385,754	388,642	437,951
outlays (dollars in millions)	509.4	532.1	666.3

SOURCE: AFDC, Medicaid, and general relief data compiled by the Office of the Budget, Ohio Department of Human Services (ODHS). Food stamp data provided by the Bureau of Reports and Statistics, ODHS.

NOTES: [a] Food stamp data shown for federal fiscal years; all other data is by state fiscal year, which begins July 1 and ends June 30.
[b] Average number of households per month.

the rule changes may have reduced the transition of single adults who marry and have children from coverage under general relief to coverage under the state's AFDC segment that provides cash assistance to two-parent families where the head of household is unemployed. (This type of welfare assistance is referred to as AFDC-U.) Specifically, because work experience under general relief is no longer counted as relevant experience in establishing eligibility for AFDC-U payments, such individuals are more likely to remain on the general relief rolls. There was also a sense that the 30 and 1/3 rule change created disincentives to reduce welfare dependency, but again, no hard data were available to estimate the magnitude of such an effect.

Locally, changes in entitlement programs were fully implemented. The state adopted and the county implemented all requirements geared toward ending support for the working poor. Early on, under the Rhodes administration, the state compounded the cuts by limiting optional family emergency assistance benefits (50 percent federal money) as well as adult emergency assistance benefits (100 percent state and local money). There was very little local opposition to most of the cuts—with the exception of the emergency assistance provisions. Cuyahoga County ended up replacing a major part of these cuts through a more restrictive emergency assistance program.

For those eligible for AFDC, the state did initiate a 5 percent increase in benefits in 1984, with another 5 percent scheduled for 1985 but conditioned on the rate of increase in case loads and AFDC spending. There was, however, no perception that these increases were intended to offset the Reagan cuts. Rather, they reflected a response by a new governor to the fact that benefit levels had not increased since 1979.

Eligibility changes in the entitlement programs had the greatest impact on the working poor. There was a general perception both within the welfare department and among public interest groups that the changes under Reagan made it more difficult to respond to their needs. The reduction in the value of assets allowed in establishing eligibility under AFDC was identified as a particularly significant change, especially for those identified as the "newly poor": persons affected by structural shifts in Ohio's economic base tied to steel and autos. While a more favorable treatment of assets in the case of food stamps allowed some relief for this group, a much greater deterioration in their overall economic condition was required than in the past in order to establish AFDC and, in turn, Medicaid eligibility.

On the other hand, some of the AFDC changes were judged to have resulted in cutbacks in aid to the non-needy. In particular, the change affecting the treatment of stepparent income was generally viewed at the state level as appropriate. However, this view is in marked contrast to the local response, where stepparent income treatment was described as the "most unfair" change.

WORKFARE

Workfare also affected AFDC recipients. The former governor adopted workfare and the new governor recommended a significant effort to implement a statewide workfare program, with proposed spending of $53 million in 1984 and $69 million in 1985. However, the workfare money for 1984 was subsequently "raided" with only $8 million appropriated to fund two or three pilot programs around the state. As to the longer-term outlook for workfare, there are conflicting philosophies represented in the legislature (those who see it in punitive terms and those who see it as job training) and it would appear that the Celeste administration, despite its proposed spending, is not strongly committed to a statewide workfare program.

MEDICAID

Developments in the Medicaid program mirror the AFDC changes. The estimated 28,178 cases that lost welfare benefits or were denied access to the AFDC program between October 1981 to February 1982 because of various rule changes translated directly into reduced Medicaid enrollments. Reductions were also recorded in blind, disabled, and elderly low-income residents of the state who as a result of 1981 federal budget reconciliation act provisions were no longer eligible for Supplemental Security Income (SSI) benefits. During the same period, however, medical payments under the state's general relief program increased sharply, mainly due to a deterioration in the state's economy, but also reflecting a shift (especially among pregnant women and in two-parent families) from AFDC to general relief. On balance, the state is estimated to have realized net savings of between $1 and $2 million per month in medical assistance payments in 1982 as a result of the indirect effects of the AFDC rule changes on Medicaid eligibility.

For 1983, total enrollment under Medicaid remained virtually unchanged, reflecting a slight increase in AFDC-related cases and a continued decrease in SSI-related cases (see table 10.1). Total outlays over this period increased by 13 percent, reflecting a general increase in health costs. Medical assistance under the state's general relief program, on the other hand, increased 50 percent between 1982 and 1983. Again, while it is not possible to systematically assess this further increase in relation to AFDC rule changes, there is certainly some association.

As the changes affecting eligibility and support provided under various federal entitlement programs became more apparent in Ohio, action was taken to limit the impact on those affected and, of even greater concern, any adverse fiscal impact on the state. For example, as part of an overall effort to constrain its own health care costs, the state intervened to include under Medicaid those persons affected by the age limitation governing coverage for dependent students under AFDC. It is estimated that 20,000 to 25,000 persons were affected by the state's decision to exercise the so-called Ribicoff option by which medical coverage was switched from the state-funded general relief program to the federally assisted Medicaid program. But, while the short-term savings were clear, there was concern about a "woodwork effect" whereby the longer-term increase in Medicaid coverage might outweigh the initial savings to the state from reducing medical assistance outlays provided under the general relief program. Another group affected by the AFDC changes and subsequently brought under Medicaid coverage by the state were women in the first five months of pregnancy.

The new governor acted to bring Medicaid outlays under control through a variety of strategies. These included a moratorium on hospital and nursing home expansion, the imposition of preadmission certification procedures for elective hospital admissions, screening for outpatient treatment, Medicaid coverage for ambulatory surgical facilities, financial incentives for doctors to provide office rather than hospital treatment, the implementation of a diagnostically related group reimbursement system, and a movement toward mandatory HMO enrollment.

The general thrust of these initiatives contrasts with those under the former governor, who placed greater emphasis on a variety of cost-shifting strategies such as imposition of copayment requirements for clients, inclusion of stepparent income in needs assessment, inclusion of medical insurance in child support orders, and increased enforcement of subrogation rights. The broader strategy of Governor Celeste, focusing on structural changes to the Medicaid-related health service delivery system, reflected his generally more activist approach.[5] In the context of Medicaid, the Reagan initiatives can be viewed as a positive force in facilitating this policy shift at the state level. It should be noted, however, that some of the increased flexibility was initially seen as more illusionary than real as needed waivers proved difficult to obtain from the federal government.

FOOD STAMPS

Enrollment in the food stamp program increased steadily from 1981 through 1983. As in the case of AFDC, however, the rate of increase between 1981 and 1982 was substantially below that recorded for the earlier and later periods, reflecting changes introduced under Reagan. More specifically, between September and November of 1981, a period of worsening economic conditions and coinciding with the implementation of the Reagan policies, food stamp case loads in Ohio declined by around 3 percent, implying a conservatively estimated reduction in food stamp coupons of around $20 million on an annualized basis.

Average monthly case loads and total outlays increased sharply in 1983 (see table 10.1). While the state made no systematic effort to analyze trends associated with food stamp participation rates, the increase appears to relate directly to underlying economic conditions. Although there was some improvement in

[5] As a basis for comparing earlier and later Medicaid policy initiatives, see "HB 694 Changes State Medicaid Program," *Budget Footnotes* 5, no. 2 (February 10, 1982), Ohio Legislative Budget Office. See also "Hospital Cost Containment Measures Readied," *Budget Footnotes* 7, no. 9 (April 25, 1984), Ohio Legislative Budget Office.

the economy in 1983, the average unemployment rate was very high during this period. Hence, given the length and severity of the recession, many families had drawn down their assets to the point where they became eligible for food stamps.

In a related matter, the emergency jobs act allocated $2,028,100 to the state in March 1983 under the Federal Emergency Management Agency (FEMA) to provide emergency food and shelter. Cuyahoga County received $268,000 from the state-administered FEMA program and an additional $643,000 from the federally administered FEMA program. FEMA monies were administered in the county by the Emergency Hunger and Shelter Board.

Prior to passage of the jobs act, the Cuyahoga Emergency Funders Coalition had been formed in response to the perceived increase in emergency food and shelter needs. The coalition collected local county monies in addition to foundation and corporate grants. The coalition coordinated their disbursement so as to extend the funding of food or shelter programs beyond the terms of the FEMA program.

Throughout the state, as was true in the Cleveland area, many of the clients served by expanded food assistance programs were not the "newly poor" but the "old poor" for whom cash and in-kind assistance was simply not adequate. This raised a serious question about the longer-term commitment by private organizations such as the United Way to "filling the gap." To continue meeting chronic subsistence level needs due to inadequate public assistance would entail a fundamental change in the traditional role of the United Way in its support of a wide variety of social services agencies targeted on a wider client population than that defined by income eligibility standards associated with AFDC and other public welfare programs.

CAPITAL PROGRAMS

Federal aid changes affecting capital programs did not figure importantly in strategic-level policy deliberations in Ohio. The uncertainty created by early Reagan efforts to cut back on highway trust fund spending was viewed as not out of line with that faced in the pre-Reagan period. Moreover, changes limiting the rate at which funds could be obligated during the budget period were viewed as beneficial to Ohio by preventing sunbelt states, which can build year round, from grabbing too much of the money.

Total aid declined between 1981 and 1982, then increased sharply in 1983, reflecting the impact of new funding under the Surface Transportation Assistance Act.[6] There was some indication from the field interviews that absent this large increase in federal aid, the state would have made an even larger commitment of state revenues to support highway construction and maintenance. Hence, while impossible to estimate precisely, at least some part of the increased federal funding substituted for state effort.

In the case of mass transit, early indications were that cutbacks in federal support proposed by Reagan would have a particularly significant impact on smaller, rural systems. The problem was not so much one of money per se, but an undermining of confidence at the local level to go forward with plans to develop local transit systems (mainly buses). Hence, while larger systems might have to cut back service in response to any substantial reductions in federal aid, smaller operations would be devastated.

The capital story in Cleveland was generally one of improvement. In the area of economic development, for example, $5.5 million in federal aid was earmarked in 1983 for industrial parks and other development activities. The federal aid changes also indirectly encouraged greater cooperation among units of local government. Uncertainty about capital programs helped solidify the work of the Community Capital Investment Strategy Group. This committee mobilized federal and state support for infrastructure rebuilding, resulting in far greater coordination of efforts among local Cuyahoga County public bodies.

OPERATING PROGRAMS

Viewed against the backdrop of the recession-induced fiscal crisis in Ohio and associated concerns over the funding of Medicaid, AFDC, and state support for local schools, reductions in federal aid affecting various operating programs ran a distant third in the reckoning of difficult budgetary choices in Ohio over the period of observation. While of major concern to program administrators and local service providers, funding cuts associated with the various block grants as well as the termination of CETA did not surface importantly in strategic-level deliberations. Moreover, even within specific program areas, the availability of carryover balances early on and the subsequent infusion of emergency jobs act money helped mitigate the budgetary impact of the federal aid cuts.

The state experienced a funding decrease in six of the seven block grants in which comparative data were available (see table 10.2). Only in the low-in-

---

[6] An analysis by the Ohio Department of Transportation of the Surface Transportation Assistance Act's fiscal impact shows anticipated federal aid to the state increasing from $220.8 million in 1982 to $333.7 million in 1983. ("Impact of 1982 Federal Surface Transportation Assistance Act on Ohio's Finances," as presented to the Ohio House Finance-Appropriations Committee, June 15, 1983.)

come energy assistance block grant was there an increase, with 12 percent growth between 1981 and 1983. Among the six programs registering decreases, cuts of around 20 percent were recorded in the social services, community services, and education block grants. Among the health block grants, the cuts were larger, ranging from 25 to 35 percent.

Again, however, carryover balances and emergency jobs act money significantly cushioned the impact of these block grant cuts. During the 1982 budget period, carryover balances were reported to have played a significant role in at least five of the block grant programs experiencing cuts in current appropriations, while during the 1983 budget period, jobs act money provided additional funding in six of the programs. The state's small-cities community development block grant and the maternal and child health block grant allocations for 1983 increased by over 20 percent as a result of the antirecession legislation. The other four programs receiving jobs act money had increases ranging from 6 to 12 percent.

While the fiscal impact of the Reagan block grant initiatives was overshadowed by the recession and the changes affecting the various entitlement programs, other aspects of these initiatives had a significant impact at the state

Table 10.2.   *Block Grant Allocations to Ohio, Federal Fiscal Years 1981–83 (dollars in millions)[a]*

Block grant	1981	1982	1983	Percentage change 1981–83	Jobs act allocation as a percentage of 1983 receipts
Social services	142.9	126.9	116.1	− 18.7	11.5
Community services	15.8	12.7	12.8	− 19.0	10.9
Education[b]	26.0	20.4	20.5	− 21.2	0
Small-cities community development	—	44.0	45.3	—	25.9
Low-income energy assistance	90.1	96.1	101.2	12.3	5.6
Maternal and child health	15.9	13.2	12.0	− 24.5	22.5
Alcohol, drug abuse, and mental health	33.1	22.7	22.4	− 32.3	6.7
Preventive health	5.8	3.8	3.8	− 34.5	0

SOURCE: Data compiled from annual state block grant reports and various internal agency documents.
NOTES: [a] Of the nine block grants established by the Omnibus Budget Reconciliation Act of 1981, Ohio assumed responsibility of all but the primary health care block grant.
[b] These amounts reflect allocations made in the respective federal fiscal year that, through forward funding provisions, will be received in the subsequent school year accounting period. Hence, actual receipts for school year 1980–81 amounted to $46 million, while new allocations in federal fiscal year 1981 to be received in school year 1981–82 amounted to $26 million.

level. In the case of education, for example, the shift to a block grant coupled with reduced funding resulted in a scaling back of support earmarked for deseg-regation efforts in larger urban school districts. In the case of maternal and child health, preventive health services, and community services, there were efforts under the new governor to allow greater discretion at the local level in the al-location of grant funds within broad program areas. Under the maternal and child health program, for instance, three separate programs (child health, per-inatal, and family planning) were to be combined into one comprehensive child and family health service program.

Only in the case of the small-cities community development block grant was there a move toward greater state control over the use of funds. This was prompted by a general dissatisfaction with the spread-it-around approach taken by the former governor, who expanded the number of small-city grant recipi-ents threefold through the use of a formula-based allocation. While the new administration was unsuccessful in its attempt to switch entirely to a competi-tively based allocation system, a significant portion of small-city funds freed by the termination of prior commitments was distributed by the state on a com-petitive, or project basis. However, even in this case the policy change reflected mainly an attempt to increase funding for larger-scale projects with greater tar-geting on low- and moderate-income families and not an attempt to exert greater state control over the local implementation process per se.

While running well behind other macro-level forces affecting the state's budgetary situation, there were some fiscal effects of note within specific pro-gram areas. In particular, the state did replace some of the cuts affecting social service and maternal and child health programs. The amount of replacement was small, however, and the reason for replacement varied. For the social serv-ices program, replacement resulted mainly from the state's effort to limit losses to individual counties caused by changes in the state's allocation formula.[7] In the maternal and child health program, additional state spending in federal fis-cal year 1984 reflected an attempt to replace previous federal aid cuts affecting perinatal and infant health care services. Overall, however, replacement was low throughout the field observation period.

Similarly, there was little evidence of efforts by the state to substitute federal for state funds in a way that could have compounded the federal aid cuts. Only in the case of the low-income energy assistance block grant, which experienced increases in federal aid in 1981 to 1983, was there any indication of potential substitution, with a proposed merging of the state's energy credit program with

---

[7] Details on the formula changes can be found in "New Social Services Formula Adopted: Losing Counties Held Harmless," *Budget Footnotes* 7, no. 3 (October 17, 1983), Ohio Legislative Budget Office.

activities funded by the block grant. Elsewhere, there was some indication, especially in the health area, that federal aid increases associated with the jobs act program were used to increase fund balances in order to spread out the effects of the longer-term cuts in federal aid. This suggests some short-run fiscal substitution, but, again, the overall rates of fiscal substitution and replacement by the state were quite low between 1981 and 1983.

Other Block Grant Initiatives

The block grant initiatives were a catalyst in forcing a review of the distribution of grant funds across local jurisdictions. In particular, the shift to state control generated a good bit of tension between large urban areas and smaller rural areas and, in general, it appeared that the issue was being decided in favor of the smaller rural places. As opposed to historical funding patterns which favored urban areas, there was a general move toward formula allocations based on population and other more specific characteristics. Such shifts occurred or were being planned in connection with the social services, community services, and preventive health services block grant programs. There was a similar shift, along with increased aid to private institutions, under the new education block grant.

The small-cities community development block grant program was an exception to the trend discussed above. Governor Celeste's effort to distribute funds on a project basis raised concerns among smaller communities that they would be at a competitive disadvantage vis-à-vis larger communities. The smaller places favored continuation of the formula-based distribution initiated by the Rhodes administration.

There were no major changes affecting the design of local service delivery systems associated with the block grant initiatives. Early on, the County Commissioners Association of Ohio attempted to gain a larger role for county governments in the administration of small-city community development and community services funds.[8] While counties were given increased responsibility in administering local community development plans, reviewing proposals submitted by townships and villages, the move toward competitively based allocations has limited growth in government control. Similarly, counties initially sought to take control of community services block grant funds, but were unsuccessful. They were subsequently given responsibility to review local com-

[8] The policy positions taken by the County Commissioners Association of Ohio on these two programs are explained in memoranda from the association's executive director dated December 15, 1981 in the case of the small-cities community development block grant program and April 6, 1982 in the case of the community services block grant program.

munity services plans and to convene public hearings, but that is no longer the case.

Administratively, the experience under the block grants was a mixed bag. For the health programs and the low-income energy assistance block grant, the results were generally positive. Within the health area there was a concerted effort to mitigate the effects of funding cuts through better targeting of health grant resources and the development of fiscal strategies to phase in cuts through judicious use of carryover balances and jobs act money.

A quite different picture emerged in connection with the social services block grant and the small-cities program. Described by one top official as a "mess," the social services program was seen as too restrictive in specifying allowed uses of funds at the local level. At the technical control level, too, intervention by the legislature in requiring unit cost criteria for purchase of service contributed to confusion and perceptions of unfairness at the local level. The lack of a good management information system significantly limited the state welfare department's ability to monitor the social services program for fraud and abuse.

In the case of the small-cities program, the mixed formula/competitive allocation system had created a management nightmare for the state. HUD's monitoring report on Ohio's small-cities program for 1983 raised serious questions about the manageability of such a system, particularly the state's "ability to monitor and assure grant compliance with federal requirements given such a large number of contacts." There was the further concern that insufficient attention to monitoring by the state "may not reasonably protect communities from adverse audit findings and the potential need for local governments to repay HUD from their general revenue for disallowed costs."

THE EMERGENCY JOBS ACT

This supplemental spending act had substantial replacement effect. As previously noted in connection with the health block grant programs, jobs act funds were used to begin special programming or to level off anticipated declines in program funding levels. In the case of the social services block grant, however, the funds were fully obligated by September 30, 1984, creating problems in some counties in fully absorbing the additional resources. While agencies were required to have planned uses of jobs act funds reviewed by the Joint Legislative Committee on Federal Funds, the plans were not very detailed, except in the case of the small-cities block grant program, where fifty-eight projects were awarded jobs act money on a competitive basis.

Nine programs in the city of Cleveland and Cuyahoga County received in excess of $20 million in jobs act money. The impact was enormous. Program cuts that were about to be made were delayed, and services for several programs were expanded. For example, social and health services were maintained, weatherization, nutrition, and community development activities were expanded, and the work of the Cuyahoga Emergency Funders Coalition was continued. The city received a critical economic development grant needed for completion of an industrial parks project. Neither spending nor control of funds generally emerged as major issues. Most of the programs had continuation/expansion needs identified or uncompleted projects. State pass-throughs were generally very timely. In some cases, jobs act money took local pressure off the state for more money. Both the women, infant, and children (WIC) nutrition program and the weatherization program received jobs act money as second increment funding; the state had been under pressure prior to the jobs act to expand programming in these areas. Both programs were very successful in expanding their services under this framework, with the number of WIC participants increasing by two-thirds.

THE JOB TRAINING PARTNERSHIP ACT

While not viewed as really "new" from the local level, for the state and the new administration, JTPA represented a major initiative. At the program level, the shift to the new federal job training programs gave the state a much greater role in policy formulation and implementation than under the CETA. Statewide JTPA receipts for federal fiscal year 1984 were estimated at $167.4 million, to be distributed among thirty service delivery areas. Under CETA there were approximately twenty-seven prime sponsors, including balance-of-state operations.

Sensitive to the audit exceptions in connection with CETA,[9] the Ohio Bureau of Employment Services gave particular emphasis to establishing sound accounting and reporting procedures under the new JTPA program. Specific policies being developed included annual visits to each service delivery area to monitor compliance and the development of a computerized information system for both compliance and performance auditing.

There was considerable sensitivity to the distributional issue and whether the Cleveland area would benefit disproportionately under title III, the JTPA program for dislocated workers. Another politically sensitive issue was the designation of local service providers in the conversion from CETA to JTPA. In terms of overall strategic planning, JTPA was seen as an excellent tool for the

---

[9] Initially estimated at $100 million, there were still $59 million in accounted for CETA expenditures in Ohio at the end of 1983 (*Columbus Dispatch*, January 5, 1984, p. 13).

new governor, who made a substantial campaign commitment to increased co-ordination and planning in connection with economic development and job training in Ohio. It was noted that the governor chaired the Employment and Training Subcommittee of the National Governor's Association and that given his commitment to the concept, if JTPA worked anywhere, it would work in Ohio.

Efficiency in Government

The shift to greater state responsibility in connection with the block grants as well as changes affecting AFDC eligibility tracking and accounting procedures and efforts to contain Medicaid costs all provided an impetus toward improved efficiency. At the technical control level, the state has long been handicapped by inadequate management-information-system (MIS) capabilities. As a result, huge backlogs have developed in closing out Medicaid audits conducted as far back as 1972, and the Medicaid division finds itself working in a very uncertain environment with respect to federal performance reviews. Similarly, the lack of a statewide computerized information system has resulted in significant audit exceptions under the AFDC program ($4 million in 1982). It is with an eye to these basic issues of financial accountability, as well as to the need to upgrade performance evaluation and policy analysis capabilities, that the new administration has moved to upgrade computerized information systems in connection with the Medicaid, cash assistance, and JTPA programs.

Other efforts to promote efficiency in part relate to the Reagan initiatives and in part to the new governor's emphasis on a more systematic approach to planning as reflected in the "cabinet cluster" formed to coordinate employment and job training policy in conjunction with JTPA.[10]

Strategy and Mix

The decision-making process at the state level varied over time and in relation to various aspects of the Reagan program. For the block grant programs, the agencies themselves wielded considerable power in shaping policy, which is not surprising given the history of how federal funds have been viewed within the overall budget process in Ohio. Only in the case of the social services block

[10] The nature of the strategic planning process in Ohio is described in *Toward a Working Ohio: A Strategic Plan for the Eighties and Beyond,* Office of the Governor, December 1983.

grant was the legislature particularly aggressive early on in shaping policy. This was explained by the fact that the legislature was already quite knowledgeable about the old title XX program and had been playing a direct role prior to Reagan. As a means of coordinating legislative action with regard to the block grant programs, the Joint Legislative Committee on Federal Funds was formed. On the executive side, a special task force was formed in the state Office of Budget and Management. In both cases, the primary function was to coordinate an information exchange about the block grant initiatives and to set procedural guidelines as to the preparation and review of block grant proposals.

Later in the process, advisory committees were established in connection with all but the low-income energy assistance block grant program. These advisory committees, with members chosen by the agencies themselves, have played a fairly active role in reviewing agency plans and, in some cases, formulating specific program proposals. Within the small-cities block grant advisory committee, for example, a split developed between those who favored a complete switch to competitive funding (a position taken by the Department of Development) and a minority view favoring a mix of competitive and formula-based allocations. The latter position was ultimately supported by the Joint Legislative Committee on Federal Funds and passed by the state Controlling Board.

Interest group activity in connection with the block grants came mainly from the Ohio Citizens Council (OCC), a nonprofit organization concerned primarily with social services and health policy, and from the County Commissioners Association of Ohio. OCC was very active early on, holding information workshops throughout the state.[11] A steering committee that included representatives from community planning councils and United Way organizations was formed for the purpose of charting policy. The main thrust of its recommendations was to spread the cuts on a pro rata basis across all programs in order to avoid sudden defunding of any agency. The steering committee recommended maintenance of state support, the elimination of matching provisions notwithstanding. As described earlier, the County Commissioners Association's main concern was to secure an increased role for county government in the administration of various block grants, particularly the small-cities and community services block grant programs.

At the departmental level, the health-related block grant programs were subject to fairly systematic analysis in deciding how to distribute the cuts over specific program areas and how carryover balances and other resources might be

---

[11] Federal policy developments and state administrative actions associated with the block grant initiatives were regularly reported by the Ohio Citizens Council in its series "Block Grant Briefs."

used to implement the cuts in an orderly fashion. In the case of the social services and community services block grants, the cuts followed traditional funding patterns and there were no major changes in the design of local service delivery systems.

Changing Roles

The Reagan changes clearly increased the role and prerogative of the state vis-à-vis local programs. At the state level, most of the initiative came from the executive. The state legislature played a more limited role, but one that seemed to be growing over time. The formation of the Joint Legislative Committee on Federal Funds was an effort by the legislature to get more involved in federal grants policy and, more specifically, in the block grant initiatives under Reagan. While establishing an oversight role in reviewing all plans submitted by the state in connection with these block grants, the committee was generally perceived as ineffective in shaping state policy. Poorly attended meetings, limited staff resources, and an emphasis on very narrowly defined programmatic issues in connection with specific block grants (for example, funding for rat control emerged as a big issue in the deliberations over the preventive health and health services block grant) all contributed to the general perception of an ineffectual committee.

During the latter part of the field study, however, there was a new push to enhance the role of the committee within the legislature. Most significantly, a new committee chair was appointed, a person who also chaired the House Finance Committee and was generally recognized as an effective and powerful member of the House. In subsequent action, the committee was able to override the new governor's proposal to change the distribution of small-city funds to a strictly competitive basis, and this was perceived as an indication that the committee intended to assert itself more forcefully in the formulation of block grant policy.

Federal aid changes indirectly encouraged greater cooperation among units of local government. Uncertainty on capital programs helped solidify the work of the Cleveland-area Community Capital Investment Strategy Group—representing both cross-public and public-private cooperation. The Cuyahoga Emergency Funders Coalition had the same dimensions. Some of the state agencies also fostered cooperation through block grant planning. For example, preventive health care funds required a countywide plan.

While moving slowly toward centralization, Ohio remains the original local control state. The state role in federally funded programs has increased, but there is continued sensitivity to local political and constituent pressures. The state has generally moved to establish broad program parameters, while allowing localities to exercise considerable discretion within those parameters. The significant event is in having the parameters at all.

Conclusion

A low rate of replacement by the state of Ohio in response to federal aid cuts persisted over the three years of analysis, 1981–83. In the entitlement area, there was no concerted effort to aid those affected by loss of eligiblity or reduced benefits under AFDC. While some of those affected were able to move on to the general relief rolls, the alternative assistance provided by the state in these cases was passive in nature, rather than a direct action to counter the federal cuts. Moreover, in response to growing general relief case loads, the state shifted more of the cost to the federal government by transferring children and teens from general relief medical coverage to Medicaid. While this afforded short-run protection to the state from the adverse fiscal impact of the changes in federal policy, the longer-term consequences are more uncertain.

Among local governments, too, there was not much in the way of replacement of cuts in entitlement programs. However, the city and county did offset some of the federal aid reductions. About one-half of the state-ratified cuts in emergency assistance were replaced by the county. Food programs were greatly expanded at the local level and targeted toward the "new" but mainly serving the "old" poor.

As in the entitlement area, there was very little replacement by the state in connection with the block grant initiatives. Fairly small amounts of replacement were identified in the social services and the maternal and child health block grant programs. In the former case, additional state funding was predicated more on a concern with limiting the redistributional impact of a new distribution formula than with a concern about inadequate funding for social services. Increased funding for maternal and child health services, on the other hand, was more a reflection of changing state priorities.

Looking ahead, there is no reason to expect the state to do more in terms of replacement, recent expansions in the state's tax base notwithstanding. Should the state's fiscal condition improve so as to provide some budgetary slack, demands for tax cuts, debt repayment to the unemployment insurance trust fund, and continued pressure for increased state aid to local schools will be accorded a much higher priority than replacement of federal aid cuts. Any future action by the state in connection with these cuts will be motivated more by a concern with protecting the state's fiscal situation than by a concern with protecting local service providers and individuals adversely affected by the cuts.

The consequences of the Reagan program for political and institutional arrangements at the state level in Ohio loom more importantly than the fiscal impact. While traditionally treated in a very decentralized fashion and apart from deliberations over general fund appropriations, a more visible institutional arrangement emerged within the legislature to coordinate policy involving federal grants-in-aid. While having relatively little impact in shaping state policies associated with the block grant initiatives during the early stages of the Reagan program, the Joint Legislative Committee on Federal Funds grew in stature over the period of the field study.

Within the executive branch, it is somewhat ironic that many aspects of the Reagan program indirectly served the interests of the new governor, who is a liberal Democrat. In the entitlement area, the governor has fully capitalized on the increased discretion afforded to states in the restructuring of Medicaid. Similarly, efforts to tighten compliance and performance evaluation procedures have been fully embraced by the new governor, as reflected in the substantial investment being made to upgrade the state's management and administrative capabilities. And in terms of longer-range strategic planning, the JTPA program is seen as a "perfect tool" for the governor's efforts to coordinate employment and job training policy in Ohio.

Locally, changes in federal policy coincided with depressed economic conditions to bring forth new and significant public-private partnerships. The Cuyahoga Emergency Funders Coalition developed and funded a network of food and shelter programs, setting the stage for smooth and effective utilization of FEMA funds. The Community Capital Investment Strategy Committee mobilized federal and state support for infrastructure rebuilding and has brought far greater coordination of efforts among local public bodies. The business community responded well to requests from the mayor for summer jobs.

A positive impact of the changes in domestic policy locally was better management of programs, partly due to new state pressures and partly to the clear need for improved efficiency. Clearly, some of the fat in operating programs was cut.

But, the overall impact upon the poor was the dominant social effect. And, this impact was largely invisible because of the recession and the "problems of the new poor." This invisibility reduces the likelihood of public concern returning to the "old poor"—those people who are socially and structurally out of the mainstream.

As to the role of state government in Ohio, the Reagan domestic policy has on balance enhanced it. In part, this reflects the consequences of macro-level policy, where recession-induced expansions in the state's tax base have increased the ratio of state-to-local tax shares. While consistent with a longer-term trend driven by increased state aid to local schools, the recent recession has given it added impetus. At the program level, the shift to JTPA has given the state a much greater role in policy formulation and implementation than under CETA. In the entitlement area, too, the state's role has been substantially expanded to include not only financing responsibility but a more direct role in the design of the Medicaid-related health service delivery system.

And finally, requirements for closer eligibility tracking and financial accountability forced the state to become more involved in the administration of local welfare and social services delivery systems. During the early stages of implementation, the state gave particular attention to these issues in connection with the various block grant programs. Beyond such technical control matters, however, there appears to be a growing sense that the state should afford greater discretion to local jurisdictions in deciding the appropriate mix of services provided under various block grants, particularly those related to health and social services. In addition to matters of technical and programmatic efficiency, there are persistent issues of fairness and equity in the design of the various block grant programs, raising longer-term questions of how willing the legislature will be to grapple with these more politically charged issues.

Washington State

V. LANE RAWLINS AND BETTY JANE NARVER

*B*etween 1980 and 1984 there were substantial changes in Washington State's delivery of federally supported goods and services. The extent to which the Reagan programs of the 1980s were responsible for all of those changes is not entirely clear since that impact must be disentangled from a variety of other economic, social, and political forces. One major difficulty pervading the analysis is that Washington State and Seattle (the case study city) experienced particularly severe financial problems during the recession of the early 1980s. Another confounding factor was a political climate in the state which conformed closely to Reagan's philosophy of eliminating waste, inefficiency, mismanagement, and governmental intrusiveness. These fiscal and political conditions, reviewed in the second section of this chapter, set the stage for the Reagan reductions and sharply limited Washington State's range of possible responses to federal cuts.

We have chosen to analyze the effects of the Reagan program by focusing on a list of key program changes that illustrates the effects of the change, and the nature of this state-local response. In general the initial state reaction to federal budget changes has been to pass them right along. State officials have stressed strong management, decreased funding, and reduction in the dependence of state citizens on government social and health programs. Emphasis has also been placed on getting the recipients of the services to pay a greater portion of the cost.

External constraints as well as the traditions, customs, and institutional

The authors wish to recognize the important research contribution of Larry Bussone and Gregory C. Weeks. Numbers and dollar figures for this report were obtained in confidential interviews and from unpublished reports. We wish to thank the many people in Washington State and Seattle agencies who provided the data and many of the ideas in this chapter.

mechanisms shaped these responses. Fundamental institutional change is rarely rapid, due to the resistance power of existing patterns of behavior, but observable change does occur. The initial state reaction to federal budget changes was to pass them along in the program pattern suggested by the cuts, taking the position that "federal" programs have been reduced by the federal government. The extent and length of time that this pattern is maintained depends on whether these programs are separately administered, the speed and effectiveness of political opposition to the reduction, and whether fiscal conditions allow for replacement of lost federal funds without actually cutting programs that are primarily funded from state and local sources.

Despite fiscal austerity and a refusal by state government to shoulder new program responsibilities, the Reagan domestic program strengthened the role and power of the Washington State government relative to that of local government. This was not a result of increased relative employment or expenditure levels. Rather, it came about by increased managerial responsibility and control over the distribution of funds.

The Setting for Federal Aid Changes

Because of heavy dependence on investment goods such as wood products and aerospace production, Washington State is subject to greater economic fluctuations than the nation as a whole.[1] The ups and downs of the state's economy reflect the fact that changes in general consumption expenditures result in magnified effects on employment, income, and spending in investment goods and primary product industries. State and local tax revenues are subject to even wider swings because the major sources of tax revenue are sales and business taxes. Both depend directly on sales, which generally fluctuate more than earnings.

The late 1970s were relatively good years for Washington. Timber prices were high and employment in the aerospace industry increased from about 45,000 in 1976 to over 80,000 in 1980 and 1981. State sales tax revenues were expanded not only by the growing income level, but also by personal income spent on taxable retail sales, which increased from 62 percent in 1975 to 72 percent in 1979. Immigration to Washington was high and the baby-boom generation was reaching an age where consumption was focused on housing and durable goods.

The impact of prosperity on state taxes was so favorable that the 1977–79

---

[1] Betty Jane Narver, "Washington's Fiscal Future," *Washington Public Policy Notes* 10, no. 3 (Summer 1982):3.

Table 11.1.   *Reduction in State Tax Revenues*

Year	Action
1972	Limit growth of local regular property tax levies to 6 percent annually.
1974	Exempt prescription drugs from the sales tax. Grant business and occupation tax credit against the business inventory tax.
1975	Cut property tax rates by 10 percent.
1977	Limit local property tax levies for schools and fund basic education from state sources.
1978	Exempt groceries from the sales tax.
1979	Allow business and occupation surtax to elapse. Limit growth of state property tax levies to 6 percent annually.
1981	Repeal the inheritance and gift tax.

SOURCE: Glenn R. Pascall, "Washington's Tax System: Choices for the Future," *Public Policy Papers* no. 17 (Seattle, Wash.: University of Washington, Institute for Public Policy Management, 1982), p. 2.

biennium closed with a $400 million surplus. Predictably, law-makers responded by reducing taxes. In fact, as table 11.1 suggests, taxes were steadily reduced from 1972 to 1981. These tax reductions drastically lowered state revenues. Official estimates indicate that if the 1972 tax structure had remained in place, there would have been nearly $2 billion in additional revenue for the 1983–85 biennium.

By the spring of 1981, there were signs that the state's economy was beginning to sputter.[2] Housing starts and aerospace employment began to decline late in 1980 and the percentage of personal disposable income spent on taxable retail sales dropped from the previously noted high of 72 percent in 1979 to 62 percent in 1981, and to 57 percent in 1983. In response, the legislature passed $250 million in additional levies in 1981. Throughout this period, the Department of Revenue attempted to forecast the economic downslide (see table 11.2), but budgeting realities continued to worsen beyond expectation. In all, the revenue for the 1981–83 biennium was more than 15 percent below the predicted (and budgeted) levels. As one would expect, the action of state government was somewhat chaotic because of unanticipated revenue shortfalls and the growing demand for state tax reform.

The legislature held two regular sessions and four special sessions in 1981 and 1982. Major newspaper editorials and broadcasts in the state implored the

[2] For an overview of Washington State's fiscal condition and tax history during this time, see Glenn R. Pascall, "Washington's Tax System: Choices for the Future," *Public Policy Paper* no. 17 (Seattle, Wash.: University of Washington, Institute for Public Policy Management, July 1982).

Table 11.2. Changes in State Revenue Forecasts, 1981–82 (dollars in millions)

Date	Estimated Reductions in Forecast 1981–83 Revenues
September 1981	602
November 1981	97
December 1981	144
February 1982	188
June 1982	353
November 1982	200

legislature to discontinue the process of tinkering with taxes and initiate major reform. However, the governor and the legislature refused to initiate any substantive changes. Instead, the legislature passed, and the governor signed, twenty-nine minor tax changes designed to increase revenues by about $1.1 billion. The two big items, raising nearly $800 million in revenue, were a one-cent increase in the sales tax, and the extension of the sales tax to food. These were supposed to be temporary measures while an agreement was being worked out for a permanent tax package. However, there is no indication that there will be a major tax reform in the foreseeable future.

The tax increases left about $500 million to be covered by budget reductions. Because of the State Supreme Court's interpretation of the state constitutional provision requiring the state to provide adequate funding for primary and secondary education, the budget cuts fell heavily on higher education, social and health services, and general government. Between September 1981 and March 1983, there were four hiring freezes and three separate rounds of budget cutting.

Washington has very strong state agencies that are accustomed to operating programs with little direct interference from the governor or the legislature. Employment Security (ES) and the Department of Social and Health Services (DSHS) are large, sprawling agencies with delivery networks that reach across the state. The superintendent of public instruction is an elected official whose budget is protected by the state constitution. The Department of Transportation's revenue sources are largely earmarked for special purposes. Each of the universities and four-year colleges in the state has its own governing board, and the statewide coordinating council, the Council for Post-Secondary Education, is notoriously weak. The other state agencies are relatively small, but also generally autonomous.

The state budget crisis forced officials to pay far more attention to planning and monitoring expenditures and programs. Governor John Spellman required each agency to develop a plan for reducing spending and formed a committee involving the heads of all major agencies to coordinate the effort. Agencies adopted more rigid accounting requirements, standards, and management information systems. The Office of Financial Management (OFM), which had historically been concerned chiefly with accountability and funding formulas, began to play a much larger management role. Legislative staff and committees also became involved with questions of management and efficiency. In short, the state government began to ask harder questions about how tax revenues were spent and imposed a system of increased accountability on all agencies.

The economy of Washington State did not recover in 1983 to the extent that was predicted. Personal income, which had declined by 1.5 percent in 1982, only regained the 1981 level. Aerospace continued to be somewhat depressed and the overall unemployment rate in the state remained at about 11 percent. In spite of this, the continuation of the tax increases passed in 1982 meant that the state was able to restore many state budget cuts and operate with a modest revenue surplus.

CHANGES IN FEDERAL FUNDS

Although initial estimates of the federal aid cuts ranged to $500 million, the actual reductions were closer to $150 million, with at least half of that occurring in social and health programs. The 1981 federal budget act came at almost exactly the same time as Washington State officials realized that there was a serious state revenue shortfall. At that time the federal reductions had been anticipated for several months and a planning process was well underway. In July 1981, the governor established two committees to plan for federal aid reductions. The first was a budget assessment team, which included membership from each of the major state agencies and representatives from counties and cities. This team had responsibility for assessing the overall dollar and program impact of the reductions. The other group was a federal relations management team comprised primarily of members of the governor's cabinet and charged with establishing state policy on federal budget reductions.

The committees got a good start when the Office of Financial Management prepared estimates of federal reductions for each agency and asked them to respond with a plan. These plans included proposals for additional state revenues, state legislation, increases in user fees and special licenses, and a list of services that could be reduced or eliminated. The plans also were to include estimates of the impact on programs, clients, and government employment.

THE SEATTLE SITUATION

As the dominant city in Washington, Seattle's problems are in close relationship with the fiscal and economic problems of the state. This fiscal interaction is magnified because the state permits only limited revenue sources to the cities and, over the past few years, has placed restrictions on local property, business and occupation, and utilities taxes. The only real option available to cities is a local sales tax; and with the state raising its sales tax and reimposing the tax on food, the city was not willing to push this option.

The federal reductions created a high level of anxiety in Seattle, and Mayor Charles Royer became one of the nation's most outspoken critics of the Reagan administration and the new variety of austere federalism. The focal point for this concern was the potential reduction of social and health services for the poor. The city raised some additional revenue with a 1981 bond issue to provide housing for the handicapped and elderly, and many local school levies passed in areas where they had failed in previous years. While this suggests some direct substitution of local funds for federal reductions, it was a relatively meager readjustment. As a percentage of income, the state and local tax burden for the people of Seattle actually declined by 20 percent between 1979 and 1982.

City officials were concerned that federal funding to Seattle would be more than proportionally reduced.[3] Because of the urban concentration of poverty in Washington State, particularly of blacks, urban Indians, and Southeast Asian refugees, federal funding for social and health programs has been focused on Seattle and the surrounding area. Fears that the distribution of funds would be altered were fueled in part by statements from state officials that the new block grants would result in a more equal distribution of federal funds across the state. This was a threat to Seattle because it had always received a majority of that money.

As an example, state administration of the maternal and child health block grant resulted in a shifting of funds away from Seattle. Although the state was able to offset some of the reduction with other funds, the city received a 25 percent cut in aid under the state's distribution of block grant funds. This did little to alleviate the feeling that more state control meant less for Seattle.

The problem was not simply one of funding. Seattle is a heterogeneous city with several easily identifiable population segments that depend upon government-supported social and health services. One such group is the city's 16,000

[3] Much of the discussion on federal aid reductions in Seattle draws from interviews with William B. Stafford, director of the city's Office of Intergovernmental Relations. The Office of Intergovernmental Relations also published reports in 1981 and 1982 entitled "Impact of Proposed Budget Reductions on the City of Seattle," which were also helpful.

Southeast Asian refugees. Federal funding reductions and regulatory changes reduced cash payments and health care coverage for refugees from a maximum duration of thirty-six months to eighteen months. Language training programs for these refugees were drastically cut. Mental health emerged as a particularly serious problem within this population, especially given recent evidence of high rates of depression, suicide, and family abuse. Similar difficulties occurred among urban Indians and other smaller, but equally distressed, subgroups. Thus, while the situation in Seattle was not fiscally different from the state as a whole, because of the traditional service provision and the geographic concentration of need, the impact of federal budget reductions on individuals, families, and neighborhoods was more readily seen.

THE CHANGING ROLE OF THE STATE

Events in Washington State since 1977 have served to strengthen the state relative to local government. In the late 1970s, the state substantially increased its financial responsibility by assuming control of funding primary and secondary education, at the same time placing additional limits on local taxing authority. Other changes in that era included limits on property taxes, which reduced the revenue flexibility of the local areas. Restrictions on local revenue flexibility resulted in complaints that the state was mandating service responsibilities to local areas, especially in King County and Seattle, without providing means for payment. The state response was a law requiring that localities must be reimbursed for costs created by state mandates. While this measure provides local relief, it is at the expense of local autonomy since the state will both decide what should be provided and pay for it.

The 1981 budget act extended the opportunity for an increased state role in managing federal grants, especially for the block grants. The federal budget reductions and the state revenue crisis were equally important because the state government made some difficult decisions that included both service reductions and tax increases. Together, these forces created a greater awareness of the importance of strict budget management, that, in this case, was accomplished by exerting greater control over local governments and local agencies actually delivering the services. The results included new regulations, tighter monitoring, and detailed systems of accountability. In short, the state increased its managerial ability and power, this being especially evident in Washington State's responses to the community services block grant, social services block grant, and jobs training partnership programs.

Changes in Federal Aid since 1981

The vast majority of federal funds coming into the state pass through state agencies. The state legislature directs the funds to qualifying agencies, which then have some flexibility in using the money. The Office of Financial Management (OFM) has monitoring responsibility to assure that the program funds are used for the intended purpose. Even so, on an agency-by-agency basis, it is possible and permissible to make internal reallocations among priorities and, therefore, state and federal funds are partially interchangeable. Thus, especially in those programs that are funded by both state and federal funds, some maintenance of service levels through shifting of funds was possible. From the time of the first notification of possible reductions in federal funding, however, the state took the general position that the fiscal condition of the state precluded replacement of federal aid reductions.

COMMUNITY SERVICES BLOCK GRANT

In September of 1981, Governor John Spellman designated the Planning and Community Affairs Agency (PCAA) to administer the community services block grant program. The state plan for the distribution of community service funds stated that the primary purpose of the grant was to help community service agencies meet the needs of low-income people. Eligible community service agencies could include: local governments, nonprofit private community organizations, and migrant and seasonal farm worker organizations. In order to be eligible, agencies were required to have a governing board with at least one-third of the members being elected public officials. Some fiscal reliability conditions were required for each of these agencies, but beyond that, they were allowed to establish their own operating procedures.

The plan also stated that PCAA would attempt to distribute community service funds across the entire state according to need. This is an important statement of a change in philosophy since, prior to 1981, most Community Service Administration funds went to agencies in the urban areas of Seattle and Tacoma.

There were rather drastic federal reductions in funding from $8.2 million in 1981 to $5.3 million in 1982, even though PCAA transferred about $1.25 million from the low-income home energy assistance block grant program to support community services. Since 1982, community services funding has stabilized. Although the original cut caused concern within operating agencies, it is significant that in 1984 all but one of the community action agencies funded in 1981 continued to receive some federal aid under state administration of the block grant. Even though there was continuity in agencies, the state made significant changes in the distribution of community services aid. At the outset of negotiations between PCAA and the operating agencies, it became apparent that, from the state's point of view, Seattle and Tacoma had been receiving a disproportionate amount of funds when the federal government had responsibility for distributing aid. This judgment was supported by data on the distribution of poverty across the state. Spokane and the rural areas had received proportionally fewer funds and PCAA wanted to take some corrective action even though the survival of the existing agencies was also an important concern.

The negotiated solution provided currently funded agencies with a base of $100,000 each to cover the costs of administration and a low level of services. The remaining funds, minus the state administrative costs, were distributed to the agencies according to the formulas based on the distribution of poverty. While this resulted in drastic cuts in Seattle and Tacoma, the most devastating effects of those cuts were mitigated by phasing them over a two-year period.

The final agreement, resulting from long and arduous negotiations, differed considerably from the distribution originally sought by PCAA. Involvement of the operating agencies in the decision-making process made them more willing to accept the reductions. Rural areas were much less affected than Seattle and Tacoma and some actually received increases. Most urban agencies, even with the negotiated buffers, took severe reductions. One agency dropped from thirty-seven staff members to eleven and discontinued some basic programs. Paradoxically, in those agencies where the largest staff reductions came, there were also reductions in volunteer hours because there were no longer enough permanent staff to coordinate and supervise volunteers.

The first services to be eliminated were administration and planning. A second major adjustment was to discontinue individualized services and to handle clients in groups. There was also a shift away from long-term assistance programs emphasizing self-help and self-sufficiency, such as employment training and counseling. Instead, community services aid came to be used primarily for the direct provision of shelter, food, clothing, and energy assistance.

The operators of these urban agencies claim that they actually served more people after the reduction, including a large influx of new poor who were formerly employed. However, these new poor tended to be relatively skilled with temporary needs. The agencies had greater difficulty dealing with the problems of the permanent underclass.

The state administration is less restrictive than the federal government had been prior to the community services block grant. The considerable bitterness resulting from the reductions is almost solely directed at the federal government. This is a little surprising in view of the fact that these urban agencies are now getting a smaller percentage of the funds than they did under federal administration. PCAA seems to have generated local support by skillfully seeking agency input into major decisions and allowing flexibility and discretion to local agencies in identifying and responding to the needs of their clients.

While PCAA has been supportive of agency efforts to gain outside support, there has been no suggestion that the state would take responsibility for replacing the federal losses. Even though this program is administered at the state level, it is still seen as a federal program in which the state is responsible only for an equitable distribution of funds.

COMMUNITY DEVELOPMENT BLOCK GRANT

Washington State did not assume responsibility for the small-cities portion of the community development block grant program until May 1982. Due to the timing of this acceptance, the agency was a year behind in its grant awards, but the transitional, administrative difficulties were eased by lumping emergency jobs act funds with community development grants.

The primary use of community development funds by small cities is for public works projects. There is a great backlog of demand for these projects and it is one of the most likely areas for future state replacement of federal reductions. Governor Spellman commissioned an inventory of public works and Washington continues to be a national leader in planning to protect its infrastructure. It was, therefore, consistent with existing plans to utilize the jobs act money for this purpose. However, the legislature did not take any steps to augment this effort or to replace projected reductions.

The small-cities community development block grant resulted in new administrative responsibility for the state. Small-city funds that had been distributed by the U.S. Department of Housing and Urban Development (HUD) are now dispersed by the state's Planning and Community Affairs Agency (PCAA). State officials expressed the opinion that HUD did a fine job with the small-cities community development program and PCAA has merely continued many of these processes. The emergence of state control, however, promoted more intercommunity dialogue. In August 1981, the state agency prepared to assume authority for the small-cities portion of the community development block grant by creating a statewide advisory committee. This committee was made up of equal numbers of city and county representatives, and its purpose was to design criteria for the distribution of small-city funds.

The committee met three or four times a year and facilitated greater representation and involvement from communities that had traditionally been underrepresented in the block grant process. Committee members pointed out that this was the first time that small towns were asked what they needed.

The PCAA staff worked with local officials, especially during the summer of 1982 after program design had been completed. In addition to technical assistance, the state held a series of meetings on the new block grant. The result of this intensified technical-assistance effort was that local expectations were raised that were difficult to meet. There were many more applications for small-city funds than there had been when HUD administered the program. In the first year of state administration, PCAA received ninety-six applications, compared with twenty to thirty under HUD. The state opted to make smaller average grant awards, spreading small-city funds over a greater number of jurisdictions.

HUD multi-year grant awards to localities helped ease transition to state administration of the new block grant. Communities that had received multi-year commitments from HUD continued to receive federal aid under state administration. Both HUD and the PCAA monitored the multi-year contracts; this enabled the state to work closely with federal officials and gain experience in administering the small-cities program.

COMMUNITY SERVICES AND COMMUNITY DEVELOPMENT IN SEATTLE

Seattle's experiences with community services and community development block grants resemble those of the state. Between 1981 and 1982 Seattle suffered a clear reduction of funding in these programs, but the trend was abated with allocations provided by the 1983 jobs act. Seattle used jobs act funds primarily to offset federal aid cuts affecting community action agencies. This money played a critical role in the survival of some of these nonprofit agencies.

Some of the new regulations affecting the community development block grant program were out of line with Seattle's long-standing priorities. For instance, the amount a recipient government could spend on public or human services was now limited to 10 percent of the grant in 1982. This was a concern to city officials, since allocation to social services has been an important vehicle for Seattle to increase the portion of the grant money targeted on low-income people.

Another regulation placed a 20 percent limitation on planning and administrative costs. Still another allowed multi-family housing complexes to be financed by community development funds if 20 percent of the units are for low-income assistance, as opposed to the 50 percent previously required. This change was justified on the basis that the old rule encouraged spatial concentration of low-income families, but Seattle officials feared that the change would result in construction of fewer low-income units. Finally, new regulations tightened auditing and reporting requirements to prevent fraud and abuse. The Seattle community development administrator feels that such requirements should not be applied to cities, like Seattle, with "clean" records.

In spite of potential difficulties, these changes have not created severe problems for Seattle; in fact, the rule changes actually simplified the administration of the block grant. The reduction in allowable spending on human services would have been a major problem because Seattle has traditionally spent a high portion of community development funds on these programs, but the impact was postponed by a temporary exemption from the 10 percent limitation, granted by HUD on the grounds that the decrease would place an unwarranted burden on the city's human service agencies and clients. The federal government subsequently raised this limit for all local jurisdictions receiving community development funds from 10 percent to 15 percent. If the exemption had not been allowed the amount going to these agencies could have been cut by $3 million and the support of health clinics and other neighborhood-based services would have been threatened. In short, the federal government regulations require less attention to services for low-income people, but the city has not been required to follow that lead. Enough flexibility exists to allow Seattle to take positive steps to protect the community-based organizations with service to the poor as their major mission.

This smooth transition by the state and city was aided by supplemental funds provided by the 1983 jobs act. Neither the state nor the city has shown any interest in replacement. As emergency jobs act funds are spent, there may be another story to tell. Some replacement is likely to occur at the state level because of the intense interest in public investment in infrastructure. However, the city has limited taxing power and an emphasis on human services that will make replacement much more difficult.

PROGRAMS FOR PRESERVATION OF NATURAL RESOURCES

Natural resource preservation is a major issue in Washington State and programs are divided among a number of small agencies. The establishment of the Land and Water Conservation Fund marked an increase in federal involvement in outdoor recreation in Washington State. This fund was designed to be a self-perpetuating source of grants-in-aid to state and local governments to "stimulate, encourage and assist local and state government agencies in creating new and expanded public outdoor recreation areas and facilities." Revenue for this comes largely from user fees at federal locations and federal funding has always required state and local matching. In 1981, the matching proportion was 23 percent federal, 27 percent local, and 50 percent state funds. The legislature has usually passed the allocation for the state share without debate.

In 1981, Washington State received $3.7 million from the federal government for this fund. In 1982, this was reduced to zero; and in 1983, it was restored to $1.3 million. Although the federal funding share for this recreational fund had been minor, when the federal funds were cut, the state simply discontinued the match. Thus, the federal cuts resulted in additional state cuts, substantially reducing services and facilities for outdoor recreation.

The federal cuts in natural resources programs were not particularly damaging but state responses have been consistent. In the Department of Game, most revenues derive from license fees and personalized automobile license plates, with estimated annual revenues of over $17 million from the state. Federal funding constitutes only a small part of the department's total revenue, but two types of programs have been severely reduced: wildlife technical assistance and research have been deeply cut, and the endangered species program was reduced more than 80 percent. Since these are programs that affect the future more than the present, the eventual damage is purely conjectural.

Likewise, in the Department of Natural Resources, only slightly more than 3 percent of the agency's funds come from federal sources. The department's primary functions, including forest management, fire protection, and insect and disease management, were virtually unaffected by any federal reductions. However, as in the case of the Department of Game, some special programs have been reduced, without state replacement. Most notable among these is the national heritage program under which endangered plant species are cataloged and recorded.

The federal reductions have not been deep or broad-based but they have resulted in selective elimination of planning and outdoor recreation programs. It is significant that even within highly integrated programs with multiple funding sources, some things are identified as state responsibilities and others as federal. Where there is federal identification, the response was consistently to pass along the cuts or augment them with state cuts, even if federal funds make up only a minor portion of previous expenditures.

HEALTH AND SOCIAL SERVICES

The period of the early 1980s was a time when significant cuts were made in social and health services in the state of Washington. However, the extent of budget cutting was more attributable to the recession than to the Reagan program.

Two examples stand out. In early 1981, before Reagan proposed any of his changes, the state legislature, at the request of the governor, eliminated two welfare programs. The first was the program known in Washington as AFDC-E (aid to families with dependent children where two parents resided in the household and the children were being deprived because neither of the parents was employed). With the elimination of that program, and the exclusion of its 26,000 beneficiaries, the remaining AFDC system served only those families where there was a single parent. At the same time, the state eliminated the general assistance program for single adults and childless couples. This step revoked eligibility for another 8,000 adults, leaving general assistance available only to those mentally or physically incapacitated and removing from eligibility those who were unemployed and had run out of unemployment benefits.

These two steps alone reduced the state budget for social and health services by an estimated $400 million. The state welfare changes preceded the Reagan reductions, overshadowing the federal reforms and making it difficult to determine the full impact of national policy affecting the AFDC program.

With the federal reductions following closely behind the state changes, Governor Spellman brought in Alan Gibbs as director of the Department of Social and Health Services (DSHS). Gibbs had considerable budgetary experience as a health administration official under Mayor John Lindsay of New York City and as the number two administrator in New Jersey's human services agency. Gibbs' early assessment of the situation was that the problems of the DSHS were major and likely to continue. He recognized that in many respects Reagan was simply continuing what President Jimmy Carter had begun and felt that the process would be continued further. In order to minimize the negative political and service effects of these cuts, Gibbs developed a detailed budget reduction planning process similar to a zero-base budgeting system. Each program director was required to prioritize the state service responsibilities of each program without regard to cost. Where programs served the same clients or responded to similar kinds of needs, the managers were expected to confer and propose coordination or consolidation.

Between June 15 and September 15, 1981, a revised budget was developed for the governor's review and approval. Important in this process was the clear indication that these budgets were to be built through negotiation with city and county officials and with coordination among program managers. Citizen advisory committees were formed and public hearings were held to give ample opportunity for feedback. With a completed plan in hand, DSHS was prepared to manage the federal reductions as they came along. The process probably would have proceeded quite smoothly had it not been for the departmental reductions precipitated by the state fiscal crisis.

The actual 1982 federal cuts for all social and health service programs amounted to approximately $70 million. Although it is generally conceded that this loss had little overall effect, some groups lost important benefits. The tightening of AFDC eligibility had a negative effect on clients but a positive impact on the state budget. The state realized a savings in matching funds by adopting federal standards that limited AFDC eligibility. Officials at DSHS explained the state's view that the AFDC program and eligibility determination should be a federal responsibility. The state responded in a similar way to tighter eligibility rules in food stamps, a program seen as exclusively federal. The state also ratified federal changes in the refugee assistance program. In fact, for all the entitlement programs it is clear that whatever the federal government decided, the state of Washington passed along.

DSHS was more creative in its management of the block grants. The $70 million cut was minimized by fortunate events and careful management. First, the actual AFDC case load was below what had been forecast for the 1981–83 biennium. This resulted in a savings of nearly $27 million, which was applied against the lost federal funds. Beyond that, because the state accepted the federal changes in the eligibility requirements for AFDC, case loads were further reduced. These two factors covered more than half of the $70 million loss.

DSHS then proceeded to reduce regulations ($1.6 million), reduce administrative costs ($1.1 million), and increase efforts to collect support payments and pursue third-party health care insurers so that the burden on Medicaid was reduced ($12 million). Fees to cover the cost of licensing, inspection, and similar activities were also increased ($2.4 million). The state also transferred federal aid provided under the low-income energy assistance block grant to support activities eligible for funding under the social services block grant.

Some minor service reductions totaling about $12 million were also made. These included such things as elimination of adoption support for healthy caucasian babies under the age of five, and reductions in technical assistance, education, and training. The agency also stopped funding alcohol and drug treatment programs in state prisons. Another tactic was to delay some of the projects in the existing budget. As an example, two new state hospital buildings were delayed by six months with substantial savings for the 1981–83 biennium.

Thus, with the exception of the impact on AFDC and food stamps, the reductions in social services funding had little effect on direct services to clients. That is not to say that the operation of DSHS was not dramatically changed during this period. On top of the $70 million federal cuts, there was a reduction of $150 million in the state budget. This was in addition to the cuts made as a result of earlier changes in AFDC and general assistance. There have been very few changes in the process since the initial cuts were made. Federal revenues were essentially stabilized and some of the state reductions have been restored, including a restoration of AFDC-E.

Maternal and Child Care Block Grant

Through Gibbs' budget reduction planning process described above, maternal and child services were maintained in federal fiscal year 1982. In the following two years, jobs act funds were used to fund prenatal care and avoid any substantial service reductions. The big issue surrounding this grant, as in many others, was its distribution across the state. The director of the Office of Community Health Services had long felt that Seattle received a disproportionate share of child care funding relative to the problems they encountered with infant mortality and considered the block grant as an opportunity to distribute funds more equitably.

The first DSHS proposal suggested a 31 percent decrease in federal funding for maternal and child health programs in King County, the county serving Seattle. This led to a battle of "statistics." Seattle officials claimed that they were being penalized for past effectiveness that had resulted in lower mortality rates and better health care. State officials countered with the argument that the distribution should be according to documented *current* need. The actual reduction to Seattle in 1982 was about 25 percent. Maternal and child health budgets in Seattle were cut in 1982 but restored when jobs act money came along.

At the state level, the maternal and child health block grant is a popular program and is seen as freeing the state from unnecessary restriction. Seattle is still smarting from its battle, but it is generally felt that prenatal care services there are quite good and that basic services are being maintained. Some hospitals are now offering free services, but this is the only evidence of replacement.

Alcohol, Drug Abuse, and Mental Health

Alcohol, drug abuse, and mental health services have received a 25 percent decrease in federal funds. These losses have been handled by user fees, reduction in hospitalization, and cutting alcohol and drug abuse programs in prisons. The cuts are controversial and generally reflect a shift from preventive activities and rehabilitation to emergency care.

Medical Assistance

Similar to the changes in AFDC and general assistance, the state began to cut back on medical assistance before the federal reductions. Throughout 1981 and 1982, the state tightened administrative and fiscal controls over health services for the poor. For instance, the deductible requirement for the state-funded medical only program was increased from $200 to $1,000. Medical services under general assistance were changed to restrict outpatient drugs, eliminate hearing aids, and reduce outpatient mental health coverage. In conjunction with the elimination of AFDC-E, medical coverage was also withdrawn. Chiropractic, podiatry, and adult dental care services were eliminated. The state adopted a new reimbursement system for hospitals that provides payments on the basis of fixed rates. Washington State also tightened restrictions on the number of reimbursable hospital days. In 1981, the deductible for the state-funded medically indigent program was increased from $500 to $1,500. On May 1, 1982, Washington State lowered the deductible back to $500, only to raise it again in October to $1,500. On July 1, 1983, the deductible was lowered back to $500.

The number of changes in rules, coverage, payment level, and eligibility is truly staggering. Medical coverage has been reduced; however, the impact is difficult to assess. One county director of health programs reported that 14 percent of patient visits were covered by Medicaid in 1983 compared with 19 percent in 1982. However, for the same period, there was an increase in the total number of encounters covered by Medicaid.

Social Services Block Grant

Of all the federal aid received by the DSHS, social services block grant funds are the most flexible; the state agency treats the funds almost like revenue sharing. The U.S. Department of Health and Human Services places few restrictions on state distribution and use of funds. Federal aid from the program is pooled with state money to enlarge the funding for social services. State officials are satisfied with the relationship between DSHS and the federal government on this grant. The federal government has relaxed auditing requirements and reduced the sample size required to show accountability.

Federal reductions resulted in a $13 million cut in social services for Washington State in 1982. Jobs act funds restored half of the cut in 1983 and the estimate for 1984 was just slightly less. While state spending increased for social services, this should not be seen as replacement, since state funding was still below the original 1981 budget.

THE DEPARTMENT OF EMPLOYMENT AND SECURITY

In contrast to the detailed advance planning for accommodation of federal budget reductions carried out by DSHS, Employment Security (ES) has been largely reactive. The state agency manages employment services, unemployment insurance benefits, and the work incentive program. In addition, it is responsible for determining food stamp eligibility and administers federal job training programs. Excluding the cuts affecting programs authorized by the Comprehensive Employment and Training Act (CETA), federal reductions in programs administered by the state's employment security department were reduced by more than $11 million in federal fiscal year 1982. The programs administered by the department are viewed as federal. There was little discussion of state replacement of the federal aid reductions.

The state department also supervised the elimination of the CETA jobs program, which had 7,000 participants throughout Washington State. Nearly 2,000 of these participants were employed by state agencies.

The Department of Employment Security was strongly affected by changes in federal employment service grants, which were cut by nearly $7 million in December 1981. Even though federal funds were largely restored in early 1982, the department reduced its staff by nearly 500 employees and cut services. In 1983, the state agency job training and placement services in smaller, more rural areas of the state tended to be cut.

Thus, the impact of the Reagan program on unemployment insurance and traditional employment services is to make services less accessible, especially in small towns and rural areas. Overall, state officials give little thought to replacing these losses. In spite of the lack of state initiative for replacement, the changes in federal funding strengthened the state office relative to local governments. The state's power was tested and reinforced when local offices were closed in 1982 despite the strong objections of local governments.

The State Role in JTPA

Federal job training programs authorized by the Job Training Partnership Act of 1982 further enhanced the role of Washington State government. In its relationship with the local service delivery areas (SDAs), the state's Department of Employment Security adopted a central management role requiring detailed plans and reports. Governor Spellman has worked to integrate JTPA resources with his plans for economic development and offender training. In 1983–84, the state mandated the following implementation procedures for title II activities: (1) The state requires an agreement that the county will abide by all state provisions for JTPA implementation. (2) The composition of the private industry council (PIC) is set by the state (emphasizing participation by women and minorities), while the county will make the actual selection. (3) The state will review all local plans. (4) The PICs may appoint grant recipients only after state approval. (5) Actual contracts are signed by the state and the grant recipient. The local areas are not happy with these arrangements, but at present they remain in force.

Even greater evidence of the state's effort to control JTPA comes from its management of title III funds for dislocated workers. None of this money was allocated directly to local service delivery areas but was instead passed on to the state's employment security offices, which have provided job training and counseling to displaced workers. This policy is so controversial that the state may have to retreat a little from that position. However, it is clear evidence of the effort to centralize JTPA control.

The impact of federal changes on Washington ES programs is clear. While the federal reductions have created some disruption in ES activities, managerial responsibility has been centralized relative to local governments and service delivery organizations. The agency is smaller than in 1981, but stronger.

HIGHWAY AID

Washington State has a strong commitment to maintaining roads, highways, and bridges, and would have probably replaced federal cuts in highway aid had they occurred. However, federal spending increased substantially between fiscal years 1982 and 1984. Washington State's estimated highway aid apportionment for 1983 increased by over 28 percent, from $214.3 million in federal fiscal year 1982 to $275.3 million in federal fiscal year 1983. The largest increases went to the interstate construction and repair program. Federal highway aid for bridge repair and replacement also received significant increases. Federal highway aid is expected to continue to increase in 1984 and 1985.

Of more immediate concern than the level of federal funding is the recent shortfall in state revenue earmarked for highway improvements. In 1983 the legislature approved a bill, which took effect in 1984 and which raised the state motor fuel tax by two cents per gallon. Washington State clearly considers the roads, highways, and bridges to be state territory and took steps to protect expenditure levels.

IMPACT OF SELECTED PROGRAMS ON SEATTLE

Educational Block Grant

In 1980–81, the Seattle school district received over $7 million federal educational aid from the categorical programs now included in the education block grant. In 1983–84, that amount had dwindled to approximately $700,000. Most of this reduction can be traced to elimination of special desegregation funding for which Seattle had received nearly $4 million in 1980–81.

The reductions result both from federal reductions in block grant funds and the way the state chose to allocate these funds. The federal categorical grants had conditions for funding, including racial mix, bilingual population, and certain staffing goals, that were not given much weight in fund distribution by the state. Although over 80 percent of block grant funds were distributed to schools on a formula basis, the state distributed discretionary funds on a competitive basis. Many districts received funds for special programs for the first time while others were severely reduced. This was an unsettling process and, in direct response to concerns originating in the Seattle school district, Washington State eliminated the state block grant competitive approach in 1985 and distributed chapter 2 money directly to remedial and bilingual programs.

Wastewater Treatment

The state department of ecology administers wastewater treatment grants. Local governments submit applications to the state agency for construction grants. The proposals are ranked according to criteria set by the state and reviewed by the U.S. Environmental Protection Agency. Current EPA-state policy requires that municipalities attain secondary treatment, get a waiver, or face enforcement action. Seattle has put all of its requests "on hold" while they await an EPA decision on a request for a waiver to their obligation to achieve secondary treatment criteria. If the waiver is not granted, the absence of state or federal funding could create a major problem for the city.

The state is concerned about federal cutbacks in wastewater treatment construction grants. This program is not seen as solely a federal responsibility. In 1981, voters in Washington State approved a bond authorization that will raise $150 million over a five-year period for the construction of treatment plants. The additional state money was seen as a response to federal cutbacks. This program is likely to be a candidate for continued replacement, although continuing fiscal difficulties have stalled major effort.

Mass Transit

The effect of federal initiatives on mass transit systems in Seattle is mixed. Operating funds were reduced by about 20 percent in 1981, and the Reagan administration stated the intent of phasing them out. For 1983 and 1984, operating assistant payments remained at about 80 percent of the 1982 level, and the losses have been replaced by a voter-approved increase in the local sales tax and some minor fare increases. Despite this replacement, there have been some service reductions and staff layoffs.

While operating support has been reduced, there has been an increase in capital funding from the new federal gas tax revenues. The end result is that the city receives about the same total as it did prior to the federal changes.

The Context for Response

In looking at the effects of federal funding changes, a major issue is whether the response of states and localities resulted in reductions in services. There are a variety of possible state responses and, as seen in the program analyses in the previous section, there are variations within the state.

The amount of time allowed for adjustment must be seen as a major factor influencing the response. In Washington, there was considerable advanced warning, and many agencies, led by DSHS, developed detailed plans for cross substitution. Even so, there is no evidence that the state or any localities actually made plans for replacement. Furthermore, only in DSHS was there any planning to prioritize existing programs and minimize negative impact. In virtually all other departments, and for the entitlement programs in DSHS, the plans provided that federal reductions would be passed along and absorbed in the programs where the federal funds were reduced.

Stringent fiscal conditions also placed a major constraint on the response to federal aid changes. Washington State found that existing revenues were insufficient to support even state services, let alone those that are seen as federal.

INSTITUTIONAL FACTORS

All factors must play out and be affected by the institutional environment within which decisions are made. Even though federal grants to Washington State increased steadily from the mid-1960s to 1980, state officials have behaved as though much of these funds were designated for special, federal, purposes. Even when grant funding was rapidly increasing, the state government did not extensively substitute these funds for locally raised revenues in support of traditional services. In fact, the use of these federal funds seems to have reflected a conscious effort to avoid dependence on federal funding.

This does not mean that the basic processes of state government were not influenced by federal grant increases in the 1960s and 1970s. New agencies emerged and old agencies expanded, with complicated delivery systems, coordinated networks, and local political involvement all keyed to the federal grants. It is remarkable, however, that many federally funded programs kept a separate identity, especially at the state level.

Some examples drawn from the programs described in the previous section illustrate this point. The activities of the Employment Security Department have always been considered federal, in part because they are funded almost entirely by the federal government. Thus, when CETA jobs were phased out and when a shortage of funding for employment services developed, Washington's response was to proportionally reduce operations while directing all complaints to the federal government. The activities of the threatened service centers included job placement, determination of eligibility for unemployment compensation and food stamps, and job training, each of which has been delivered by state agencies. Yet the federal identity has been maintained and there was no consideration of state replacement.

The AFDC program is jointly funded and the heart of the state's welfare system. But it falls in the welfare category which Washington State sees as triggered by federal initiative. When the federal government changed eligibility rules for AFDC, the state avoided replacing the lost benefits and received a revenue savings as a result. Outdoor recreation programs operated on a matching grant where the federal share was only about one-quarter of the total. However, when the federal portion was eliminated, the state simply eliminated this "federal" program and saved its matching share.

Even in the area of education, where the state assumes primary responsibility, federal programs and funds are kept separate. These included desegregation funds, impact aid, and subsidies for the school lunch program. When these subsidies were reduced, they were passed through in clearly identifiable programs. Another example is the food stamp program. Officials at DSHS indicated that there would never be replacement because food stamps are not a state responsibility.

Program identity by level of government seems to be firmly rooted in the minds of state officials and legislators. However, it is not shared by all administrators and was not a dominant force, for instance, in the early DSHS plan for prioritization of services. Secretary Gibbs gave high priority to the vocational rehabilitation program in spite of the fact that prior to federal cuts the program funding was 87.5 percent federal. The plan called for a shift of state money to vocational rehabilitation to offset federal losses. Characteristically, though, when the legislature reviewed spending proposals during the state revenue crises, they attacked this replacement recommendation and made further reductions to the program. The legislative view, made explicit in the budget hearings, was that vocational rehabilitation was a federal program and state funds should not offset the federal cuts.

For capital projects, the situation is less clear. The state and the city of Seattle have shown a willingness to replace losses when funds for roads, streets, sewers, or housing were threatened, although there has been less concern over housing for poor families, which has been viewed as a poverty program and a federal rather than a state responsibility. In these areas, the predictions concerning replacement are largely conjectural because most of the threatened reductions did not materialize. However, unlike income support or training programs, it is evident that state and local officials think of capital programs as state and local responsibilities, and so replacement would probably occur.

Thus, programs are identified by revenue source and by the level of government that originated the program. The choice of what to cut when federal funds are reduced is essentially dictated by this institutional framework. In one sense, this is a politically smart way to handle problems since protest is channeled to the federal government. The efforts of the Reagan administration to shift the focus of responsibility, by suggesting that many federally funded services really should be assumed by state and local governments, have not yet been accepted in Washington State. Even though it is possible to maintain something like a CETA training program by eliminating some community colleges or by reducing local street repair, the political identity of these programs precludes such action. For state and local governments to admit, by their actions, that programs that have been federally funded may now become state or local responsibilities is tantamount to accepting an entirely new configuration of government responsibility. That would be significant institutional change, and it is not likely to happen suddenly.

In 1983 there was almost no replacement of federal funds except in capital projects and jobs act funding allowed some hard choices to be postponed. But the discontinuance of that funding will lead to some recommendations for replacement and in the 1984 special session of the legislature, some attention was directed to restoration of lost social and health services. But these questions were of minor consequence compared with the pressure to restore funding for education and infrastructure support, the more traditional state responsibilities, which were lost as a result of cuts in state budgets. These latter issues will dominate the next legislative session, and budget surpluses or new revenue sources are already being earmarked to meet these needs.

Conclusions

Perhaps the most evident effects in Washington of federal aid changes are on the government operations at the state level. Managerial procedures have been strengthened and the state agencies are more involved in prioritizing services, instituting user fees, and increasing the accountability of funded organizations. The tendency of both state and local government in Washington to ratify and compound federal changes has been clear. Some view this as a position dictated by the recession, but that is not the sole explanation. Washington State had always kept most federally funded activities somewhat separate from those financed by state and local sources. Rather than prune all programs, the federal branches were simply allowed to wither in proportion to the changed revenues. The burden was eased by the availability of emergency jobs funds and few programs were allowed to completely die in federal fiscal years 1982 and 1983.

The block grants administered by DSHS were treated in a somewhat different manner, and funds were moved around to minimize impact. This was almost entirely the result of a rigorous planning process that was carried out before the reductions occurred. The outcome was shifting funds across federally funded activities—although replacement still did not take place. This example illustrates the fact that new leadership, not bound by state traditions, can facilitate the process of change and accelerate institutional adjustment. In 1981 and 1982, the general opinion of government officials in Washington was that the block grants were merely a mask for the reductions, but by 1984 it was evident that the state was making full use of the flexibility allowed by the block grants. Time has shown that the more flexible block grant approach does provide a partial offset for cuts, and that the block grant money is being used in some imaginative ways.

Another outcome of the block grants was a reduction in what state officials called "urban bias" in the distribution of federal funds. Prior to 1981, Seattle's share of federal funds far exceeded its share of the population, poverty families, or any other objective measure of need. State administration of federal aid has resulted in a redistribution of funds that is more favorable to smaller cities and rural areas. This has especially been the case under the maternal and child health, community services, and education block grants. As a result, the federal reductions had a disproportionate impact on Seattle; many other areas actually received increases and a few areas got money for the first time. This change is likely to persist because it reflects the current distribution of state political power and because small towns and rural areas are building an institutional framework for absorbing the funds.

There is tension between the state and localities as a result of this change and the situation is not yet at equilibrium. Disputes over JTPA funds and federal aid from the maternal and child health and the community services block grant programs are continuing, and the state will probably retreat from the position it now holds. Even so, there is a general awareness among state politicians and officials that the role of the state is increasing. There is a growing tendency to assume more authority over social and capital programs and to do more state-level planning and programming in education and health. As the reduced role of the federal government becomes clearer, the state seems to increase its willingness to fill the gap.

The federal reductions in Washington State created some individual hardship. The trend in social and health services has been to provide basic services (à la "safety net") and to sacrifice planning, rehabilitation, preventive, and training activities. The results of such changes are long term and difficult to predict, but it is the working poor and those who need preventive care who are most affected.

The reductions and administrative changes initiated by the Reagan administration should be seen as validating a trend in Washington State that was already underway in early 1980. That trend was manifested by reductions in social and health services, higher user fees, tightened management procedures, and an insistence that communities, organizations, families, and individuals become more self-reliant. Each step within the trend has been relatively small. Most services continue at about the same level and are delivered in the same way as before. Whether the adjustments that have taken place are indications of a long-term trend or a one-time adjustment depends largely on upcoming elections. However, it is unlikely that there will be a quick return to the 1979–80 situation because the new approaches are settling in.

12

Arizona

JOHN STUART HALL AND RICHARD A. ERIBES

State government in Arizona became more centralized in the 1980s. The state has assumed new responsibilities and the executive branch has gained authority relative to the legislature. The Reagan domestic policy changes of the early 1980s played a part in these shifts. Many of the effects of the changes in federal grant programs, however, were merely "icing on the cake." Reagan's initiatives enhanced, and in some cases speeded up, state and local actions and responses, but were not primarily responsible for these changes. Rather, other recent political and economic developments have driven institutional change in the state.

The most important such factor was the national economic downturn of the 1980s. After thirty years of almost constant growth, the 1981–82 recession showed Arizona to be vulnerable to national economic trends. State and local officials learned that public sector budgets would not expand inevitably or automatically. They faced problems that were new to Arizona: service reductions, layoffs, reorganization, and the need for major tax increases.

If the public sector revenue decline was not enough, Arizona officials were also forced in the early 1980s to deal with the short- and long-term consequences of more stringent fiscal limitations. Tax limits imposed in 1980 effectively capped property taxes and placed restrictions on local expenditures, thus placing a ceiling on overall public program growth. Fiscal limits were in sync with the national "Proposition 13" movement and in keeping with a sentiment of fiscal conservatism that had marked Arizona politics throughout the history of the state.

Authors would like to acknowledge the assistance of Pam Eck.

Indeed, because of Arizona's traditional fiscal conservatism, the idea of national retrenchment was well received in the state. For the most part, the federal cuts were ratified, though the state's growth and own priorities led to increased state and *federal* spending in some areas.

Fiscal and Economic Conditions

A conservative political and fiscal tradition is rooted in Arizona culture, and has been a dominant theme of state politics, regardless of party and position. Populism, Arizona style, provides a somewhat negative image of government and expenditures for public services. As one writer put it: "Public policies are hard to promote in a part of the country where rugged individualism is the old religion and growth is the new one."[1]

But up until the last few years, fiscal reality actually clashed with political rhetoric. The public sector in Arizona grew at rates in keeping with the state's population boom and economic development. Between 1966 and 1976, state and local taxes increased 265 percent, while population increased 49 percent and personal income increased 238 percent.[2] The state's budget more than doubled in the past ten years, between state fiscal years 1974 to 1984. This was also true for the city of Phoenix.

Why did this expansion of the public sector occur, given the seemingly overriding political importance of the philosophy of fiscal restraint? The answer to the question has two parts. In the first place, revenue generation in recent decades in Arizona has been almost automatic. Secondly, fiscal restraint was until very recently an abstract philosophy more than a practical policy.

The principal reason for the growth of the Arizona public sector is that the revenue structures of Arizona state and local government are relatively balanced, diverse, and elastic. For state fiscal year 1984, general fund revenue came from the following sources:

Sales/use tax	47.0%
Income taxes	33.2%
All other taxes	9.5%
Other revenue transfers	5.7%
General property tax	4.6%

[1] Michael T. Kaufman, *New York Times*, April 5, 1975.
[2] Frank J. Sackton and David Jankofsky, "Revenues, Economic Projections and Tax Elasticity," in Frank J. Sackton, David Jankofsky, and Nicholas Henry, eds., *Toward Tax Reform* (Phoenix: The Arizona Academy, 1979), p. 96.

Similarly, the city of Phoenix and other local jurisdictions rely heavily on sales tax and their share of the state income tax, which is reallocated to localities on a population basis. As a result, local governments in Arizona do not rely as heavily as localities in other states on local property tax revenues and therefore benefit quickly from population and economic increases, and industrial relocation to the Sunbelt.

The story of public sector growth in Arizona is perhaps most interesting because it took place despite formal limits on taxation and government spending. A 1921 statute, which remained in effect until 1978, limited annual growth in local budgets to 10 percent. The measure also restricted annual increases in local property tax rates by the same percentage.

Local governments, however, have rarely been constrained by these limits. Important revenue categories, such as most intergovernmental revenues, were exempted. Furthermore, knowledge of loopholes and adept accounting enabled local financial officials to exclude "half or more" of local expenditures from the constraints.[3] Similarly, the 10 percent limit on property tax rate increases was an easy ceiling to live with since Arizona's ever-expanding tax rolls ensured rapid actual growth in tax collections.

Regardless of their limited efforts, these constraints—as well as similar limitations on local school districts—were popular among elected officials, who were able to point to the limits as legal checks on the expansion of government.

In Arizona, elected officials were ahead of the fiscal constraint wave that reached the rest of the country in the late 1970s. In 1974, the state legislature proposed a measure to limit state spending. But this was defeated by the Arizona voters.[4] By 1978, however, the mood of the Arizona electorate had shifted. The same year that California passed Proposition 13 Arizona voters approved a constitutional amendment limiting the amount of state revenues that could be appropriated by the legislature to 7 percent of the state's estimated total personal income during each year. That limit can be exceeded by approval of two-thirds of each house of the legislature on each appropriation.

In a 1979 special session, the Arizona Legislature imposed spending and tax limits on local school districts. These measures led to greater centralization of education funding at the state level. In 1973, just prior to the 1974 special session action, state funds accounted for only 37.4 percent of the local school district expenditures. By 1983, state revenues comprised over one-half of the rev-

[3] Anthony H. Pascal et al., *Fiscal Containment of Local and State Government* (Santa Monica, Calif.: Rand Corporation, 1979), p. 71.

[4] For that story, see Brent W. Brown, John Stuart Hall, Thomas Goodwin, and Sandra Day O'Connor, *Arizona's Expenditure and Tax Limitation Proposal: An Analysis of "Proposition 106"* (Tempe, Ariz.: Center for Public Affairs, Arizona State University, 1974).

enues needed to run the state's public schools, with increases compensating for cuts in property tax support and allowing an expansion in local education spending. During this same ten-year period federal aid to the state's local public schools has accounted for a modest and stable amount of the total secondary and elementary education expenditures, between 8 and 10 percent.

Another tax-limitation measure approved by Arizona voters in a 1980 special election closed some of the loopholes that had enabled local governments to get around the 10 percent limit on budgetary growth. Annual increases in local budgets were limited to a rate based on annual population and inflation adjustments that are applied to spending levels from a 1979–80 baseline period. Various sources of funds, however, are still exempted from the budgetary limit, including federal grant-in-aid. Furthermore, local governments can override spending limits with the approval of county or municipal voters. Many communities have been successful in securing such overrides. For example, on November 30, 1981, Phoenix voters elected to allow the city to exceed state expenditure limits through 1985–86 for spending in connection with the large capital budget programs of aviation, water, wastewater, and civic plaza programs.

Thus, in recent years, Arizona's state and local spending and taxing limits have become more stringent. Yet economic growth and personal income increases still provide the opportunity for public sector growth. For example, the limitation on overall state expenditures is 7 percent of the state's estimated *total personal income*. As that total increases, so does the state expenditure limit. This situation led to a legislative referral to voters of a proposal to tighten this limitation further to 6.5 percent.[5]

These current limitations, particularly the property tax limit of 1980, have put teeth into the past political symbolism of fiscal constraint. As such, they probably please fiscal conservatives and perplex some who are responsible for providing state and local government services.

RETRENCHMENT IN THE EARLY 1980S

The early 1980s' revenue picture for the state, and to some degree, for local governments contrasted sharply with state and local fiscal conditions in the preceding decades. The obvious common villain for all jurisdictions was the national recession. The lesson for the Arizona public sector of the recent national recession is really quite simple. The tax structure that responded to the extended pe-

[5] Arizona voters rejected this proposal (Proposition 108) in the November 1984 elections by a 73,000 ballot margin. Keven and Ann Willey, "Extension of the One Percent Sales Tax Hike Advances," *Arizona Republic*, April 21, 1984.

riod of economic growth in Arizona by expanding revenues responded equally quickly to major economic decline. Shortfalls in revenues ensued. The reliance of Arizona governments on sales and income taxes for well over half of their income makes those governments very dependent on economic forces. Fortunately, the recent recession did not last too long in Arizona. Resulting fiscal problems for Arizona state government were more significant and longer lasting than for the city of Phoenix.

Differences in the current fiscal conditions of these two jurisdictions are attributable to the way in which they responded to the tax revolt of the late 1970s and the economic slowdown of the early 1980s.

At the state level, the legislature eliminated the state sales tax on food (resulting in a loss of approximately $90 million in state fiscal year 1982) and indexed the state's income tax. On the other hand, state legislative "reforms" in recent years required large increases in state expenditures for local public education and for indigent health care. The state's new experiment in indigent health, the Arizona Health Care Cost Containment System (AHCCCS), has been particularly costly and troublesome, and has, more than any other recent policy, affected state and local finance and the relationship between state and county governments.[6]

This combination of economic forces and fiscal limits required Arizona state officials to make substantive changes in their revenue structures. At the state level, an increase in the sales tax from 4 to 5 percent was passed in 1983. This was originally to be a "temporary" tax but became permanent in 1984, when legislators meeting in special session determined that they could not balance the state budget without the $118 million in additional revenue provided by the sales tax hike. A series of revenue-raising tactics were enacted that included a hike in the hotel/motel room tax and tighter restrictions on tax credits for rental income, purchases of solar energy devices, as well as certain out-of-state purchases. The recent tax initiatives raised approximately $260 million in additional revenue in state fiscal year 1984–85, when the state budget totaled approximately $2 billion.[7] Tax increases of this magnitude are rare in Arizona and run counter to the state's widespread conservative political and fiscal traditions. The spending increases, however, have been large enough to eat up this added income and continue fiscal pressures on state government.

The city of Phoenix responded quickly but differently to the perceived de-

---

[6] Until October 1, 1982, Arizona was the only state without a Medicaid program. Before then, indigent health care was the responsibility of county governments.

[7] Richard R. Robertson, "Here's How the Taxpayers Will Foot the Bill for the Budget," *Arizona Republic*, May 4, 1984. Keven and Ann Willey, "Extension of the One Percent Sales Tax Hike Advances."

mand for tax and expenditure limitation. A blue ribbon commission and city officials responded to the perceived strength of the tax revolt of the late 1970s[8] by adopting an even lower local property tax rate. In 1980, the city began to wean itself even further from dependence on that revenue source. In 1979–80, property tax revenue accounted for 11 percent of the city's general fund budget. By 1983–84, only 8.4 percent of general-fund expenditures were supported by that revenue source. The conscious policy of city officials to increase user fees over the past four years, along with increased sales tax revenues, has allowed the city to maintain and in some cases expand existing services. However, in contrast to state government, the city has been more reluctant to add new programmatic functions in this period of fiscal uncertainty. This is partly because of the constitutionally prescribed role of city governments in Arizona and partly a conscious choice of city officials to resist the temptation to augment or replace services reduced by other levels of government.

The Arizona Intergovernmental Setting

The subjects of our story—the state of Arizona and the city of Phoenix—are but two of over 850 units of government in Arizona. A central feature of the Reagan domestic program is the promotion and enhancement of the power of state government. To determine the extent to which that objective is being met in Arizona requires an understanding of the exercise of political power within and between these two jurisdictions and the remainder of governments in Arizona.[9]

To begin with, a good case can be made to the effect that Arizona is really two states: one urban and one rural. Over one-half of the state's 1982 population of 2,886,600 resides in the Phoenix metropolitan area. Another 567,000 people live in the Tucson metropolitan area. The remainder of the state's population reside in small municipalities and unincorporated areas, which are ru-

---

[8] Interestingly, this commission, its recommendations, and measures taken by city management in keeping with the commission's report were in response to state tax and expenditure limits and preceded the revenue shortfalls occurring in 1981. Because many of these measures were put in place just prior to unanticipated declines in sales tax revenues, they greatly cushioned the effects of the recession for the city of Phoenix. These measures included: (1) a $253 million bond issue approved in 1979; and (2) enhancement of a productivity program that one writer has described as "one of the best governmental productivity programs in the country." See Jeremy Main, "Why Government Works Dumb," *Fortune*, August 10, 1981, p. 156.

[9] Much of this section is condensed from Frank J. Sackton, *Arizona Government in the National Context* (Tempe, Ariz.: Center for Public Affairs, Arizona State University, 1980), chapters 3 and 4. In addition, good sources on Arizona state government structure are Nicholas Henry, ed., *Of, By and For the People* (Tempe, Ariz.: The Arizona Academy, Arizona State University, 1977), and Ray Everett, *Arizona History and Government*, 2nd ed. (Tempe, Ariz.: Center for Public Affairs, Arizona State University, 1982).

ral in nature. Although it is difficult to generalize about the relationship between local jurisdictions, their representatives, and agencies, and officials of
state government, it is fair to say that rural Arizona has had more reason to interact with state agencies, programs, and officials than have officials from the
cities of Phoenix and Tucson and their host counties (Maricopa and Pima).
Historically, Phoenix and Tucson have had substantial experience in dealing
directly with federal agencies such as the U.S. Department of Labor and the
U.S. Department of Housing and Urban Development. These cities have had
less interaction with their own state agencies. In fact, by 1979 some of these
experienced city officials viewed the state as at best not involved in their program and at worst an obstructionist jurisdiction.

Rural Arizona jurisdictions had been involved with state agencies as partners
in such programs as the balance-of-state job training program authorized by the
Comprehensive Employment and Training Act (CETA) and areawide planning and economic development activities. In addition, despite legislative reapportionment and adoption of population-based criteria for both houses of the
legislature, rural interests continued to be well represented in the state house.
In sum, rural Arizona had more reason to be supportive of devolution of power
and dollars to the state than did urban officials and interest groups such as those
involved in federal programs in Phoenix.

The state's role in funding and administering public services had been growing prior to the grant-in-aid changes enacted in the first term of the Reagan
administration. This was especially true of two program areas: elementary and
secondary education and indigent health care.

State funding for public education increased during the last twenty years in
response both to state and federal court decisions in other states and decisions
by the U.S. Supreme Court. Prior to 1968, state funding for local school districts in Arizona was based on a flat grant per student amounting to not more
than $200 per enrollee. Since this amount did not go far in covering educa-
tional costs, local school districts generated most of their operational revenues
through the local property tax. In 1974, state legislation reformed the school
finance system, greatly increasing the level of state support, thereby decreasing
reliance on local property taxes.[10]

Many contend that the general shift from primarily local property tax funding to primarily state general fund revenues to support public education in Arizona has been accompanied by a commensurate loss in local control of public

[10] For details on the history of school finance reform in Arizona, see John Stuart Hall and Al-
bert K. Karnig, eds., *Phoenix Decade of Change: Education* (Phoenix, Ariz.: Phoenix Together,
1983).

education. The accuracy of that charge may be debatable, but the financial trend in Arizona has been toward greater centralization.

Similarly, there can be doubts about the magnitude of differences but no doubt about the direction of the change in Arizona's approach to indigent health care. Although the state provided some aid, counties bore the brunt of the administrative and financial responsibilities for providing medical care for the poor.

The state substantially increased its role in indigent care in 1983, however, when it began administering a three-year experimental program, the Arizona Health Care Cost Containment System (AHCCCS). The system relies on competitive bids from public and private health care providers to extend health care services to the poor. In the first year of the AHCCCS program, the state contributed $22.1 million and by the end of state fiscal year 1984 that amount had grown to over $80 million.

In 1984, the state assumed full responsibility for administering Medicaid. In the first year of the AHCCCS program, the state had subcontracted administrative duties to a private firm. This simply did not work. The program incurred huge cost overruns, estimated at $40 million in 1984. Fee-for-service charges were about $34 million, more than twice the amount expected. The state is currently embroiled in legal actions with the private firm. As a result of first-year problems, management and administrative responsibilities were assumed by the state's health department.

Other more subtle political shifts in Arizona have been in the direction of increased centralization of public finances and services. From 1968 through 1975, the legislature placed under direct control of the governor eleven major agencies previously reporting only to independent boards created by statute. These agencies included the state departments of Corrections, Public Safety, Land, Economic Planning and Development, Emergency and Military Affairs, Administration, Economic Security, Health Services, Transportation, Revenue, and Real Estate.[11]

In addition, Governor Bruce Babbitt has focused attention on his office not only by capturing control over federal funds, but by becoming prominent in intergovernmental relations. A member of the U.S. Advisory Commission on Intergovernmental Relations in the early 1980s, Governor Babbitt was the democratic governor cited by President Reagan in his 1982 State of the Union "New Federalism Speech" as favoring a new division of federal and state functions. Although the governor has for some time suggested the need to re-sort governmental functions, he disagreed with the swap proposal presented by the

[11] Sackton, *Arizona Government in the National Context*, p. 29.

president and argued that all welfare functions (in the general sense of the word) should remain at the national level. He suggested that states take full control of more traditional state and local functions, such as education, libraries, roads, water systems, and airport construction.

Arizona's legislature took a back seat to the executive branch and its effort to shape state responses to the federal aid changes made under Reagan. The state legislature has historically been reluctant to become involved in federal aid decision making. Given the interest and experience of the state's current governor, it was no surprise that the executive branch of state government moved quickly to develop distribution processes and strategies for the new block grants. In the course of Reagan's changes, Babbitt seized considerable control over state affairs.

All of this means that Arizona state government has become more centralized, with respect to decision-making authority, financial responsibility, and organizational structure of state government. This centralization has occurred on different levels. The executive's role has grown relative to that of the rural-dominated legislature. Furthermore, the state's financial and programmatic responsibilities have grown in comparison with local governments.

The Reagan initiative promised further intergovernmental change: a diminished national government presence accompanied by stronger state and local government responsibilities. Arizona's increased capacity for financing and managing programs facilitated a shift in responsibilities. But government operates through public programs, and programs require funds. The Reagan approach to decentralization reduced federal aid for state and local programs, and thereby raised real questions about the actual intergovernmental effects of the 1981 reconciliation act.

Changes in Federal Aid

For the city of Phoenix and the state of Arizona, 1982 was an important year in their fiscal history. This was the year of the initial impact of the Reagan domestic budget cuts, and the period of greatest effect of the national economic recession. To understand better the consequences of these two major events for Arizona fiscal policy, we constructed several time-series graphs.

Figure 12.1 shows own-source revenues and federal aid for Arizona for a period of time immediately before and after enactment of the 1981 budget act. State own-source revenues and total state expenditures of own-source and federal funds increased in a fairly continuous fashion from 1975 through 1983. In 1982, there were only modest increases in state own-source revenues compared

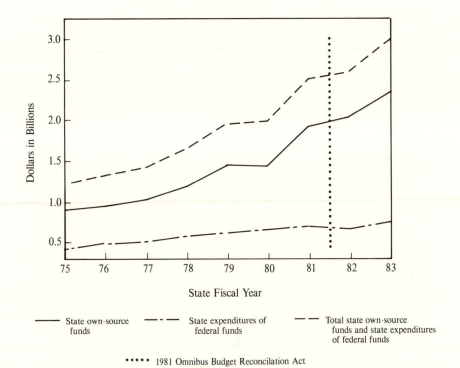

FIGURE 12.1. Arizona expenditure of own-source funds and federal aid, state fiscal years 1975–83
Source: State of Arizona, *Executive Budget*, various years; and State of Arizona, *Federal Programs Report*, various years.

with other years. Thus, when we look at overall state revenues it would appear that the recession had some leveling effects on state revenues. Figure 12.1 also shows a modest increase in state expenditures of federal aid. Not surprisingly, a modest dip in that trend appears in 1982, as a result of the spending cuts in the 1981 federal budget act.

In figure 12.2 we place the spotlight on federal aid expenditures to examine what happened more precisely between 1981 and 1982. Real cuts are evident at this point. As shown in figure 12.2, 1982 marked the only year in which federal expenditures to Arizona state and local jurisdictions declined. This $40.4 million reduction, from $620 million in 1981 to $580 million in 1982, also resulted in the lowest ratio of federal to state funds over the last ten years. Perhaps the most interesting feature of figure 12.2 concerns 1983 expenditures of federal aid by the state. Federal expenditures in 1983 increased at a level that made up for the modest reduction in 1982 and placed federal expenditures back

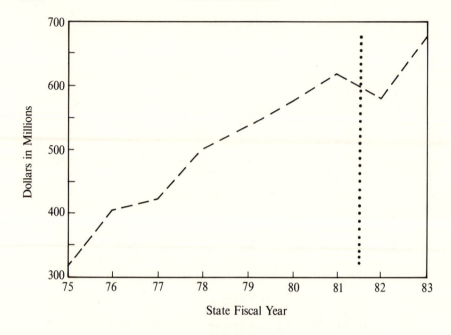

••••• 1981 Omnibus Budget Reconciliation Act

FIGURE 12.2.   Arizona expenditures of federal aid, state fiscal years 1975–83
Source: State of Arizona, *Federal Programs Report*, various years.

virtually on the trend line that had been developing since 1975. This figure and
figure 12.1 demonstrate that both state and federal expenditures in 1983 can be
connected to their 1981 takeoff point by a straight line of virtually the same
slope as the trend line of the preceding five years. This kind of macro-analysis
shows that something important did happen in 1982 to Arizona fiscal policy.
But perhaps more importantly, these overall patterns suggest that 1982 was an
anomaly.

A similar but not identical pattern occurred in Phoenix. Figure 12.3 shows
the pattern of growth for the city from 1970 through 1983. Figure 12.4 shows
an earlier reversal in the federal grants pattern than is seen by examining Arizona state data.

Similar to the state pattern, however, federal aid to the city increased in
1983. This examination of the pattern of change begins the process of understanding overall fiscal effects of shifts in national policy. But other important
organizational, institutional, and client effects cannot be discerned from these
totals and patterns. Nor can the fiscal effects of particular program changes be
separated from the totals shown here. Accordingly, we need to examine more

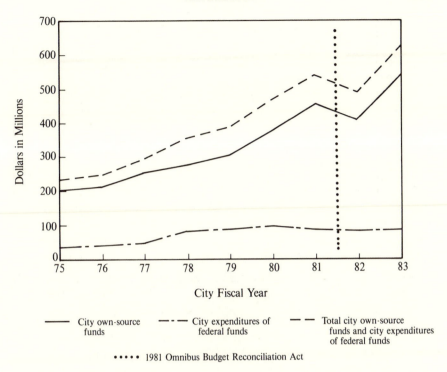

FIGURE 12.3. Phoenix expenditures of own-source funds and federal aid, city fiscal years 1975–83
Source: City of Phoenix, *Annual Financial Report*, various years.

closely, in the Arizona and Phoenix setting, the effects of major federal program changes.

FEDERAL FISCAL YEAR 1982

The major domestic budget cuts that reached Arizona in federal fiscal year 1982 were for the most part accepted and ratified. Table 12.1 shows that the largest cuts in terms of percentage reductions were in job training, maternal and child health, and the community services block grant program. Federal spending for entitlement programs to the poor increased. A number of factors accounted for this: a lean existing AFDC (aid to families with dependent children) program; initiation of a Medicaid program (AHCCCS); a substantial population growth, which was advantageous in a formula-driven revenue system; and a severe economic recession, which increased some social benefits.

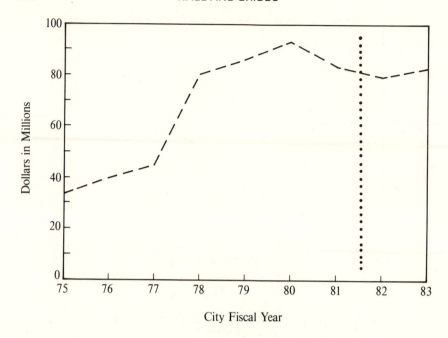

••••• 1981 Omnibus Budget Reconcilation Act

FIGURE 12.4.   Phoenix expenditures of federal aid, city fiscal years 1975–83
Source: City of Phoenix, *Annual Financial Report*, various years.

COPING WITH CUTS

Reagan domestic budget changes in 1982 had little impact on Arizona's major public assistance entitlement programs. Federal AFDC and food stamp grants increased in federal fiscal years 1982 and 1983. These increases reflect the structure of the entitlement programs already in place in the state prior to the 1981 reconciliation act. Compared to other states, Arizona's AFDC program provides a low level of benefits. Welfare benefits are paid primarily to people who have no source of earned income. Thus, federal policy designed to reduce the number of working poor who received entitlement benefits had little effect in the state. In fact, the 1981–82 recession, along with rapid population growth in the state resulted in growing case loads.

With respect to capital and operating programs, unspent funds available from prior years helped reduce the effects of the 1982 cutbacks. Federal spending for many of the capital and operating programs viewed in this study increased in 1983 as a result of passage of the emergency jobs act and other federal spending legislation. If these cuts had been continued at the national level in

Table 12.1. *Federal Aid to Arizona, Federal Fiscal Years 1981–84 (dollars in millions)*

Program	1981	1982	1983	1984
Small-cities community development block grant	6.0	6.0	8.7	6.4
Community services block grant	3.1	2.3	2.8	2.6
Social services block grant	31.3	28.6	32.3	32.4
Education block grant	3.8	4.5	5.1	5.3
Highway aid	118.3	104.0	158.8	161.8
Mass transit	—	11.6	14.3	19.1
Aid to families with dependent children	29.1	30.7	36.9	42.0
Food stamps	128.6	131.5	150.8	157.2
Maternal and child health block grant	4.0	3.2	3.2	3.5
Alcohol, drug abuse, mental health block grant	8.9	9.3	10.8	9.5
Medicaid	0	15.4	41.0	66.4
Job training	48.6	27.7	25.9	24.9

SOURCE: Interviews with and budget data provided by state agencies.

federal fiscal year 1983, it is likely that much of the carryover would have been depleted and real effects have been visible. For the most part, however, 1983 in Arizona and Phoenix was a year of federal funding restoration. Secondly, in this period of intense economic recession, state replacement was viewed as "pie in the sky" by many Arizona policy makers. Finally and fortuitously, the emergency jobs act and other federal spending bills enacted after the 1981 federal budget act brought an increase in funds to the state.

State agencies, particularly the Department of Economic Security, which was responsible for the largest portion of the state allocation of jobs act money, viewed the antirecession funds as a temporary, one-time bonus. Agency recipients were encouraged to spend the money on services rather than temporarily beefing up staff. There was substantial variation by program areas in the speed with which jobs act money could be planned for and used.

One of the more innovative uses involved allocating the entire $2.9 million supplement to the social services block grant program. This jobs act money was used for support services for dislocated workers, who were participating in training programs authorized by the Job Training Partnership Act (JTPA). Under JTPA job training programs, support stipends are not normally available. Yet, the emergency jobs act revenues were mixed with JTPA training funds to assist dislocated workers in severely impacted industries such as copper mining.

Institutional and intergovernmental issues—not funding—were at the heart of the JTPA programs. Officials in the governor's office, the Office of Economic Planning and Development (OEPAD), and the state Department of

Economic Security (DES), all saw JTPA as different from job training programs that had been authorized by the Comprehensive Employment and Training Act (CETA), and, an important new resource. Prior to JTPA, employment and training functions in Arizona were split between these two state agencies. OEPAD staffed the state's job council and administered the balance-of-state program. Other prime sponsors located in the state dealt with the U.S. Department of Labor.

Both OEPAD and DES led strong campaigns to try to persuade the governor and his staff to make a decision in their favor. Because of state political conflicts, the program got a late start. The governor was placed in a quandary and postponed his decision until January of 1983. At that time the governor decided to locate JTPA in DES, arguing that JTPA needed to be integrated with other social welfare programs like AFDC and the work incentive (WIN) program. The decision was bitterly opposed by the old CETA planning staff in OEPAD and required a period of transition and reorganization before the state could operate in its new role.

The intent of JTPA is to improve the private sector partnership with government in employment and training areas and it does appear in Arizona that private-sector interests are somewhat better represented at both the state and local level than they had been in the past. Yet the public sector continued to dominate employment and training programs, particularly in more established and professional jurisdictions of the state that were certified as service delivery areas (SDAs). In these SDAs such as the city of Phoenix, existing employment and training of professional staffs carried over the CETA experience and continued to dominate planning and reorganizational activities under JTPA. The private industry council (PIC) in Phoenix, for example, served more as a consultant to the program than as a decision maker. In addition, although there is increased private-sector representation on both the state jobs training council and the PIC serving the city of Phoenix, that representation has not been of either the quality or quantity to date to ensure a true partnership between the public and private sectors. Professionals in this area have a major resource: technical knowledge. To date, in the established urban SDAs, this knowledge has been used to promote continuation of existing employment and training programs and contractors from the CETA days. The representation of the private sector appears to be improving as they learn more about public-sector employment and training activities. Presently, however, the public-sector professionals at both the state and local level hold sway over the development of JTPA and have done a reasonable job of protecting their interest while admitting new representatives to the area of public employment and training programs.

GRANT CHANGES IN 1983 AND 1984

If our initial look at the 1982 consequences of Reagan domestic policies appeared to reveal minimal state and local financial effects, our second look at later years produced even less evidence of important federal aid reductions or consequences in Arizona. In the two years following the 1981 reconciliation act, federal aid to Arizona and its localities increased for many grant programs. One national study, which tracked the overall change in federal aid between federal fiscal years 1982 and 1984, showed federal increases for the fifty states on the average of 4 percent between federal fiscal years 1982 and 1983 and 8 percent between federal fiscal years 1983 and 1984. Arizona's overall increases in federal aid between federal fiscal years 1982 and 1984 were 26.5 percent; the largest among the fifty states.[12] Tables 12.1 and 12.2 show a somewhat uneven pattern of restoration and increases in federal spending for many of the programs reviewed in this study. Comparing 1983 allocations with those for 1982 shows increases in federal spending for most of the programs. This pattern generally held true for the Phoenix area and the state of Arizona. For the state and the city the biggest percentage increases came in the education block grant, highway, and mass transit programs. Thus, in the few areas in which Reagan domestic program cuts penetrated Arizona in 1982, restorations were evident

Table 12.2. *Federal Aid to the City of Phoenix and Maricopa County, Federal Fiscal Years 1981–84 (dollars in millions)*

Program	1981	1982	1983	1984
Community development block grant—entitlement	13.0	12.8	11.4	11.2
Community services block grant	1.0	0.8	0.7	0.7
Social services block grant	1.2	1.1	1.4	1.1
Education block grant	0.1	0.1	0.2	0.3
Highway aid	3.0	3.1	4.5	4.2
Mass transit	6.6	5.8	7.4	8.9
Housing	6.1	5.4	5.8	6.0
Maternal and child health block grant—Maricopa	0.9	0.7	0.6	0.7
Alcohol, drug abuse, mental health block grant—				
Maricopa	0.2	0.2	0.4	0.5
Job training				
Phoenix	13.7	8.7	7.8	5.5
Maricopa	9.4	5.7	5.0	6.1

SOURCE: Interviews with and budget data provided by city of Phoenix and Maricopa County.

[12] Rochelle Stanfield, "Federal Aid to States Resumes its Upward Course, But Not for All," *National Journal*, December 17, 1983, p. 2640. Based on information from *Federal Funds Information for States*.

in 1983. The clear direction of the one-year change between 1982 and 1983 is revenue growth, not decline.

As can be seen from tables 12.1 and 12.2, overall funding changes projected for federal fiscal year 1984 for most of the programs viewed in this study equalled or exceeded allocations to the state for federal fiscal year 1981. The message again is one of restoration and growth rather than programmatic reduction. The only major exceptions to this pattern are found in the city of Phoenix's community services block grant program and Maricopa County's maternal and child health block grant program, which were relatively small by comparison to the other major federally funded activities.

The Arizona and Phoenix Response to Grant Changes

The Arizona experience is the dramatic counter to the expectations of Reagan domestic budget architects for several reasons. In the first place, Arizona got its share of restorations based on national budget decisions. But Arizona did particularly well in the functional areas, like transportation, in which formula changes made Arizona's population increase particularly valuable. In addition, state spending on some federally aided programs also increased. Numerous domestic programs were beneficiaries of increased public revenues. For example, from federal fiscal years 1981 to 1984:

1. In mass transit, federal fund increases for the city were 33.7 percent and for the state of Arizona 64.1 percent. Over that same period state funds for mass transit increased by 71.3 percent. A newly implemented state lottery yielded nearly $4 million for mass transit for the city of Phoenix alone.

2. Another example of the state's proactive response occurred in 1981 when the state legislature enacted a measure which increased numerous transportation user fees that netted an increase of about 60 percent in state revenues for transportation purposes. This action predated the 1982 federal increase in gas tax.

3. In AFDC, federal funds increased by 44.4 percent and state funds increased by 43.1 percent. For food stamps, federal funds increased by 22.2 percent while state funds increased by 45.1 percent.

4. In the new AHCCCS program, federal funds increased from $41 million to $66 million between 1983 and 1984 while state funds increased from $22 million to approximately $80 million for the same

period. A temporary 1 percent sales tax was in part justified to assist in financing this indigent health care program.

Many of the other major federal aid programs previously examined in this case study were solely federally funded. Shifts in funding levels in those programs were generally accepted at the state and local level without replacement or augmentation of state and local revenues. As mentioned earlier, the conservative political culture of the area required a view of federal programs that differentiates them from local programs. The combination of this view and service emphasis means that as federal programs expanded or contracted there was minimal impact on the recipient government.

As one would expect, cooperative programs between the public and private sectors are much more acceptable in Arizona, especially those efforts that purport to tighten eligibility requirements for welfare programs. This is why the state's WIN experiment, the work incentive demonstration program (WIDP), generated enthusiastic support from the governor and Department of Economic Security officials. Under WIDP, clients receive regular wages through their employer, usually a public agency. Unlike other states with large welfare grants where "workfare" can become an actual disincentive, Arizona's welfare benefits are so low (the maximum AFDC grant is $180 per month) that WIDP is a better option for AFDC clients.

WIDP began in June 1982, with the goal of removing 4,000 people from welfare. The program attempts to place participants in jobs with state agencies and private employers. Thus far, the program has met its goal of placement with the public sector. The state has had less success in obtaining a significant number of pledges with private sector employers to hire WIDP participants. The poor economy at the start of WIDP played a part in this. In spite of the state's strong interest in involving the private sector, it is important to understand that WIDP is perceived as basically an entitlement program and therefore regarded as a federal, not a state priority. The program now receives $1.7 million in federal aid, with the state matching 10 percent of the total funding. It is unlikely that the state would pick up any reduction in federal funding should it occur.

The block grant movement was welcomed in Arizona by the governor and has enhanced the ability of his office and state agencies to be involved in major domestic programs. The state's increased general prominence raises issues of real power versus symbolic change. At the outset of the Reagan program many wondered whether states would become the "new oppressors." Would they regulate just as their federal agency counterparts did? Would they be arbitrary or fair? The Arizona State response to its newly found programs, resources, and responsibilities sheds some light on these questions and clearly varies across programs. It is important to consider whether block grants are blocks in name only, carrying significant funding, or true block grants that provide states with real fiscal discretion. The state-local relationship can be characterized by the distribution of money and administrative power between them in a given program area.

In the area of education, local districts generally favored the block grant process. This is primarily because they received more money under the formula-driven allocation system. For example, between 1981 and 1984, education block grant aid to the Phoenix Union High School increased by over 200 percent. This increase has been accompanied by decreased rules and regulations. Local public school officials tell joyfully of needing only a two-page application form to secure increased funds from the state education department. In contrast these districts endured much more cumbersome, competitive procedures when they received funding from the federal Department of Education. The formula basis for current educational block grants assumes need exists everywhere, thereby insuring funding for all districts. From the perspective of many local school districts in Arizona, increased revenues have been accompanied by increased latitude in spending for programs to meet local needs.

In transportation, the relationship between the state Department of Transportation and local jurisdictions seems to have improved, despite the fact that the state agency developed new regulations and criteria for evaluating local projects and project applications. The lesson of the Arizona transportation experience is that more rules are easier to accept when there is more money. The increase in overall highway funds available for use in local jurisdictions from 1981 to 1984 was $43 million, a 37 percent increase.

One of the ironies of the highway aid program is that it has increased the cooperation between Arizona local units of government and the Arizona State Department of Transportation. Local governments have been forced to band together in competition with other states. This is because of the discretionary features of the highway aid program which pits states against each other. Competition has been spirited and worked well for Arizona.

Other federal program changes have meant that local jurisdictions are interacting with state agencies on a totally new basis. The state has forged a new role in its administration of JTPA programs and the small-cities portion of the community development block grant program. When evaluating the state-local relationship under these programs, the reviews are mixed. A major dimension in different patterns of cooperation and conflict appears to be the urban-rural differences in the state.

In the small-cities program, the state Office of Economic Planning and Development has final responsibility for approving grant applications received from eligible communities throughout the state. The state agency has delegated some of the early screening for these programs to local councils of governments (COGs), which in Arizona are made up of local elected officials from every area of the state. This new procedure has resulted in a greater role for the COGs. They serve as the first level at which proposals from eligible small communities are screened in the state's competitive allocation process. Because of representation from all local jurisdictions within each region, COGs generally are predisposed to spread allotments to many jurisdictions. By bringing the COGs into the process, the new small-cities community development block grant program automatically ensures representation of mayors and council members of many Arizona small cities. Accordingly, this particular program and its administration increases state and local political interaction, though it has significantly politicized the planning function of regional councils.

In addition to spreading dollars and projects around, state administration of the small-cities program has resulted in the creation of guidelines, rules, and regulations that are not universally popular throughout the state. Some local governments have been critical of new state guidelines. On balance, however, more communities are involved with the process even though grants are relatively modest in many cases, and elected officials are particularly pleased with the state and its role as dispenser of community development funds.

The new JTPA program also enhanced the role of the state in intergovernmental relations. Under CETA, the state's rural jurisdictions dealt with the state Department of Economic Security, while the state's two urban areas, Phoenix and Tucson, were individual prime sponsors working directly with the U.S. Department of Labor. Thus, the new JTPA program administered by DES represented a major change in authority relationships for employment and training officials in Phoenix and Tucson. Not surprisingly, these officials tend to view state implementation of JTPA as cumbersome and somewhat confused. Yet the state's assumption of power in this area again has the effect of expanding the training pie by creating new SDAs in rural areas of the state and increasing funding to them. In summary, state administration of this program appears to have improved relationships between officials from rural jurisdictions and the state Department of Economic Security while it has had a reverse effect in the urban areas.

American Federalism in Arizona

National economic changes and important state and local political battles have
resulted in political and governmental changes in Arizona with the direction of
change toward assumption of new functions by the state. However, it is important to recognize that in Arizona, power and centralization are distinguishable
concepts and that the movement toward greater state capacity is not always followed by an exercise of political power. Experience, in fact, has demonstrated
just the opposite, with the state making a conscious choice not to flex its political muscle in many programmatic areas. Within the state today, one can find
a mixed strategy with regard to the delegation and use of power and influence.

One reason that federalism is working in Arizona is that many of the programmatic decisions have been allowed to flow to the level of government most
capable of handling the problem. The conservative philosophy of the state, as
one might expect, tends to recognize those units of government that can best
deliver the required service. This has produced a curious mix of service providers, both public and private, state and local, county and municipal, even
though responsibility has progressively become more centralized.

However, a discussion concerning the shifts of power and responsibility must
not only address the changes between governments, but also the changes within
governments. The most visible of these within Arizona has been the change in
the interaction between the state's executive and legislative branches. Throughout the history of the state the Arizona legislature has been the dominant
branch of government.

Recent fiscal and political events described increased not only the state role
but the role of those who administer at the state level—the executive branch.
Executive agencies in education, health, and social services are all more powerful because of actions of the state legislature. As the governor's responsibility
has increased, so has his power. In 1970, the Arizona executive office was
largely perceived to be a center of symbolism and the primary activity of the
incumbent was often that of ribbon cutting. At the end of the 1984 session of
the Arizona legislature the governor threatened to veto the majority party's tax
and budget package if the temporary 1 percent sales tax was not changed to a
permanent one. Although this was not the favorite position of legislative leaders
it was the final outcome. The executive's assumption carried over to federal aid
programs—especially the block grants—and may in the long run lead to increased legislative involvement in these varied programs. Proposition 101,
which would have permitted the legislature to exercise control over federal
funds, was defeated in November 1984, but the political message is obvious.

The potential for increased conflict between the executive and the legislature over the planning of programs receiving significant federal funding is clear.

Many different federal programs have arrived in Arizona and been accepted in recent years because they were needed. The Phoenix metropolitan area of over one million residents exists in the middle of a natural desert. Much of the physical infrastructure and economic developments that have converted this geographical space into an urban area are in one way or another the result of federal programs and assistance. Other federal programs in areas such as housing, community development, and employment and training have arrived in Arizona and in Phoenix more recently and have been accepted for the same reason. They were needed. Arizona officials attempted to fit federal aid to state and local problems. In some cases the federal programs helped to identify the problems.

When the Reagan policy changes shifted discussion to reduction of federal assistance, state and local officials prepared to cope. They coped by using carry-overs in 1982 and were not surprised greatly by restoration of funds in 1983. They also coped by responding early, wisely, and conservatively to discussions of retrenchment and the symbolic politics of budget cutting.

Arizona officials have been realistic enough to know that they needed assistance to solve certain problems. In the midst of the Reagan domestic budget cuts discussions, they also appeared to accept a theory of American federalism that revolves around an *assistance relationship*. Students of politics and government often focus on the conflicts and tensions within the American federal system. So do some policy makers. Yet, when the dam breaks someone has to fix it. When children need an education, school districts conduct classes. When poor people must eat, food is distributed. In essence, when national goals require implementation the federal government turns to state and local agencies. In these instances and in many others, federal funds are fitted to local functions. The fitting process takes time, discussion, and analysis. This is a sometimes awkward process that can seem cumbersome and inefficient. In Arizona there is some adjustment taking place as state and local officials remind one another of the cooperative basis of American federalism. But our belief is that adjustment will take place and that federal financial and problem identification assistance will continue to be important.

At the end of our first observation of the impact of the Reagan domestic budget program in Arizona we concluded:

> What seems enduring in the history of American government is the federal-state-local assistance relationship. The understanding, tolerance, and anticipatory behavior required to make this unique arrangement

work does not seem in danger of drastic change in Arizona. From this early admittedly limited perspective the old federalism seems alive, well, and necessary.[13]

That paper was written at a time when the rhetoric of the "new federalism" was at its high point. But that paper argued that something neat, clean, and decisive such as the Reagan administration's proposed separation of national, state, and local functions was not likely given the reasons for the assistance relationship in the first place. At the end of this study, we believe that the rationale for a cooperative intergovernmental assistance relationship remains and is even more firmly entrenched. The old federalism is at work in Arizona because it allows for the maximum use of the talents, skills, resources, and synergism of all levels of government to attack our most pressing problems. The various levels of government are obviously not always successful in solving those problems, but many in Arizona continue to believe in the strength and capacity of a cooperative American federalism.

[13] John Stuart Hall, "The Reagan Domestic Program in the Arizona Context," paper delivered at 1982 meeting of the American Political Science Association, Denver, Colorado, September 1982.

Illinois

CHARLES J. ORLEBEKE

*T*he budget cutback numbers which registered so impressively on the Washington scoreboard in August 1981 did not automatically translate into public service cutbacks at the state and local levels in Illinois. Although there were indeed some service reductions, Illinois political leaders—and their often resourceful program managers—had many techniques for smoothing out federal aid reductions and blunting their impact. Moreover, there was a general upward trend in federal grants in 1982 and 1983, as Congress turned back the much-feared second wave of cuts sought by the Reagan administration. The result was that the landscape of public and private agencies in Illinois, and the services they provided, were remarkably unchanged at the end of the first Reagan term.

With regard to the enhancement of state leadership, the evidence in Illinois is mixed. The state government, led by three-term Republican Governor James Thompson, supported the Reagan economic program including the budget cutbacks, and also welcomed the administration's "new federalism" initiatives. On the cutbacks, the state's policy response was to accept them, cope with them as best as possible, but not replace lost federal dollars with state dollars. On the new block grants, the state moved quickly to assume administrative control, but generally was careful not to disturb existing allocations and institutional arrangements very much. (The community services block grant was a striking exception.) The state also took charge promptly of implementing the Job Training Partnership Act (JTPA) programs, which included a controversial decision by the governor to alter previous service delivery boundaries in Cook County surrounding Chicago. An aggressive attack on rising Medicaid costs also marked the first Reagan term in Illinois.

Some things have not changed. The Reagan program had no effect on the dominant fact of political life in Illinois—the three-way competition between Chicago (the case-study city), its surrounding suburbs, and downstate Illinois; state government continued as broker rather than organizer and leader. Moreover, state fiscal policy as it relates to the support of local governments and school districts showed no signs of an increased state role, and was in fact far less assertive than in the early 1970s.

State government in Illinois did extend its administrative reach into a number of program areas as a result of the Reagan initiatives. Sometimes this reach was defensive—a way to deflect the damage to programs vulnerable to federal cutbacks; sometimes the reach was prompted by the sheer administrative necessity to take over a responsibility devolved from Washington. In both situations, the controlling impulse was to limit change to small incremental steps. Only rarely—the assault on Medicaid costs may be the best example—did the state government reach out to change policy course in a big way. However, the machinery to do more in the future was put in place.

Setting

State government is the arena where Illinois politicians, divided along rough geographical lines, contend for shares of resources raised at the state level. The main competitors are the city of Chicago, the suburban areas surrounding Chicago, and "downstate" Illinois—all the rest of the state in any direction from Chicago, including north. In population terms, the three areas divide Illinois' 11.4 million persons as follows: Chicago has 3 million, the Chicago suburbs have 4.1 million, and downstate Illinois has 4.3 million. Only two downstate cities have populations exceeding 100,000: Rockford (139,712) and Peoria (124,160). In this three-cornered contest, it is the city of Chicago with which the other two parties must come to terms. This is not to say that Chicago dominates Illinois politics. It is in fact far outnumbered in the legislature. But the city is so large relative to any other city and the state as a whole; it is such a major economic and cultural force in the state; and its legislative block, especially during Mayor Richard J. Daley's era (1955–76), is sufficiently cohesive, that its claim on statewide resources must at least be confronted, if rarely satisfied entirely. Once Chicago has its "share" of the money for school, roads, health, or any other purpose, the city expects the state to stay out of its internal political decision making.

THE STATE ROLE IN THE 1970S

Illinois is a politically conservative state with a strong tradition of local control. There is no real political market for the idea that the state should exercise strong leadership in comprehensive planning or service delivery. The most activist period in recent Illinois history for state government occurred during the administration of Richard Ogilvie, a progressive Republican elected in 1968. Having inherited a billion-dollar budget deficit, Ogilvie pushed for an income tax as the way out of the state fiscal crisis, and also as a way to ease the upward pressure on the local property tax.[1] The legislature responded with a 2.5 percent tax on individual income and 4 percent on corporate income; one-twelfth of the individual tax levy was set aside for return to local governments based on population.

In 1970 Illinois overhauled its state constitution, giving automatic home-rule status to all cities over 25,000 population, empowering them with wide tax-levying discretion and borrowing authority. Other communities could achieve home-rule status by local referendum. The new constitution also conferred broad new powers on the governor, particularly amendatory veto power over both substantive legislation and appropriation bills.

Also during the Ogilvie administration, the state increased its role in infrastructure financing: $750 million in general obligation bonds was authorized for water-pollution control facilities; and $1.9 billion for roads, mass transit, and aviation facilities. These funds were used throughout the 1970s in combination with federal grants which were rapidly increasing during the same period.

A growing state economy in the early 1970s helped build receipts from both the income and sales taxes. In state fiscal year 1972, the combined growth in the two sources was $208 million; this performance was repeated in state fiscal year 1973, but in the following year, the combined increase vaulted to $332 million. Augmenting these larger yields was general revenue sharing from the federal government. Local public schools became the main beneficiary of a flush state treasury. In a single jump, between the 1974–75 and 1975–76 school years, state aid to local schools rose to $662 million (a 50 percent increase), and the state share of total school spending increased from 34.4 to 48.4 percent.[2] In the same year, local property tax support for schools declined by $454 million.

Also in the 1970s, state government took over administrative control of the aid to families with dependent children (AFDC) and the Medicaid programs.

[1] *Illinois State Budget, Fiscal 1970*, p. A-2.
[2] *State of Illinois Fiscal Condition Report*, State Comptroller, February 28, 1984, p. 3.

The transition from welfare board administration in 101 counties to a state-run system was completed on January 1, 1974, when about 5,000 welfare employees in Cook County transferred to the state payroll.

In spite of the relative activism of the 1970s, the state began to pull back toward the end of the decade. The economic recession and fiscal stress of the early 1980s coincided with a resurgence of the strong tradition of local control in Illinois.

CHICAGO POLITICS AND FINANCES BEFORE REAGAN

Chicago during the 1950s and 1960s experienced many of the trends typical of other frostbelt cities: population decline, rapid racial change, and loss of manufacturing jobs—particularly to the flourishing suburbs. Yet, in contrast to such cities as New York, Cleveland, Newark, and Detroit, Chicago by the mid-1970s was still able to project a credible image of urban vigor and fiscal stability. Its economic base was well diversified beyond manufacturing in such growth sectors as banking, insurance, real estate, tourism, transportation, and communications. Under Mayor Daley, the city also established a tradition of fiscal conservatism. Daley believed that city government should stick to the basics: police and fire protection, garbage collection, street cleaning and maintenance, and public transit. Taxes should be kept moderate. Daley was also unabashedly pro-business and provided a hospitable climate for private investment, especially in Chicago's architecturally dramatic downtown "Loop" area.

Although Chicago was doing well enough to earn an upgrading in its municipal bond rating (to AA) in 1974, the city was in fact under moderate and increasing fiscal pressure during the 1970s. Inflation was pushing up the cost of municipal services year by year just a little faster than revenues from "own sources." Daley was unwilling to raise property taxes, and even less willing to cut back on the city work force—the backbone and muscle of the Daley political organization. To ease the fiscal pressure, the city resorted to a series of relatively low yield "home-rule" taxes (or tax increases) on car rentals, hotel bills, cigarettes, parking lots, and pinball machines.

Chicago Finances and Federal Grants

For basic city services, the most important federal grant was general revenue sharing, which in 1975, poured about $76 million directly into the city's corporate (or general) fund, thereby reducing the pressure for more local taxes. In relative terms, however, federal grants were much more crucial in city activities outside of the basic operating services: social services, and capital development such as urban renewal, housing rehabilitation, roads and transit, and economic development.[3]

The antipoverty and model cities program of the 1960s occupied an important part of the Chicago political landscape. Because Daley made hardly any room in his budget for social services, these federal programs were eagerly sought by the city to fund a wide array of services such as day care, neighborhood health centers, educational enrichment programs, youth recreation, job counseling, and supportive services for the elderly. Federal grants paid virtually all the operating costs of these programs. Frequently, federal money also paid for constructing facilities such as neighborhood health centers and senior citizen centers. Most of these facilities funded city jobs for thousands of administrators, social workers, community aides, youth workers, health professionals and aides, clerks and janitors.

During the 1960s and most of the 1970s, social programs supported by federal grants existed in a shroud of political and fiscal ambiguity. Political leaders fostered the notion that these were the "mayor's" programs, but the city's official budget documents contained no information on federal program sources, grant amounts, or numbers of personnel paid with federal dollars. Keeping federal grants outside the official budget made them easier to manage because it was hard for anti-machine critics to figure out exactly what was going on. But there was another reason, always unspoken, which was that social services were not really legitimate municipal functions unless another level of government pays the cost. Everyone hoped—perhaps assumed—that federal social programs would go on forever; but if they did not, the city had no explicit obligation to continue them.

Although, compared to social services, Chicago has been somewhat less dependent on the federal government for support of capital programs, the city's reliance on federal grants has still been extensive. For example, the urban renewal program, enacted in 1949, delivered over $150 million dollars in grants for a variety of slum clearance, redevelopment, and neighborhood conservation projects before being folded into the community development block grant in 1974. The community development program, which was also important in supporting social programs started under model cities, provided a rapidly growing source of funds for all kinds of capital projects, from pothole filling and sewer repair to housing rehabilitation and commercial strip development. In a single year, Chicago's community development allotment jumped from $61

[3] For a more detailed analysis of federal grants to Chicago, see Charles J. Orlebeke, *Federal Aid to Chicago* (Washington, D.C.: The Brookings Institution, 1983).

million to $114 million following a change in the program's distribution formula enacted by Congress in 1977.[4]

Chicago has also benefited significantly from federal grants for transportation. The interstate highway program paid for most of Chicago's expressway system, and the federal grants for urban highway systems brought well over $100 million to Chicago in the 1970s. In the area of mass transit, Chicago has also been an aggressive and successful grant getter: between 1965 and 1980, the city received over one billion dollars for bus and transit car purchases, major system additions, and a variety of other improvements.

Chicago's carefully cultivated image of robust self-sufficiency—"the city that works"—prevented the city's leaders from joining in the kind of "urban crisis" rhetoric that declares dependence on the federal government for survival. But federal aid did make a big difference during the 1960s and 1970s. Federal grants paid the cost of rising social services demands associated with a changing population. They helped the city cope with its aging public facilities and housing stock. They provided strategic capital for the city's more activist role in economic development. They generated thousands of jobs, directly and indirectly, at a time when the city's industrial base was eroding. And they helped contain tax increases affecting Chicago citizens and commerce.

Overlying Governments Serving Chicago

A distinguishing feature of the local government structure in Chicago is the extent to which overlying governments finance and administer services provided in the city. The most important governments are: the Board of Education, Cook County, Metropolitan Sanitary District of Greater Chicago, City Colleges of Chicago, Chicago Housing Authority, Chicago Park District, and the Chicago Transit Authority. Cook County and the sanitary district are governed by boards of elected commissioners. The mayor of Chicago controls appointments to the governing boards of all the other entities.

During the 1970s, the combined operating budgets for the seven major overlying governments were approximately double the city government's budget. The Board of Education, with a budget of $1.1 billion in 1980, was the biggest spender; the smallest agency in dollar terms was the housing authority with a budget of $110.7 million. Expenditures for all governments grew steadily at an average rate of 9.5 percent in the 1970s, ranging for individual governments

---

[4] For additional information on Chicago's use of community development block grants, see Charles J. Orlebeke, "CDBG in Chicago: The Politics of Control," *Publius* 13, no. 3 (September 1983):57–72.

from 14.9 percent for the city college system to a low of 8.4 percent for the Board of Education.[5]

The revenue sources underpinning Chicago's multigovernmental structure are complex and not readily summarized. The most important local revenue source shared by the city government and most of the overlying governments is the property tax. Public schools and the community colleges are largely dependent on a combination of state aid and the local property tax. Neither the transit authority nor the housing authority has the legal power to levy property taxes. The transit authority's ability to pay its own way through fares—still possible in the 1960s—rapidly deteriorated in the 1970s, and it had to rely on federal and state subsidies passed through the regional transit body, as well as on regional tax levies on gasoline and retail sales. The housing authority receives no state or local support, and is entirely dependent on federal operating subsidies to fill the growing gap between rental income and operating costs. Cook County Hospital, an agency of county government, received significant support through Medicaid and Medicare payments. The largest capital project in the Chicago area is the sanitary district's controversial tunnel and reservoir plan (TARP), a network of huge tunnels and reservoirs capable of storing excess storm water following heavy rains. During the 1970s, the sanitary district spent about one billion dollars on the first phase of TARP. The federal government picked up about 75 percent of the cost.

FISCAL SLIPPAGE AT THE END OF THE DECADE

For most of the 1970s, both the state government and Chicago appeared to enjoy a solid business-as-usual fiscal situation: no major changes in services, regular salary raises for public employees, no significant tax increases. The state treasury appeared in especially good shape as it cruised toward a $390 million surplus in state fiscal year 1980. But in Chicago, two important components of its intricate fiscal system—public education and public transit—tumbled into crisis in late 1979 and early 1980. Both naturally turned to the governor and legislature for help; the answer was "no."

The Board of Education's fiscal health had been precarious for several years, and the schools had been kept afloat by using fiscal gimmickry: interfund transfers of revenue dedicated to bond retirement, adroit timing of tax anticipation notes, and delayed payments to vendors. Moody's Investors Service abruptly pulled the trigger when it gave its lowest credit rating to a planned issue of

[5] Arthur Lyons and Charles J. Orlebeke, *Chicago Area Public Finances, 1970–1990: Trends and Prospects*, Report no. 3, Metropolitan Housing and Planning Council, MAP 2000 project, October 1981, p. 6.

$124.6 million in tax anticipation notes, making them unmarketable. The School Board chairman resigned, as did the school superintendent and his top financial officers. School employees had payless paydays.

Marathon crisis sessions—involving the School Board, Mayor Byrne, Governor Thompson, teachers' union leaders, bankers, and consultants from New York City—eventually produced a complex bailout plan calling for deep cuts in the school budget, an emergency issue by the city government of tax anticipation notes backed by the school's property tax levy for 1980, and the creation by the state of a new Chicago School Finance Authority to oversee the board's finances and issue $500 million in long-term bonds, again backed by local property taxes. Significantly, there was not a dollar of state cash in the deal, only a willingness by the state to reorganize and stretch out the fiscal burden.

The transit system also careened toward fiscal collapse as the gap between fare revenues and operating costs grew from $62.6 million in 1974 to $213.8 million in 1979. Chicago political leaders pleaded for additional state subsidies, but were unwilling either to impose fare increases, cut services, or resist the demands of transit unions for continued cost-of-living adjustments which were guaranteed in their contracts. A ten-cent fare increase (to sixty cents) was finally imposed in late 1979. The legislature also permitted the regional transit authority to levy a 1 percent sales tax in Cook County, and 0.25 percent in the five surrounding counties, provided that a 5 percent gasoline tax was cancelled. As with the school crisis, the state's policy was to grant Chicago citizens the privilege of raising their own taxes rather than distributing the burden of urban services statewide.

In summary, three forces combined in the 1970s to keep Illinois and Chicago in satisfactory, if not robust, fiscal health. The first was the state income tax enacted in 1969; the second was a state economy sufficiently strong to pump up revenue yields without increasing tax rates. Federal grants were the third force contributing to solvency in the 1970s; the explosion of federal programs for both operating and capital purposes brought in billions of dollars in revenue which did not need to be raised from state and local sources. By 1980, however, the three forces supporting Illinois' fiscal health were weakening. Economic decline and fiscal stress in Illinois coincided with Ronald Reagan's victory in 1980.

THE EARLY 1980S

As the Reagan program was being implemented in 1981 and 1982, the financial position of both the city and state government was slipping toward crisis. However, their fiscal problems were unrelated to federal grant changes.

At the state level in the late 1970s, there was little turbulence on the surface. But underneath, the trends were ominous. The state comptroller reported at the end of state fiscal year 1981–82 (June 30), that the state's fiscal health, "while appearing to be on a par with the previous fiscal years was unfortunately in a somewhat precarious position."[6] Total general fund revenues had come in $538 million less than estimated in the governor's budget, a $333 million short-fall in sales tax revenues alone. And although the general fund showed a paper balance of $187 million, this was only possible because of the deferral of such obligations as a school aid payment, retirement system contributions, and other commitments adding up to about $500 million. In essence, the state had run through its reserves, run out of band-aid options, and would need to raise taxes in 1983.

Governor Thompson presented the legislature in spring 1983 with a "doomsday" budget for state fiscal year 1983–84 which called for decreases in state school aid, elimination of state revenue sharing of the income tax, elimination of the general assistance program, and sharp cutbacks in social services. He followed this with a $1.6 billion proposal for new revenues, including an increase in the personal income tax from 2.5 to 4 percent. On the eve of the new fiscal year, the legislature passed a much smaller package—$963 million—built around an eighteen-month temporary increase (expiring June 30, 1984) in the income tax to only 3 percent, a one-cent increase in the state sales tax to 5 percent, and a five-and-a-half-cent increase in the state gasoline tax. The revenue package included an $85 million subsidy to the regional transportation authority. "Doomsday" had been averted, but there was only a 1 percent increase in state school aid, and no increases for AFDC and general assistance recipients.

In Chicago, Mayor Byrne had to deal in the late 1970s with gradually increasing fiscal stress in the city government, and she was also forced to intervene in public school and transit crises. Her basic strategy was to raise local taxes and avoid major layoffs of city workers assigned to the basic services. Additional revenue flowed from higher property taxes, increased water and sewer fees, and a doubling of the cigarette tax. In mid-1981, the City Council passed both a 1 percent city sales tax and a 1 percent tax on professional services which were intended to bolster city revenues and rescue the transit authority. However, the State Supreme Court threw out the service tax five months later as unconstitutional, so the mayor cut out the transit subsidy, saying the state would need to provide funds for transit.

Chicago's new mayor, Harold Washington, inherited a serious deficit in the

---

[6] *State of Illinois Fiscal Condition Report*, State Comptroller, July 23, 1982, p. 1.

city budget from his predecessor, who loaded several hundred new employees on to the city payroll before leaving office. To get through 1983, Mayor Washington laid off over 1,000 city workers, cancelled half of a scheduled property tax decrease, and took other stopgap measures—which still left a year-end deficit of about $40 million. For 1984, the mayor proposed a $1.9 billion budget, which was 2.5 percent less than 1983, froze salaries of all city employees, and also called for new taxes. After a long debate in City Council—uncharacteristic for Chicago—a $98.3 million batch of taxes was passed, increasing levies for the employers' head tax, city auto sticker, parking, cigarettes, boat mooring, and other miscellaneous items.

The scale of the fiscal problems in Illinois and Chicago dwarfed any changes in federal aid occurring in the same period. In addition, tax increases were not part of a strategy to respond to federal grant changes, but rather were aimed at keeping primary state and local funded services at politically acceptable levels. Nevertheless, federal cuts took their toll as well, and significantly reinforced already existing trends toward fiscal austerity and local responsibility.

Interplay of Reagan Themes and Illinois Politics

In Illinois, the decline of heavy manufacturing industries is part of a long-term trend affecting older industrial regions. However, the 1981–82 recession intensified the state's economic problems, causing sharply increased unemployment with all its sad and disruptive effects on people and communities. Illinois' unemployment rate in 1979 was a moderate 5.5 percent, but by 1982 it had risen to 11 percent. Individual cities with high percentages of manufacturing workers suffered unemployment rates well above the state average: Peoria was over 14 percent; Decatur, 16 percent; Rockford and Kankakee, about 17 percent; and Chicago, 12 percent.

The message from Washington, D.C. was that a revived economy would spring from the Reagan policies of tax cuts, constrained government spending, and less government interference generally. But it would take time, and require patience.

Many of the most visible political leaders in Illinois were ready to accept the essentials of that message. Governor Thompson and his fellow Republicans supported the president with predictable enthusiasm; the governor had campaigned hard for the Reagan ticket, and applauded especially the president's economic and new federalism initiatives.

Mayor Byrne's support of the president was more surprising. She criticized his policy of a large state role, but was willing to give his economic strategy a chance to work. Speaking to a conference of fellow big-city mayors in November 1981, the mayor said: "It may be too early at this point to tell if current Federal policies will represent a step toward solving the nation's ills. However, these policies should be given a chance."[7]

The mayor was particularly vigorous in echoing Reagan administration themes on big, wasteful government. She characterized her proposed 1982 budget as her response to Chicagoans' belief that "there is too much government."[8] And in a March 1982 speech to the Institute for Socioeconomic Studies, she specifically linked government waste to the availability of federal grants:

> Padding the municipal payroll with unnecessary workers and cramming departments with excess personnel, simply because the federal government supplied the cash, were practices I have always had trouble accepting. Then, and especially now, I ordered heads of city departments to take a fresh look at their activities and to find ways of maintaining essential services by means of sound management and a sharp knife.[9]

ELECTORAL POLITICS

During the first two Reagan years, Governor Thompson and Mayor Byrne were both running for re-election, the governor for a third term in November 1982, and the mayor for a second term in April 1983. The two politicians were very much absorbed in their own contests. Thompson faced a strong opponent in Adlai Stevenson III; Byrne was challenged in the February 1983 Democratic primary by Cook County States Attorney Richard Daley (the former mayor's son) and Congressman Harold Washington, a leader of Chicago's black community. Both incumbents were eager to avoid either tax increases or major public service disruptions until they were safely past the elections. The governor and mayor tended to accommodate each other by supporting stopgap measures in the legislature, such as allowing the regional transportation authority to borrow $100 million to meet cash flow needs in 1982 and 1983.

As campaign issues, the Reagan administration's reductions in specific programs did not figure prominently, either in the Chicago mayoral contest or the gubernatorial race. However, "Reaganomics," as a political symbol for insensitivity and even hostility to the poor and minorities, was important in galvanizing black and Hispanic communities to register and vote against the incumbents. For the governor, a Republican who had in the past run quite well

[7] *New York Times*, November 14, 1981.
[8] *Chicago Sun-Times*, November 14, 1981.
[9] Press release, Office of the Mayor, March 4, 1982.

among black voters, the November 1982 election was a cliffhanger. Although his opponent was not personally popular among black voters, Stevenson carried the black wards of Chicago with 90–98 percent margins.

A few months later, Mayor Byrne was beaten in a bitter three-way Democratic primary by Washington. Byrne's defeat was the result of many complex local political forces, among which her initial support of the Reagan program was a minor one. But "Reaganism" as a code word certainly helped mobilize minority voters. After the primary, the suddenly credible Republican candidate, former state senator Bernard Epton, and Washington engaged each other in a nasty, racially charged contest which Washington narrowly won.

Major Findings

Because of the dramatic legislative success of the Reagan program in 1981, "the Reagan cutbacks" became code words—often invoked without reference to specific dollar amounts and programs. This section summarizes for selected federal grant programs what was cut and by how much. It also examines state and local responses to the changes in grant-in-aid policy.

ENTITLEMENT PROGRAMS

The major entitlement programs—AFDC, food stamps, and Medicaid—account for the largest flows of federal dollars to Illinois—over $1.6 billion in federal fiscal year 1981. Despite Reagan administration efforts to contain costs in these programs, federal spending in Illinois for AFDC and food stamps increased each year. The AFDC rise was modest—only 2.6 percent between federal fiscal years 1981 and 1982, and a slightly larger increase in 1983—but food stamp spending went up at a much faster rate with increases of 7.8 percent in federal fiscal year 1982 and 18.6 percent in 1983 (see table 13.1). The Reagan strategy on Medicaid was somewhat more successful: the state imposed a long list of benefit reductions and cost controls for Medicaid. The result was that federal spending for Medicaid declined by 2 percent in federal fiscal year 1982 before returning in 1983 to basically the same level as in federal fiscal year 1981. Overall, Illinois ratified federal cuts in entitlements, and used its increased administrative discretion to decrease and control costs.

WELFARE PROGRAMS

In Illinois there was general receptivity to the administration's views on welfare. As the Illinois director of public aid remarked wryly: "Contrary to some popular

Table 13.1.   *Federal Aid to Illinois for Selected Entitlement Programs,*
Federal Fiscal Years 1981–83 (dollars in millions)

Program	1981	1982	1983
Aid to families with dependent children	390.9	401.1	411.8
Food stamps	505.7	545.6	647.4
Medicaid	743.6	728.1	742.9
TOTAL	1,640.2	1,674.8	1,802.1

SOURCE: Illinois Department of Public Aid; U.S. Department of Health and Human Services, Region 5.
NOTE: Amounts are for benefits only, and do not include federal grants for cost of administration.

myths, the Department of Public Aid does not put anyone on easy street."[10] Illinois AFDC payments are "near the bottom among the industrial states"[11] and well below other midwestern states with similar standards of need.

Illinois accepted and implemented the AFDC provisions in the 1981 federal budget act without any deliberate attempt to cushion their impact. One change made by the state was coincident with the implementation of the 1981 federal budget act: the standard of need for an AFDC family of four persons was raised from $368 to $593 effective October 1, 1981. Although the increase was planned prior to the 1981 budget act and was not specifically designed to offset federal efforts to tighten eligibility, the higher needs standard did have the effect of protecting from automatic ineligibility those persons—an unknown number—whose total income exceeded 150 percent of the previous standard of need.

Four of the twenty-two AFDC changes in the 1981 budget act were specifically aimed at eliminating or reducing welfare benefits to people earning income—about 5 percent of Illinois' total case load in September 1981. According to a special study done by the Department of Public Aid, the number of people who both worked and received AFDC benefits declined by 43 percent in the first year of implementation. "Overall," the study reported, "the changes affected all family sizes but the most vulnerable were those with full-time jobs earning at least the minimum wage and those earners with more than three dependents and a job paying above the federal minimum wage."[12] The provision

[10] Remarks by Gregory L. Coler, Director, Illinois Department of Public Aid, to Illinois Campaign for Family Stability, February 6, 1984, p. 1.
[11] Ibid., p. 2.
[12] *Impact of the OBRA [Omnibus Budget Reconciliation Act] Changes*, AFDC Earned Income Case Load Monitoring Project. Bureau of Planning and Evaluation, Illinois Department of Public Aid, December 1983, p. 22.

which dropped the largest number from the rolls (2,182 cases) was the four-month limit on the 30 and 1/3 earnings disregard.

Other provisions in the 1981 budget act which affected relatively large numbers of cases in federal fiscal year 1982—through terminations or grant cuts—were the inclusion of stepparent income in eligibility determination (5,581 cases); the ineligibility of 18–20-year-olds as dependents (1,623 cases); and the ineligibility of first-time pregnant women in their first six months of pregnancy (3,600 cases). All told, it is estimated that the reconciliation act affected about 20,000 cases and reduced federal fiscal year 1982 expenditures by about $25 million.[13]

The general assistance (GA) program is the state's "safety net" for the poor who do not qualify for one of the federal income assistance programs. Although many Illinois communities run their own GA programs independent of state government, the state administers GA in Chicago and about forty other communities. Primarily a program for single, childless adults, the GA case load grew rapidly, from about 60,000 cases in 1980 to over 100,000 cases in 1983.[14] Generally, around 80 percent of the persons receiving GA live in the city of Chicago.

Like the Reagan administration, the Thompson administration has tried to get spending under control for the state's own-income assistance program. In 1980 a single adult receiving GA could get a monthly grant of $184. This level was cut to $162 in January 1982 and cut again to $144 in May 1982. In the process, the state's attempt to establish a new category of "employable" recipients to receive only $128 monthly was prohibited by court order.

In Illinois a link between general assistance and workfare existed well before the Reagan administration. Home-grown workfare programs were common in downstate Illinois, and in 1979, the legislature passed with huge bipartisan majorities a statute urging local governments to set up workfare programs for general assistance recipients. For the city of Chicago, the governor directed the state-operated program to develop "a comprehensive plan specifically tailored to workfare for large metropolitan areas."[15] A pilot workfare program was begun in Chicago four days before the Reagan inaugural, and was expanded citywide in October 1981.

---

[13] *A Review of Studies: The Impact of the Reagan Budget Cuts in Illinois,* Legislative Advisory Committee on Public Aid (March 19, 1984 draft of report), p. 42. Data cited in report are from Illinois Department of Public Aid response to a U.S. General Accounting Office Survey, July 1983.

[14] Illinois Department of Public Aid, *1984 Plan Part I,* Transmitted by IDPA director Jeffrey C. Miller to the Illinois General Assembly, April 1983, p. 24.

[15] *Flat Grant in the General Assistance Program,* The Legislative Advisory Committee on Public Aid, February 1982, p. 1.

The Chicago GA workfare program assigns all "employable" GA applicants to a job placement unit that guides the applicant through an intensive sixty-day job search effort. If unsuccessful, the applicant is assigned to a workfare site to work off his or her benefits at the minimum wage. After ninety days of working, the recipient is cycled through another job search or may be assigned to another site. "Non-cooperative" persons have their benefits cut off for ninety days.

An evaluation conducted by the public aid department indicated that the Chicago workfare program was working quite well. Although the study could not establish that the program had any effect on total GA case load, its cost-benefit analysis did conclude that "for every dollar the Department invested in GA jobs, it received $3.36 in savings."[16] This was because workfare, on average, was credited with shortening a person's stay on the case load by five months.

The bureaucratic environment for the Chicago workfare program appears to be positive. An assessment by the Legislative Advisory Committee on Public Aid—which has been more skeptical about workfare than the public aid department—acknowledged that the program seemed "well-managed." "The overwhelming majority of the counselors interviewed expressed positive attitudes toward the program, its potential for success and its value in helping recipients toward self-sufficiency."[17] In general, program staff feel that the GA program and its clientele are well suited for the workfare approach. They have been more cautious about extending it to the AFDC case load, but a pilot program in Chicago was begun in February 1984.

Medicaid

As the state's fiscal position was deteriorating, Governor Thompson became a harsh critic of Medicaid as a program essentially out of control. In 1982 and 1983, the state used the increased flexibility granted in the 1981 federal budget act to cut outpatient services, and limit hospital and nursing home reimbursements. The state also sharply reduced coverage for the general assistance population, for which there is no federal matching.

Cost control measures were applied across the board, from small items like eliminating aspirin and dandruff shampoo, to a major attack on hospital costs, which account for almost half of the state's total Medicaid expenditure. In state fiscal year 1982, the state "capped" Medicaid payments to hospitals at $843 million—achieving an estimated savings of $106 million—by reducing each hos-

[16] *1984 Plan for the Department of Public Aid*, Part II, Chicago General Assistance Jobs Program: Client Job Placement Plus Workfare. Final Evaluation Report, p. 2.

[17] *Workfare in Illinois*, The Legislative Advisory Committee on Public Aid, March 1982, p. 17.

pital's reimbursement rate by 14.27 percent.[18] For the following state fiscal year, the state's principal cost-saving strategy was to impose a reduction averaging 18 percent statewide on the number of patient days the state would pay for.[19] This strategy was followed later in the fiscal year (February 1983) by a set of "emergency" Medicaid cuts totaling $54.6 million; these included a 7.5 percent cut in rates to medical providers, and a $500 limit on hospitalization coverage for general assistance recipients—enough for a day or so.

BLOCK GRANTS AND OTHER OPERATING PROGRAMS

Generally, Illinois received less federal aid in 1982, the first year of the block grants, compared with funding levels under the predecessor programs that were in place in 1981. In federal fiscal year 1983, some, or all of this loss was restored. For example, one of the largest programs, the social services block grant, took a 20 percent cut, from $149.5 million in 1981 to $120.3 in 1982, but then recovered about half of the reduction in 1983, when social services aid amounted to $135.6 million (see table 13.2).

Other reductions between federal fiscal year 1981 and 1982 were 24 percent for the maternal and child health block grant; 22 percent for the alcohol, drug abuse, and mental health block grant; and 15 percent for the community services block grant. But again, federal appropriations for 1983 partially restored the cutback in each case.

Some federal grant programs to the state were increased. The low-income energy assistance block grant, a program giving payments to help cover the high cost of heating and cooling bills, increased in federal fiscal years 1982 and 1983. The special supplemental food program for women, infants, and children (WIC) also increased slightly in federal fiscal year 1982 and then jumped by 30 percent in fiscal year 1983. The compensatory education program for disadvantaged school children also increased both years.

An enthusiastic supporter of the new federalism, Governor Thompson took control of the new block grants as soon as possible. The emphasis, however, was on continuity of support for existing programs, rather than on using the state's new authority to shift program priorities. The governor's general approach to implementation was to create a task force or advisory committee for each block grant, the members of which consisted of persons representing public and pri-

---

[18] *State of Illinois Fiscal Condition Report*, State Comptroller, October 26, 1982, p. 6.

[19] Laura B. Landrum, D. Patrick Lenihan, and Philip R. Davis, *An Analysis of the Impact on Chicago of FY 1983 Reductions in the Illinois Medicaid Program*, Chicago Center for Health Systems Development, June 1983, p. 4.

Table 13.2. *Federal Aid Allocated to Illinois State Government for Major Operating Programs, Federal Fiscal Years 1981–83 (dollars in millions)*

Program	1981	1982	1983
Social services block grant	149.5	120.3	135.6
Maternal and child health block grant	19.3	14.1	16.8
Community services block grant	20.5	17.3	17.2
Child nutrition	165.9	152.6	169.8
Alcohol, drug abuse, and mental health block grant	20.0	15.7	17.4
Low-income energy assistance block grant	106.9	108.6	114.7
Supplemental food—women, infants, and children (WIC)	33.0	35.0	45.5
Preventive health block grant	2.1	2.0	2.1
Older Americans Act	30.0	28.0	29.0
Compensatory education (chapter 1)	117.1	111.5	120.4
Education block grant (chapter 2)	30.4	18.9	21.2
TOTAL	694.7	624.0	689.7

SOURCES: U.S. Office of Management and Budget, Office of the Governor, Illinois State Board of Education, and Princeton Urban and Regional Research Center.

NOTE: For the block grants, federal fiscal year 1981 data are estimates of equivalent categorical programs.

vate agencies most directly affected by a particular block grant. The effect of this approach (with one exception, the community services block grant) was to maintain the support of established programs and service delivery agents.

Community Services Block Grant

Prior to the enactment of the community services block grant, Illinois received about $20.5 million from the predecessor community action program operated by the federal Community Services Administration. About 70 percent of the grant was normally allocated by the federal agency to the city of Chicago.

For federal fiscal year 1982, Illinois' share of the new block grant was only $17.2 million—a $3.3 million cut. The governor appointed a committee of community services directors (chaired by the Cook County director) to advise him on allocating the grant. Not surprisingly, there was a strong sense among the committee that Chicago had taken the lion's share of Community Services Administration funds for several years, and that it was time to spread the money around more evenly. The committee recommended that instead of passing on a proportional cut to existing community action agencies serving 61 counties, the state should use an entirely new formula, which spread the block grant over all of the state's 102 counties, and which also based distribution on each county's share of the state's poverty population. The effect of the formula would have reduced Chicago's previous 70 percent share to 40 percent of a smaller pot. Chicago's Department of Human Services, which was represented on the committee, objected to the proposed formula on the grounds that the city had a high percentage of the state's income assistance recipients and other dependent poor. But the simple poverty-based formula also had a certain plausibility that was difficult to deny, and the governor decided to go along with the advisory committee, thereby taking money away from Chicago and providing small windfalls to many county social service programs. In order to cushion the severity of the impact, the state split the difference in the first year, awarding Chicago 55 percent of the state's grant. This still left Chicago with an abrupt 32 percent reduction in 1982. Ironically, the new formula brought a 32 percent *increase* to the Community and Economic Development Association of Cook County, an agency which operates nine community service centers in the suburbs surrounding Chicago—an example of how a cut enacted in Washington does not necessarily carry through to the local level.

Social Services Block Grant

In contrast to the community services block grant program, the state adopted its more characteristic strategy of stressing continuity in its implementation of the social services block grant. Like "title XX"—the similar predecessor program replaced by the 1981 budget act—the social services block grant provides approximately one-half the funding for twenty-five to thirty social services programs operated by nine separate state agencies. The state agencies, in turn, distribute funds through grants and contracts with thousands of local governments and nonprofit organizations which actually operate day care, foster care, family planning, and many other services.

Social services block grant funds are difficult to track from source to destination because most of them (about three-quarters) are deposited directly into the state general fund. The rest are deposited into state agency accounts where they are mixed with various types of local matching funds. Thus, block grant funds lose identity at the state level, and at the local level are frequently intermingled with funds from other sources including local revenues, private donations, United Way, fees for service, and rummage sales. Because social services grants are elusive, one cannot readily make direct connections between the federal fiscal year 1982 cutback of about 20 percent and services at the local level. Although some agencies undoubtedly suffered some reductions, especially when the state was also fiscally strapped, the governor's general policy has been to keep the title XX-social service block grant delivery system intact.

Dodging the Cuts with Fiscal Footwork

Like community services and social services block grant (SSBG) programs, block grants for maternal and child health and for alcohol, drug abuse, and mental health also suffered cuts in the 20–25 percent range between federal fiscal years 1981 and 1982. These reductions, however, did not hit programs with the force that the raw numbers suggest. One key reason is that the cuts took effect on October 1, 1981—the beginning of the federal fiscal year—but the state organizes its planning and allocations around the state fiscal year which begins July 1. When a federal cut beginning October 1 is imposed, therefore, the state has a full quarter (July–September) of its own fiscal year under the previous higher grant amount. In addition, some agencies receiving federal funds do not spend all the money allocated to them and are able to carry forward unused funds into a leaner year. Finally, some programs had funding contracts from pre-block grant funds which supported them for part of the new fiscal year; this was true of the federally funded community mental health centers which were covered through March 1982 by funds appropriated for federal fiscal year 1981. In this instance, the mental health block grant actually provided a windfall of about $9 million in federal fiscal year 1982. The combination of unspent carryover funds and overlapping fiscal years had a general cushioning effect on the federal fiscal year 1982 cuts.

With respect to SSBG-funded programs, the governor used another technique to relieve budget pressure: this was to shift selected programs out of the SSBG group and into an entitlement category, thereby attracting a 50 percent federal match. There have been two such shifts. First, in 1982, the Department of Public Aid stopped using social service funds to contract directly with day-care providers for AFDC recipients. Instead, AFDC recipients take a $160 deduction from income for child care expenses and pay the day-care provider directly. The recipient gets a larger grant, but the higher amount is federally matched so the state achieves a net savings of about $5 million annually. The second program shifted was home health care as an alternative to the usually more expensive group or institutional care. In federal fiscal year 1983 Illinois obtained a waiver from the U.S. Department of Health and Human Services that allowed the state to charge home health care to Medicaid as an eligible program expense. Savings to the state are estimated in the $5–$10 million range annually.

If federal fiscal year 1982 federal cutbacks had been followed by a similar round of reductions in 1983, such footwork would have merely postponed more drastic effects on service. But this did not happen. Each of the block grants had at least a partial restoration in 1983 of the fiscal 1982 reductions. Much of this restoration was the result of the emergency jobs act passed by the Congress in March 1983.

When the jobs act augmented the social services block grant to Illinois by $13.8 million, the governor was quick to take control of these "off-cycle" funds and apply the bulk of them ($12 million) to a high profile program called "Parents too Soon." According to the governor, the program involves several state agencies in an effort to "prevent unwanted pregnancies, prevent the risks associated with teen births and assist teen parents" with their problems. [20] "Parents too Soon" demonstrated the program flexibility of block grants for an alert chief executive.

JOB TRAINING PARTNERSHIP ACT

In Illinois, Governor Thompson assigned the lead responsibility for Job Training Partnership (JTPA) programs to the Department of Commerce and Community Affairs, which had also administered job training programs that were authorized by the Comprehensive Employment and Training Act (CETA). Well before the passage of JTPA, commerce and community affairs staff had organized working groups built around the various versions of JTPA pending in Congress, so when the act was signed, Illinois was ready to make a fast start toward putting the new job training programs in place.

The implementation timetable was tight and involved many procedural steps of considerable complexity and political sensitivity. The most important of these early steps was the division of the state into service delivery areas (SDAs) and the creation of private industry councils (PICs). In general, where there had been well-established CETA "prime sponsors" in urban areas, state program staff recommended similar boundaries for the new SDAs. In the rural areas of the state which had been CETA "balance-of-state" regions, state officials acted as brokers among local officials supporting a variety of SDA configurations. The outcome was an SDA "map" consisting of twenty-six areas.

The most controversial SDA boundary designation was in Cook County. Local officials in the northern section of the county—supported by local business groups and educators—petitioned the state for separate designation of an area previously incorporated under the Cook County prime sponsor. The gov-

[20] Press release, Office of the Governor, April 27, 1983.

ernor's preliminary SDA map had kept Cook County intact; however, vigorous lobbying by Republican legislators helped persuade the governor to approve separate designation. Cook County government appealed the governor's ruling to the secretary of labor, who upheld the governor.

Once the SDA map was settled in June 1983, the state program staff went ahead with the tasks of issuing guidelines for the appointment of PICs by local elected officials, and for the joint agreements by which PICs and local elected officials would determine actual responsibility for program administration. Again, the state's general approach was to set the procedural terms, allow local interests to bargain among themselves, and intervene only where an impasse threatened to hold up implementation. In several SDAs, the state had to act as a broker where there was conflict between former CETA organizations, local officials, or business groups over control of the program.

A third major component of the state's task was to establish the framework for the job training programs; this included guidelines for program planning documents, program management, determination of eligibility for job training participants, and program evaluation criteria. The state's policy was to give wide latitude with respect to the types of training programs to be undertaken locally.

In summary, the year-long transition period to JTPA was largely absorbed by the mechanics of establishing a new program structure consisting of both "old" CETA elements and the new elements of state responsibility, as well as a strong private sector role in job training. Given the complexity of the task, the state's ability to fasten the structure into place by October 1, 1983 was a considerable accomplishment.

CAPITAL PROGRAMS

Transportation

Although there are separate federal programs for highways and mass transit facilities, the single largest source of funds for both in the Chicago region was the interstate transfer program. These funds, roughly $2 billion, became available in 1979 when the city and state governments agreed to cancel the Crosstown Expressway, and reallocate the funds to other transportation projects. Under the Crosstown agreement, the funds were split fifty-fifty between the city of Chicago and its surrounding counties. The city programmed about 70 percent of its share for mass transit projects, and the suburban counties about 90 percent for street and highway projects. Crosstown funds were regarded as a binding federal commitment, although Congress retained control of the rate of spending through annual appropriations.

Chicago area elected officials and transportation planners were concerned about Reagan administration intentions to stretch out interstate transfer payments and to eliminate the "federal aid-urban" component of the Highway Trust Fund. Rather than alter project plans for the 1980s, however, their posture was to stick with their plans, and hope—as well as vigorously lobby Congress—for a reversal of Reagan administration cutback proposals.

Illinois officials, meanwhile, became preoccupied with the state's rapidly deteriorating road system and the prospect that reduced federal funds would exacerbate the problem. Adding to the squeeze on road funds were steady declines in two major revenue sources: the motor fuel tax and motor vehicle license fees. Because of these declining revenues, the state in 1980 began diverting 5 percent of sales tax revenues from the general fund to the road fund—a clear indication of the high priority placed on roads.

The anxieties of 1981 about federal transportation funding gave way to happy relief in 1982 and 1983 as the president yielded to pressure both for an increase in the federal gasoline tax and for emergency jobs legislation. Federal spending for highway programs increased by 50 percent in Illinois between federal fiscal years 1981 and 1983. Total spending on highway programs increased by more than $150 million in this period (see table 13.3). In addition, the Chicago region benefited from substantial increases in interstate transfer funds which more than doubled between federal fiscal years 1981 and 1983, increasing by $190 million (see table 13.4). State transportation spending increased along with federal aid. In 1983 Illinois passed a five-and-a-half-cent increase in the state motor fuel tax. Traditional "road politics" and concern for "jobs" combined to put transportation in very good shape for the rest of the 1980s.

Wastewater Treatment

Illinois' allocation of wastewater treatment construction grants declined by 15 percent between federal fiscal years 1981 and 1983 (see table 13.3). The Met-

Table 13.3. *Federal Grants to Illinois for Major Capital Programs, Federal Fiscal Years 1981–83 (dollars in millions)*

Program	1981	1982	1983
Small-cities community development block grant	32.4	33.7	38.5
Highways	316.3	289.3	468.9
Wastewater treatment	130.5	122.7	110.6

SOURCES: U.S. Department of Housing and Urban Development, Illinois Environmental Protection Agency, Illinois Department of Transportation, and Metropolitan Sanitary District.

Table 13.4.   *Federal Grants to Chicago Area for Major Capital Programs,*
Federal Fiscal Years 1981–83 (dollars in millions)

Program	1981	1982	1983
Community development block grant[a] (capital programs)	84.7	80.5	95.3
Urban development action grants[b]	22.1	15.2	13.7
Urban mass transportation administration (capital grants)[c]	102.0	92.4	139.3
Interstate transfers (highways and mass transit)[c]	150.0	185.0	340.0
Federal aid for urban highway systems[c]	31.7	28.3	28.6
Wastewater treatment (Metropolitan Sanitary District)[d]	32.4	24.9	—

SOURCES: U.S. Department of Housing and Urban Development, Illinois Environmental Protection Agency, Illinois Department of Transportation, and Metropolitan Sanitary District.

NOTES: [a] Chicago's entitlement grant under the community development block grant program.

[b] Urban development action grants awarded to Chicago.

[c] Grant allocation shown for six-county Chicago area.

[d] Metropolitan Sanitary District serves an area approximately the same as Cook County.

ropolitan Sanitary District, which serves the city of Chicago and surrounding Cook County suburbs suffered a severe cut as its allocation of federal funds from the state Environmental Protection Agency was cut from $32.4 million in federal fiscal year 1981 to zero in 1983 (see table 13.4). Understanding this apparently harsh cutback requires going back to the pre-Reagan 1970s when the sanitary district was getting much more than half of the proceeds from the sale of state bonds. In those years, the sanitary district was spending federal money for its controversial "Deep Tunnel" and other projects at the rate of $150–$175 million annually. With federal funds declining in the 1980s, the state decided to help communities outside Chicago play catch-up. Since the reconciliation act the state has not replaced federal dollars for Chicago's sanitary district, nor can the district possibly raise property taxes enough to proceed with its plans, except in very small steps.

THE REAGAN PROGRAM IN THE CITY OF CHICAGO

Economic distress aggravated by the recession, and reductions in federal entitlement programs brought hardship to large numbers of Chicago citizens, especially the working poor. Cuts in operating programs hit Chicago as well, especially the elimination of the CETA public service employment (PSE) program. Aside from PSE, however, cuts in other grant programs were smaller, and the negative effects on services and people were harder to define and document. Also, partially offsetting the general downward trend in grants were increases in energy assistance grants and public housing operating subsidies (see table 13.5).

According to a November 1981 analysis by the city budget office, about three-fourths of the city government's entire loss of federal grant funds for federal fiscal year 1982 was estimated to be in employment programs. Social services were identified as the other main area to be affected. From the outset, however, the city government tended to downplay the effects of the cuts, and to draw a distinction between "essential services" and those services supported by federal grants. The following statement from the budget office is indicative:

> These fiscal 1982 cuts will *not* prevent the city of Chicago from delivering necessary public services to its residents...the response to these cuts must

Table 13.5. *Federal Aid to Chicago for Major Operating Programs, Federal Fiscal Years 1981–83 (dollars in millions)*

Program	1981	1982	1983
Community development block grant (operations)	43.3	41.7	52.5
Comprehensive Employment and Training Act— public service employment grants	57.1	0	0
Comprehensive Employment and Training Act— job training programs	47.9	33.3	30.5
Social services block grant[a]	13.0	13.1	13.5
Community services block grant[a]	13.0	8.8	7.8
Maternal and child health block grant[a]	6.5	6.5	6.5
Compensatory education (chapter 1)	63.7	59.9	64.2
Education block grant (chapter 2)[a]	5.2	5.4	6.3
Regional transportation authority operating subsidy	79.9	72.6	73.9
Special rail grant	0	20.0	15.0
Chicago public housing authority operating subsidy[b]	63.5	86.9	83.3
General revenue sharing[c]	70.2	66.3	62.7
Low-income energy assistance block grant[a]	13.5	17.0	19.2
TOTAL	476.8	431.5	435.4

SOURCES: U.S. Department of Housing and Urban Development, Illinois State Board of Education, interviews with city agencies, and the state comptroller's report.

NOTES: [a] Federal fiscal year 1981 data are for equivalent categorical programs.
[b] Federal fiscal year 1982 includes special allocation of $7 million for housing authorities.
[c] City fiscal year, January 1–December 31.

be through administrative improvements in the delivery of essential services, and, in some instances, a redefinition of the proper role of city government in the area of human and community service delivery.[21]

The emphasis clearly was to be on accepting cutbacks where they could not be avoided, and to use managerial agility to soften the effect of cutbacks whenever possible.

Public Service Employment

PSE was one of the few federal programs where city officials knew exactly what was going to happen and when. In the six months prior to closing on September 30, 1981, about 4,800 persons were phased out of the program. These were persons employed by city government, the public schools, community colleges, the housing authority, and about one hundred nonprofit organizations (see table 13.5). They included janitors, health clinic aides, dogcatchers, typists, artists, safety aides, child-care workers, and teacher aides. No other operating program cutback came close to PSE in dollar amount ($57.1 million) or in the number of persons, agencies, and organizations directly affected by an interruption in federal support. The most serious impact was on PSE participants themselves; only a small fraction could be absorbed by the agencies which had hired them with federal funds, and the rest were released into a worsening economy. Apparently, most public agencies adapted to the loss of PSE workers without serious disruption. The adjustment was more difficult for those nonprofit organizations which had come to depend on PSE for a significant part of their work force.

Community Services Block Grant

Although much smaller in dollar terms than the PSE termination, Chicago's $4.1 million cut in community service grants was a sharp blow to the department of human services. The block grant reduction forced the layoff of 450 persons out of a total departmental work force of about 1,600, as well as the closing of four community service centers and five youth service centers.

Although traumatic to the employees involved, the extent to which this cutback reduced services needed by Chicago citizens is unclear. The city budget office, at least, was almost upbeat as it referred to "streamlining operations" and "greater coordination" so that "impact on actual service delivery should be minimal."[22] The city made no effort to replace federal funds with local funds;

---

[21] City of Chicago, Office of Budget and Management, "Impact of the Federal Government's Economic Program on the City Budget," p. 1. Photocopied staff report released by the city, November 1981.
[22] Ibid., p. 5.

in fact, the human services department took a further cut in Mayor Washington's 1984 budget.

Feeding the Hungry

If there were less money and fewer jobs for the poor, there was also by all accounts more food being distributed by a plethora of public and private agencies. The city of Chicago increased its own general fund budget for emergency food, and supplemented that with allocations from community development block grant funds including $1.3 million from the emergency jobs act. From its sixteen neighborhood distribution centers, the city human services department gave emergency food parcels to a rapidly growing number of persons; for example, the department reported serving about 4,000 persons in September 1981 and 36,211 persons in April 1983.[23]

The Greater Chicago Food Depository serves as the main food bank for the Chicago area; it receives and distributes donated food from corporate sources, food drives, and surplus government commodities. Growth in the depository's program has been spectacular, from 1.6 million pounds of food handled in 1980 to 6.1 million pounds in 1982, and 11 million in 1983.[24] In mid-1983 the depository was distributing food to 490 member pantries and congregate feeding sites, and this number was growing at a rate of 10 agencies monthly while 284 agencies remained on a waiting list. The Church Federation of Greater Chicago itself had 116 pantries in 1983, many of which gathered food from church sources as well as from the depository. There is no way to pin down exactly how many people were helped, how desperate they were, how many people were still hungry. What is clear is that many were needy and many reached out to help. As the head of a large social agency remarked, "It doesn't matter what business we *say* we are in; we are all in the emergency food business."[25]

Public Health Services

Service changes in the Chicago Department of Public Health illustrate the frequent confusion surrounding federal grant changes, and the difficulty of sorting out federal grant effects from other events. In January 1982, the department—citing "funding cutbacks"—announced personnel reductions and selective cuts in health services, including the closing of eight "well-baby" clinics that had been open only one or two days a month, and making some physician special-

---

[23] Tom Fox, Kent Peterson, and Lauren Hughes, eds., *Chicago Hunger Watch Report: 1983* (Chicago: Hunger Watch Task Force, October 1983), p. 32.

[24] *Chicago Hunger Report: 1983*, p. 21.

[25] From my notes taken at a meeting at the Taylor Institute, Chicago, January 15, 1982.

ists assigned to the city's seven comprehensive neighborhood health centers re-
dundant.[26] In contrast to the human services department, however, there appeared to be no clear connection between specific federal aid reductions and the
department's action. Indeed, the health commissioner stated that some changes
were decided long before federal budget cuts were known, and were "just a co-
incidence."[27] The commissioner also acknowledged that he really did not know
how much the federal cuts would be, but that his Washington sources warned
him they could amount to a 50 percent loss in projected federal support. A dep-
uty commissioner, referring to "inside sources" in Washington, also stated
"there is only bad news coming" and that "the cuts are going to be much deeper
than anticipated."[28] These dark forebodings turned out to be wrong, so what
happened in early 1982 had more to do with carrying out previous departmental
plans and with the fear of federal cutbacks than with the actual loss of federal
support.

   Since 1982, the health department has raised clinic fees, for those who can
afford them, from a maximum of $14 per visit to a maximum of $41. The department is also tapping the federal entitlement programs for more revenue by
improving its Medicare and Medicaid collection process and renegotiating
higher reimbursement rates. These revenues were needed to help offset an 8
percent reduction of city government funds in the department's 1984 budget.

Community Development Block Grant

Since the beginning of the community development block grant in 1975, Chicago mayors have relied on community development entitlement grants as a
source of flexible funds for both capital and operating purposes. For federal fiscal year 1982, Chicago's entitlement was reduced to $122.2 million, $5.8 million less than the 1981 grant—threatening the city's social services programs,
which had already been hit by the community services block grant cutback.
However, the impact of the entitlement cut was nullified as a practical matter
when the U.S. Department of Housing and Urban Development permitted
Chicago to move its community development program year forward from October 1 to July 1, 1982. Chicago's receipt of federal fiscal year 1983 funds on
July 1 had the effect of "double funding" the community development program
from July through September 1982.

   With the added flexibility provided by this maneuver, the city was able to
maintain operating services at existing levels, and at a minimum, postpone the

[26] Press release, Department of Health, City of Chicago (undated).
[27] *Chicago Tribune*, December 13, 1981.
[28] Ibid.

impact of the reduction. The emergency jobs act extended the reprieve by adding an additional $37.6 million to Chicago's 1983 community development
entitlement grant of $110.2 million. But the city's federal fiscal year 1984 en-
titlement was cut to only $103 million, threatening further layoffs, particularly
in the much-battered Department of Human Services.

The election of Harold Washington in April 1983 caused more important
changes in the community development program than anything the federal
government has done. The City Council, which was controlled by an anti-
Washington faction, took a much more active and interventionist role in block
grant planning and allocation decisions since Washington's election. For the
city's 1983–84 fiscal year, the council limited the mayor's community development reprogramming flexibility to 10 percent of any program allocation and
also required council approval of any grants or contracts over $50,000. Effec-
tively broken is Chicago's long tradition of virtually complete executive control
of community development block grant programming.

Conclusion

Political leaders in Illinois were generally caught up in the driving momentum
of the Reagan administration's push for reduced spending and "less government." They looked for opportunities to echo similar themes in their own do-
mains. President Reagan made cutting back fashionable, and the initial reductions were not so severe that they could not be absorbed with little political
damage. A more serious problem was the recession, which undermined state
and local fiscal strength and finally made large tax increases unavoidable. Although revenue shortages were not directly related to federal grant reductions,
the resulting fiscal stress made any replacement of federal cuts unlikely.

The multitude of federal budget changes in 1981, 1982, and 1983 created a
management environment of profound uncertainty and confusion in many
agencies. Responses varied widely: some overreacted to cutbacks or the fear of
further cuts, some stretched out program spending as a precaution, some assumed—not always incorrectly—that cuts would never come. It was a time of
administrative turmoil.

The state government in Illinois readily took administrative control of the
new block grants and JTPA without much fanfare and without much disturb-
ance of established political arrangements. The governor took the lead; the state

legislature was only marginally involved. Although the governor asserted himself on a few specific issues and took initiatives on "off-cycle" federal funds when available, the state's traditional role as political broker between Chicago, suburbs, and downstate was unchanged. But, the possibilities for a stronger state role in the future have been enhanced.

14

California

CRISTY JENSEN AND RUTH ROSS

The Reagan domestic program had modest institutional impacts in California. While program beneficiaries and program personnel were significantly affected, the 1981 federal budget act was not central to the politics, policy making, structures, or overall activities of the California state and Los Angeles local governments. Certainly, California public officials had expected substantial effects from the president's initiatives. Both the California Legislative Analyst and Department of Finance even established small units to monitor changes in federal programs in 1982. But the Legislative Analyst's unit was abolished in 1983, and the Department of Finance's unit faded into the routine of incorporating the flow of federal funds into the state's accounts.

The primary reason that Reagan's initiatives had few repercussions in California is that they were minor compared with more significant fiscal, economic, and political forces operating at the state and local levels. The most obvious of these larger events was the succession of blows to the California public treasury resulting from initiatives that cut property taxes (Proposition 13, 1978), constrained expenditures (Proposition 4, 1979), imposed indexing of the personal income tax (Proposition 7, 1982), and abolished the inheritance tax (Proposition 6, 1982). Moreover, the recession of 1981–82 lowered state revenues below anticipated levels for three fiscal years. Finally, the politics of California, particularly at the state level, but also in local governments, were particularly tumultuous in the early 1980s.

Beset by fiscal constraints and consumed with partisan wrangling over reapportionment, California state officials essentially ratified the funding and program changes of the Reagan domestic program. Local officials were even more pressed fiscally than was the state, and they also were frequently caught up in larger political controversies, so they also commonly implemented the changes with as little disruption to established patterns as possible. Even when fiscal stress eased, as it has for the state since 1983, California governments did not restore earlier cuts made in national programs.

Much has changed in the policies and politics of California since the early 1980s. The state government has become more dominant in both policy choice and public finance. The initiative process is encouraging the pursuit of major policy shifts, the best example of which was Proposition 41 (defeated in November 1984), which would have required a reduction in public assistance welfare and medical payments to the average in the other forty-nine states plus 10 percent. The conflict over reapportionment has become even more acrimonious. An initiative (Proposition 24, 1984) to reform the rules of the California Legislature and reduce its funding was passed and partially implemented and was the subject of litigation. None of these events has been stimulated by Reagan's actions. These state actions, not changes in national grants policy, dominated the attention of California policy makers and shaped their actions.

However, the consequences of these indigenous conflicts and dynamics have affected the implementation of federal grant programs. Partisan wrangling between the Democratically controlled legislature and Republican Governor Deukmejian contributed to the lack of initiative in assuming Reagan's block grants.[1] The success of spending and taxing limitations in California indicated a willingness on the part of state and local officials to ratify and even compound federal cuts. And the recession-induced fiscal stress sharply limited California's options for replacing cuts.

The California Setting

Both political and fiscal factors reduced the importance of the Reagan domestic program for California public officials. The two are intertwined, of course. As an example, the inability of state legislators to provide property tax relief spurred the passage of Proposition 13, which reduced property tax revenues available to local governments by $7 billion, approximately one-half their previous level. And that event stimulated further centralization of fiscal and policy-making power in the state legislature.

[1] Dale Rogers Marshall, "Block Grants: Reagan's, Deukmejian's and Choices for the Future," in John J. Kirlin and Donald R. Winkler, eds., *California Policy Choices, 1984* (Sacramento, Calif.: University of Southern California, 1984), pp. 166–67.

CALIFORNIA POLITICS

Largely as a result of the Progressive legacy, California legislative bodies are more dominant than in most states. Political parties are weak and executive powers limited and fragmented. Beyond these structural attributes, California legislatures have been strengthened by development of large, full-time staffs at the state level and in the larger local governments.

A good rule of thumb is that elected officials will choose the policy option that increases their ability to raise campaign contributions or to mobilize votes from specific constituencies. The Reagan policy initiatives provided few new resources to California legislators. Instead, the changes threatened relationships already established. State legislators responded by defending interest groups supportive of them. For instance, by 1984, no state legislator had taken any initiative to respond in an innovative manner to the Reagan block grants; rather, they accommodated old interests, since no additional political advantage could be extracted.[2]

The distinctive fiscal situation of California also bears brief mention. From a period of increasing revenues at both state and local levels in the early 1970s, California governments became buffeted by reduced revenues and much greater uncertainty in the late 1970s and early 1980s. The fiscal limits movement reduced revenues available to California governments more than in other states. No other state experienced four successful initiatives to reduce/control revenues and expenditures. Moreover, future revenue-cutting initiatives are always a possibility.

Two specific points about fiscal affairs in California are important to understand the context in which the Reagan program was implemented.[3] First, while total own-source revenues of all California governments measured in constant dollars per capita declined by 12 percent between state fiscal years 1977–78 and 1981–82, total expenditures measured similarly declined only 8 percent. The 1981 federal budget act took effect at a time when revenues and expenditures were both falling, and there was a shortage of current revenues to cover current expenditures. This imbalance was accommodated by drawing down surplus state funds. By 1982, however, the surplus was exhausted and the recession further eroded revenues, particularly those raised by the state, whose dependence upon personal income and sales taxes make its tax receipts fluctuate with economic cycles. For example, revenues available to the state of California in state

[2] Cristy Jensen, "Legislative Response to Cutbacks in California," *Journal of Public Budgeting and Finance* 4, no. 2 (Summer 1984):71–72.

[3] John J. Kirlin, "The Fiscal Context of California Policy Choices," in John J. Kirlin and Donald R. Winkler, eds., *California Policy Choices* (Sacramento, Calif.: University of Southern California, 1984), pp. 7–35.

fiscal year 1982–83 fell $2.8 billion short of those originally projected in the governor's budget presented in January 1982.

Second, while overall revenues declined, counties and community colleges bore most of the brunt of the decrease. The cities generated sufficient revenues from special taxes, fees, and enterprise activities to actually increase their constant dollar per capita expenditures. The state accelerated revenue collections, shifted funds from special to general purposes, deferred capital expenditures, and reduced subsidies to local governments to also achieve increased constant dollar per capita expenditures. The state protected elementary and secondary education from revenue losses through increased transfers. Community colleges were the big losers; constant-dollar expenditures declined by 18 percent between state fiscal years 1977–78 and 1981–82. Importantly for implementation of federal grant programs, the expenditures of counties (which deliver most of the nationally funded programs) fell by 10 percent in constant-dollar per capita terms between state fiscal years 1977–78 and 1981–82. The state increased transfers to counties for its health and welfare programs, but provided essentially no support for other county functions, and few counties were able to replace losses in federal aid.

Since the late 1970s, the state has dramatically increased its domination of the political system in California. That change is not fully analyzed here because it was not caused, or even stimulated, by changes in national policy and funding. Kirlin provides an analysis of changes in the fiscal context of California policy making since 1970.[4] The sources of the state's ascendance are its constitutional superiority over local governments, its more elastic revenue system, the reduction in property tax revenues received by local governments caused by tax-cutting initiatives (Jarvis-Gann), and the needs of legislators to bring more policy issues into their orbit so that they may be used to generate campaign contributions and/or votes.

CENTRALIZING TRENDS IN CALIFORNIA

The state's control over counties has increased. One cause is increased financing of county activities. The state has directed such transfers to the programs it gives the highest priority, effectively reducing the proportion of county budgets over which local officials have substantial discretion. But the state legislature found ways to direct the activities of counties long before Proposition 13, through the imposition of state mandates upon counties. Even without Reagan's attempts to return to a dual federalism and to reduce the powers of the

[4] Ibid., pp. 7–35.

national government, which in combination give more powers to states, the state would have played an increasing role in the administration of national policies in California. The 1981 federal budget act could only reinforce the institutional changes already occurring.

STATE AND LOCAL GOVERNMENTAL RELATIONSHIPS

In California, it is usually local governments which ultimately implement most of the national programs funded through intergovernmental grants. California's State Constitution creates three major forms of local government: cities, counties, and special districts (such as the Los Angeles Unified School District and the Southern California Rapid Transit District, LAUSD and SCRTD, respectively). The most numerous special districts in the state are the 1,028 school districts. Cities hold "police powers," to make and enforce all local police, sanitary, and other ordinances not in conflict with state laws. These powers include general government, police, fire, solid and liquid waste, streets and other public works, parks and recreation, libraries, community development, and land use.

Notably absent from this list of city services are those relating to the major policy changes and budget cuts of the 1981 reconciliation act. In California, health and welfare services are provided not by cities, but by counties. Thus, funds for major programs affected by Reagan changes—aid to families with dependent children (AFDC), food stamps, Medicaid, and the health and social services block grants—flow from the national government through the state to counties.

County governments are not only political subdivisions of the state; in many regards, they are administrative agencies of the state. Although the California Constitution allows county governments to exercise police powers independent of an act of the legislature, their other actions derive authority from specific state statutes or constitutional provisions. Most of the federally funded programs fall into this latter category, where county activity is tightly controlled by explicit state statute.

LOS ANGELES AREA GOVERNMENTS

Los Angeles County has an annual budget of more than $5 billion, more than 70,000 employees, and a population approaching 8 million. It is the second largest provider of urban services in the nation, exceeded only by the city of New York. Nearly three-fourths of the county's revenues come from federal, state, and other earmarked funds. The state of California provides 58 percent of the county's revenues, and approximately half of its own-source revenues are committed to mandatory matching of major state or federal programs.[5] Thus, the county must be considered to be largely the local implementor of programs designed and funded in Washington, D.C., or Sacramento.

In his 1983–84 budget recommendation, the county's chief administrative officer (CAO) noted an "us versus them" philosophy between the state and local governments as the state's fiscal problems deepened. In particular, the CAO worried about the instability of incoming state funds, perceiving them to be subject to immediate call by the state if needed for its programs. This concern was substantiated during the fiscal crisis between 1982 and 1984, when the state reduced statutorily required subsidies to local governments by $1.4 billion.[6] The state effectively borrowed $200 million from Los Angeles County by delaying payment of that amount owed the county for provision of health services to medically indigent adults from state fiscal years 1982–83 until 1984–85.[7]

By 1983, the county had become the direct provider not only of local, but also of state and federal services.[8] At the same time, the county had reduced its operations more since passage of Proposition 13 than had the state. For example, budgeted positions in state employment have increased by approximately 1,000 since 1978–79, while Los Angeles County's budgeted positions decreased by approximately 5,000 in the same period. The decline in county employment began in 1974, and Reagan-era national budget reductions have played only a minor role in the personnel decrease. The state's increased fiscal assistance after passage of Proposition 13 was directed to continuation of state-mandated services. As a consequence, "local-option" services, those carried out under the county's police powers or permissive state statutes, have borne the brunt of budget, staff, and service reductions.

The city of Los Angeles, with a population of nearly 3 million, aggressively sought federal aid in the 1970s. Since the beginning of the Reagan administration, federal funds coming to the city government have dropped from $275 million (28 percent of the city's own-source revenues) to $252 million, largely because of cuts in job training grants.[9] In spite of the sizable fraction of activities funded by intergovernmental grants, those funds were not used to support basic city functions. This is in sharp contrast to Los Angeles County, where federal

---

[5] County of Los Angeles, *Proposed County Budget: Fiscal Year Ending June 30, 1984* (Los Angeles, Calif.: County of Los Angeles, 1983), p. 23.

[6] Kirlin, "The Fiscal Context of California Policy Choices," p. 17.

[7] Legislative Analyst, *Analysis of the Budget Bill for the Fiscal Year July 1, 1983 to June 30, 1984* (Sacramento, Calif.: Legislative Analyst, 1984), p. 779.

[8] County of Los Angeles, *Proposed County Budget*, pp. 19–21.

[9] Ruth Ross, *The Impact of Federal Grants in the City of Los Angeles* (Washington, D.C.: U.S. Department of Labor, 1980), p. 30.

(and state) funds were integrated into core health and welfare activities. On the whole, the city prefers to avoid dependence on intergovernmental transfers for basic services. (General revenue sharing and wastewater treatment funds are notable exceptions.)

Changes in Federal Aid in the Reagan Years

In federal fiscal year 1982, the state of California experienced a reduction in federal aid of approximately 2 percent from President Carter's budget proposal for 1982. Actual receipts of federal funds increased in every state fiscal year during the early 1980s. It is difficult to measure precise fiscal impacts because of carryover funding, forward funding, and lack of comparable data. California had not maintained data on categorical programs previously awarded directly to local governments from Washington, making any analysis of receipts where federal funds were redirected from local governments to the state problematic. Nonetheless, all analyses conclude that the cuts were not as substantial as most commentators had expected (see table 14.1).

Changes in entitlement programs are perhaps most complex. Although eligibility changes in entitlement programs reduced the rate of growth of the AFDC case load, program expenditures increased by 17 percent during the period. This was due to rising unemployment. Clearly, without the Reagan changes, case loads and expenditures would have been even higher. Similarly, state reforms in Medi-Cal (California's Medicaid program) reduced the rate of increase in Medicaid expenditures, but they still rose by 13 percent. State officials devoted great attention to the entitlement program changes because of the financial magnitude and the implications for individuals.

The smaller block grants generally received the greatest percentage cuts in 1982, but by 1983, each of the primary health care, community development, and community services block grant programs showed marginal increases over 1982 spending levels, even without emergency jobs act funds. The larger operating programs, such as social services, education, and job training, were not as successful in recouping lost federal revenues. Even though the state did not replace lost operating funds, a significant amount of political energy was expended on block grant assumption and implementation. Legislation was enacted in fall 1981 authorizing assumption of two mandatory block grant programs (the social services block grant and the low-income energy assistance block grant programs) and forming a block grant advisory task force to develop plans for future state assumption of the remaining block grants. By October 1983, California had assumed all blocks except for primary health care.

Table 14.1. *Federal Aid to California, State Fiscal Years 1980–83 (dollars in millions)*

Program	1980–81	1981–82	1982–83
Entitlement Programs			
Aid to families with dependent children	1,297	1,427	1,521
Food stamps	530	535	710
Medicaid (Medi-Cal)	1,904	2,075	2,083
Operating Programs			
Job training (state only)	118	67	50
Social services block grant	296	249	255[a]
Small-cities community development block grant	23	25	27[b]
Compensatory education	299	272	258
Education block grant	60	57	34
Community services block grant	36	29	29[c]
Alcohol, drug abuse, and mental health block grant	50	41	42[d]
Maternal and child health block grant	21	18	18[e]
Preventive health block grant	6	6	6
Primary health care block grant	—	26	29
Capital Programs			
Highway aid	498	520	482
Mass transit	284	395	276
Wastewater treatment	350	338	347

SOURCE: Interviews with state officials.

NOTES: [a] Does not include $27 million in social services block grant funds provided by the 1983 jobs act.
[b] Does not include $8 million in small-cities community development block grant funds provided by the 1983 jobs act.
[c] Does not include $3 million in community services block grant funds provided by the 1983 jobs act.
[d] Does not include $3 million in alcohol, drug abuse, mental health block grant funds provided by the 1983 jobs act.
[e] Does not include $6 million in maternal and child health block grant funds provided by the 1983 jobs act.

Cuts in capital outlay programs were the least significant. Highway aid, mass transit, and wastewater treatment grants were reduced 3.2, 2.8, and 0.8 percent during the course of the study period.

AID TO LOS ANGELES GOVERNMENTS

The story of federal grant-in-aid to Los Angeles area governments is a complex one. Los Angeles County, City, and special districts have an excellent record in obtaining discretionary grants through skilled responses to federal requests for proposals. In federal fiscal year 1978, Los Angeles governments received a

Table 14.2. *Federal Aid to Los Angeles Local Governments, Federal Fiscal Years 1981–83 (dollars in millions)*

Program	1981	1982	1983
Entitlement Programs			
Aid to families with dependent children	473.5	532.8	568.5
Food stamps	216.9[a]	199.7	261.3
Medicaid (Medi-Cal)	59.3	83.0	86.5
Operating Programs			
Job training	107.4	41.9	40.3
Social services block grant	64.6	50.9	49.3
Community development block grant (entitlement)	56.9	54.8	49.5
Compensatory education	54.3	50.6	52.2
Education block grant	19.8	10.5	8.0
Community services block grant	9.4	5.4	3.4
Alcohol, drug abuse, and mental health block grant	2.5	1.2	8.0
Capital Programs			
Highway aid	8.5	12.2	7.4
Mass transit	183.9	107.8	89.6
Housing	58.8	76.4	86.5
Wastewater treatment	6.9	23.7	38.4
Urban development action grants	13.5	15.1	—

SOURCE: Interviews with local officials.

NOTE: [a] Yearly estimate based on data for January 1981–September 1981.

total of 110 federal grants.[10] The move toward formula allocations has decreased local government entrepreneurship. Program planning and innovation by local governments have also been reduced because of the complex interdependence of state and local finances, the restrictions on raising taxes since Proposition 13, and the recession-induced reduction in the local sales tax. Los Angeles area governments have had no alternative in many cases except to pass federal and state funding through to recipients.

As table 14.2 indicates, Los Angeles area governments received more federal funds over the period between federal fiscal years 1981 and 1983 in entitlement programs. Federal funding grew for AFDC, food stamps, and Medi-Cal. These increases occurred because of the 1981–82 recession and the steady influx of low-income people into the county. These data are not adjusted for price changes nor for changes in case load, so they may well mask declining levels of constant dollar funding per unit of service rendered.

[10] Ibid., pp. 18–24.

The State-Local Responses

California's responses to these cuts tended to be cautious and conservative. The state generally ratified federal cuts and also delayed long-term decisions whenever possible. The conservative response and failure to replace fund cuts were due in large part to the seriousness of the state's own fiscal crisis. At the state level there was virtually no structural change, either in state-local or executive-legislative relationships that might be expected in response to a national strategy affording new opportunities for state control. Rather, the norm was accommodation to varied demands—a political response. This accommodation was especially apparent in the case of the block grants, but was also evident in the AFDC and Medi-Cal reforms where there was no real effort to replace aid cuts.

ENTITLEMENT PROGRAMS

Income maintenance and health services for the poor consume 30 percent of the state's budget, the second highest category behind support for elementary and secondary education. California has historically provided a high level of state support for the poor, frequently exceeding the federal contributions in these entitlement programs.

Aid to Families with Dependent Children

In large part because of the recent political history of California, Democratic Governor Jerry Brown did not want to embrace the president's welfare cuts and so took no action initially to prepare the necessary state conforming legislation and regulations. During a special session of the legislature in the fall 1981 to discuss reapportionment, legislators became aware of the potential loss of federal funds that would result from the state's non-conformity with federal eligibility criteria and benefit levels. Appropriate legislation was enacted to achieve conformity, only to have the implemention delayed as a consequence of court challenges to county implementation. Implementation of the changes did not occur until April and May of 1982. Though there was some controversy at the time over federal payment for the period of non-compliance, the state was eventually reimbursed by the federal government.

Though California ratified the federal changes in benefit levels and eligibility criteria in the AFDC program, it remains more liberal than many states by providing state-funded benefits to first-time mothers during the first six months of pregnancy and eligibility of two-parent families for state-only assistance where federal eligibility criteria of "recent work experience" are not met. Since the eligibility changes have taken place, the proportion of AFDC recipients with earned income declined from nearly 19 percent in July 1981 to 5.6 percent in April 1983. (Part of this decline is as likely to be attributable to the recession.) A Department of Social Services survey of AFDC recipients before and after the 1981 eligibility changes sought to determine the impacts of the 1981 federal budget act changes on AFDC recipients. The survey found that families whose AFDC assistance was discontinued because their gross income exceeded the limit were no more likely to return to AFDC than those discontinued for other reasons (14 versus 15 percent). The data suggest that some AFDC families were less likely to continue working after the 30 and 1/3 income disregard expired at the end of four months.

The numbers of persons on AFDC in Los Angeles County increased from 517,118 in September 1981 to 549,376 by September 1983. The gross increase in numbers, however, does not reveal the effects of the Reagan welfare changes. The county estimates that impacts of the reconciliation act upon AFDC were 42,094 reductions in the level of aid and 12,424 terminations. Within six months of the federal changes nearly 60 percent of those removed from the welfare rolls had been reapproved for some type of public assistance. Five out of six of the terminees were cut from AFDC because of the 1981 budget act restrictions on earned income, but six months later one-fourth were reapproved for AFDC earned supplemental income. Overall, 10 percent of the terminees came back on AFDC, another 49 percent returned to the Medi-Cal rolls as recipients of only Medicaid, and 7 percent were reapproved for food stamps.[11]

A recent study of AFDC by the Los Angeles County Department of Social Services identified the following changes in welfare services. First, the stricter eligibility standards resulted in a loss of benefits for some welfare families. Second, staffing cutbacks reduced staff-recipient contact levels and increased error rates. Third, implementation of tighter quality control (audit) standards could result in future reductions in funding.[12]

The many changes in the welfare rolls created net cost savings of approximately $60.5 million to the county from December 1981 through November 1982 after accounting for reopened cases.[13] An additional county cost savings of $750,000 resulted from "Operation Intercept," a program by which the State

[11] Joseph Guerra, June 16, 1982 memorandum from the Los Angeles County Department of Public Social Services. See also "Impact of Reagan Administration Changes on AFDC: Omnibus Budget Reconciliation Act of 1981 (OBRA)" (Los Angeles, Calif.: Los Angeles County Department of Public Social Services, 1983).

[12] "Impact of Reagan Administration Changes on AFDC."

[13] Tom Joe, *Effects of Federal AFDC Policy Changes: A Study of Federal State Partnerships* (Washington, D.C.: Center for Study of Social Policy, March 1983), p. 78.

Franchise Tax Board deducts child support obligations of delinquent parents from state income tax refunds. On the other hand county spending increased when approximately 2,000 persons shifted from AFDC to the totally county-funded general relief program.

Food Stamps

Food assistance programs aid one in ten Los Angeles County residents. Approximately 600,000 receive food stamps and an additional 225,000 on Supplemental Security Income receive a monthly cash supplement in lieu of food stamp coupons. Approximately 180,000 persons had their benefits reduced or terminated. By December 1983, the overall number of people in the county on food stamps increased by 13 percent over the case-load levels during the years prior to the 1981 budget act, primarily as a result of the state's economic condition (9.7 percent unemployment in 1983). The county's Department of Public and Social Services periodically receives reports from line staff and community-based organizations, which indicate that more than 100,000 eligible needy persons do not even apply for food stamps; thus, case-load figures alone do not reveal the full magnitude of the population in need of food assistance services.

Medi-Cal

For three years, the state sought to control expenditures in the Medi-Cal program. The Medi-Cal reforms enacted in 1982 were not caused by federal funding cuts or program changes, but rather by state budget pressures. The most significant reform enacted in 1982 was the establishment of a selective provider contracting process to determine which acute care hospitals would serve the state's Medicaid population. The authority to enter into prospective rate reimbursement contracts with acute care hospitals for providing inpatient care to Medi-Cal beneficiaries was assigned to the governor's office. Subsequent legislation established the California Medical Assistance Commission comprised of seven members which assumed the function. The commission's first report issued in May 1983 estimated that as a result of the competitive contracting for inpatient hospital service, Medi-Cal savings would amount to $41.7 million in state fiscal year 1982–83 and $238.1 million in state fiscal year 1983–84.

Contracts are negotiated in a geographic area by the commission's staff. The responsibility for implementing and monitoring contracts rests with the state's Department of Health Services. The contracts, which are negotiated on a bid or no-bid basis, impose a duty on the contract hospital to provide inpatient services in a nondiscriminatory manner at a fixed per diem rate. Hospitals are expected to assume as much risk as possible.

A second feature of the Medi-Cal reforms has possible long-term implications for state-local relations. Statutes direct the Medical Assistance Commission to negotiate contracts with counties for the implementation of countywide health systems for Medi-Cal beneficiaries within their jurisdiction. A number of counties are currently pursuing the development of county health systems, and requests for waivers of federal regulations to allow systems to begin operation have been submitted. These local health systems have exclusive contracts negotiated with the state, in a fashion similar to hospital contracting, to provide health care to Medi-Cal beneficiaries. A contracting county may provide services directly to recipients or arrange for any or all of the services to be provided by subcontracting with primary care providers, health maintenance organizations, insurance carriers, or other entities or individuals. Four of these county systems have received state and federal approvals. San Mateo County, an urban county on the San Francisco peninsula, was the first to receive approval and was scheduled to begin operation in January of 1986. It has been suggested that countywide health systems for Medi-Cal beneficiaries may encourage integrated public health care systems where county employees and Medi-Cal beneficiaries are both enrolled in the same system.

The state reduced Medi-Cal costs by shifting responsibility for the medically indigent adult (MIA) program to counties. (MIA never received federal funds.) It appears, though, that the game goes both ways. In Los Angeles, an aggressive county policy sought to move people from the state-mandated, but county-funded, MIA program to the state- and federal-funded Medi-Cal program of health care for the poor.

Two of the changes in financing health care are particularly important to Los Angeles County. First, the state changed benefits and reduced reimbursements through stricter controls, limitation of specialized services, and changes in the definition of medical necessity. Second, it changed Medi-Cal eligibility by increasing patient co-payments and by transferring to the counties the responsibility for medical care of approximately 280,000 MIAs whose total care had been previously funded by the state. The state cut its transfer payments to 70 percent of what it would have spent if MIAs were still covered by Medi-Cal, and forced the counties to absorb the remaining 30 percent. To help offset the difference, Los Angeles shifted its MIAs from private providers to the county hospitals, health centers, and clinics. Additionally, the county aggressively encouraged enrollment of indigent patients which it felt were eligible for Medi-Cal in order to shift their health care costs to the state and federal governments.

OPERATING PROGRAMS

Block Grants

The legislature's decision to give significant power to seasoned, urban, community-based organizations as the dominant faction in the block grants advisory task force was symbolic of the Democratic legislature's political alliances with community-based organizations. In turn, the dominance of community-based organizations influenced the choice of an implementation strategy which protected existing local grantees, primarily community-based organizations.

The state administrative machinery maintained basic control over the new block grants, carrying out the block grant task force's recommendations of pro rata reductions to existing grantees in all of the health block grants. The legislature rejected alternative legislation sponsored by the United Way of California, which would have given substantially increased power to counties. Under the defeated legislative proposal, county-appointed human services commissions would have prepared needs surveys and then recommended appropriate providers to the local county board of supervisors.

The legislature failed to agree upon a long-term plan for implementation of the three health block grants, suggesting a broad accommodation to the federal program changes. The task force protected the funding status, and the very survival, of several urban minority mental health centers, primarily in Los Angeles County. The funding changes in these three programs have been fairly significant—funding dropped from a 1981 level of $77 million to $56 million in 1983 ($65 million if jobs act funds are included). What began as a one-year transition from federal to local funding has settled into an accommodation which allows existing community-based service providers to survive, maintains previous levels of county involvement, and protects an administrative allowance for state departments. But another effort to negotiate a longer-term plan including transfer of administrative responsibility for several grants to county government and a reduced state role in monitoring and evaluation failed in January 1984.

If the Reagan strategy to increase the states' role in domestic programs has a major institutional impact, it will be an indirect one. Republican Governor Deukmejian, a supporter of the president's ideology, has proposed state block grant programs to local governments in his two state budgets. The moves have generally failed in the Democratically controlled legislature, in large part because of alliances with community-based organizations. Observers expect the governor to continue efforts to consolidate state programs into block grants.

Prior to the Omnibus Budget Reconciliation Act of 1981, the state required counties to use social service funds to provide a range of services, including the in-home supportive services program (IHSS) and other county supportive services (OCSS). As an initial response to the funding cuts, in 1981 the California Department of Social Services reduced the number of state-mandated elements in the OCSS program from ten to six, ostensibly to allow counties greater flexibility in the use of the reduced funds. In 1982 the state passed the Family Protection Act, dramatically reversing this earlier move toward flexibility for counties, while at the same time providing a guaranteed cap on the county costs for the OCSS program.

This legislation suggests that a pattern of state mandating of local program priorities remains strong, and that federal block grants have facilitated new state mandates. The state helped counties by replacing the 25 percent county cost-sharing requirement with a guaranteed cap on county costs; but the state also took advantage of its new-found flexibility under the social services block grant to fund its own program priorities, thereby reducing county discretion. Flexibility received by the state became strictures imposed upon counties; states can apparently pursue "creeping categorization" as effectively as did the national government.

Funding to Los Angeles County increased dramatically under the alcohol, drug abuse, and mental health block grant. Prior to the block grant, both the state- and the county-administered federal drug abuse programs, and local providers sought funding from both levels of government. As part of the state cost cutting, California turned all drug program administration over to the county governments. The effect for the county Department of Health Services was an increase from $2.5 million in federal fiscal year 1981 to $11.0 million in federal fiscal year 1984; the effect on community-based organizations was program funding and administration by one, rather than two governments. The county feels that drug abuse programs are now more efficiently managed because of the centralization of the flow of funds to providers. While funding comes from the alcohol, drug abuse, mental health block grant, actual program administration at both state and county levels remains "categorical." Historic program separation continues.

Los Angeles County's allocation of social services block grant funds declined by 24 percent, from $64.6 million in federal fiscal year 1981 to $49.0 million in federal fiscal year 1983. In 1984, the county received an increase in funds, $62.4 million. Case-load and population increases boosted the county's share of social services aid distributed by the state.

Funding for the community services block grant has declined because of federal policy changes. This program was not a state priority. By January 1984 the state still had not created regulations to implement the program, and the county was running the program based upon its own interpretation of the state and federal laws. California community action agency directors, however, are a strong influence in Sacramento. They meet monthly, and as lobbyists, drafted the state legislation which passes federal funds through the state to them with safeguards to protect community action agencies. Thus, in the case of community services, unlike some of the social services, the state did not take advantage of its chance to mandate county services. Rather, counties retained discretion even after the reconciliation act, and continued to utilize already existing service providers.

The major federally funded block grant programs administered by the city of Los Angeles are the community development block grant program and the job training partnership act (JTPA) program. The city's Community Development Department administers community development and job training grants. Federal aid is isolated in this agency and kept separate from regular city operations.

The city community development grant has generally increased in recent years, reflecting a variety of factors. Population growth and the reallocation of unobligated funds earmarked for entitlement communities throughout the state has brought an increase in funds to the city. Use of the 1980 census in the U.S. Department of Housing and Urban Development's formula distribution of grants resulted in the city receiving a 27 percent increase in federal aid.

Transition from the Comprehensive Employment Training Act (CETA) to the Job Training Partnership Act had little effect on city staffing, but had a major impact on community-based organizations. When Congress terminated the public services employment program in the spring of 1981, the city subcontracted 5,620 positions to other entities and employed only 708 CETA-funded personnel in its own work force.[14] The majority of the subcontracted slots, 2,943, went to community-based organizations for social services and arts-related programs.

Under state administration of the education block grant, California school districts have wide latitude over how they use federal funds. For the Los Angeles Unified School District (LAUSD), however, funding declined from $19.8 million in 1981 to $7.2 million by 1984. In 1981 and 1982 nearly 80 percent of the funds came from the Emergency School Assistance Act (ESAA), which severely limited the use of this aid in school integration programs. These funds could not, for example, be used for the court-ordered busing program the district was required to run in 1981. The district, instead, used the ESAA funds to supplement its magnet school program. Mandatory busing for integration

[14] Ruth Ross, "Field Research Report on Public Service Employment Titles VI and II-D: Los Angeles," in Robert F. Cook et al., eds., *Public Service Employment in Fiscal 1981* (Washington, D.C.: U.S. Department of Labor, 1982).

ended in 1982 and the magnet schools had been sufficiently strengthened so
that some extra state and local funds were freed up; thus, the ESAA cut was not
central to the LAUSD voluntary integration programs. Furthermore, the district viewed a few million federal dollars as minuscule in the context of a 1983–
84 operating budget of $1.943 billion. LAUSD feels it has actually gained be-
cause there was very little money in the prior categorical programs and because
many were discretionary allocations, requiring proposal writing.

CAPITAL PROGRAMS

California's response to federal changes in funding of wastewater treatment
plants reveals preoccupation with state and local issues. Reduction in federal
funding was not significant to California. However, federal plans to reduce the
matching rate of wastewater treatment grants from 75 to 55 percent of eligible
construction costs, effective in October 1984, led the state and local governments to consider replacement activities. Historically, the state government has
helped localities pay part of the matching share of federal wastewater treatment
construction grants. The state contribution has been funded from bond authorizations, while localities generally have had to rely on own-source revenue
sources and the bond market to pay their share of the nonfederal cost of construction. Proposition 13 reduced local bonding capacity. The state bond authorization for wastewater treatment facilities is nearly depleted. Because of
both of these factors, along with the reduction in the federal matching share,
state and local officials focused upon securing the November 1984 passage of a
new $450 million state revenue bond authority. Essentially, the reduction in
federal funds and share is accepted as a reality and attention has shifted to developing a state-local system that can interact with the federal program and
funding.

Wastewater treatment, urban highway systems, and mass transit grants received by Los Angeles local governments are increasing. Rising expenditures
for wastewater treatment reflected construction of a city project that was just beginning after a seven-year delay due to legal battles.

Expansion in mass transit grants (administered by a special district, the
Southern California Rapid Transit District—SCRTD) resulted from more attention to infrastructure repairs and preliminary allocations for a subway project along Wilshire Boulevard. Continued federal assistance for the multibillion
dollar subway project is uncertain. The Urban Mass Transportation Administration has only approved enough funds to support construction of 4.5 miles of
the proposed 18.6 miles of the Wilshire corridor line. Federal funding for
SCRTD has declined, primarily because of major federal cuts in UMTA sec-

tion 3 capital grants. However, the total revenues available to SCRTD have increased from receipt of an extra half-cent sales tax approved by Los Angeles County voters in 1980. It is clear that capital programs have shouldered fewer cuts than entitlement or operating services and, moreover, that capital programs receive a high priority in California.

Conclusions

The state of California basically accepted the changes made in the 1981 federal budget, making only modest modifications in program design and virtually no decisions to either replace federal funds or to cut state funding. However, reductions in state funding for a program sometimes occurred as a result of the state continuing to provide a constant share match to a reduced federal program. These combined federal and state policy choices passed the cuts down to the local governments (and non-governmental bodies) actually implementing the programs.

Because of their own fiscal strain, limited revenue generating options, and beliefs that these were "federal" programs, local governments also accepted and implemented the funding reductions. The only instance of replacing lost federal funds with local revenues discovered is in the Southern California Rapid Transit District, but this was the consequence of funds coincidentally made available as the result of a voter-approved increase in the sales tax to provide transit funding, not as a response to Reagan policies.

California local governments seek to isolate themselves from fluctuations in federal funding or changes in program design. Their ability to do so varies according to their legal status relative to the state and whether or not federal funding is for activities they define as "core."

It is important to note that while fiscal stress is one of the reasons why California governments did not replace any of the federal funds cut with their own funds, neither have they proposed such replacement now that their fiscal fortunes have improved. Governor Deukmejian would probably oppose such action. But the Democrats in the legislature have not made this a visible, high priority, either. Federal programs simply did not have sufficient indigenous political and popular support for state or local governments to replace funding. However, there was enough political support from the providers and clientele of the federal programs affected by Reagan that they secured continuation of the old program designs, although they commonly bore the full brunt of whatever funding reductions occurred. By and large, all that changed was funding levels, not program designs, implementing organization, or political dynamics.

Five factors contributed to the modest impact of revisions in grants-in-aid. First, the federal cuts were far outweighed by austerity measures already enacted by California state and local governments. California is the leader in fiscal limits, with voters having passed four tax reduction or limitation initiatives since 1978. These actions reduced revenues available to California governments by $14 billion in state fiscal year 1982–83, more than twice the amount of the nationwide reductions in intergovernmental aid that occurred between 1981 and 1982. Cuts in federal aid received by local governments or individuals may have been about $1 billion. These cuts pale into insignificance in comparison to the nearly $7 billion lost in property tax revenues resulting from Proposition 13.

A second explanation for the modest and declining importance of national grants is based on the relative proportion of national grants when compared with the total resources available to states and localities. Federal aid peaked at 26 percent of total state and local own-source revenues in 1978 and declined to 20 percent by 1983.[15] As a percentage of total state expenditures in California, a precipitous decline in federal funds occurred in the Carter presidency, when federal funds as a percentage of total funds declined from 40.5 percent in state fiscal years 1975–76 to 27.7 percent in 1979–80.

Third, fluctuations attributable to economic cycles often have a greater impact relative to changes in national grants. In California, recession-caused shortfalls in 1981 to 1983 were ten times as large as reductions in grants-in-aid from the national government. In response to this shortfall, in 1983 the state adopted a revenue-raising package that included no increases in general taxes, yet increased revenues nearly $800 million.

A fourth reason that changes in national grants are not central concerns of California state and local governments is that the largest transfers are in programs where state and local officials have little latitude for policy making. In 1972, only 10 percent of all grants were "general-purpose" or "broad-based," providing state and local officials with substantial policy-making latitude. The advent of general revenue sharing and the Nixon-Ford block grants increased the portion of general-purpose grants to 22 percent in the late 1970s. In 1981, broad-based grants decreased to 18 percent before rising again to 20 percent in 1982 as a result of the Reagan initiatives.[16] Since state and local governments have restricted discretion in the other 80 percent of grant programs, they remain

---

[15] U.S. Advisory Commission on Intergovernmental Relations, *Significant Features of Fiscal Federalism, 1984* (Washington, D.C.: Government Printing Office, March 1984), p. 63.

[16] Congress of the United States, Congressional Budget Office, *The Federal Government in a Federal System: Current Intergovernmental Programs and Options for Change* (Washington, D.C.: Government Printing Office, August 1983), p. 25.

forever "federal" programs, "theirs" not "ours" in the perception of state and local officials.

Finally, state and local officials have, in some places and with differing degrees of success, developed routine strategies to cope with changes in the design or funding levels of national grant programs. Some are best considered "isolation" strategies, where the nationally funded activities are kept as separate as possible organizationally and fiscally. For example, a separate organization may be established to operate the grant-funded activity and staffed by personnel without civil service status. Another strategy is to contract out the activity to non-governmental entities (community-based nonprofit organizations, for example), who then must cope with the vicissitudes of program design and funding. Yet another strategy, favored where the dollar amounts are relatively small, is to use them as an "add-on" to already established activities.

These five factors suggest a complex set of interactions among state, federal, and local governments, which generate incentives and disincentives important to understanding the success and failure of policy initiated at any one level of government. While some shifts in the balance of state and local government responsibilities occurred in California, these changes were due more to events within the state than to the 1981 reconciliation act. In California, both state fiscal conditions and the state's political climate limited state fiscal and policy options in responding to federal initiatives. Certainly looming budget deficits closed out any options for replacement of federal cuts by either state or local governments.

But California's political leaders have also not taken any dramatic actions to respond to the institutional challenges of the Reagan domestic program. Here the state's experience highlights the importance of political traditions—the historic state-local and legislative-executive relationships as well as the extent of the preexisting state role in human services programs.

California's historically strong commitment to human service programs means there were existing relationships prior to 1981 between state and local governments with significant state funding, mandating of local activities, and an accompanying technical assistance and oversight function. The history of state funding meant political alliances existed prior to 1981 between clients, community-based organizations, interest groups, and members of the state legislature. The state legislature was already an arena for decision making in human service programming.

The importance of the state legislature was strengthened by Proposition 13, which curtailed local revenue-raising capabilities and increased reliance on the state as a source of funds for local governments. This post-Proposition 13 tension in state-county relations predominated over any national initiatives to encourage a new state role toward localities. Another impact of the strong legislature is evident in the intense period of partisan conflict between the Republican governor and the full-time Democratically controlled legislature, which has thwarted the governor's initiatives aimed at further devolving power to the local level.

California's modest response to the Reagan program can be seen both as a consequence of a constrained fiscal environment *and* of a political history of strong state involvement in human services.

Conclusions

RICHARD P. NATHAN AND FRED C. DOOLITTLE

Implications for Federal-State Relations

*L*ooking across the landscape of federal grants-in-aid, the incidence of the benefits and services of a grant-in-aid program was the most important factor in determining what happened to the program in the Reagan first term. At the national level, programs that are most highly redistributive to politically vulnerable groups among the poor were most likely to be cut. This was true of all four of the types of grants examined.

Among entitlement grants, the most important exception to these findings was the degree to which the Medicaid program was exempted from cuts. However, on examination, we noted that in important respects the beneficiaries of the Medicaid program are different from the recipients under the other programs in this group; they are both less poor and politically less vulnerable. Specifically, the elderly, who are a major recipient group under the Medicaid program, often become poor because of their need for long-term nursing home services. Furthermore, the provision of these services to this group relieves the burden on their offspring, who often are not poor.

The Medicaid program also differs from other entitlement programs in the political strength of its constituency groups and its structure, two other factors that were found to be important in determining the fate of a grant-in-aid program in the 1980s. In the case of Medicaid, the states strongly opposed the president's proposed cuts. These cuts threatened a program that supplemented and substituted for state and local spending for services in a functional area in which state governments have traditionally played a strong role in policy formulation and program design, as well as in program administration. The support of politically powerful provider groups (hospitals and medical practitioners) was also important in explaining the high level of resistance to cuts in Medicaid spending. Taken together, these factors help to explain why the Medicaid program was insulated to a higher degree than other entitlement grants-in-aid programs from the effects of federal budget cuts.

In the case of operating grants, the big cuts under Reagan that were made at the federal level and tended to stick at the state and local levels were also in programs where the services provided are targeted on the poor. This was true, for example, in the case of the people who lost public service jobs under the Comprehensive Employment and Training Act (CETA). It was also true of people who received social services from community action agencies, which were sharply cut at the national level with the creation of the community services block grant. There was a strong tendency for state and local governments, using our terminology, to "ratify" these cuts—that is, pass them along to the beneficiaries of the grant programs reduced in the federal budget.

And finally, in the case of capital grants, we found that the biggest cuts in services at both the federal and state-local levels were in the housing programs. Housing programs are far and away the most redistributive of the grant-in-aid programs considered under this heading.

Despite David Stockman's expressed hope in what he thought was a private moment that the Reagan budget cuts would curtail "weak claims rather than weak clients," the combined incidence of the 1981 Reagan budget cuts in federal grants had a sharp focus.[1] The cuts in AFDC and food stamps, the CETA jobs program, the child nutrition programs, many social services, and the increase in rent levels in public housing all hit hardest on the able-bodied, nonaged poor and their children, the group commonly referred to as the "working poor." This is the most controversial group aided by social programs in the United States. Such an incidence pattern should not surprise us. It occurred in a conservative period in which there has been an increasingly strong backlash in response to a decade of substantial growth in redistributive social spending at all levels of government.

At the state and local levels, we found what can best be characterized as "modest" or "limited" levels of federal aid replacement out of own funds plus generally much higher levels of activity associated with coping strategies to prevent federal aid cuts from causing reductions in the level of service provision. These replacement and coping actions were more prevalent for programs with

---

[1] William Greider makes this point several times in his account of David Stockman's role in the federal budget process. "To reject weak claims from powerful clients—that was the intellectual credo that allowed him [Stockman] to hack away so confidently at wasteful social programs, believing that he was being equally tough-minded on the wasteful business subsidies. Now, as the balance was being struck, he was forced to concede in private that the claim of equity in shrinking the government was significantly compromised if not obliterated." *The Education of David Stockman and Other Americans* (New York: E. P. Dutton, 1982), p. 55.

the broadest incidence patterns and highest levels of political support; however, efforts were also made to protect some redistributive social services and social benefits programs on the part of state governments.

What are the implications of these findings for federal-state relations? We are impressed by the way in which our findings raise questions about the conventional wisdom of the late 1960s and 1970s regarding the allocation of domestic program responsibilities in American federalism. Since the 1960s, the strong tendency has been for liberals to favor greater responsibility for social programs at the national level, whereas conservatives (Ronald Reagan included) have generally supported devolutionary proposals highlighting the role of state governments. It is ironic in this context that Reagan in his first term achieved his biggest cuts in actual dollars in the grant-in-aid programs, particularly entitlement grants, where eligibility requirements and benefit levels are most heavily controlled by the national government—AFDC, housing, food stamps, and the child nutrition programs. By contrast, in the case of the Medicaid program, where Reagan achieved much less of what he sought in cutting and controlling spending, state governments have a stronger role in setting policies and providing services and the constituencies involved are also much stronger.

The lesson for liberals of this period may be that centralization of policymaking and financing responsibility for programs targeted on the poor in the long run has greater costs than had previously been realized. In liberal periods, the federal government may well be the best locus of responsibility from the vantage point of liberals. But when the country is conservative, federal programs that involve state governments in policy making and financing, as well as administration, and have built up a constituency and tradition of service, may be more likely to receive support at the state and local levels even if they are losing favor at the national level. When the recipient governments under federal grant-in-aid programs have a stake in the programs and identify them as "their" activities and services, they are more likely to support the program in the face of external threats, such as the federal aid policy retrenchment efforts of the Reagan administration.

These findings reveal what we call "a paradox of devolution" under Reagan. The phrase refers to the ways in which Reagan's goals of social program retrenchment and devolution worked against each other. To the extent that state and local governments responded to Reagan's devolutionary initiatives by increasing their own support for programs cut at the federal level, the Reagan goal of social program retrenchment was undercut.

On an overall basis, the experience of the Reagan period shows the way in which political factors combine with economic and social conditions to influence the character and size of federal grant-in-aid programs and the nature of underlying intergovernmental relationships. These observations about the Reagan period need to be viewed in relation to theories of American federalism; we focus in the analysis that follows on the pivotal role of state governments in American federalism.

Theories of Federalism

Theories of American federalism cluster around two main approaches:

1. a traditional position, which is the legalistic, dual (federal-state) approach; and
2. a dynamic position, which tends to emphasize a three-level (federal-state-local) view of American federalism.

The first approach, the traditional view of federalism, highlights the Tenth Amendment to the U.S. Constitution, which states that powers not explicitly assigned to the national government reside with the states and with the people. Although many politicians and experts in the field have in recent years moved away from this theory, both as a normative and a descriptive model,[2] Ronald Reagan has consistently been an adherent of this traditional position. He has frequently referred to the importance of the Tenth Amendment to his "theory of federalism." Basic to this traditional view of federalism is a legal doctrine that defines different functions of government as intrinsically the proper role of particular levels of government, not to be intruded upon by other levels.

Among political scientists, the 1950s mark the turning point in the way the federal system has been viewed. The writings of Columbia University political scientist Arthur W. Macmahon reflect the dominant view in the field up to the late 1950s. Macmahon, in the lead essay of a major collection of essays on American federalism published in 1955, described a federal system as one that "distributes power between a common and constituent governments under an arrangement that cannot be changed by the ordinary process of central legislation."[3] The Constitution must be changed to adjust these relationships. Furthermore, according to Macmahon, "the powers entrusted to the constituent units (whether their powers are residual or delegated) must be substantial and

---

[2] Robert Freilich et al., "The Demise of the Tenth Amendment: An Analysis of Supreme Court Decisions Affecting Constitutional Federalism," *The Urban Lawyer* 17, no. 4 (Fall 1985):651–732.

[3] Arthur W. Macmahon, "The Problems of Federalism: A Survey," in Arthur W. Macmahon, ed., *Federalism Mature and Emergent* (Garden City, N.Y.: Doubleday, 1955), p. 4.

not merely trivial."[4] This theory is often described as the layer cake theory of federalism, involving clear separations between the layers of government.

The contrasting academic theory of federalism that emerged in the late 1950s and early 1960s is also identified by a cake metaphor, in this case the marble cake. According to the position advanced by Morton Grodzins, new governmental structures and activities are continuously adopted and existing arrangements modified as social and economic issues come to public attention and new or different forms of governmental action are deemed necessary. This theory of federalism is often seen as evolutionary, as *a process* of building a community on a basis that leads to greater political integration. Morton Grodzins' famous essay on this position was published in conjunction with the work of Eisenhower's national goals commission, despite the fact that Eisenhower consistently favored the traditional federal-state concept of federalism. Grodzins in his essay depicted governmental functions and responsibilities as intrinsically intermixed in "vertical and diagonal strands and unexpected whirls," as in a marble cake.[5] A common feature of this dynamic and evolutionary position on federalism is the idea that the U.S. federal system is a three-part (rather than dual) system, what Roscoe Martin has called an "expanded partnership."

> The open marriage of the federal government and the cities cannot but have strengthened American democracy. It has brought into close collaboration the two most democratic governments in a way that has resulted in the invigoration of both, but especially of the city.[6]

Other writers in the field have contributed important points to this conventional view of federalism among political scientists. Daniel J. Elazar, a student of Grodzins', maintains that cooperative federalism (the marble cake model of federalism) is not a recent development. Rather it has been the dominant pattern since colonial times; the principal difference over time is not the degree of

[4] Ibid.

[5] Morton Grodzins, "The Federal System," in U.S. President's Commission on National Goals, *Goals for Americans, The Report of the President's Commission on National Goals* (New York: Columbia University Press, 1960), p. 265. Aaron Wildavsky has gone the cake bakers one better, with his simile of "fruitcake federalism (that is, being bogged down in governmental plums and puddings)." Aaron Wildavsky, "Birthday Cake Federalism," in Robert B. Hawkins, Jr., ed., *American Federalism: A New Partnership for the Republic* (New Brunswick, N.J.: Transaction Books, 1982), p. 184. The title of Wildavsky's chapter in this book refers to his argument that federalism should be diverse, varied, and competitive, so that each citizen can pursue his or her individual just deserts.

[6] Roscoe C. Martin, *The Cities and the Federal System* (New York: Atherton Press, 1965), p. 192. See also Paul E. Peterson, *City Limits* (Chicago: University of Chicago Press, 1981). Peterson emphasizes economic and structural problems related to the inability of municipal governments to finance redistributive programs. He proposes enhanced federal support for state and local governments to deal with this problem. See especially chapter 11.

sharing according to Elazar, but the number of governmental activities that are shared.

> From the first days of American independence, the controversy as to the scope of national vis-à-vis state powers has been part and parcel of the American political scene. While the controversy has continued to rage unabated, the American people have by and large endeavored to use both federal and state governments as a means to achieve specific ends, rather than as ends in themselves. When problems arose, solutions were sought that would harmonize with the reality of the times, involving government whenever and wherever necessary, generally at every level. Out of these attempts to solve actual problems, there evolved a series of cooperative re-lationships between all levels of governments.[7]

Samuel H. Beer has added another important dimension to the Grodzins-Elazar analysis. Beer contends that what emerged in the 1960s was a new form of "technocratic federalism" characterized by the rise of politically powerful groups of professional specialists in major domestic program fields.

> In the 1960s and on into the 1970s, new federal programs draw heavily upon the "professional specialisms" in the field of health, housing, urban renewal, transportation, welfare, education, the environment, energy and poverty.[8]

According to Beer, the result was that "social programs typically followed a serv-ices strategy."[9] This strategy was reinforced by categorical grants-in-aid from the national government to state and local governments. These particularistic in-tergovernmental payments were often used to create and stimulate programs fa-vored by what Beer calls "professional specialisms."

In essence, the debate between the traditional and more dynamic positions can be seen as one between *structuralism* (federalism as a governmental system of divided responsibilities between the national and state governments) and *in-strumentalism* (federalism as a tool for solving problems that change over time). The instrumental position gained influenced in the sixties in a context of the growing strength of liberal ideas on social policy issues and an increased role for the national government in the domestic public sector.

However, there was another shift in thinking on federalism issues in both the

---

[7] Daniel J. Elazar, *The American Partnership: Intergovernmental Co-operation in the Nine-teenth-Century United States* (Chicago: University of Chicago Press, 1962), pp. 297–98.

[8] Samuel H. Beer, "Foreword," in John William Ellwood, ed., *Reductions in U.S. Domestic Spending* (New Brunswick, N.J.: Transaction Books, 1982), p. xviii.

[9] Ibid.

academic and public policy communities. The shift which occurred in the late sixties and seventies was a reaction to the burst of new social programs of the federal government that occurred under Lyndon Johnson's "Great Society." Both liberals and conservatives expressed concern about the effects of the "proliferation" of federal grant-in-aid programs and the increases in their size and scope. Proposals were made to *"rationalize"* the domestic programs of the federal government. Frequently, this is referred to as *"sorting out"* functions, a phrase that has come into wide usage in this field. The U.S. Advisory Commission on Intergovernmental Relations (ACIR), an agency of the federal government that includes among its members both Democrats and Republicans, emphasized the problem of "proliferation" and the need to "sort out" functions. David B. Walker, for many years a member of the staff of the ACIR, calls this condition, "system's overload." Viewed from the local perspective, Walker says, "the ever-increasing number, variety, fiscal significance, and administrative complexity of these vastly expanded contacts with the federal government suggest a basically transformed rather than merely adapting pattern of intergovernmental relations."[10] In essence, the overload position and the associated idea that we need to sort out functions represent a shift on the federalism continuum away from the Grodzins-Elazar view and back toward the traditional Macmahon model of federalism.

Three-Dimensional Federalism

In an effort to provide a system for understanding Reagan's contribution in this field, we find it helpful to highlight the three-part analytical framework used at a number of points in our analysis. All governmental activities have three dimensions: (1) policy making, (2) financing, and (3) administration. Reagan's "swap and turnback" plan and his 1976 campaign proposals for reforming federalism strongly reflect the traditional Eisenhower-Macmahon federal-state view of American federalism. They would have turned over to state governments the responsibility for all three dimensions of certain programs and taken on the full three dimensional responsibility for others at the national level. However, when we look closely at the federalism policy changes that actually occurred during Reagan's first term, they are of a much more indirect, *incremental*, and Grodzinian character. For the programs affected by changes made under Reagan, one or more of the three program dimensions continue to be shared between the federal government and states and localities. Even Reagan's

[10] David B. Walker, *Toward a Functioning Federalism* (Cambridge, Mass.: Winthrop Publishers, 1981), p. 5.

new block grants still have the federal government involved in financing and policy making (although to a lesser degree), with administrative responsibility assigned to a greater degree at the state level. These are important, but not far-reaching changes of the type Reagan had previously proposed.

Under most federal grant-in-aid programs, the federal government plays a role in setting policy, costs are shared with states and in some cases localities, and administrative responsibility rests with states and localities, primarily with the states. The changes that ultimately came to pass in the intergovernmental field during the Reagan first term shifted the way these three dimensions of governmental activities are arranged for a number of programs, but they did not mark a sharp departure from past practice.

The most important federalism change brought about by Reagan's policies—one that was probably unanticipated by Reagan and his advisors—was the way in which the combination of Reagan's social program retrenchment goals and his block grant and related devolutionary policy initiatives *activated state governments and enhanced their role in the nation's governmental system.* The equilibrating tendency revealed here between the reactions to Reagan's retrenchment and devolutionary policies shows how hard it is to make sharp changes in the American political system. Ronald Reagan has been an effective leader in Washington. He has put his stamp on the domestic, and particularly the social, policies of the national government. But in a real sense his stamp appears to have been cancelled—not fully, but partially—by state government policies and actions.

Looking to the future, we draw this lesson from our study. There is no one scheme for all time for arranging governmental responsibilities in American federalism. The role of state government as the middleman of American federalism has changed over time in a way that reflects this observation. Generally speaking, the states tend to be more prominent in domestic policy in conservative periods than in liberal periods.[11] On the other hand, in liberal or pro-government periods, we have seen the accretion of the role of the central government. There is a nice, almost mathematical, explanation for this situation. In liberal periods, the proponents of increased governmental activity find it possible and efficient to lobby for their interests at one place, the center. Our advice to politicians would be for liberals to support state role enhancement in policy making and administration in conservative periods, like the present one, and for conservatives to be cautious about strengthening the states under these conditions. Ronald Reagan, adhering to the received theory in his presidency, may

[11] For further discussion of this generalization, see Richard P. Nathan, "America's Changing Federalism," in Anthony King, ed., *The American Political System* (Washington, D.C.: The American Enterprise Institute, forthcoming revised edition).

have missed a signal to the extent he pushed in his first term for devolutionary reforms in the assignment of program responsibilities in American federalism. In fact, officials of the Reagan administration appear to have pulled back from their efforts to devolve policy-making and programmatic responsibility to the states, perhaps in part in response to the "paradox of devolution" under Reagan. This tendency for devolutionary policies and actions to undercut retrenchment goals is the most recent example of a central characteristic of American federal-state relations—the energizing role played by state governments in conservative periods of our history.

Index

Library of Congress Cataloging-in-Publication Data

Nathan, Richard P.
Reagan and the States.

Includes index.
1. Budget—United States. 2. Grants-in-aid—
United States. 3. Intergovernmental fiscal
relations—United States. 4. United States—
Economic policy—1981– . 5. Finance, Public—
United States—States—Case studies. 6. Local
finance—United States—Case studies. I. Doolittle,
Fred C. II. Title.
HJ2051.N167 1987   353.0072′5   87–45529
ISBN 0–691–07748–7
ISBN 0–691–02273–9 (pbk.)

Richard P. Nathan is Professor of Public and International Affairs at the Woodrow Wilson School, Princeton University. Fred C. Doolittle is Senior Research Associate at the Manpower Demonstration Research Corporation in New York City.